FLOYD CLYMER'S MOTORCYCLIST'S LIBRARY

The Book of the
A.J.S.

A PRACTICAL GUIDE ON THE HANDLING AND MAINTENANCE OF ALL 1945-60 350 c.c. AND 500 c.c. O.H.V. TOURING SINGLES EXCEPT THE 1960 350 c.c. MODEL 8

BY

W. C. HAYCRAFT

F.R.S.A.

ANNOUNCEMENT

By special arrangement with the original publishers of this book, Sir Isaac Pitman & Son, Ltd., of London, England, we have secured the exclusive publishing rights for this book, as well as all others in THE MOTORCYCLIST'S LIBRARY.

Included in THE MOTORCYCLIST'S LIBRARY are complete instruction manuals covering the care and operation of respective motorcycles and engines; valuable data on speed tuning, and thrilling accounts of motorcycle race events. See listing of available titles elsewhere in this edition.

We consider it a privilege to be able to offer so many fine titles to our customers.

FLOYD CLYMER
Publisher of Books Pertaining to Automobiles and Motorcycles

2125 W. PICO ST.   LOS ANGELES 6, CALIF.

INTRODUCTION

Welcome to the world of digital publishing ~ the book you now hold in your hand, while unchanged from the original edition, was printed using the latest state of the art digital technology. The advent of print-on-demand has forever changed the publishing process, never has information been so accessible and it is our hope that this book serves your informational needs for years to come. If this is your first exposure to digital publishing, we hope that you are pleased with the results. Many more titles of interest to the classic automobile and motorcycle enthusiast, collector and restorer are available via our website at www.VelocePress.com. We hope that you find this title as interesting as we do.

NOTE FROM THE PUBLISHER

The information presented is true and complete to the best of our knowledge. All recommendations are made without any guarantees on the part of the author or the publisher, who also disclaim all liability incurred with the use of this information.

TRADEMARKS

We recognize that some words, model names and designations, for example, mentioned herein are the property of the trademark holder. We use them for identification purposes only. This is not an official publication.

INFORMATION ON THE USE OF THIS PUBLICATION

This manual is an invaluable resource for the classic motorcycle enthusiast and a "must have" for owners interested in performing their own maintenance. However, in today's information age we are constantly subject to changes in common practice, new technology, availability of improved materials and increased awareness of chemical toxicity. As such, it is advised that the user consult with an experienced professional prior to undertaking any procedure described herein. While every care has been taken to ensure correctness of information, it is obviously not possible to guarantee complete freedom from errors or omissions or to accept liability arising from such errors or omissions. Therefore, any individual that uses the information contained within, or elects to perform or participate in do-it-yourself repairs or modifications acknowledges that there is a risk factor involved and that the publisher or its associates cannot be held responsible for personal injury or property damage resulting from the use of the information or the outcome of such procedures.

WARNING!

One final word of advice, this publication is intended to be used as a reference guide, and when in doubt the reader should consult with a qualified technician.

PREFACE

My first practical experience with an A.J.S. was in 1927 when I bought a "big port" O.H.V. 350 c.c. model. Even then A.J.S. performance was very high. Today A.J.S. motor-cycles have a world-wide reputation for high performance, mechanical quietness, reliability, and economical running. Appearance and general finish too are excellent.

It has always been, and still is, the policy of A.J.S. Motor Cycles of Plumstead Road, London, S.E.18, to develop and perfect their machines gradually, and to embody in the standard touring models their experience gained through participation in racing *and* trials events.

As hitherto, the object of this handbook is to help *you* to obtain the maximum pleasure, mileage, m.p.h., m.p.g., and m.p.£ from your mount, and to reduce depreciation to the minimum.

If you have never before handled an A.J.S., turn direct to Chapter I which deals with preliminaries, starting-up, gear changing, running-in, etc. A useful book for novices (and experienced riders) is *The Art of Motor Cycling*, published by Pitman at 5s. Also read and thoroughly digest the latest edition of the *Highway Code*. I also recommend the wearing of a crash helmet. Chapters II–V deal comprehensively with the maintenance and overhaul of the following four-stroke O.H.V. single-cylinder touring models—

1. The 1945–55 347 c.c. rigid-frame Model 16M.
2. The 1945–55 498 c.c. rigid-frame Model 18.
3. The 1949–60 347 c.c. spring-frame Models 16MS, 16.
4. The 1949–60 498 c.c. spring-frame Models 18S, 18.

Except where otherwise stated, the instructions given apply to 1945–60 inclusive. Machines *not* covered in this handbook are: the 1960 348 c.c. Model 8, the 1959–60 248 c.c. O.H.V. Model 14, the Trials models, the overhead-camshaft racing models, and the twin-cylinder O.H.V. machines. The competition models, by the way, have engines similar to the touring models dealt with in this handbook, but they have, of course, specialized equipment.

In conclusion I thank A.J.S. Motor Cycles (and various accessory firms) for their kindness in providing technical data, and for according me permission to reproduce many copyright illustrations.

W.C.H.

CONTENTS

CHAP.
I. HANDLING AN A.J.S. 1
   Essential preliminaries—Starting the engine—Gear changing—General driving hints

II. ALL ABOUT CARBURATION 12
   Amal standard carburettor—Amal "Monobloc" carburettor—Tuning Amal carburettor—Carburettor maintenance—The air filter

III. THE LIGHTING SYSTEM. 25
   Illumination—The lamps (1945–8 models)—The lamps (1949 onwards)—Maintenance of battery—Maintenance of dynamo—The alternator and rectifier (1958–60)—The horn—The wiring system

IV. CORRECT LUBRICATION. 53
   Engine lubrication—Motor-cycle lubrication

V. GENERAL MAINTENANCE 75
   Engine maintenance—Sparking plugs, contact-breaker, etc.—Timing the magneto (1945–57 models)—Timing the ignition (1948–60)—Tappet adjustment—Decarbonizing and valve grinding—Valve timing—Motor-cycle maintenance—Tyre pressures, wheel alignment—Brakes—The transmission—The frame, etc.—Wheel removal

Index 151

CHAPTER I

HANDLING AN A.J.S.

AN A.J.S. O.H.V. single is easy to handle, and even the absolute novice quickly acquires confidence in the saddle. Beware, however, that you do not indulge in big throttle openings *until you have had ample road experience*. Also do not forget to follow the advice given in the *Highway Code*.

FIG. 1. A FLEXIBLE AND FAST TOURER WITH CLEAN LINES AND MECHANICAL QUIETNESS—THE 1960 MODEL 18

The 500 c.c. A.J.S. model shown is similar to the 350 c.c. Model 16. Both models have snappy push-rod O.H.V. engines with light-alloy cylinder heads," Monobloc" carburettors, hairpin valve-springs, and automatic-ignition control. Their specification includes: "Teledraulic" front forks, Girling rear-suspension units, a quickly-detachable rear wheel, die-cast light-alloy hubs, a deep secondary-chain guard, an A.M.C. four-speed gearbox, Lucas headlamp, Lucas coil ignition, and other attractive features.

Essential Preliminaries. Before you can legally ride on the road—

(1) Insure against all *third-party* risks and obtain the vital "certificate of insurance." With a new machine you cannot get this until the machine is licensed, and an insurance "cover note" must be obtained. If you have a valuable machine, you are advised to take out full comprehensive insurance.

(2) Obtain the registration licence and registration book (Form R.F.I/2)* or renew the licence (Form R.F. I/A).

* The A.J.S. engine and frame numbers required on Form R.F. I/2 will be found on the near-side of the crankcase and the off-side of the saddle lug, or on the main frame head lug (1958–60).

(3) Obtain a six months "provisional" or a three year annual driving licence (Form D.L.1).

(4) Fit a reliable speedometer if one is not fitted (not *essential* if machine registered prior to 1st Oct., 1937).

(5) If you carry a pillion-passenger, see that he or she sits *astride* a proper pillion seat securely *fixed* to the machine (all "springers" have dualseats), and that the passenger holds a current three-year driving licence for Group G if you are a "learner."

(6) If you are ineligible for a three-year driving licence, attach "L" plates to the front and back of the machine.

(7) If not already provided, fit a red reflector ($1\frac{1}{2}$ in. minimum diameter) *vertically* at the rear of the motor-cycle and, on a sidecar outfit, an additional red reflector and rear lamp at the rear of the sidecar and at the same height as those on the motor-cycle.

(8) Use an ignition-suppression type sparking plug or terminal cover if the machine was registered for the first time after 1st July, 1953.

All the official forms referred to above may be obtained from any money-order post office. See also footnote,* with reference to Forms R.F. 1/A or R.F. 1/2.

You are not eligible for a three-year driving licence for Group G *unless* you are 16 and have complied with one of these conditions—

(*a*) You have held a licence (other than a provisional or Visitor's licence) authorizing the driving of vehicles of the class or description applied for within a period of ten years ending on the date of coming into force of the licence applied for.

(*b*) You have passed the prescribed driving test (this includes a test passed while serving in H.M. Forces) during the said period of ten years.

STARTING THE ENGINE

First verify that there is sufficient petrol and oil in the tanks. Handlebar controls are shown in Figs. 2, 3; oil tank and gearbox replenishment are dealt with on pages 58 and 65 respectively. Check that the gear-change pedal *is* in neutral (*see* Figs. 5–7).

Adjusting the Controls. If the engine is cold—

(1) Set the throttle so that it is slightly open by turning the twist-grip *inwards* about *one-sixth* of its total movement.

(2) Completely close the air-control lever.

(3) Turn the ignition switch on 1958–60 models to the "IGN" position.

(4) Fully advance the ignition-control lever (where fitted) by pushing it *outwards* to its *full extent*, and then retard it by about *two-fifths* of its total movement by pulling it *inwards*. 1945–52 models: pull *inwards* to advance.

---

* All 350 c.c. and 500 c.c. models are taxed at £3 15s. per annum, with £1 5s. extra duty for a sidecar.

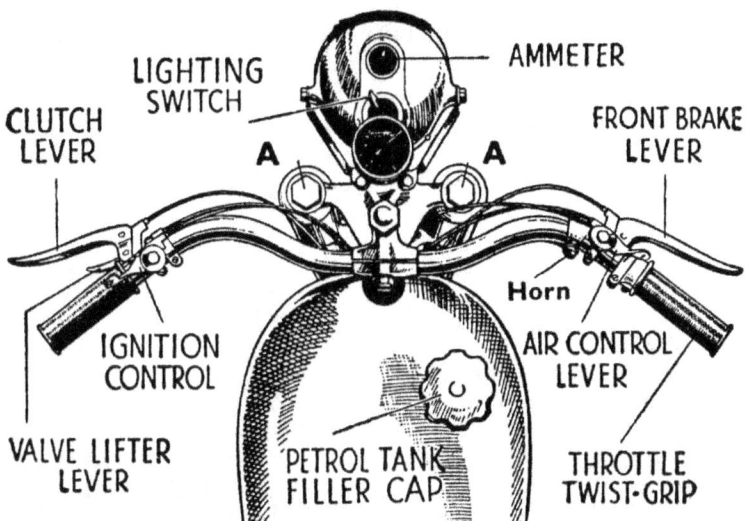

FIG. 2. LAYOUT OF HANDLEBAR CONTROLS (1945–53 MODELS)

This also applies to the 1954 350 c.c. models, which have manual ignition control. All controls operate by inward movement and the handlebar clips are adjustable for angle. The dipping switch (not shown) is mounted close to the ignition control. A A are shown the filler plugs for the front forks.

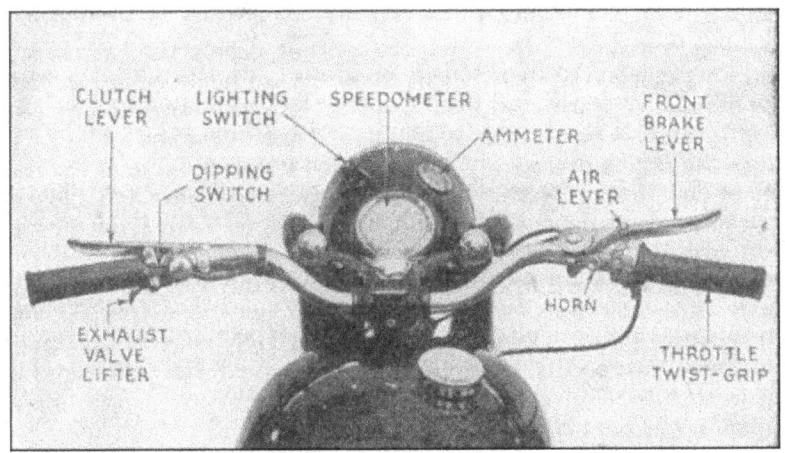

FIG. 3. LAYOUT OF HANDLEBAR CONTROLS (1954 ONWARDS)

Automatic ignition-advance mechanism was not fitted to the 1954 350 c.c. model, and this had manual ignition control as shown in Fig. 2. As hitherto all controls are adjustable for angle and are operated by inward movement. 1956–60 models have a combined dipping-switch and horn push and 1958–60 models have an ignition key in the centre of the lighting switch.

If the engine is already warm, open the throttle about a quarter and the air-control lever half to three-quarters.

The Petrol Tank Filler Cap. Some riders find that the filler cap does not come away instantly. On A.J.S. machines, to release the filler cap quickly, depress it slightly, then turn it fully anti-clockwise and withdraw the cap. It has two locking positions.

Main and Reserve Petrol Taps. Many A.J.S. singles have down-draught type Amal carburettors and on such machines it is important when leaving a machine standing for more than a few minutes always to turn off both the main and reserve-supply petrol taps.

Both taps are of the horizontal-plunger type. To open (1945–54), push the *hexagon* knob marked PUSH-ON towards the tap body. To shut the tap push the *knurled* knob marked PUSH-OFF towards the tap body. As mentioned in a later paragraph, it is advisable normally to run with only the off-side tap open. Refuelling should be undertaken as soon as possible after being forced to draw upon the reserve fuel supply. The reserve supply tap should then be shut immediately. On 1955 and later models, to close either tap, push the plunger right in; to open it, pull the plunger right out.

If Engine is Cold. If the engine (especially a new one) is stone cold, it is generally advisable to free the piston before attempting to start up. Raise the exhaust-valve lifter and kick the engine over smartly about three times.

Starting Procedure. After setting the controls, depress the float chamber "tickler" momentarily, but do not flood the carburettor so that petrol drips from it. It is assumed that the petrol has been turned on by using the *off-side* tap. Use the other to maintain a reserve supply.

Turn the engine over slowly with the kick-starter pedal until the resistance of compression is felt. Raise the exhaust-valve lifter and allow the piston just to pass the position of full compression. Then allow the kick-starter pedal to return almost to its normal position.

Release the exhaust-valve lifter and simultaneously kick the engine over sharply with a long swinging kick. If nothing happens, repeat the procedure until something does! When the engine fires, fully open the air-control lever slowly, advance the ignition lever (where fitted) fully, and open the throttle slightly to give even running on the pilot jet. Check the oil circulation (*see* page 58).

Emergency Starting (1958–60 A.J.S. Models). On the coil-ignition models the ignition switch (in the centre of the lighting switch) has an emergency starting position. Should the battery for some reason become badly discharged, turn the ignition switch to the "EMG" position. This connects the alternator direct to the ignition coil and enables the engine to be started independently of the battery. Immediately the engine starts turn the ignition switch to the "IGN" position, otherwise misfiring will develop.

Avoid Force on Kick-starter Pedal. It is very important not to exert excessive force on the kick-starter pedal (*see* Fig. 4) until the toothed quadrant (*A*) has moved in the direction of the arrow sufficiently to bridge the gap (*C*) between the quadrant and the kick-starter ratchet pinion (*B*).

Until the gap (*C*) has been bridged and full engagement has been obtained and felt, a slow, gentle operation of the kick-starter is essential to prevent wear and damage. *Never use excessive force.*

Excessive Flooding is Risky. Do not adopt the pernicious habit of swamping the carburettor with petrol before starting up. Such flooding incurs a grave risk of neat petrol entering the cylinder from a downdraught carburettor and destroying the vital oil film between the piston and cylinder. Dripping petrol also causes a slight fire risk.

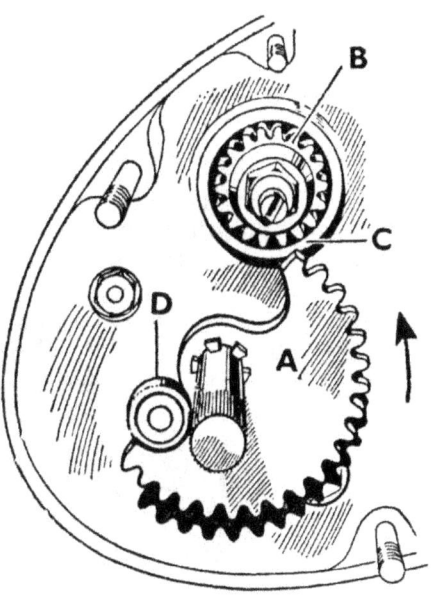

FIG. 4. THE KICK-STARTER (1945-51)

A, B, C show the quadrant, ratchet pinion, and the gap between them, respectively. *D* is the quadrant stop.

If Engine Refuses to Start. If the engine refuses to start at the third kick, verify that petrol is reaching the float chamber by depressing the tickler. When you are satisfied on this point, remove and carefully inspect the sparking plug. Clean the plug, check its gap, and replace it (*see* pages 77-80).

Correct Method of Warming Up. Do not race the engine immediately after starting up from cold, as it takes some time for the oil to circulate properly. Running the engine too fast also generates excessive heat. On the other hand, do not warm up the engine too slowly, or the pump will not work fast enough to circulate the oil properly and the combustion of a rather cold mixture will be incomplete, with the result that condensation on and corrosion of the cylinder walls may occur. Never allow the engine to idle for long, especially in hot weather, and do not travel fast until the oil has warmed up.

Speedometer Readings. The top set of figures on the dial records the total mileage and automatically returns to zero when 100,000 miles is recorded. The bottom set of figures records the mileage since the trip was set to zero, and the red figures indicate tenths of a mile. It is a good plan to set the trip to zero before driving off on each run. To do this, pull and turn to the *right* the knob (protruding from the lower part of the speedometer unit) until "000·0" appears.

GEAR CHANGING

Ease the A.J.S. off its stand, with the engine ticking over and the foot gear-change pedal in neutral, sit astride the machine, and disengage the clutch, using the handlebar lever (*see* Figs. 2, 3).

Engaging First Gear. Raise the foot gear-change pedal *fully* with the toe of the foot and engage first (bottom) gear (*see* Figs. 5–7). Slight

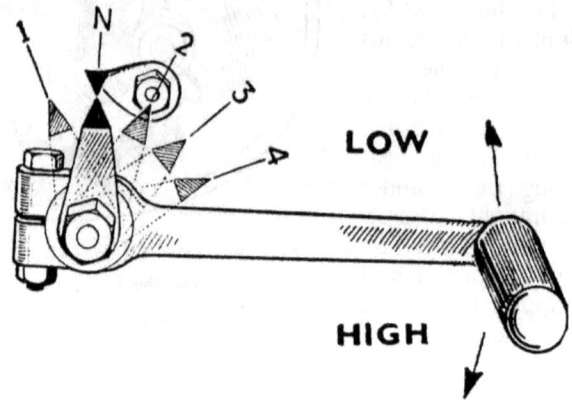

FIG. 5. THE FOOT GEAR-CHANGE INDICATOR (1945–51 MODELS)

All changes up to a higher gear are made by *depressing* the pedal with the toe, and all changes down to a lower gear by *raising* the pedal with the toe. Internal springs return the pedal to the horizontal position after each gear change is made.

backward or forward movement of the machine often facilitates engagement. As soon as first gear is *felt* to engage, remove the toe from the pedal.

If difficulty is experienced in engaging first gear, wait a few seconds before making another attempt. Initial difficulty in engaging first gear on a *new* machine usually cures itself quite soon, and sticking clutch-plates can be rectified by stopping the engine (by raising the exhaust-valve lifter) and smartly operating the kick-starter several times with the clutch fully disengaged.

To Move Off. Having engaged first gear, move off by slowly releasing the clutch lever. As the machine gathers speed and the engine takes the

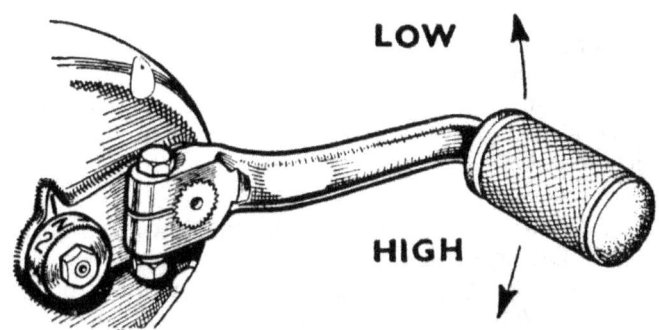

FIG. 6. THE FOOT GEAR-CHANGE INDICATOR (1952–6, 1958–60)

The indicator itself comprises a small drum having the gear positions marked as shown. *N* (neutral) is shown aligned with the dash mark on the gearbox shell.

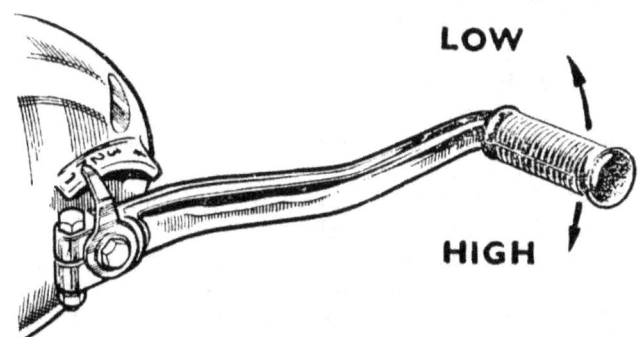

FIG. 7. THE FOOT GEAR-CHANGE INDICATOR (1957 MODELS)

The indicator comprises a pointer on the gear-change lever shaft, and a marked quadrant on the gearbox.

full load, gradually increase the throttle opening by means of the twist-grip, so as to maintain a progressive rise in the speed of the engine and machine.

Changing Up (First to Second). As soon as your A.J.S. has reached a speed of about twelve m.p.h. in first gear, change up into second gear. Once again disengage the clutch, slightly close the throttle, pause a second, and then *depress* the gear-change pedal to its *full extent* with the toe, until second gear is *felt* to engage perfectly. Then engage the clutch and also remove the toe from the pedal to allow the pedal to return to its normal position.

Changing Up (to Third and Fourth). Progressively increase the throttle opening until about twenty m.p.h. is obtained. Now disengage the clutch, throttle down slightly, pause a second, and then smartly, but without force, *depress* the gear-change pedal fully until third gear is *felt* to engage perfectly. Engage the clutch, remove the toe from the pedal, and throttle up to maintain a good road speed without any tendency for the engine to "knock." To change into fourth (i.e. top gear) repeat the procedure at nearly thirty m.p.h.

To Change Down (Fourth to Third). Throttle down to a normal speed for third gear. Disengage the clutch, throttle up slightly, pause a second, and *raise* the gear-change pedal to its *full extent* with the toe of the foot until third gear is *felt* to engage. Immediately afterwards engage the clutch, remove the toe from the pedal, and throttle up to compensate for the increase in the speed of the engine relative to rear-wheel speed.

To Change Down (to Second and First). The required procedure is similar to that just described for changing down from fourth to third gear. With the toe of the foot *raise* the gear-change pedal to its *full extent* during each gear change. Each full movement of the pedal engages the *next* gear in the gear-change sequence as shown by the indicator in Figs. 5–7.

To change from fourth or third gear into first (bottom) gear, it is not *essential* to complete the full gear-changing procedure for each intermediate gear, although this should be done when hill climbing. The method which can be used is to bring the machine to a crawl by means of the throttle and brakes, disengage the clutch, and then raise the gear-change pedal to its *full extent*—three times or twice (in quick succession), according to whether top or third gear was previously engaged. Each time you raise the gear-change pedal "blip" the engine, i.e. throttle up slightly. Then gently re-engage the clutch.

Silence Is Golden. Noisy gear changing is bad for sensitive ears, and worse still for the gearbox! Learn to change gear silently. Here are a few golden rules—

(1) Make full use of the four gear-ratios provided. The gear-change pedal always returns to the same position, but do not forget where it is

(2) Do not "bully" the machine up a steep incline in top gear.

(3) Change gear *before* your mount gets "hot and bothered."

(4) Use a nicely co-ordinated and almost simultaneous movemen when operating the clutch, throttle, and gear-change pedal.

(5) Keep a steady pressure on the gear-change pedal and hold the clutch out *until the gear is felt to engage*. At other times remove the foot.

(6) Do not race the engine in the lower gears to "impress the lads." They may like it (perhaps) but your engine will hate you!

(7) Be kind to the gearbox and give it its oil ration occasionally (*see* page 65).

GENERAL DRIVING HINTS

Negotiating Hills. Your A.J.S. will romp up gentle gradients, but maintain the engine r.p.m. high by making full use of the gearbox where necessary and *in good time*. On no account permit the engine to labour. Be liberal with the throttle opening, and do not retard the ignition-control lever (where fitted) unless this is essential (to ward off a "knock"), as this reduces power output.

When descending steep hills, open the air lever wide and close the throttle. This will not only cool the engine, but it will enable engine compression to exert a powerful braking effect.

Use of Brakes. Acquire the habit of using *both* brakes simultaneously, as this gives powerful braking with minimum and even wear of the brake linings and tyres.

Excessive and fierce brake application plays havoc with the tyres and transmission, and for this reason you should learn to *drive on the throttle* and use the brakes as little and as seldom as possible. Make use of engine compression as a brake when descending hills (*see* previous paragraph), but never use the clutch, ignition switch (1958-60), or exhaust-valve lifter for controlling speed. This places a motor-cyclist beyond the pale.

To Stop the Machine. To effect a normal stop on the road, use the following procedure—

(1) Close the throttle by means of the twist-grip.

(2) Fully disengage the clutch.

(3) Apply *both* brakes simultaneously, increasing the hand and foot pressure as the brakes take effect.

(4) Raise the gear-change pedal fully once or several times (according to which gear is already engaged) until you get into first gear. Then depress the pedal *very slightly* with the toe until "neutral" (*see* Figs. 5-7) is obtained.

(5) Engage the clutch by gently releasing the lever.

To Stop the Engine. After bringing the motor-cycle to a halt with the throttle closed (as far as the throttle-stop permits*), it is only necessary to

---

* The correct throttle-stop setting is such that when the engine is warmed up and the throttle is closed, the engine ticks over smoothly (*see* page 18).

raise the exhaust-valve lifter for a few seconds in order to extinguish all signs of life. On 1958–60 models it is not necessary to use the exhaust valve lifter; just turn the ignition key to the centre. Before you leave your machine, turn off the petrol tap to prevent accidental "flooding."

Running-in New Machine. On covering 1,000 miles it is not harmful to step up the speed of a *new* machine gradually, but refrain from using full throttle until about 2,000 miles have been covered. A new A.J.S. must be properly run-in, or it may be permanently spoiled. Here is some sound advice—

(1) Don't exceed one-third full throttle for 1,000 miles.

(2) Don't "over-rev." the engine when idling or on the road, especially in the lower gears.

(3) Don't often exceed 30 m.p.h. in top gear.

(4) Don't permit the engine to labour or "knock." Change down in good time.

(5) Don't run the engine with the machine stationary for more than a minute or two.

(6) Don't forget to keep the engine, gearbox, and machine correctly lubricated (*see* Chapter IV).

While the running-in process is taking place, engine performance will be helped considerably by the use of Acheson's Colloidal Graphite, together with engine oil, as this will aid the cylinder and bearing surfaces.

After Covering 400–500 Miles. A certain amount of bedding-down occurs, and it is important to check the adjustment of the following: (*a*) tappets, (*b*) contact-breaker points, (*c*) steering-head bearings, (*d*) primary and secondary chains, and (*e*) brakes. Steering-head bearing adjustment is very important, as slack bearings will suffer. After the initial bedding-down and necessary adjustments have been made, further adjustment is needed much less frequently.

Colloidal Graphite Beneficial for Running-in. It is beneficial during the running-in period to mix *one pint* of Acheson's Colloidal Graphite with each *gallon of engine oil.* This benefits the cylinder and bearing surfaces. If the compound (obtainable from most garages) is used after running-in, reduce the amount by one half.

Advice on Avoiding Accidents. Accidents on the road occur atrociously often. Below is some sound practical advice.

(1) Wear a crash helmet. A fractured skull and severe concussion can cause a shocking "hangover" for a long period and can easily be fatal.

(2) Do not speed on major roads, or apparently major roads, having minor cross-roads. This can lead to being rammed at right-angles.

(3) Exercise special care at cross-roads and roundabouts.
(4) Keep a good distance behind car drivers.
(5) Always give *clear* hand signals in *ample* time.
(6) Do not cut in or indulge in "stunt" riding.
(7) Never apply the brakes fiercely on wet roads.

CHAPTER II

ALL ABOUT CARBURATION

A STANDARD type Amal needle-jet carburettor is fitted to all 1945-54 single-cylinder 350 c.c. and 500 c.c. A.J.S. engines but all 1955 and later engines have the "Monobloc" type Amal needle-jet carburettor fitted.

AMAL STANDARD CARBURETTOR

An understanding of the working of the standard Amal carburettor is desirable before considering its tuning and maintenance. Referring to Fig. 8, showing a sectional view of the Amal semi-automatic carburettor, (A) is the carburettor body or mixing chamber, the upper part of which has a throttle valve (B), with taper needle (C) attached by a needle clip. The throttle valve regulates the quantity of mixture supplied to the engine. Passing through the throttle valve is the air valve (D), independently operated and serving the purpose of obstructing the main air-passage for starting and mixture regulation. Fixed to the underside of the mixing chamber by the union nut (E) is the jet block (F), and interposed between them is a fibre washer to ensure a petrol-tight joint.

On the upper part of the block is the jet-block barrel (H), forming a clean through-way. Integral with the jet block is the pilot jet (J), supplied through the passage (K). The adjustable pilot-air intake (L) communicates with a chamber, from which issues the pilot outlet (M) and the by-pass (N). A throttle stop (*see* Fig. 9) is provided on the mixing chamber, by which the position of the throttle valve for tick-over is regulated independently of the cable adjustment.

The needle jet (O) is screwed in the underside of the jet block, and carries at its bottom end the main jet (P). Both these jets are removable when the jet plug (Q), which bolts the mixing chamber and the float chamber together, is removed. The float chamber, which has bottom feed, consists of a cup (R) fed with petrol through union (S). It contains the float (T) and the needle valve (U) attached by the clip (V). The float chamber cover (W) has a lock screw (X) for security.

The petrol tap having been turned on, petrol will flow past the needle valve (U) until the quantity of petrol in the chamber (R) is sufficient to raise the float (T), when the needle valve (U) will prevent a further supply entering the float chamber until some in the chamber has already been used up by the engine. The float chamber having filled to its correct level, the fuel passes along the passages through the diagonal holes in the jet plug (Q), when it will be in communication with the main jet (*P*) and the pilot feedhole (*K*), the level in the needle and pilot jets being, obviously, the same as that maintained in the float chamber.

Imagine the throttle valve (*B*) very slightly open. As the piston descends,

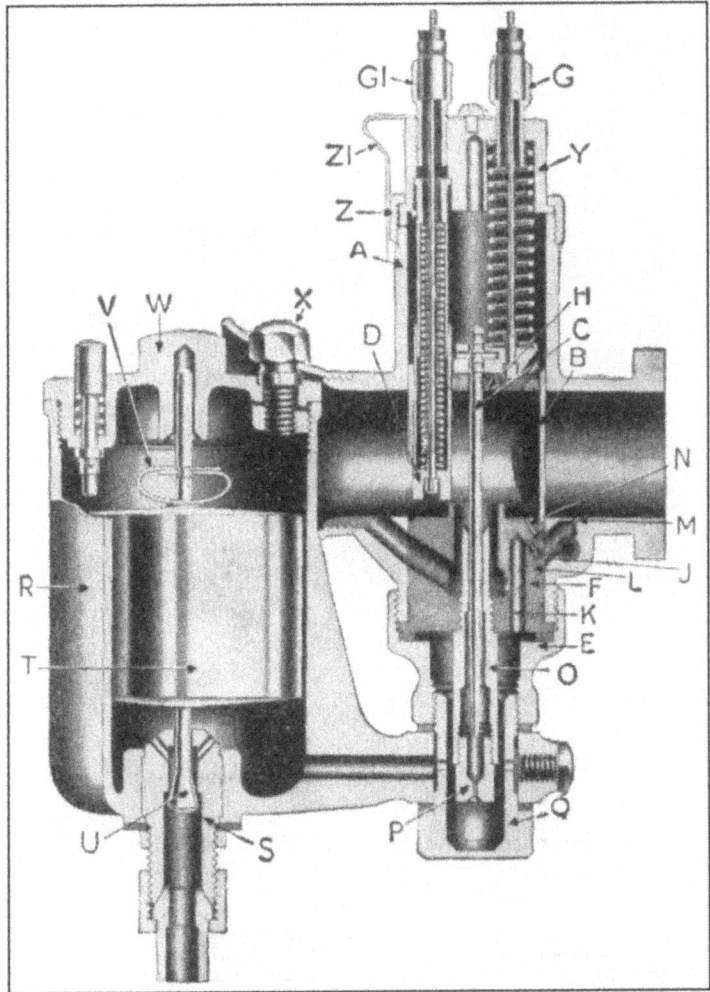

FIG. 8. SECTIONAL VIEW OF AMAL STANDARD NEEDLE-JET CARBURETTOR FITTED TO ALL 1945–54 MODELS

a partial vacuum is created in the carburettor, causing a rush of air through the pilot-air hole (*L*) and drawing fuel from the pilot jet (*J*). The mixture of air and fuel is admitted to the engine through the pilot outlet (*M*) which has a pilot-air screw adjustment (*see* Fig. 9), used in conjunction with the throttle-stop screw to obtain a good slow-running mixture. The quantity of mixture capable of being passed by the pilot outlet (*M*) is insufficient to run the engine. This mixture also carries excess of fuel. Consequently,

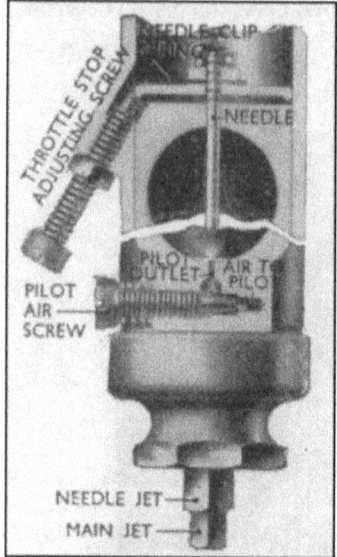

Fig. 9. Throttle Stop and Pilot-air Screw

(Standard Carburettor)

before a combustible mixture is admitted, throttle valve (*B*) must be slightly raised, admitting further air from the main air-intake.

The farther the throttle valve is opened, the less will be the depression on the outlet (*M*), but, in turn, a higher depression will be created on the by-pass (*N*), and the pilot mixture will flow from this passage as well as from the outlet (*M*).

The mixture supplied by the pilot and by-pass system is supplemented at about one-eighth throttle by fuel from the main jet (*P*), the throttle valve cut-away determining the mixture strength from here to one-quarter throttle.

Proceeding up the throttle range, mixture control by the needle position occurs from one-quarter to three-quarters throttle, and from this point the main jet is the only regulation.

The air valve (*D*), which is cable-operated like the throttle valve, has the effect of obstructing the main through-way and, in consequence, increasing the depression on the main jet, enriching the mixture. Two cable adjusters (*G*), (*G*1), are provided.

AMAL "MONOBLOC" CARBURETTOR

The Amal "Monobloc" carburettor specified on all 1955 and later A.J.S. O.H.V. singles differs from the standard type, used before 1955, in several

Key to Fig. 10

1. Mixing-chamber cap.
2. Mixing-chamber cap ring.
3. Air valve.
4. Jet-needle clip.
5. Jet block.
6. Air passage to pilot jet.
7. Tickler assembly.
8. Banjo securing-bolt.
9. Float needle.
10. Float.
11. Float-chamber cover screws.
12. Float-chamber cover.
13. Float chamber.
14. Needle jet.
15. Main-jet holder.
16. Main jet.
17. Pilot jet.
18. Throttle-stop adjusting screw.
19. Jet-block locating screw.
20. Pilot-air adjusting screw.
21. Mixing chamber.
22. Fibre seal.
23. Jet needle.
24. Throttle valve.
25. Throttle return-spring.

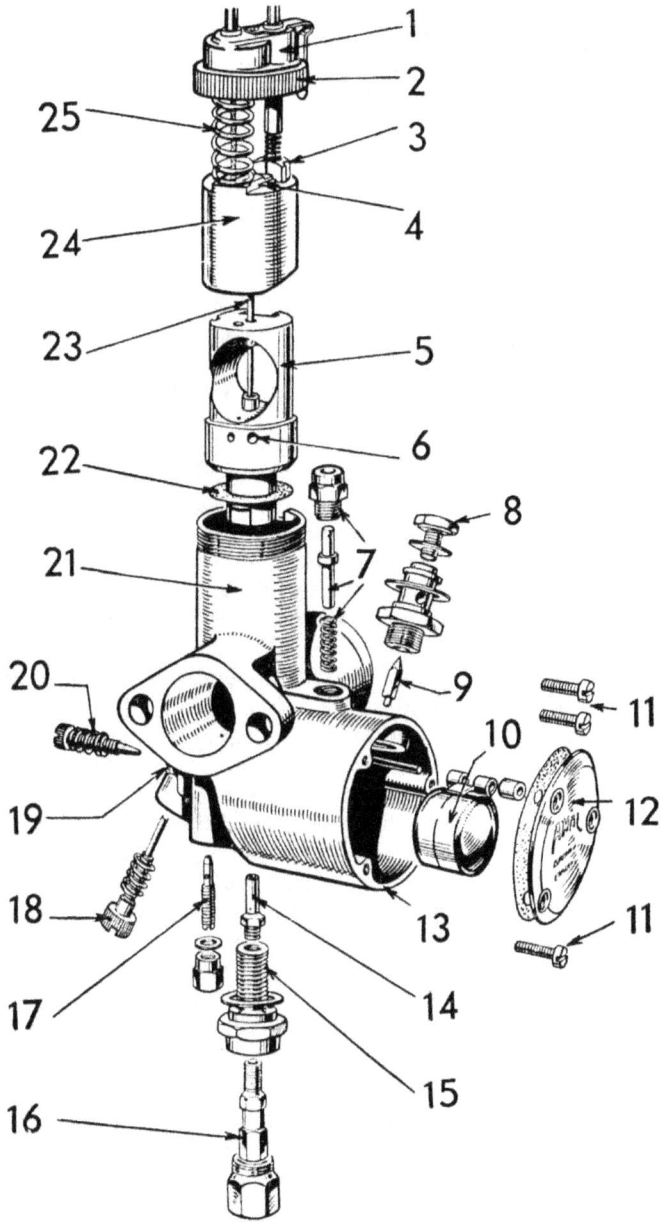

Fig. 10. Amal "Monobloc" Carburettor (1955 Onwards) Shown Dismantled
(*By courtesy of B.S.A. Motor Cycles, Ltd.*)

respects. But its general functioning is similar. The "Monobloc" design includes: a horizontal float chamber made integral with the carburettor body; a float needle of moulded nylon; a top petrol-feed; a needle jet with bleed holes giving two-way compensation; and a detachable pilot-jet which can be easily cleaned.

Fig. 10 shows all the essential parts of the instrument. The float chamber (13) and needle (9) maintain a constant level of petrol in the needle jet (14) and the pilot jet (17). The selection by the makers of the appropriate jet sizes and main-bore choke ensures a proper atomizing and proportioning of the petrol and air sucked into the engine.

The air valve (3) is normally kept fully raised, and the throttle valve (24) controlled by the handlebar twist-grip controls the volume of mixture, and therefore the power. At all throttle openings a correct mixture is automatically obtained.

The "Monobloc" carburettor, like the standard instrument, operates in four stages. When opening the throttle from the fully closed position to one-eighth open (for tick-over) the mixture is supplied by the pilot jet (17), and the strength of the mixture is determined by the setting of the knurled pilot-air adjusting screw (20) which has a coil locking-spring to facilitate adjustment. As the throttle is opened slightly farther, the main jet system comes into action, the mixture being augmented by the main jet (16) through the pilot by-pass.

The amount of cut-away on the atmospheric side of the throttle valve regulates the petrol-to-air ratio between one-eighth and one-quarter throttle. The needle jet (14) and the jet needle (23) take over the mixture regulation between one-quarter and three-quarter throttle, and the mixture strength is determined by the relative position of the needle in the clip (4) attached to the throttle valve (24). When the throttle is opened beyond three-quarters, the mixture strength is determined only by the size of the main jet. Note that the main jet (16) does not spray petrol direct into the carburettor mixing-chamber, but discharges through the needle jet into the primary air-chamber. From there it enters the main choke through the primary air-choke. The latter has a two-way compensating action in conjunction with the "bleed" holes in the needle jet. Pilot and main jet behaviour are not affected by this two-way compensation which governs only acceleration at normal cruising speed.

TUNING AMAL CARBURETTOR (STANDARD AND "MONOBLOC" TYPES)

The same tuning instructions apply to the standard and "Monobloc" instruments. Normally *it is unwise to interfere with the maker's carburettor setting* (*see* Tables I-III) unless there is a very special reason for doing so. However, it is sometimes desirable to make a slow-running adjustment with the pilot adjusting-screw and throttle-stop screw.

ALL ABOUT CARBURATION

Table I
AMAL CARBURETTOR SETTINGS FOR 1945-54 SINGLES

Model	Carburettor	Main Jet	With Air Filter	Throttle Valve	Needle Position
350 c.c. O.H.V.	76AE/1AK	150	130	6/4	3*
500 c.c. O.H.V.	89B/1AK	180	160	29/4	2

Table II
AMAL CARBURETTOR SETTINGS FOR 1955-6 SINGLES

Model	Carburettor	Main Jet	Pilot Jet	Throttle Valve	Needle Position
350 c.c. O.H.V. (no air filter)	376/5	210	30	376/3	3
350 c.c. O.H.V. (with air filter)	376/33	200	30	376/3	3
500 c.c. O.H.V. (to engine 27000)	376/14	240	30	376/3	2
500 c.c. O.H.V. (after No. 27000)	389/1	260	30	389/3	3

Table III
AMAL CARBURETTOR SETTINGS FOR 1957-60 SINGLES

Model (No air filter)	Carburettor	Main Jet	Pilot Jet	Throttle Valve	Needle Position
350 c.c. O.H.V.	376/5	220†	30	376/3½	3
500 c.c. O.H.V.	389/1	260	30	389/3½	3

* Where an air filter is fitted, the needle position should be No. 2, not No. 3. The type numbers of the 1954 350 c.c. and 500 c.c. Amal carburettors are 76AV/1ED and 89N/1ED respectively.

† On 1958-60 350 c.c. models the correct main jet size is 210. Where an air filter is fitted, reduce the main jet size by 10. This applies to all 350 c.c. and 500 c.c. models.

To vary the strength of the running mixture (rarely necessary), it is necessary to adjust the height of the needle in the throttle valve, or else to fit a larger or smaller size main-jet. The condition of the sparking plug will provide an excellent guide to the condition of the mixture (*see* page 77).

To Make a Slow-Running Adjustment. This should be effected with the engine already *warmed up*. If the adjustment is appreciably at fault, screw home the pilot-air adjusting screw fully and then unscrew it (usually about two complete turns) until the engine idles at an excessive speed, with the throttle twist-grip closed and the throttle slide abutting the throttle-stop screw. The air lever should be fully open and the ignition lever (where automatic ignition-advance is not provided) should be set to obtain the best slow-running (half to two-thirds advanced).

Loosen the nut (omitted on the "Monobloc" carburettor) securing the throttle-stop screw, and unscrew the latter until the engine slows up and begins to falter. Then screw the pilot-air adjusting screw in or out as required to enable the engine to run regularly and faster. To weaken the mixture, screw the pilot-air adjusting screw *outwards*.

Slowly lower the throttle-stop screw until the engine again begins to falter. Then lock the throttle-stop screw (standard carburettor) with the lock-nut and reset the pilot-air adjusting screw to obtain the best slow-running. If after making this second adjustment the engine ticks over too fast, repeat the adjustment a third time. The combined adjustment sounds complicated but in practice is quite simple. It is important to avoid excessive richness of the slow-running mixture, especially if much riding is done on small throttle openings; if the mixture is too rich, considerable running on the pilot jet will occur while riding, with consequently a high fuel consumption.

Aim at obtaining the best tick-over, preferably on a mixture just bordering on the weak side. The engine should be on the point of spitting-back.* When perfect slow-running has been obtained, tighten the lock-nut (standard carburettor) on the throttle-stop screw without disturbing the position of the screw.

Obstructed Pilot Jet. If the adjustment of the pilot jet does not obtain the desired results and the engine will not idle nicely with the throttle almost closed, the air lever fully open, and the ignition lever (where fitted) half to two-thirds advanced, it is possible that the pilot jet is obstructed. The jet passage (on the standard carburettor a duct drilled in the jet block) is very small and can readily become choked.

* Rev the engine up and down sharply several times (while at rest and while riding) and note whether the exhaust is nice and crisp, with no "flat spots" as the twist-grip is turned. It is essential to combine good tick-over with good acceleration.

ALL ABOUT CARBURATION

To gain access to the pilot jet on the standard carburettor (*see* Fig. 8), remove the jet plug (*Q*) and the float chamber (*R*), and then detach the jet block (*F*) by pushing or tapping it out of the mixing chamber. The pilot jet (*J*) can then be cleared by blowing through it, or by means of a *very* fine strand of wire.

With the "Monobloc" carburettor (*see* Fig. 10) to remove the pilot jet (17), remove the pilot jet cover-nut and then unscrew the jet itself which should be thoroughly cleaned in petrol and then blown through. See that the air passage (6) to the pilot jet, and also the pilot outlet, are quite clear.

Bad Slow-running. If it is found impossible to obtain good slow-running by making the pilot-air adjustment as described on page 18, it is probable that some defect other than carburation is responsible for preventing the engine running smoothly at low revolutions. Air leaks or badly-seating valves may weaken the mixture. Defects in the ignition system may also be responsible for poor tick-over. The sparking plug may be oily, or the points set too close (*see* page 77). Possibly the spark is excessively advanced or the contact-breaker needs attention (*see* page 80).

Also examine the h.t. cable for signs of shorting.

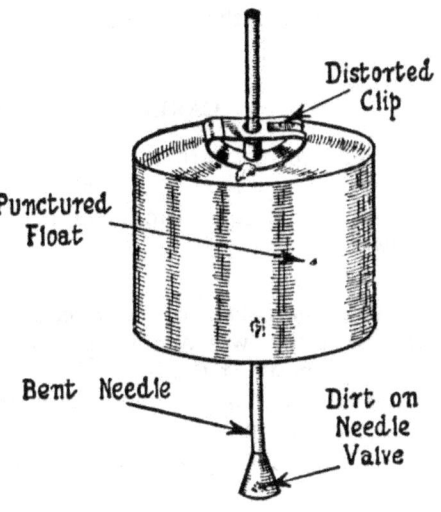

FIG. 11. IF PERSISTENT "FLOODING" OCCURS, LOOK FOR THESE DEFECTS
(Standard type carburettor)

Excessive Fuel Consumption. If in spite of careful checking on the tuning of the carburettor, high fuel consumption continues, it is likely that one or more of the under-mentioned causes is responsible for wastage of precious fuel. Late ignition timing will eat into your petrol supplies quickly. The same applies to poor engine compression due to badly-fitting piston rings or valves. Also take into consideration the question of flooding due to a faulty float, air leakage at the joint between the carburettor and the engine, weak valve springs. See that no wastage is caused by slack petrol pipe union-nuts.

Twist-grip Adjustment. Adjustment should be such that the grip is free and easy to twist, but "stays put." The spring tension on the twist-grip rotating sleeve is regulated by a screw incorporated in one-half of the twist-grip body. To increase the tension, loosen the lock-nut and turn the screw into the body as required.

It is possible to move the complete twist-grip on the handlebars by slackening the two screws which clamp it in position. The best position of the twist-grip is that which gives the cleanest and straightest path to the throttle cable between the handlebars and the under-side of the petrol tank.

On 1945–53 models the throttle cable is initially coated with graphite lubricant which suffices for an indefinite period, but when a new cable is fitted it should be similarly greased. On 1954 and later models a nipple is provided for lubricating the throttle cable, and so ensures smooth throttle operation. If any stiffness or jerkiness occurs, inject a little engine oil through the nipple. When doing this, apply the gun as nearly vertically as possible, with the nozzle downwards.

CARBURETTOR MAINTENANCE

To ensure correct carburation it is advisable occasionally to remove the carburettor from the engine, strip it down completely, and then thoroughly clean it. It is a good plan to do this about every six months as described below.

Dismantling Standard Carburettor. First close both petrol taps and disconnect the twin petrol pipes from the carburettor by undoing the single union-nut at the base of the float chamber. Referring to Fig. 8, loosen the jet plug (Q) and slacken the mixing chamber union-nut (E).

Unscrew the mixing-chamber knurled cap-ring (Z) held by the retaining spring ($Z1$) at the top of the carburettor, and remove the two nuts securing the carburettor flange to the face of the inlet port. Now remove the body of the carburettor, complete with the float chamber, from the engine.

When removing the carburettor, pull the air valve (D) and the throttle valve (B), together with the jet needle (C), from the mixing chamber (A); temporarily tie up the slides out of the way. It is not necessary to remove the air and throttle slides from the control cables unless it is desired to renew the slides or control cables. The jet needle (C) can be adjusted for position in, or removed from, the throttle slide by removing the spring clip from the top of the slide. Examine the carburettor-flange washer, and, if damaged, renew it.

With the carburettor removed from the engine, proceed to remove the jet plug (Q) and the float chamber (R). Also remove the main jet (P) and the needle jet (O). Then completely unscrew the mixing-chamber union-nut (E) and push the jet block (F) right out; if stiff, tap the jet block out gently with a wooden stump. Unscrew the float-chamber cover (W) after loosening the locking screw (X). Then withdraw the float by pinching the clip (V) inwards, and pull gently upwards.

Dismantling "Monobloc" Carburettor. Close both petrol taps and disconnect the twin petrol pipes by undoing the banjo bolt (8) over the float chamber (see Fig. 10). Referring to Fig. 10, unscrew the mixing-chamber knurled cap-ring (2) on top of the carburettor and remove the two nuts securing the carburettor flange to the face of the inlet port. Then remove the body of the carburettor (21), complete with the integral float chamber (13). While removing the carburettor, pull the air valve (3) and the throttle valve (24) from the mixing chamber and tie them up temporarily out of the way. As mentioned in the instructions for the standard type carburettor, it is rarely necessary to disconnect the slides from the cables. Check that the flange washer is sound.

Further dismantling is straightforward. Referring to Fig. 10, to remove the jet needle (23), withdraw the jet-needle clip (4) on top of the throttle valve, and remove the needle. To obtain access to the float (10), remove the three screws (11) securing the float-chamber cover (12). Lift out the hinged float (10) and withdraw the moulded-nylon needle (9). Lay both aside for cleaning. The float-chamber vent, by the way, is embodied in the tickler assembly (7), and the top-feed union houses a filter element of fine gauze which is rapidly accessible for cleaning.

To remove the main jet (16), remove the main-jet cover and unscrew the jet from the jet holder (15), which should also be unscrewed. Remove the jet-block locating screw (19) to the left of and slightly below the pilot-air adjusting screw. Then push or tap out the jet block (5) and fibre seal (22) through the large end of the mixing chamber (21). To remove the pilot jet (17), remove the pilot-jet cover nut and unscrew the jet.

To Clean the Carburettor. Wash all the carburettor components, thoroughly clean with petrol and blow through the various ducts and passages to make sure they are quite clear. Avoid using a fluffy rag for drying purposes. Pay special attention to the small pilot-jet passages in the jet block on both the standard and "Monobloc" type instruments. See that all impurities are removed from inside the float chamber. On the "Monobloc" carburettor do not forget to clean the detachable pilot jet and the filter gauze inside the top-feed union for the float chamber.

Inspecting the Parts. When dismantling the carburettor it is advisable to make a close inspection of the various parts if the carburettor has been in continuous service for a considerable period.

1. THE FLOAT CHAMBER. Examine the components very carefully and check that the vent is unobstructed. The float must be in perfect condition. Clean the moulded-nylon needle on the "Monobloc" carburettor very thoroughly, and be careful not to damage it. On a standard carburettor hand-polish the valve part of the float needle by rotating the needle on its seat while pulling it vertically upwards. If a distinct shoulder is visible on

the needle where it seats, renew the needle at once. Check for any sign of bending or distortion of the clip.

2. THE THROTTLE VALVE. Test this for fit in the mixing chamber. Should excessive play exist, renew the slide forthwith. See that the new slide has the correct amount of cut-away.

3. THE JET-NEEDLE CLIP. The spring clip securing the tapered needle to the throttle valve must grip the needle firmly, and free rotation must *not* occur, as this causes the needle groove to wear. Always be careful to replace the needle with the clip in the correct groove (*see* page 16).

4. THE JET BLOCK. Before tapping this home in the mixing chamber verify by blowing that the pilot-jet ducts are clear and that the jet-block fibre seal is in good condition.

5. THE CARBURETTOR FLANGE. Examine this for truth with a straight-edge. Distortion sometimes occurs, and this may cause an air leak. If the flange is slightly concave, file and rub down the face with emery cloth until it is dead flat and smooth.

Assembling Standard Carburettor. Referring to Fig. 8, refit the jet block (*F*) with the fibre washer on its under-side, and screw on lightly the mixing-chamber union nut (*E*). Screw in the needle jet (*O*) and the main jet (*P*). Open the air lever $\frac{7}{8}$ in. and the throttle twist-grip half way; grasp the air slide between the thumb and the finger and make sure that the jet needle enters the central hole in the barrel (*H*). Slightly turn the throttle slide until it enters the barrel guide when, on pushing down the slides, the air valve should enter its guide. If not, slightly move the mixing-chamber cap (*Y*), when the air valve will slide into position. Screw home the mixing-chamber knurled cap-ring (*Z*). No force is necessary.

Replace the carburettor-flange washer, offer up the carburettor body and secure in position by tightening the two nuts evenly. Replace the float and needle in the float chamber, holding the needle against its seating with a pencil until the float (*T*) and needle clip (*V*) are slipped into position. See that the spring clip enters the needle groove. Then screw home the float-chamber cover securely and lock in position by tightening the lock-screw (*X*).

Insert the jet plug (*Q*) in the union nut (*E*) and very firmly tighten the union nut with a suitable spanner. Remove the jet plug, fit the float chamber, and secure with the jet plug. Be sure there is a fibre washer above and below the float-chamber lug as shown in Fig. 8. When the float chamber has been correctly positioned, tighten the jet plug firmly. Finally reconnect the twin petrol pipes and tighten the union nut at the base of the float chamber. In the event of the pilot-jet adjustment having been disturbed, re-tune as described on page 18.

Wear of Jet Needle. The needle itself does *not* wear, though some wear of the groove may occur if the jet-needle clip is not grasping the needle firmly. If the mixture is too rich with the clip in No. 1 groove (nearest the top), it is probable that the needle jet needs to be renewed because of wear. It is assumed that the carburettor is correctly tuned and that no flooding occurs (*see* page 18).

Assembling "Monobloc" Carburettor. Do this in the reverse order of dismantling. Referring to Fig. 10, screw home the pilot jet (17) and the pilot jet cover-nut, not omitting to replace its washer. Push or tap home the jet block (5) and fibre seal (22) through the large end of the mixing chamber (21). Check that the fibre-seal fitted to the stub of the jet block is in good condition. Then fit the jet-block locating-screw (19). Screw the main-jet holder (15) into the jet block, after checking that the washer for the holder is sound. Next screw the main jet (16) into the jet holder.

Replace the moulded-nylon needle (9) in the float chamber (13), and fit the hinged float (10) with the *narrow* side of the hinge uppermost. Afterwards fit the float-chamber cover (12) and secure by means of the three screws (11). Verify that the cover and body faces are undamaged and quite clean. Renew the washer.

If previously removed, attach the jet needle (23) to the throttle valve (24) and secure with the jet-needle clip (4), making sure that the clip enters the correct groove. (*See* page 16.)

Position the carburettor-flange washer, and offer up the carburettor to the face of the inlet port after easing the air and throttle valves (3) and (24) down into the mixing chamber (*see* hints on page 21 concerning the standard carburettor). When easing the throttle valve home, make sure that the tapered jet-needle (23) really enters the hole in the jet block (5). Secure the carburettor flange firmly to the engine by means of the two nuts, and tighten these evenly. Tighten down firmly the mixing-chamber knurled cap-ring (2) and see that the throttle slide works freely when this is tightened down.

Finally reconnect the twin petrol pipes by tightening the banjo bolt (8) over the float chamber (13).

THE AIR FILTER

Maintenance. An air filter of the "oil-wetted" type is fitted as an optional extra to A.J.S. models. In the United Kingdom the roads are excellent and the air comparatively free from dust, and it is questionable whether the fitting of an air filter, except for use abroad in countries where the roads are poor and dusty, will appreciably prolong the life of the cylinder and piston.

Where an air filter is fitted, it is advisable about every 2,500 miles to withdraw the filter element; wash it thoroughly in petrol, paraffin, or other suitable solvent, and allow to dry. Then submerge the element completely for a few minutes in thin oil (SAE 20) of the type recommended on page 65 for the "Teledraulic" front forks. Remove the element, allow all surplus oil to drain off, and afterwards replace in the air-filter case. It is desirable to renew the filter element about every 10,000 miles.

To Remove Filter Element (1956–60 Models). First pull the rubber hose off the air-intake of the "Monobloc" carburettor after releasing the clip (1957). Next remove the frame cover and pull off the hose end from the air filter. Then remove the bolts which secure the air filter to the oil tank and remove the complete filter assembly. Note that the filter element is secured in its cage by bolts, nuts, and locking washers.

After cleaning the filter (*see* a previous paragraph) replace it. When replacing the hose on the filter, see that it is properly located. The end of the rubber hose is split along the edge of the lip, and it is important to make sure that the neck of the filter assembly enters this groove.

CHAPTER III

THE LIGHTING SYSTEM

To ensure maximum illumination from the lamps at all times, a little attention to the equipment is normally necessary and in practice is generally confined to: keeping the lamps clean; renewing dud bulbs; topping-up the battery regularly; taking occasional specific-gravity readings; periodically inspecting the dynamo brushes and commutator (particularly important on 1945–51 models, but not applicable to any 1958–60 models); the keeping of all connexions clean and tight; and the prevention or repair of frayed leads by taping where necessary.

ILLUMINATION

The Switch Positions. The lighting switch (*see* Figs. 2 and 3) situated on top of 1945–60 headlamps causes the dynamo to charge in all three switch positions, which are as follows—

"OFF"—No lights on.

"L"——Headlamp pilot, rear, and speedometer bulbs on.

"H"——Headlamp main, rear, and speedometer bulbs on.

Headlamp Alignment. Incorrect headlamp alignment and/or an out-of-focus main bulb give reduced road illumination and liability to dazzle other road users. Both faults are simply rectified. 1951–60 headlamps have a "pre-focus" main bulb.

To check the headlamp alignment, take your A.J.S. to a straight, level stretch of road, turn the lighting switch to the "H" position, and operate the dipping switch so that the main driving light is switched on. The beam of light should, if alignment is correct, be straight ahead and slightly below the horizontal. If the headlamp is mounted so that the beam of light is elevated or projects too much on the road, slacken the mounting bolts or nuts which secure the headlamp to its brackets and then tilt the headlamp slightly down or up until correct alignment is obtained. Afterwards secure the headlamp firmly.

Headlamp Focusing. On 1945–50 A.J.S. machines the double-filament main bulb (movable) is focused to give the best illumination. Provided genuine Lucas bulbs of the correct wattage and number are fitted as replacements, subsequent refocusing should be unnecessary. Where a Lucas bulb is not available, or the focusing adjustment has been disturbed, it is necessary to re-focus. At the same time it is desirable to check the headlamp alignment as previously described.

The headlamp is correctly focused when the reflected rays of light are almost parallel and when the beam, projected upon a wall (30–40 ft from the machine) illuminates brightly a circular area of minimum diameter. The filament for the main driving light should be as near as possible to the focal point of the reflector in order to obtain a parallel beam. If the filament is positioned in front of the focal point, a converging beam (with dark centre portion) results. If, on the other hand, the filament is positioned behind the focal point, a diverging beam is obtained.

Both converging and diverging beams are highly undesirable as they illuminate the road poorly and are liable to dazzle other road users. Adjust the focus of the headlamp immediately if its beam is not uniform, is of short range, and has a dark centre. To focus the headlamp it is obviously necessary to move the main bulb backwards or forwards on the reflector axis according to whether the beam is converging or diverging respectively.

THE LAMPS (1945–8 MODELS)

To Focus DU-42 Headlamp (1945–8). You should take your machine to a level stretch of road and focus the headlamp against a wall some distance (say 30-40 ft) from the machine. The lamp front and reflector must first be removed. To do this, release the front fixing-clip (*see* Fig. 12) which secures the base of the lamp front and pull the latter outwards. As the lamp front and reflector come away together, free the top tag of the lamp front from the body of the lamp by lifting the lamp front slightly upwards.

The double-filament main bulb holder is adjustable in the plate fitted to the back of the reflector, and as may be seen in Fig. 12 there is a clamping clip for focusing adjustment. To focus the bulb, loosen the clamping screw on the clip and push the bulb-holder in or out of the clamping clip as required. Several focusing adjustments may be needed. After making each adjustment, replace the lamp front and reflector and test the beam for focus (*see* earlier paragraph). When the correct focus is obtained, tighten the screw on the bulb-holder clamping clip firmly.

When fitting the lamp front and reflector, first locate the top tag in the slot of the lamp body and then press home the lamp front towards the body. Finally, fasten the lamp front by means of the spring fixing-clip at the base of the lamp.

Lamp Bulb Renewal (1945–8). If a bulb "goes west," fit a bulb of the correct type. Most large garages and accessory dealers stock genuine Lucas bulbs, which are all specially tested to check that the filament is correctly positioned to give maximum results *with Lucas reflectors.*

THE LIGHTING SYSTEM

It is advisable not to wait till bulbs actually burn out but to renew them after long service. This avoids the risk of incorrect focusing caused by filaments sagging, which sometimes occurs after extensive use.

Lucas bulbs have their metal caps marked with a number for identification purposes and it is important when renewing a bulb to see that it has the correct number on its cap. The correct headlamp double-filament main bulb is No. 168; and that of the headlamp pilot-bulb and sidecar lamp bulb, 200. The number 168 bulb is 6 V., 24 W., S.B.C. The number 200 bulb is 6 V., 3 W., S.B.C. Fit a No. 205 (6 V., 6 W.) rear-lamp bulb.

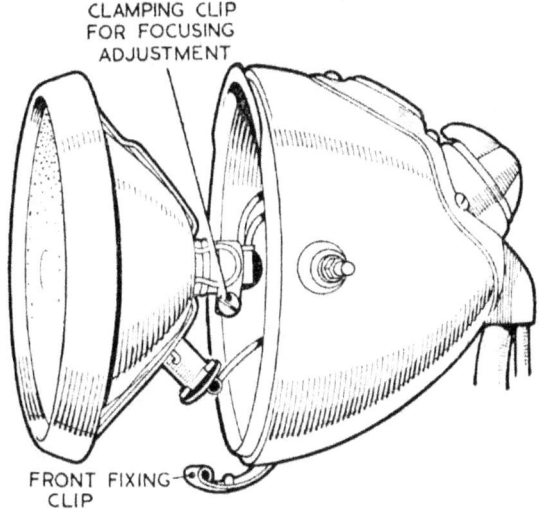

FIG. 12. LUCAS DU-42 HEADLAMP (1945-8 MODELS)

The lamp front and reflector are shown detached from the lamp body to reveal the clamping clip, which must be loosened to enable the bulb-holder to be moved for focusing.

The headlamp main and pilot bulbs are fitted in holders attached to the plate secured to the rear of the reflector by two spring wires. To remove the plate, complete with the two holders and bulbs, it is only necessary to spring the two wires outwards until they are clear of the plate.

To remove the headlamp main bulb or pilot bulb from its holder, it is only necessary to release the bayonet fixing and withdraw the bulb.

It is essential when fitting a new main bulb to see that it is the correct way round, i.e. with the dipped beam filament *above* the centre filament. The word "Top" is etched on Lucas main bulbs to indicate the correct position in the bulb holder. After fitting a new main bulb it is advisable to check the focus of the headlamp (*see* page 25).

Removing Reflector (1945–8). Remove the four spring clips that secure the reflector and glass to the headlamp front and detach the reflector the cork packing strip between the reflector and glass, and the glass itself.

To assemble the reflector and glass, the following procedure is necessary. First position the glass in the lamp front. Next, fit the cork packing strip to the reflector edge by pressing it into the pins which are integral with the lamp front. Then place the reflector assembly (complete with bulb holders) on top of the glass. Make sure that the top of the reflector registers with the top of the lamp front. Finally, replace the four spring clips so that they are about equally spaced.

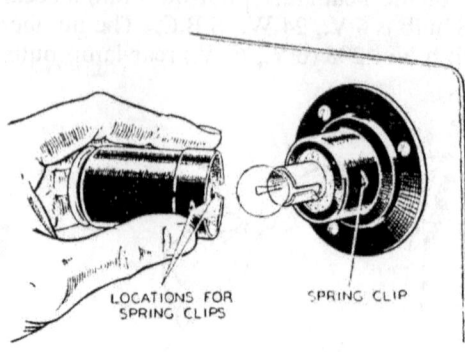

FIG. 13. LUCAS REAR LAMP (TYPE WT203)

The lamp shown is fitted to some 1945–8 models. For details of later design rear lamps, *see* page 35.

The WT203 Rear Lamp (1945–8). The lamp body, with bulb holder, is secured to the rear number plate by means of three bolts with appropriate washers and nuts. To detach the portion of the rear lamp housing the red glass, give it a *half-turn* to the left and then pull it outwards, as shown in Fig. 13. When replacing the outer portion of the lamp, engage the slots in the body of the lamp with the two spring-clips on the body of the lamp and push right home to effect full engagement.

Cleaning Lucas Lamps. Clean ebony black surfaces with a good type of car polish. Chromium-plated surfaces do not tarnish and should be wiped over with a damp cloth occasionally to remove dirt or dust. Care must be taken when handling a reflector not to scratch it accidentally, and *on no account must metal polish be used to clean it.*

A fine, colourless and transparent covering is provided on the Lucas reflectors for protection purposes, and this covering can readily be cleaned without any risk of damaging the actual surface of the reflector. Polish the reflector covering lightly with a clean, dry, soft cloth or a chamois leather. No other treatment is desirable.

Ammeter Readings. This centre-zero instrument shows a charge on one side and a discharge on the other and is provided to give a reading of the amount of current flowing to or from the battery.

For instance, if the dynamo output is 3 amp. at a certain speed, and the pilot bulb and rear lamp are on, thereby absorbing, say, 1 amp., then 2 amp. remain for battery charging, and the ammeter will therefore indicate 2 amp.

At very low r.p.m. the ammeter reading is zero because the dynamo armature is not rotating fast enough to generate sufficient current to give a battery charge. (*See also* page 40).

Ammeter Removal (1945–54 Models). Should it be necessary for some reason to remove the ammeter, this can readily be effected. Referring to Figs. 14 and 20, detach the panel from the top of the Lucas headlamp by unscrewing the three retaining screws. Then unscrew the two ammeter terminal screws shown at A and disconnect the wires. Next bend back the four metal tags shown at B. When these have been dealt with, ammeter C can be removed bodily from the panel. Replace the ammeter, in the reverse order of removal. Do not touch switch D.

THE LAMPS (1949 ONWARDS)

The headlamp and rear lamps fitted 1949 onwards are different from previous types and the following notes should be studied by owners of 1949 and subsequent models.

Focusing SSU700P Headlamp (1949–50). Focusing should always be effected on a level stretch of road with the headlamp beam directed against a wall some 30–40 ft distant from the machine. Note the general remarks on page 25 concerning focusing, and see that the headlamp is aligned correctly. On the SSU700P headlamps, the lamp front and the light-unit assembly (reflector and glass) are removed together.

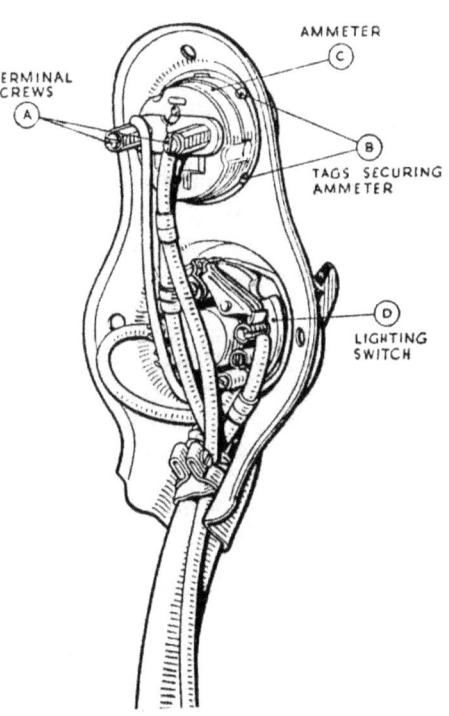

Fig. 14. Ammeter and Switch Panel Removed (1945–50 Headlamps)

To remove the lamp front, loosen the screw on top of the headlamp body, withdraw the rim outward from the top, and as the lamp front emerges raise it a little to free the lower tag from the shell of the headlamp. The double-filament main bulb is adjustable in its holder and has a clamp tightened by one screw. To focus the main bulb, loosen this screw and push the bulb holder inwards or outwards until the correct focus is obtained. Afterwards firmly retighten the screw which clamps the bulb holder.

Next engage the lower tag on the lamp rim with the small slit in the lamp shell and carefully press the top of the rim back into the lamp shell. Finally retighten the screw on the top of the lamp body.

The "Pre-Focus" 1951 SSU700P Headlamp. On the 1951 models the Lucas SSU700P headlamp has a "pre-focus" main bulb, and no focusing adjustment is provided. Details of the bulb holder assembly are shown in Fig. 19. The "pre-focus" bulb filament is in permanent focus relatively to the reflector, and the pilot bulb mounted on the top of the back shell provides illumination through a transparent window in the reflector.

To obtain access to the main and pilot bulbs, remove the lamp front, with light-unit assembly as previously described for the SSU700P headlamp fitted to 1949–50 models.

The 1952-3 SSU700P/1 Headlamp. This headlamp (*see* Fig. 17) is identical to the 1951 SSU700P "pre-focus" type headlamp just described except that instead of the pilot bulb being mounted above the "pre-focus" main bulb as shown in Fig. 16, it is mounted in an inverted position in a detachable carrier-plate at the base of the lamp and shines through an underslung pilot lens, not perhaps an ideal arrangement.

If desired, suitable pilot lamps can be substituted (*see* Fig. 18) for the underslung pilot light. Access to the "pre-focus" main bulb and the pilot bulb is obtained by removing the lamp front (with light-unit assembly) as already described for the 1949–50 SSU700P headlamp.

The 1954-7 Headlamps. These Lucas headlamps are basically similar to the 1952-3 SSU700P/1 "pre-focus" type headlamp, but the pilot-light arrangement is quite different. As may be seen in Fig. 18, two smart torpedo-shaped pilot lamps are secured to the front-fork lamp supports by tubular bolts, through each of which a lead passes to the adjacent pilot lamp. On 1954 headlamps the ammeter and lighting switch are mounted, one behind the other, on a panel on top of the headlamp, but on 1955-7 headlamps the arrangement is as shown in Fig. 18.

On all 1954–7 headlamps, to obtain access to the double filament "pre-focus" main bulb, remove the lamp front (with light-unit assembly) as described on page 29 for the 1949–50 SSU700P headlamp. To get at the bulb in each streamlined pilot bulb, remove the screw at the rear and gently pull forward on the glass rim.

The 1958–60 MCH57 Headlamp. Details of the Lucas MCH57 headlamp fitted to 1958–60 A.J.S. machines are shown in Fig. 15. As may be observed, the arrangement of the light-unit assembly and main bulb is similar to that provided on earlier "pre-focus" type headlamps (*see* Fig. 17), but the parking bulb and lighting switch arrangement differs.

The single pilot or parking bulb is fitted *inside* the headlamp and is a plug-in or push fit in the reflector. The lighting switch has three positions

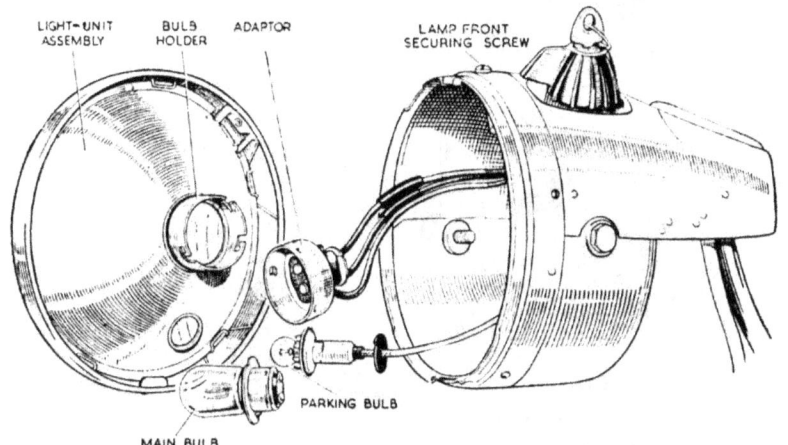

Fig. 15. Lucas MCH57 "Pre-Focus" Headlamp with Light-unit Assembly, Main Bulb, and Parking Bulb Withdrawn (1958 Onwards)
Note the ignition switch fitted in the centre of the lighting switch.

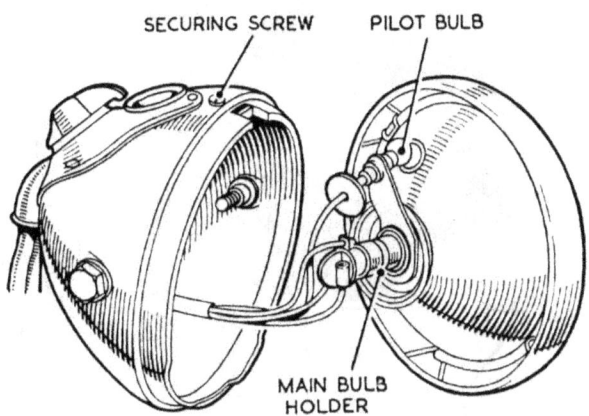

Fig. 16. Lucas SSU700P Headlamp with Front and Reflector Removed (1949–50 Models)

On 1951 A.J.S. machines with SSU700P headlamp the lamp glass and reflector are not detachable from each other; the two components comprise the "light unit" assembly, secured to the rim by spring clips. A back shell houses the pilot bulb and a "pre-focus" main bulb.

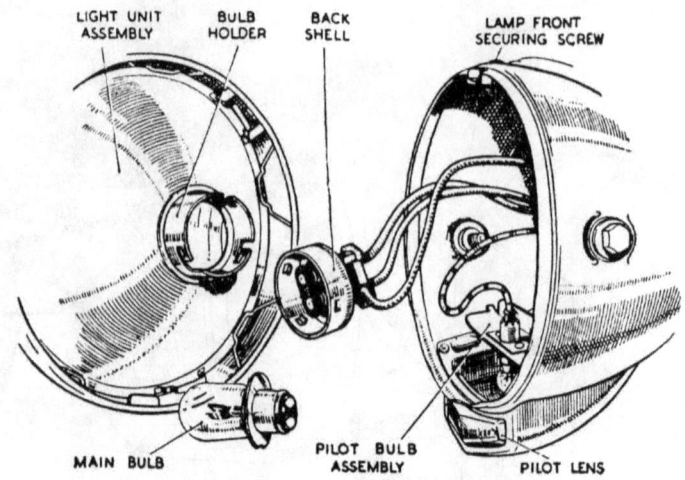

FIG. 17. LUCAS SSU700P/1 "PRE-FOCUS" HEADLAMP WITH FRONT (LIGHT-UNIT ASSEMBLY INCLUDED) AND MAIN BULB WITHDRAWN (1952–3 MODELS)
Note the remarks below Fig. 16 concerning the light unit.

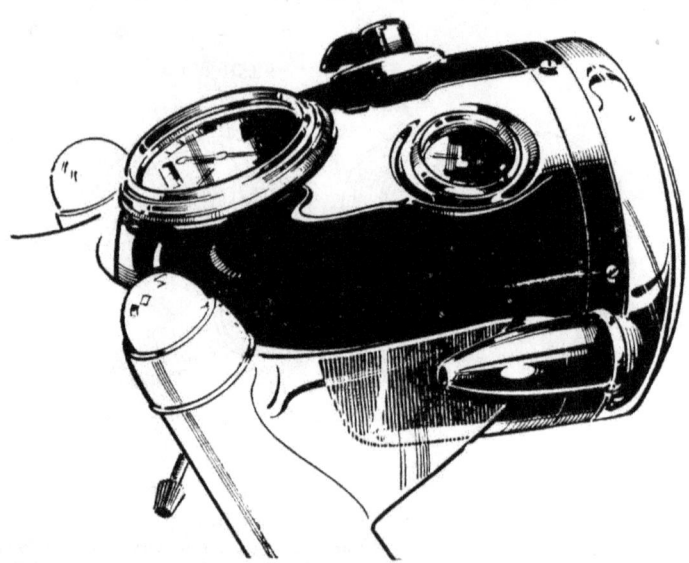

FIG. 18. LUCAS "PRE-FOCUS" HEADLAMP HOUSING AMMETER, LIGHTING SWITCH, AND SPEEDOMETER (1955–7)
Streamlined twin pilot-lamps were introduced in 1954 and are made to A.M.C. specification.
(*By courtesy of "Motor Cycling"*)

THE LIGHTING SYSTEM   33

which are the same as those mentioned on page 25. An ignition key (*see* page 4) is provided in the centre of the lighting switch.

To remove the lamp front (i.e. the light-unit assembly) to get access to the main and pilot bulbs, release the screw securing the lamp rim with one hand and support the light unit with the other. Then withdraw the light-unit assembly. Main bulb removal and fitting are effected as described below. To replace the light-unit assembly, engage the bottom tag on the lamp rim with the small slit in the lamp shield and gently press the top of the rim back into the lamp shell. Afterwards retighten the retaining screw on the top of the lamp body.

Separating Light Unit from Rim. On all Lucas 1949–50 type headlamps, and 1951 and later models, the front glass and reflector are made as one assembly (the "light-unit") and cannot be separated. The light-unit, however, can be removed from the chromium-plated rim by disengaging the spring clips from the turned-up inner edge of the rim by pressing with the blade of a screwdriver, working away from the edge.

To fit the light-unit assembly to the rim, lay the unit in the rim so that the location block on the unit engages the forked bracket on the rim, and then spring home the spring clips. See that they are spaced at equal distances around the rim.

Headlamp Bulb Renewal. Fit *genuine* Lucas bulbs if occasion arises to renew them, and do not defer renewal until actual bulb failure occurs (*see* page 27). To remove the cap (non-"pre-focus" headlamp) which carries the bulbs, depress one of the two spring plungers which secure the cap to the reflector and tilt the cap bodily. When replacing the bulb holder, engage the holder carrier-cap in the position at which the pilot bulb is against the small window in the reflector.

When fitting a non-"pre-focus" main bulb, see that it is fitted with the dipped beam filament *above* the centre filament. Lucas main bulbs have the word "TOP" etched to indicate the correct position in the bulb holder. Check the main bulb for focus after renewing it.

When fitting a "pre-focus" bulb (*see* Fig. 19) turn the back shell anti-clockwise and withdraw it. You can then remove the bulb from the back of the reflector. Insert the correct Lucas-type bulb replacement in the bulb holder with its locating flange positioned, engage the projections on the inside of the back shell with the slots in the bulb holder, press on, and secure by turning clockwise.

Correct Bulb Renewals. The 1949–50 Lucas type SSU700P headlamp (with focusing adjustment) takes a 6-volt, 24/24-watt No. 168 S.B.C. double-filament main bulb (bayonet-fixing type), and a 6-volt, 3-watt No. 988 M.C.C. pilot bulb. The 1951–60 headlamps ("pre-focus" type) require a No. 312 (30/24-watt) Lucas double-filament main bulb which has a broad locating flange on the cap. An alternative bulb to the 6-volt

No. 312 is the No. 373 (6-volt, 30/24-watt) Lucas double-filament bulb. Both bulbs are suitable for "pre-focus" lamps with block lens light units, but the No. 373 bulb has a left-hand dip and is now recommended by A.J.S. Motor Cycles for use in Great Britain. On continental models fit a Lucas No. 403 (6-volt, 35/35-watt double-filament bulb which has a vertical dip. Note that a No. 312 or 373 bulb cannot be used in a "focusing" type lamp, nor

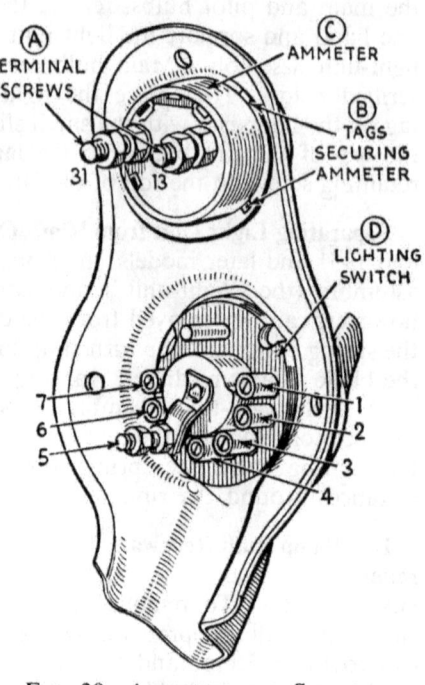

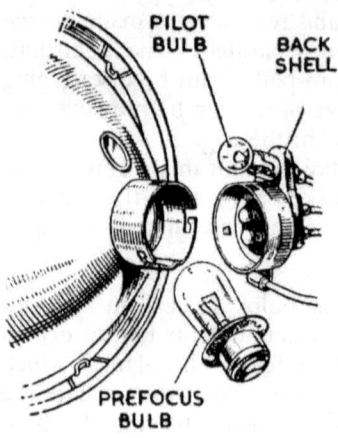

Fig. 19. Lucas Light-unit Assembly and Back Shell with "Pre-focus" Main Bulb and Pilot Bulb (1951 Models)

Fig. 20. Ammeter and Switch Panel Removed (1951–4)

The cable harness (see Fig. 14) is not shown. For location of numbered parts, see wiring diagram (Fig. 30)

can a No. 168 bulb be used in a "pre-focus" type headlamp incorporating a Lucas light-unit assembly. All 1951–60 headlamps require a No. 988 pilot bulb. This is not suitable for 1949–52 rear lamps which require a 6-volt, 6-watt, No. 205 or 951 bulb. 1953 and later Lucas stop-tail lamps require a 6-volt, 18/6-watt, No. 384 double-filament bulb. The correct speedometer bulb is a 6-volt, 1·8-watt No. 53205 M.C.C.

The Ammeter. The sketches numbered Figs. 14 and 20 show the back of the panel housing the ammeter and lighting switch on 1945–50 and 1951–4 models respectively.

1955–60 models have the ammeter and lighting switch built into the Lucas headlamp as shown in Fig. 18. Note the remarks on pages 28 and 42 concerning ammeter readings. Do not meddle with the ammeter. If its needle sticks or "flutters," take the motor-cycle to the nearest Lucas service depot.

THE LIGHTING SYSTEM

Cleaning Lucas Lamps. Observe the instructions given on page 28, but note that on 1949 and later "sealed beam" Lucas headlamps (with Lucas light-unit) the reflector cannot be detached for cleaning.

The MT211 Rear Lamp. This rear lamp, of Lucas design, is secured to the rear number plate of some 1948–9 models by means of a three-bolt fixing. To remove the cover carrying the red glass, push in and turn in an *anti-clockwise* direction. To replace the cover of the lamp, locate the slots in the front portion over the retaining pegs in the lamp body, push inwards, and turn in an *anti-clockwise* direction.

The 467/1 Rear Lamp. The Lucas rear-lamp body, complete with bulb holder, is secured on 1949 models to the rear number-plate by means of two nuts and spring washers. To remove the cover securing the red glass, loosen the captive screw which secures it, and withdraw the cover.

The 467/2 Rear Lamp. On 1950–52 A.J.S. models a Lucas type 467/2 rear lamp is secured to the rear number-plate by two nuts and spring washers. A sleeve nut secures the cover (carrying the red glass) to the body of the lamp. To fit a replacement bulb, remove the sleeve nut and withdraw the cover and glass.

Stop-tail Lamps. 1953 and later A.J.S. machines have Lucas stop-tail lamps of type 525 (564, later models). The lamp has a double-filament 6-volt, 18/6-watt bulb; the 6-watt filament serves as the normal rear light and the 18-watt filament is illuminated only when the rear-brake pedal is depressed. To obtain access to the bulb it is only necessary to remove two screws and withdraw the thermo-plastic cover. To prevent incorrect fitting of the No. 384 bulb, its securing pins are offset.

MAINTENANCE OF BATTERY (LEAD ACID)

Neglect of the battery quickly brings trouble, and correct attention in regard to its maintenance is *vitally* important. Upon it depend the lamps and horn.

Topping-up the Battery. Examine the acid level about every four weeks, and even more frequently in tropical climates. Unscrew the battery clamping screw and remove the battery after first disconnecting the battery positive and negative leads. On 1956–60 models the Lucas battery is housed in a front compartment of the tool box as shown in Fig. 23.

To remove the battery on 1956 models, first release the rubber strap by grasping the loop attached to its lower end; pull downwards until the strap and loop are freed from the retaining clip at the platform base, and permit the rubber strap to slacken. Then lift the battery out.

To remove the battery on 1957–60 models, grasp the rubber strap with the fingers between the battery case and rubber strap. Push the strap downwards until it is possible to free the metal toggle from the strap retaining-clip, then carefully take the battery out.

Take off the battery lid and remove the three vent plugs. Inspect the hole in each vent plug and make certain that is is not obstructed. A choked vent plug hole will result in an increase of pressure in the cell owing to "gassing," and this may cause trouble. Wipe the top of the battery clean

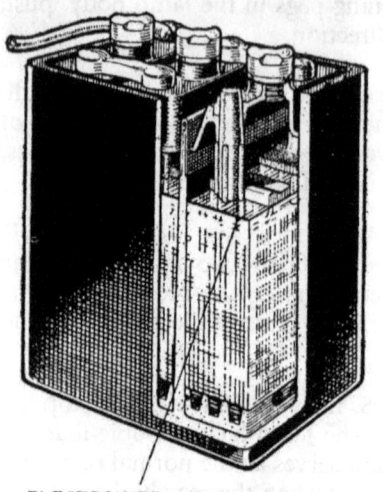
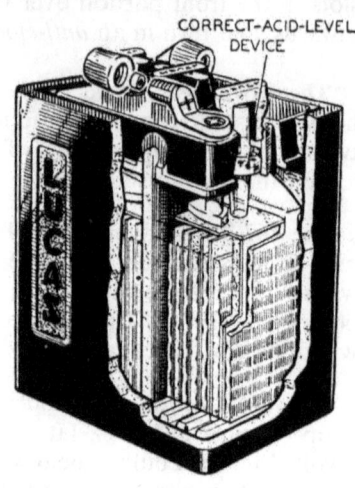

ELECTROLYTE LEVEL

Figs. 21 and 22. Keep the Electrolyte Level with the Tops of the Plate Separators

On the left is shown the Lucas type PUW-7E-4 battery fitted prior to 1954, and on the right the Lucas PU7E/11 battery with correct-acid-level device, fitted to 1956–60 models. The PU7E/9 battery fitted to 1954–5 models is similar except for modified terminals and the omission of external cell connectors.

with a rag and verify that the washer (where fitted) beneath each vent plug, to prevent leakage, is in position. After wiping the top of the battery, either destroy the rag or wash it thoroughly, using several changes of water. See that a supply of clean distilled water is to hand. Topping-up is necessary because the distilled water, unlike the acid, is gradually lost through evaporation.

Be careful not to hold a naked light near the vents. If the level is below the tops of the separators, add *distilled* water as required to bring the level correct (*see* Figs. 21 and 22). This should be done just *before* a charge run, as the agitation due to running and the gassing will thoroughly mix the solution. Acid must not be added to the electrolyte unless the solution has been spilled. If the solution has been spilled by accident, add diluted sulphuric acid of specific gravity equal to that in the cells.

Undoubtedly the best way to top up a PUW-7E-4 type battery is to use a Lucas battery filler. Insert its nozzle into each cell, with the nozzle resting on the separators. Hold the battery filler in this position until air bubbles

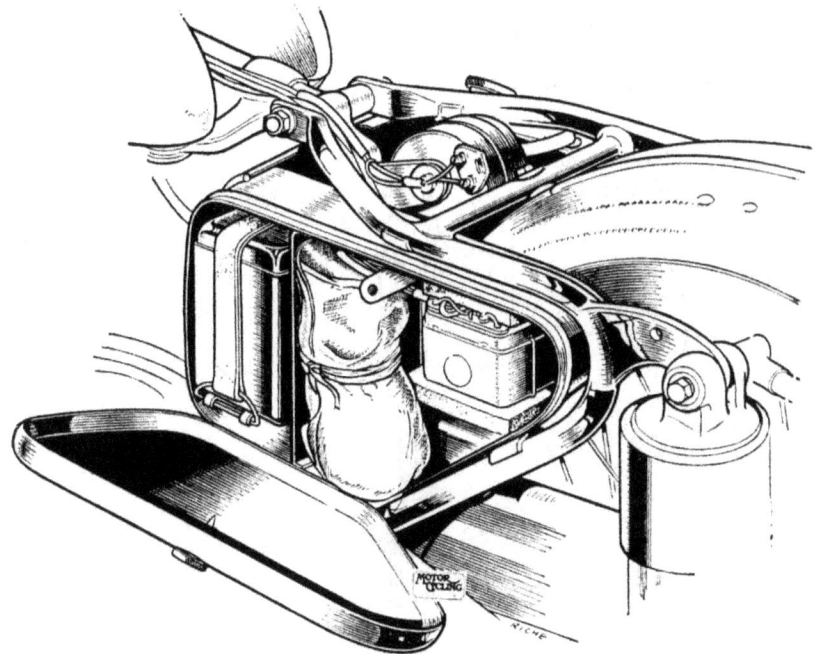

FIG. 23. A 1956–60 REFINEMENT—NEAT ENCLOSURE OF THE BATTERY AND C.V.C. UNIT IN THE TOOL BOX

The compensated-voltage-control unit is, of course, omitted on 1958–60 models with coil ignition. The battery must be fitted with the negative terminal on the right-hand side.

(*By courtesy of "Motor Cycling"*)

cease to rise in the glass container. The electrolyte level should then be correct, but examine it to make sure.

On 1954–60 machines with the PU7E/9 or PU7E/11 battery, pour distilled water round the flange (not the tube) of the acid-level device (*see* Fig. 22) until it ceases to drain into the cell. Then lift the tube slightly to enable the small amount of water in the flange to drain into the cell. The electrolyte level should then be correct. Inspect to make certain.

If the battery needs to be topped up very often, it is possible that the C.V.C. unit (1945–7) needs to be adjusted; if one cell requires more frequent topping up than the others, probably the battery case or container is cracked, and battery renewal is called for.

Checking Specific Gravity. Very occasionally, hydrometer readings (specific-gravity values) should be taken of the solution in each of the cells. The method of doing this is shown in Fig. 24. The Lucas hydrometer contains a graduated float which indicates the specific gravity of the battery cell from which a sample of electrolyte is taken.

After a sample has been taken and checked, it must, of course, be returned to the cell. The taking of S.G. readings with a hydrometer is the most efficient way of ascertaining the state of charge of the battery. The S.G.

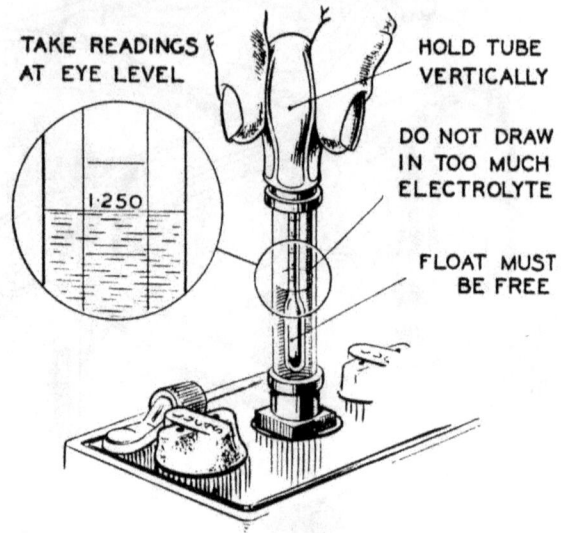

Fig. 24. Lucas Hydrometer being used to Check Specific Gravity of Battery Electrolyte

readings should be approximately the *same for all three cells*. Should the reading for one cell differ substantially from the readings for the others, probably some acid has been spilled or has leaked from the cell concerned. There is also a possibility of a short circuit between the battery plates. In the latter case it will be necessary to return the battery to a Lucas service depot for attention.

Under no circumstances must the battery be permitted to remain in a discharged condition for long, or serious deterioration will occur. After checking the S.G. readings and topping up the cells, wipe the top of the battery and remove any spilled electrolyte or water; replace the three vent plugs and the battery lid. Then fit and tighten the battery clamping screw, or secure with the rubber strap (1956–60 models).

Battery Connexions. Always keep the battery connexions clean, free from corrosion, and tight, otherwise the ammeter readings will *not* indicate

THE LIGHTING SYSTEM

the true state of charge of the battery and proper battery charging may not occur.

Correct Readings. With Lucas batteries fitted to A.J.S. machines, the specific gravity readings at an acid temperature of approximately 60°F. should be: 1·270–1·290, battery fully charged; about 1·190–1·210 battery half discharged; 1·110–1·130 battery fully discharged. If the temperature exceeds 60°F., add 0·002 to the hydrometer reading for each 5 degrees rise in temperature above 60°F. Similarly if the temperature is below 60°F., deduct 0·002 for each 5 degrees decrease in temperature.

Never leave the battery in a discharged state for any appreciable period. A low state of charge often is caused through parking the machine for long periods with the lighting switch in the "L" position, unaccompanied by much daylight running. The remedy is, of course, to undertake more daylight running and to keep the switch in the "Off" position as much as possible until the battery regains its normal state of charge. If overcharging occurs, have the setting of the compensated-voltage-control unit checked in the case of 1945–57 models.

MAINTENANCE OF DYNAMO (1945-7)

It is not necessary to take any special precautions when merely inspecting the commutator, but on making adjustments to the wiring circuit, it is essential to take steps to prevent accidental "shorting." Disconnect the lead from the lighting switch at the battery *positive* terminal (*negative* terminal where the battery positive is earthed). Push back the rubber shield and then unscrew the cable connector (where fitted). When doing this be sure that the cable does not make contact with any metal part of the frame, otherwise a "fat" spark will indicate that the battery *was* well charged! When reconnecting the lead, pull the rubber shield well over the connector.

General Overhaul. It is a good plan every 10,000–15,000 miles to entrust the dynamo to a Lucas service depot for dismantling, cleaning, servicing, and lubrication. Lubrication is referred to on page 65.

The Commutator and Brushgear. The Lucas E3AR and the E3-N dynamos will run satisfactorily for thousands of miles without attention other than occasional inspection of the commutator and brushgear. It is advisable about every 5,000–6,000 miles, to remove the metal cover-band from the dynamo and make a careful inspection.

The Brushes. The brushes must make good electrical contact with the commutator. They must be absolutely clean and able to move freely in their box-type holders, on holding back the retaining springs and gently pulling the leads and then releasing them. There must also be perfect contact between both the brushes and the copper segments of the commutator; the brush faces in contact with the segments should be uniformly polished. Clean the brushes with a petrol-moistened cloth after removing them. To do this, pull back each brush-retaining spring (*see* Fig. 25) and remove the brush by pulling on its lead, being careful to see that the brush pressure spring is clear of the brush holder.

Examine the carbon brushes for wear and unevenness, and true them up if necessary. Generally it is best to renew the brushes *before* serious wear develops, as this prevents sparking, which causes blackening of the commutator and an unsteady charging current. Always replace brushes in their original positions.

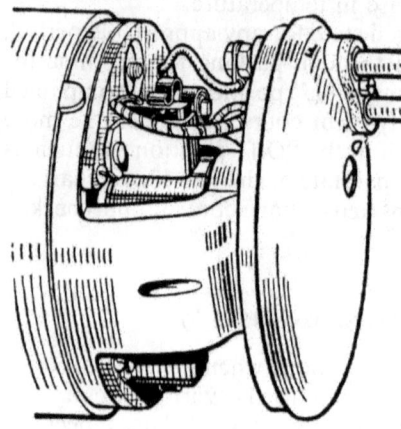

Fig. 25. Commutator End of the Lucas Dynamo with Cover Band Removed

If Lucas brushes become so badly worn that it is necessary to remove them, this can easily be done as follows: Release the eyelet on the brush lead by unscrewing the hexagonal nut or screw at the terminal; then, holding back the spring lever out of the way, withdraw the brush from its holder. Renew with genuine Lucas brushes.

The brush springs should be inspected occasionally to see that they have sufficient tension to keep the brushes firmly pressed against the commutator when the dynamo is running. It is particularly necessary to keep this in mind when the brushes have been in use a long time and are very much worn down.

It is unwise to insert brushes of a grade other than that supplied with the dynamo, or to change the tension springs. The arrangement provided has been made only after many years' experience and will be found to give the best results and the longest life. It is really best, when the brushes become so worn that they no longer bed down on the commutator, or their flexible leads are exposed on their running faces, to have new brushes fitted at a Lucas service depot, as this ensures the brushes being properly "bedded."

The Commutator Surface. The surface of the commutator segments should be kept clean and free from oil or brush dust, etc. Should any grease or oil work its way on to the commutator through over-lubrication, it will not only cause sparking, but, in addition, carbon and copper dust will collect in the grooves between the commutator segments.

The best way to clean the commutator is, without disconnecting any leads, to remove from its box-holder one of the main brushes and, inserting a fine dry duster, hold it, with a suitably-shaped piece of wood, against the commutator surface, causing the armature to be rotated by the kickstarter.* If the commutator is very dirty, first moisten the cloth with petrol. The segments should be *dark bronze* and highly polished.

To Adjust Dynamo Chain. The tension of the dynamo chain which lies behind the primary chain (*see* Fig. 75) should be checked occasionally, after removing the oil-bath case inspection cap (*see* page 68). Chain whip with the chain in its tightest position, mid-way between the sprockets, should be approximately ¼ in.

To make an eccentric adjustment for chain tension, first slacken the strap bolt clamping the dynamo in its housing. Then apply (1945–51) the spanner (Part No. 017254) to the flats cast on the dynamo end-plate, on the left-hand side of the dynamo. Now rotate the dynamo *anti-clockwise* (with the fingers, 1952–7 models) until chain tension is felt to be correct on passing a finger through the inspection-cap opening. Be careful not to confuse the primary chain with the dynamo chain which lies *behind* the former (*see* Fig. 75). Afterwards retighten the strap bolt and again check the tension of the dynamo chain. If found to be correct, replace the inspection cap on the oil-bath chain case (*see* page 68).

Dynamo Removal. Removal of the dynamo on 1945–51 models is a little difficult, but is greatly simplified on 1952 and later models where the magneto is in front of the cylinder instead of over the dynamo. Full instructions for 1945–57 models are given on pages 42–3.

Compensated Voltage Control. All 1945–57 A.J.S. motor-cycles incorporate compensated voltage control. The C.V.C. unit consists of a cut-out and voltage-regulator unit in a box beneath the saddle, beside the battery carrier, or (1956–7) in the tool box. It is connected between the dynamo and battery and ensures that the battery is automatically charged the right amount by varying the dynamo output according to the state of charge of the battery and the load imposed on it.

Current is prevented from flowing back from the battery to the dynamo at low r.p.m. by means of the cut-out which opens. As soon as the r.p.m. rise high enough to enable the dynamo to charge the battery, the cut-out closes and completes the circuit.

In all three lighting-switch positions (*see* page 25) the dynamo gives a controlled output and thus relieves you of responsibility in regard to charging. The regulator begins to operate when the dynamo voltage reaches about 7·3 volt. During daylight running with the battery well charged and the switch in the "Off" position, the dynamo gives only a

* Slow rotation is assisted by removing the sparking plug.

trickle charge, and the ammeter reading is unlikely to exceed 1–2 amp. There is no danger of overcharging.

The regulator provides for an increase of dynamo output as soon as the lamps are switched on. The effect of switching the lamps on after a long run with the battery voltage high is often to cause a temporary discharge reading at the ammeter, but fairly soon the voltage falls and the regulator responds, thereby causing the output of the dynamo to balance the load of the lamps.

When the battery is in a discharged state, the regulator increases the dynamo output and restores the battery to its normal state of charge in the shortest possible time.

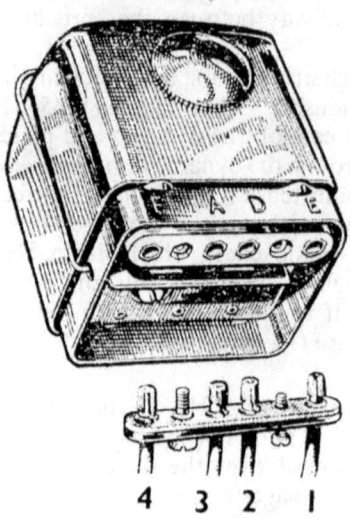

FIG. 26. CONNEXIONS TO COMPENSATED VOLTAGE-CONTROL UNIT
1. To earth.
2. To terminal D on dynamo.
3. To terminal 3 on switch.
4. To terminal F on dynamo.

Do Not Tamper with C.V.C. Unit. The unit is sealed by the makers, as it should not need adjustment once it is correctly set. If, however, the battery (in good condition) is persistently under-charged or over-charged, suspect the C.V.C. unit setting and have it checked, preferably at a Lucas service depot. Note that the C.V.C. unit is retained by self-locking nuts, except on 1956–7 models where it is retained in a sponge-rubber holder in a partition at the rear top corner of the tool box (see Fig. 23). To remove the C.V.C. unit on a 1956–7 model, grasp it between the fingers and thumb of one hand, and gently and firmly pull it away from the sponge-rubber holder.

As may be seen in Fig. 26, the four terminals of the C.V.C. unit are clearly marked by the letters F.A.D.E. Leads from the F and D terminals are attached to similarly marked terminals on the dynamo. The terminal marked A is connected to one of the ammeter terminals, and the terminal marked E is earthed.

To Remove the Dynamo (1945–51). On machines with the magneto positioned above the dynamo, the following procedure is necessary to remove the dynamo. First remove the magneto chain-case cover (secured by six screws). Also remove the nut and washer securing each magneto sprocket. Next with a sprocket-withdrawal tool, or by the application of suitable wedges, free both magneto drive sprockets. Remove both sprockets and the chain, taking them off together. Remove the timing-

THE LIGHTING SYSTEM 43

case cover (secured by five screws). When doing this be careful not to allow the two camwheels to disengage from the small engine pinion. Remove the outer portion of the oil-bath chain case (see page 135). Now remove the spring circlip, lock-washer, nut, and plain washer below the nut which secures the chain sprocket to the dynamo-armature shaft. With a sprocket withdrawal tool, or using suitable wedges, between the dynamo body and sprocket, free the sprocket from the dynamo armature spindle.

Loosen the nut on the off-side end of the gearbox upper fixing bolt. Also remove the nut on the near-side end of the gearbox lower fixing bolt and drive out the bolt. To do this it may be necessary to disconnect the oil-return pipe from the oil tank. Unscrew the central fixing bolt securing the retaining plate to the dynamo end-cover, and disconnect the electrical leads. Then unscrew the bolt which clamps the dynamo in the rear engine-mounting plates sufficiently to permit of the dynamo being free to move. Pull backwards the bottom of the gearbox as far as possible. Finally rotate the dynamo until the locating plate on its body is in a position to allow it to pass the cut-away portions of the engine plates. and withdraw the dynamo from the off side of the motor-cycle.

To Replace the Dynamo (1945-51). Proceed in the reverse order of removal. If the camwheels have been disengaged from the small engine pinion, it is necessary to retime the valves (see page 109). Having disturbed the magneto drive, it is also necessary to retime the magneto (see page 86). Also check the tension of the dynamo chain (see page 128).

To Remove the Dynamo (1952-7). On machines with the magneto positioned in front of the engine, dynamo removal is very straightforward and no retiming of the magneto is necessary.

First remove the near-side footrest arm. Lay a drip-tray beneath the oil-bath chain case to receive the oil, and remove the outer portion of the oil-bath chain case (see page 135). Next remove the spring circlip, the locking plate, and the nut securing the dynamo sprocket, and with a suitable tool withdraw the sprocket. While slackening the sprocket-retaining nut, hold the sprocket with the appropriate spanner (Part No. 017254). This prevents any bending stress being imposed on the spindle of the dynamo.

Disconnect the dynamo leads and slacken the dynamo clamping-bolt fully. Now twist the dynamo by hand until the locating strip on its body aligns with the key-way cut-away in the rear engine plate housing the dynamo. Then withdraw the dynamo, tilting it upwards so as to clear the gearbox.

To Replace the Dynamo (1952-7). Observe the removal instructions in reverse. Be careful to locate the dynamo-sprocket key accurately when fitting the dynamo sprocket. Also check that the dynamo chain is correctly tensioned (*see* page 86), and follow the instructions given (page 138) for replacing the outer half of the oil-bath chain case. Before fitting this outer half, make sure that the dynamo sprocket securing-nut is firmly tightened prior to the fitting of the locking plate and the retaining circlip.

Removal of Dynamo Chain (1945–57 Models). First remove the outer half of the oil-bath chain case (*see* page 138). Next remove the nut retaining the engine sprocket. This is facilitated by engaging top gear and applying the rear brake. Withdraw the shock-absorber spring, cupped washer, and cam. Now remove the primary chain to obtain access to the dynamo chain. Remove the spring circlip from the nut retaining the sprocket on the dynamo armature. Also detach the locking washer or plate which surrounds the nut. With the appropriate spanner (Part No. 017254) applied to the two flats on the back of the dynamo sprocket, hold the sprocket and unscrew the dynamo-sprocket retaining nut. With a suitable extractor tool release the dynamo sprocket from the armature. Now remove in one operation the dynamo sprocket, "endless" dynamo chain, and the engine sprocket assembly.

Replacing Dynamo Sprocket, Chain, and Engine Sprocket (1945–7). Check that the key for the dynamo sprocket is in position on the armature location. Also verify that the spacing collar (between the crankcase ball bearing and the back of the engine sprocket) is replaced on the engine driving-side mainshaft. Next engage the dynamo driving chain with the teeth of the dynamo driving sprocket (the smaller sprocket of the engine-sprocket assembly) and the sprocket which fits on the dynamo armature. In one simultaneous operation replace the two sprockets (and chain) on the engine mainshaft and dynamo armature. Then replace the plain washer and sprocket retaining nut on the dynamo armature. Tighten the nut finger-tight only.

While preventing the dynamo armature from turning by applying the appropriate spanner (Part No. 017254) to the flats on the back of the sprocket, tighten the dynamo sprocket retaining nut firmly. Replace the locking washer or plate for the retaining nut, also the retaining circlip. Make sure that the latter beds down properly in the nut groove. Finally replace the cam of the engine shaft shock-absorber, the spring, cap washer, and retaining nut. Also replace the primary chain and check its tension (*see* page 124). The outer half of the oil-bath chain case can now be replaced (*see* page 136).

THE ALTERNATOR AND RECTIFIER (1958–60)

The Lucas RM15 Alternator. The alternator on 1958–60 models comprises a spigot-mounted 6-coil laminated stator bolted to the oil-bath chain case cover (*see* Fig. 76), with a rotor carried on and driven by an

THE LIGHTING SYSTEM

extension of the crankshaft. The aluminium rotor has a hexagonal steel core, each face of which carries a permanent magnet keyed to a laminated pole tip.

Because, unlike the Lucas dynamos fitted to 1945–57 models, the alternator and stator have no rotating windings, commutator, brushgear, bearings, or oil seals, no maintenance whatever is called for other than to see that the three snap-connexions in the output cables (*see* Fig. 27) are tight and clean, and the leads unfrayed. The snap-connexions, by the way, are located behind the frame cover which is located by two knurled screws.

Should it be necessary for any reason to withdraw the rotor, there is no need to fit keepers to the rotor poles. After removing a rotor wipe

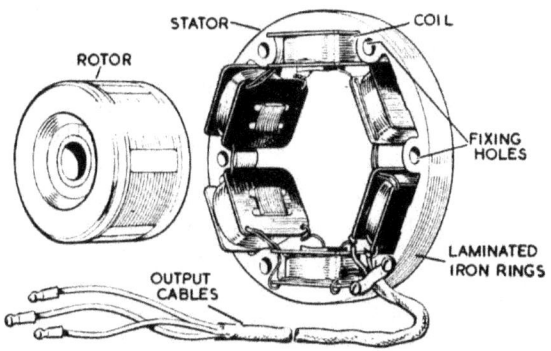

FIG. 27. SHOWING DETAILS OF LUCAS RM15 ALTERNATOR
Applicable to 1958–60 A.J.S. Models 16, 18. For position on machine, *see* Fig. 76. The colours of the output cables (top to bottom in above sketch) are: light green; dark green; dark green and yellow.

off any metal swarf which may have collected on the pole tips. Place the rotor in a clean place.

To Remove A.C. Rotor. The rotor is keyed to the engine shaft. If removal is required for some reason, first remove the outer half of the oil-bath chain case (*see* page 135). Next engage top gear and apply pressure to the rear brake pedal. Then unscrew the lock-nut and the nut securing the rotor. Withdraw the washer and pull off the rotor.

The Alternator Output Control. While riding normally with the ignition switch in the "IGN" position the rate of output depends on the position of the lighting switch, electrical energy passing through the battery from the alternator in the form of rectified alternating current.

When the lighting switch is turned to the "OFF" position the alternator output supplies the ignition coil and trickle-charges the battery. When the lighting switch is turned to the "L" or "H" position the alternator output is automatically increased to meet the extra load.

Altering the Alternator Connexions. In the event of the battery becoming discharged it is possible to effect a temporary boost by altering the alternator connexions behind the frame cover after removing the two knurled screws and removing the cover. Alter the connexions in the following manner. Disconnect the dark green and dark green and yellow cable connectors. Reconnect the dark green cable connector to the dark green and yellow cable connector. Do not interfere with the light green cable. Note that prolonged use of the machine with the alternator connexions altered is not recommended and will *harm the battery*.

The Lucas Rectifier. The Lucas rectifier is housed on the tool-box below the dualseat. The rectifier consists of four plates (coated on one side with selenium) and functions like a non-return valve, permitting current to pass in one direction only. The alternating current from the alternator is thus converted to unidirectional (d.c.) current for charging the battery. The rectifier needs no maintenance other than to keep the connexions clean and tight, and to check periodically that the nut securing the rectifier to the frame of the motor-cycle is tight. *Do not in any circumstances loosen the nut which clamps the rectifier plates together*. The nut is most carefully adjusted during manufacture to give optimum performance.

FIG. 28. THE LUCAS RECTIFIER CONNEXIONS

The Rectifier Connexions. Should the leads be disconnected from the rectifier it is vital to see that they are reconnected correctly. Fig. 28 shows how the coloured cables should be connected to the rectifier. Never alter this arrangement.

THE HORN

Careful adjustment of the Lucas horn is made at the works, and subsequent adjustment is rarely called for. Normally the horn should give long service without any attention whatever. The vibrating parts do, however, gradually wear and, after very considerable usage, some roughness and loss of tone may develop. This necessitates an examination being made at a Lucas service depot.

If Horn Fails Completely or Partially. Do not immediately infer that the horn has broken down or needs adjustment. Possible causes of the trouble are: a loose fixing bolt; vibration of some adjacent part; a discharged battery; a loose connexion; a short circuit in the wiring; or a defective push-switch. The last-mentioned may be occasioned through poor electrical contact with the handlebars.

THE WIRING SYSTEM

No Fuse. There is no fuse incorporated in the wiring circuit, which is purposely simplified, and capable of being understood by those with elementary electrical knowledge. If care is taken to keep the various wires correctly connected, and to maintain the connexions clean and firm, there is no risk of an excessive current damaging any of the equipment or wiring.

Inspect the Wiring Occasionally. It is advisable occasionally to make a careful inspection of the wiring, especially of the wires from the battery, the leads from the dynamo to the C.V.C. unit or the alternator output cables (1958-60). See that the insulation is sound and not chafed and that all connexions are clean and tight. Should the dynamo fail to charge, this may be due to dynamo trouble, a faulty lead, or a faulty C.V.C. unit. Tape up any loose or frayed leads.

As may be seen in Figs. 29-32, the ends of leads can be identified for connexion purposes by means of their coloured sleeves. This greatly facilitates reconnecting the wiring circuit in the event of the wires being disconnected from the various terminals.

The leads connected to the terminals marked *D* and *F* on the dynamo and C.V.C. unit must on no account be reversed. To prevent this being done, the screw in the dynamo terminal-block is off-centre, and the screws securing the regulator clamping-plate are of different size.

An Important Precaution. It is extremely important to disconnect one of the battery leads (*see* page 39) if making any alterations to the wiring or removing the lighting switch from the Lucas headlamp. *On all* 1952-60 *models the battery positive terminal is earthed.* The earth connexion is connected to the dualseat lug tube. The dualseat must be removed to obtain access to it.

The Battery Lead Connexions. On all later (PU7E/9, PU7E/11 type) Lucas batteries detachable lead-connectors are provided at the battery terminals. To make a lead connexion, unscrew the knurled terminal nut and withdraw the collet or cone-shaped insert. Note that the inserts for the two terminals are not interchangeable. After baring the lead end for about an inch, thread the bared end through the knurled nut and collet. Then insert the collet and cable into the terminal block after first bending the wire strands over the narrow end of the collet. Tighten the knurled nut firmly to secure the connexion.

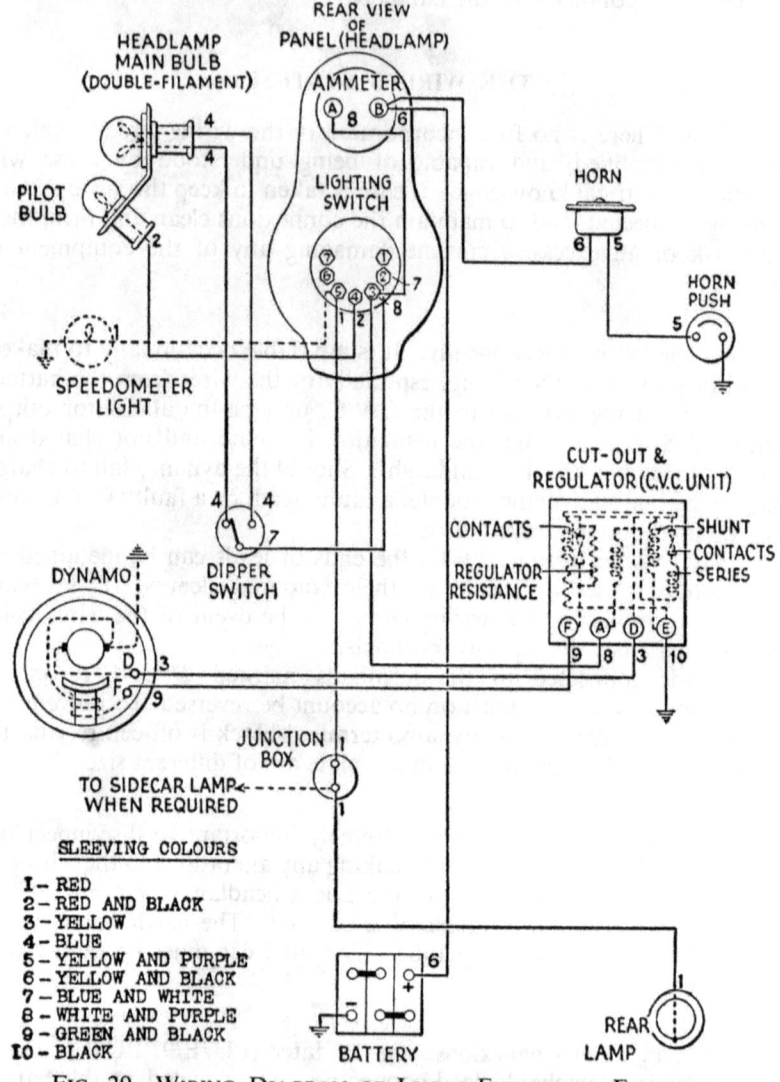

FIG. 29. WIRING DIAGRAM OF LUCAS ELECTRICAL EQUIPMENT FITTED TO ALL 1945–50 MODELS (NEGATIVE EARTH)

On earlier type batteries other than those just referred to, detachable connectors are not provided at the battery terminals. Instead, short lengths of cable are permanently secured to the terminals, one for the

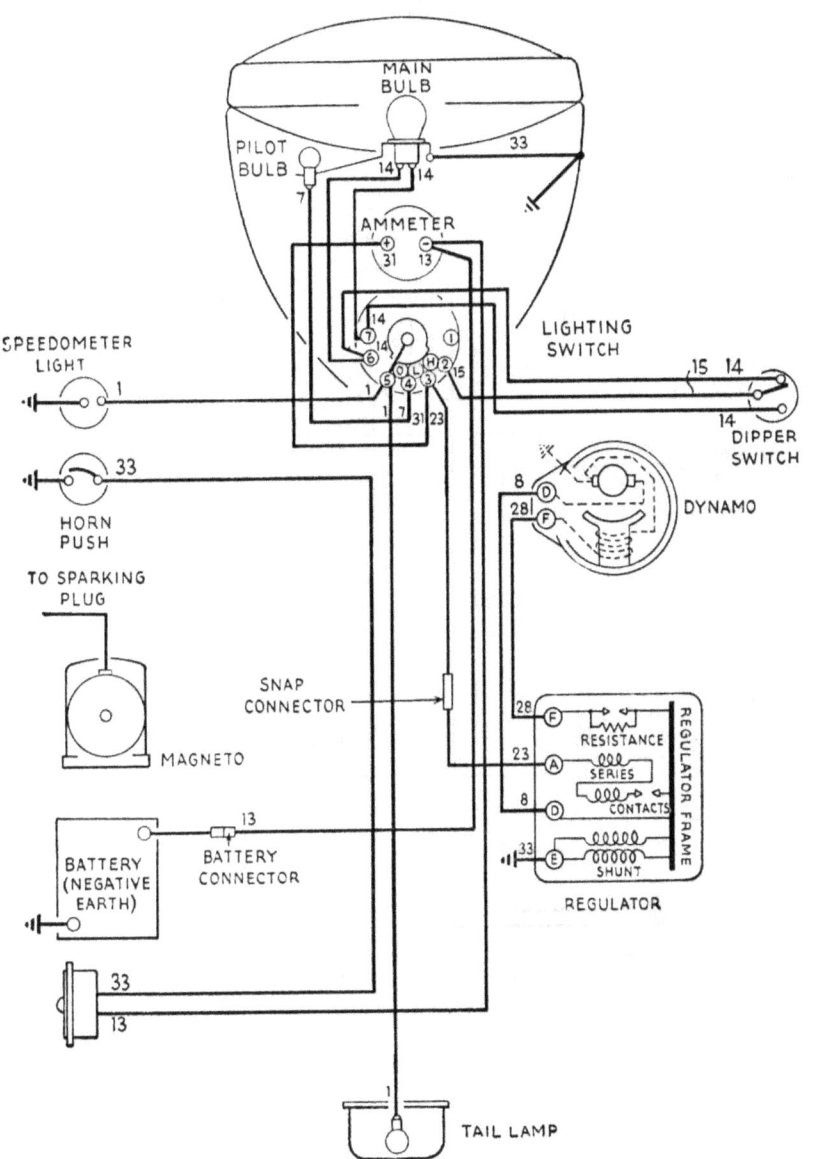

FIG. 30. WIRING DIAGRAM FOR ALL 1951 MODELS
(NEGATIVE EARTH)

KEY TO COLOURED SLEEVES

1. Red
7. Red and black
8. Yellow
13. Yellow and black
14. Blue
15. Blue and white
23. White and purple
28. Green and black
31. Purple
33. Black

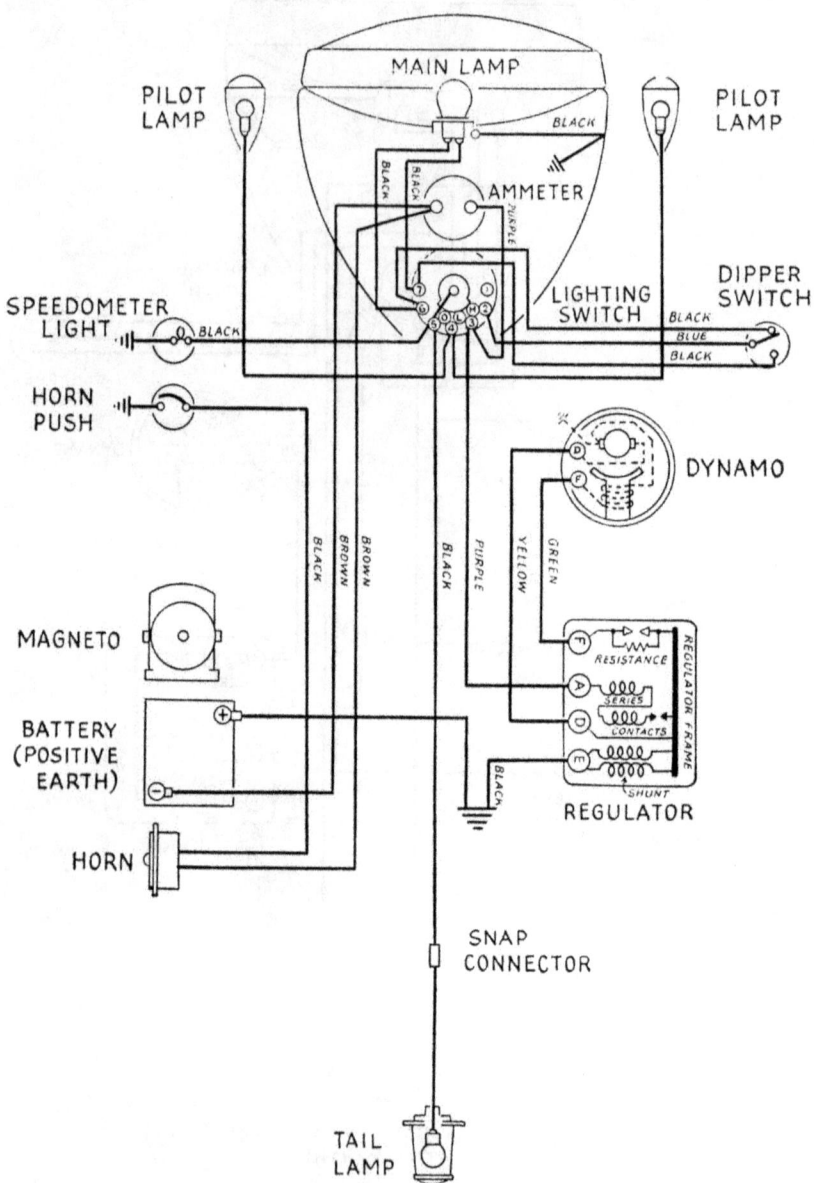

Fig. 31. Wiring Diagram for all 1954–7 Models
(Positive Earth)

This diagram applies also to all 1952–3 models (positive earth) but on these machines a single underslung pilot-bulb (used instead of the twin pilot-lamps shown) has its lead connected to No. 4 switch terminal.

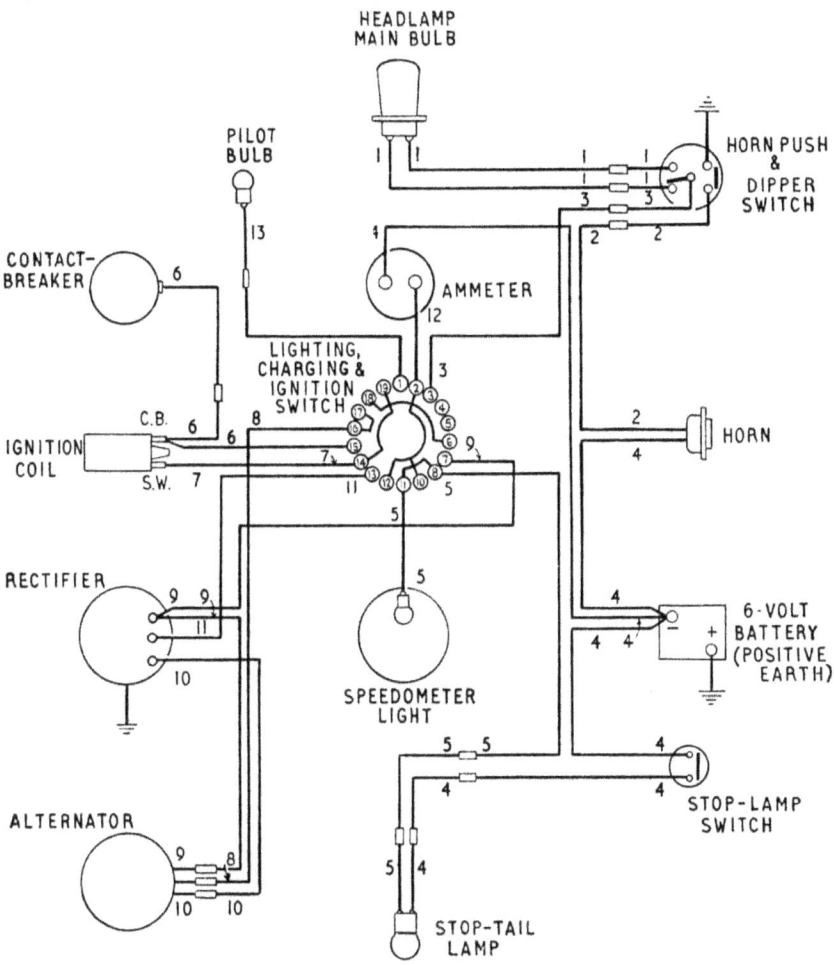

FIG. 32. WIRING DIAGRAM FOR ALL 1958–60 MODELS (POSITIVE EARTH)
KEY TO SLEEVE COLOURS

1. Black.
2. Brown and black.
3. Blue.
4. Brown and blue.
5. Brown and green.
6. Black and white.
7. White.
8. Green and yellow.
9. Dark green.
10. Light green.
11. Purple.
12. Brown and white.
13. Red.

earth connexion, and the other for connecting to the lighting-switch cable by means of a screwed-type brass connector. This is accessible on pushing back a protective rubber-sleeve. It is vital that this sleeve is always kept pulled well over the connector.

The Dynamo and C.V.C. Unit Connexions. The dynamo and C.V.C. unit connexions (*see* page 42) are readily connected, but note the warning on page 47 concerning incorrect (reversed) connecting of the dynamo *D* and *F* terminals.

CHAPTER IV

CORRECT LUBRICATION

THE A.J.S. design dept. have done their best to ensure that correct lubrication involves the minimum attention by the rider. This attention, however, is *absolutely vital* and is dealt with in detail in this chapter. A summary of lubrication requirements will be found on page 67.

Neglect to lubricate the engine and machine properly causes excessive friction and head, accompanied by undue wear of the contacting bearing

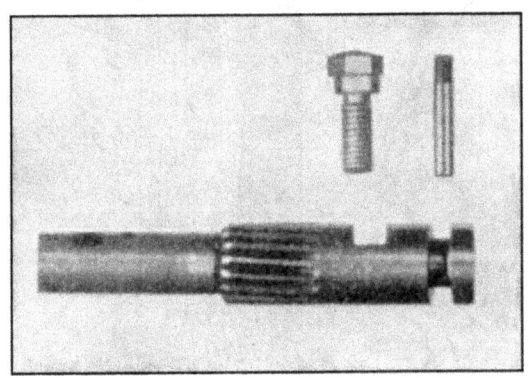

FIG. 33. THE "HEART" OF THE A.J.S. LUBRICATION SYSTEM

The oil pump is positioned on the engine as shown in Fig. 34. Above are shown the pump plunger, the guide screw, and the steel pin which fits inside the hollow guide screw with the relieved end (shown dark) *away from* the plunger. The plunger and the guide screw should not be disturbed during routine maintenance.

surfaces. Such neglect can rapidly spoil a good motor-cycle and cause heavy repair bills, besides reducing performance.

ENGINE LUBRICATION

The engine lubrication system on all A.J.S. O.H.V. models is of the full dry-sump (D.S.) type, where *all* oil in the engine and oil tank is kept in constant circulation while the engine is running. Its functioning is entirely automatic, but a little regular attention is *essential*.

The A.J.S. Oil Pump. The oil pump in the crankcase has a horizontal-type steel plunger (Fig. 33) which combines rotary motion with reciprocating movement. Rotary motion is imparted to the plunger by a worm on

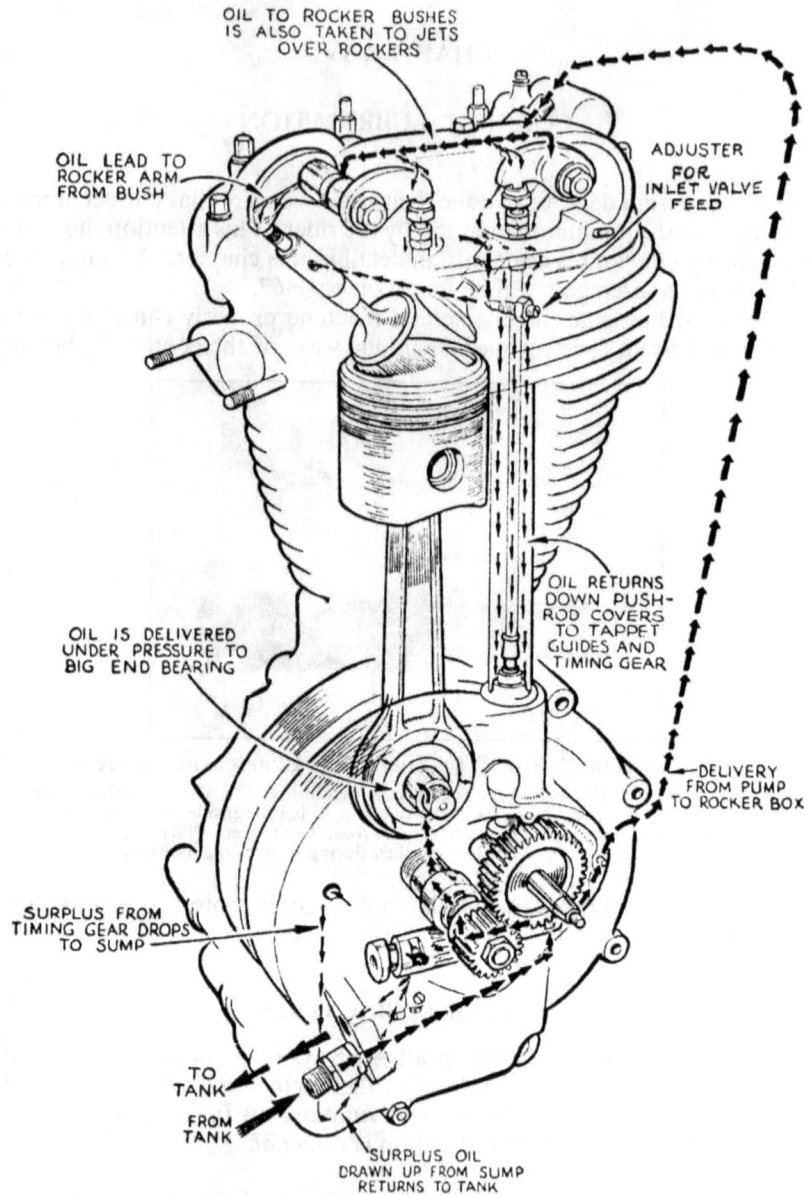

FIG. 34. OIL CIRCULATION DIAGRAM (1956–60 ENGINES)

This diagram also applies to 1945–55 engines except for the following: 1945–55 engines have a circular channel in the cylinder base feeding holes in the cylinder wall; 1945–53 engines have no oil lead to each rocker arm from the spindle bush.

the timing-side engine main-shaft. The reciprocating motion is obtained by the hardened pin in the hollow guide screw (*see* Fig. 33) engaging the profiled cam-groove cut on the (larger) scavenge end of the plunger.

The profiled cam-groove is designed so that the opening and closing of the two main ports, and a small auxiliary port, are synchronized with the pumping impulses obtained by plunger reciprocation. The scavenge (rear) end of the plunger (which is totally enclosed in its housing by two end-caps) has a greater capacity than the delivery end, and in consequence it keeps the crankcase sump in a "dry" state, all oil being returned to the tank for further circulation.

How the Oil Circulates. Fig. 34 shows at a glance how the oil circulates in the A.J.S. engine with D.S. lubrication. The filtration of the oil in the tank (capacity: 3 pt., 1945-8; 4 pt., 1949-51; $4\frac{1}{2}$ pt., 1952-5; 5 pt., 1956; 4 pt., 1957-60) is shown (1945-60 tanks) in Figs. 35 and 36.

The delivery (front) end of the plunger shown in Fig. 33 feeds oil under pressure to the timing-side main bearing and connecting-rod big-end bearing through a passage cut in the timing-side main shaft, flywheel, and crankpin. The piston and cylinder bore are lubricated by surplus oil splashed from the big-end bearing. Further provision for lubrication of the cylinder is included on 1945-55 engines. The oil pump forces oil through a passage (equipped with ball-valve control) in the crankcase to a circular channel in the cylinder base. The oil reaches the cylinder bore through a number of small holes drilled in the channel. Surplus oil automatically drains down into the sump of the crankcase.

The A.J.S. plunger pump also feeds a secondary oil supply to the timing gear and rocker-box. The supply to the timing gear is fed through a passage in the timing-gear case. The oil collects in the timing-case until a pre-determined level is reached. As may be seen in Fig. 34, an external pipe connected to the front of the oil-pump housing conveys the secondary oil-supply direct to the rocker-box and push-rod ends.

The overhead inlet and exhaust-valve rockers inside the rocker-box are thoroughly lubricated by means of jets above them. In addition, oil is fed to the rocker bushes and (1954 onwards) each rocker arm. The surplus oil drains to and lubricates both valve guides. The oil supply to the guide for the inlet valve can be regulated by means of a needle-pointed screw adjuster. This oil-supply adjustment is the only one provided on the A.J.S. dry-sump lubrication system.

Surplus oil from the valve guides passes down the push-rod covers and the tappet guides and enters the timing case. Here all engine oil, beyond that needed to keep the level at the predetermined height, drains down into the sump of the crankcase. The large-capacity scavenge end of the plunger pump sucks up the oil collected in the sump from various parts of the engine and pumps it back via the upper pipe into the oil tank for filtering and further circulation.

56   THE BOOK OF THE A.J.S.

The whole of the oil in the tank and the engine is thus kept in constant circulation and the sump remains practically "dry." Up to 1952 an external engine-breather pipe was fitted, but from 1952 onwards the crankcase pressure-release valve has been incorporated in the driving-side main shaft.

The Tank Filters. Clean every 5,000 miles. A cut-away view of the A.J.S. oil tank is shown in Figs. 35 and 36. As may be observed, a metal

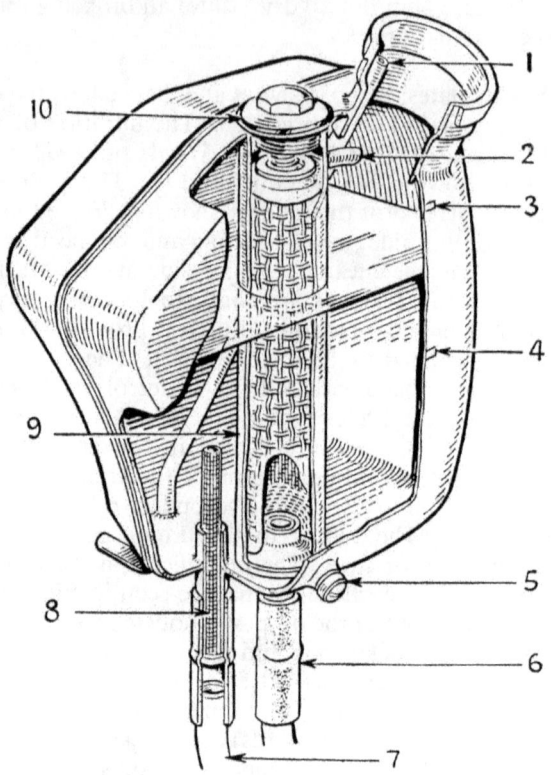

FIG. 35. CUT-AWAY VIEW OF OIL TANK SHOWING THE FILTERS, ETC. (1952-5)

On 1945-51 tanks the smaller gauze-filter was integral with a screwed feed-pipe union (Fig. 37), and the drain plug was at the rear. On 1956-7 models a pannier-type tank (Fig. 36) with a metal-gauze filter was introduced. Prior to 1954 the rubber connexion for the oil-return pipe was omitted.

KEY TO FIG. 35

1. Vent pipe (to prevent air locks).
2. Oil-return pipe orifice.
3. Top-level mark.
4. Low-level mark.
5. Drain plug.
6. Oil-return pipe.
7. Oil-feed pipe.
8. Gauze filter.
9. Tube enclosing felt element.
10. Cap on main filter.

gauze filter is incorporated in the delivery or feed-pipe union. It should be noted that the sole object of this filter is to trap any dirt, pieces of fluff, etc., which may get into the oil tank while it is being replenished.

The main filter (1945–55 models) is a detachable fabric-type. It comprises a long felt-element contained within an upright tubular wire-cage. As may be noticed in Fig. 35, all the engine oil returned to the scavenge end of the pump has to percolate through the felt element and wire cage which are supported by a cylindrical housing inside the tank. Very

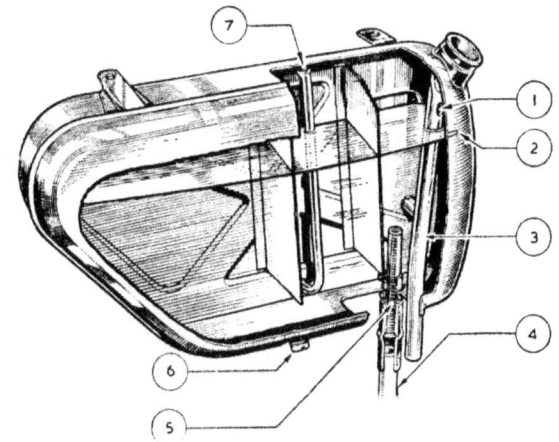

FIG. 36. CUT-AWAY VIEW OF OIL TANK ON 1956–60 MODELS

KEY TO FIG. 36

1. Oil-return pipe orifice.
2. Top level mark.
3. Oil-return pipe.
4. Oil-feed pipe.
5. Gauze filter (metal).
6. Drain plug.
7. Air vent pipe.

thorough filtering results. On 1956–60 models a fabric-type filter with felt element is omitted. Instead, a cylindrical filter of fine metal-gauze is secured in the tank end of the feed-pipe union.

Always purchase engine oil in sealed containers or replenish from branded cabinets. Specify clearly the brand and grade which you require, and refuse firmly but politely the "just as good" type.

Suitable Engine Oils. To ensure easy starting, maximum performance and minimum wear, the safest policy is to use one of the brands and grades officially recommended by A.J.S. Motor Cycles. They recommend the use of one of the following engine oils—

(a) Castrol "Grand Prix" (summer) or "XL" (winter).
(b) Mobiloil "D" (summer) or "A" (winter).
(c) Shell X-100 50 (summer) or X-100 30 (winter).

(d) B.P. Energol SAE 50 (summer) or B.P. Energol SAE 30 (winter).
(e) Essolube 50 (summer) or Essolube 30 (winter).

It should be noted that the above recommendations are not tabulated in any priority order. It is for the rider to choose which brand he prefers. All the five mentioned are thoroughly sound.

Oil Level in Tank. Remove the filler cap and inspect the level of oil prior to every ride. Always verify the level very carefully before a long run and top up with suitable engine oil (*see* previous paragraph) if necessary. Sufficient oil must be kept circulating to ensure correct lubrication of the engine and its proper cooling.

Never allow the oil level to fall below the low level mark, otherwise the oil in circulation is apt to become hot, dirty, and diluted. As far as possible maintain the oil level at or near the top level mark on the outside of the tank (1952–60), but do not allow the level to rise above this mark, or (1945–51) above 1 in. from the filler-cap orifice. This is important for the following reason.

On stopping the engine, no further pump action occurs, but the oil continues to drain into the sump from various parts of the engine. When the engine is subsequently started there is obviously surplus oil accumulated in the sump and this is immediately pumped back into the tank by the large-capacity scavenge end of the pump plunger. The effect is to cause an excessive rise in the level of oil in the tank, and possibly oil leakage via the tank air-vent (provided to avoid air locks).

Checking Oil Circulation. Verify the oil circulation before *every run*, immediately after starting up the engine from cold. Remove the oil tank filler-cap and observe the oil flow from the small spout (*see* Fig. 35) about 2 in. below the filler-cap orifice. If no oil can be seen emerging from the spout, raise the exhaust-valve lifter and stop the engine immediately.

The oil flow immediately after starting up the engine from cold should be *steady*. An erratic or weak flow is abnormal and requires investigation. After a brief period of warming up the engine, the surplus oil in the crankcase sump is disposed of, and thereafter the oil flow from the spout of the return pipe decreases somewhat and may become irregular. Some froth may be noticeable caused by the presence of air bubbles, but this is normal and can be disregarded, once the engine gets into its stride.

If you suddenly accelerate the engine and then close back the throttle, you may observe first a marked decline, or even cessation, of the oil flow and then a considerable increase in the flow.

No Pump Adjustment. The A.J.S. oil pump is capable of delivering the correct volume of oil to the engine at *all* throttle openings. Consequently there is no adjustment provided for the main oil supply. To ensure correct lubrication of the engine, however, it is essential to keep the two end-caps of the plunger housing quite airtight. Check the securing nuts periodically for tightness with a spanner. (*See also* page 62.)

Oil Supply to Inlet Valve Stem. The adjuster for the oil supply to the inlet valve stem comprises a needle-pointed screw (Fig. 34) situated on the off-side of the cylinder head. If the engine is mechanically sound, the approximately correct setting of the adjuster screw is *one-sixth of a complete turn from the fully closed position*. Once the correct setting has been obtained, it should not be necessary to interfere with the adjustment.

The adjuster screw is secured by a lock-nut, which prevents accidental alteration of the adjustment. To *increase* or decrease the oil supply to the inlet-valve stem, the adjuster screw must be turned slightly *anti-clockwise* or clockwise respectively, after first loosening the lock-nut.

What symptons indicate that an adjustment is called for? An excessive oil supply is denoted by blue smoke at the exhaust, high oil consumption, and a tendency for the sparking plug to oil up and become dirty. An insufficient oil supply is indicated by the inlet-valve stem developing a mouse-like squeak.

The Exhaust Valve Stem. No adjustment is provided for the oil supply to the exhaust-valve stem. The stem is automatically lubricated by oil fed through a channel drilled in the cylinder head. Surplus oil from the exhaust-valve stem and from the stem of the inlet valve is by-passed back into the chamber responsible for lubricating the timing gears.

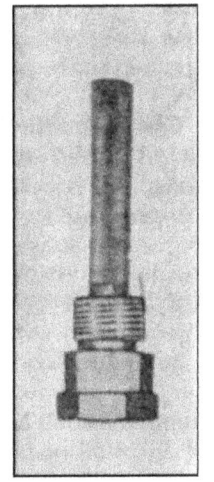

FIG. 37. GAUZE FILTER INTEGRAL WITH FEED PIPE UNION (1945-51 only)

Changing the Oil. With a brand-new A.J.S. it is advisable to empty the oil tank and replenish it with fresh oil after covering 500 miles and again at 1,000 miles. After this, change the oil once every 5,000 miles. If a machine is only used for short runs, renew the oil every three months. Also clean the tank filter(s).

Before draining the oil tank, make sure that your A.J.S. is level, with both wheels on the ground or with the stand down. Then to drain the tank, place a suitable receptacle below the drain plug to catch the oil and unscrew the plug from the off-side (1952-60) or rear (1945-51) edge of the tank. Be patient and allow all the oil to drain away.

Having drained the oil tank, also remove the drain plug from the bottom of the crankcase sump (on the off-side), and permit any accumulation of oil to drain off. There will not be a large amount, but it is desirable to remove what there is. A powerful magnetic filter is fitted to the crankcase drain-plug on 1956 and later models and it is important to see that the accumulation of any fine metallic particles is completely removed. Finally, make sure that both drain plugs are replaced and firmly tightened.

The Magnetic Crankcase-Filter (1956–60). To obtain access to this filter for cleaning, it is only necessary to unscrew the crankcase drain-plug which embodies the magnetic filter.

Forcibly wipe off with a greased rag all metal particles adhering to the magnetic filter (they adhere strongly). If you place the filter on the bench see that the magnet does not come into contact with large iron or steel objects, such as a vice, otherwise some loss of magnetism may occur. Also avoid placing the magnet close to iron or steel filings, which will be attracted to the magnetic filter and need removing.

The Tank Filters. Thorough and regular cleaning of the two filters in the oil tank (one, 1956–60) is most important and must never be overlooked. It is best to remove and clean the filters when the engine oil is changed. Advice on removing the filters is given in subsequent paragraphs. As regards actual cleaning, this should be done thoroughly with petrol, but do not attempt to remove the felt element of a large cartridge-type filter from its tubular wire-cage, and do not use a fluffy rag when cleaning a gauze filter. Allow to dry afterwards.

Inspect the cork washer fitted below the hexagon cap of a fabric filter (Fig. 35) and renew the washer if it is not in perfect condition. Also examine the felt element very carefully. Fit a new element if its ends are at all distorted or perforated.

It should be observed that a choked gauze-filter can completely or partially starve the engine of oil, since it is secured to the feed-pipe union and all oil entering the engine has to pass through it.

On the other hand, choking of the above gauze can be caused only through replenishing the tank with impure oil. The whole of the oil returned by the pump from the engine to the tank is effectively cleaned by means of the large fabric or gauze (1956–60) filter, assuming the felt or gauze (1956–60) element is sound.

If the felt element of a fabric filter is clogged up with impurities, excessive lubrication can occur owing to resistance offered to the returning oil causing a "build-up" of oil in the sump. Renew the filter element if its condition is poor.

To Remove Felt Element (1945–55). First raise (1945–7) the rear of the saddle after removing the two saddle-spring securing bolts. On 1948 and later machines this is not necessary.

Unscrew and remove the hexagonal cap from the oil tank filler-orifice. Next withdraw the dished washer and the filter spring.

On 1945–53 models insert a finger inside the felt element and gently raise the element until the top end touches the underneath of the saddle. Now encircle the filter with the hand and exert sufficient upward pressure on the flexible saddle-top to enable you to withdraw the filter without distorting it. Take great care not to kink or damage the element when withdrawing it.

On 1954–5 models, after withdrawing the dished washer and filter spring, insert a finger in the exposed open end of the felt element and gently strain inward and backward (rigid-frame models) to avoid fouling the saddle frame, or outward and forward (spring-frame models) to avoid fouling the dualseat. Be most careful not to kink the element when doing this.

The procedure for replacing the filter element is the reverse of that just described. On a 1945–7 model, where the rear of the saddle is assumed to have been raised, replace the saddle in its normal position and fit and securely tighten the two saddle-spring securing bolts.

To Remove Gauze Filter (1945–51). To remove a filter (Fig. 37) for cleaning *after* draining the oil tank, the following procedure is necessary. Disconnect the oil-feed pipe from the union screwed into the base of the oil tank by unscrewing the union nut from the pipe nearest the rear wheel. Spring the feed pipe away from the union and then unscrew the union and remove this complete with the integral filter. To replace the gauze filter, union, and feed pipe, reverse the above instructions.

To Remove Gauze Filter (1952–60). The small gauze filter on the delivery side is not integral with a detachable union as on the 1945–51 models. Referring to Fig. 36, first drain the oil tank and then (1952–6) free the oil-feed pipe from the rubber connecting-sleeve on the small oil-feed pipe which projects from the base of the tank. If the gauze filter comes away with the rubber connecting-sleeve (1952–6) or feed pipe (1957–60), do not disturb it. If, however, the filter remains in the small pipe attached to the tank, grasp the ringed open end and pull the filter out of the pipe. Replace the filter in the reverse order of removal. On 1957–60 models all oil pipes are of the Neophrene push-on type.

Splitting the Crankcase. Should it be necessary for any reason to separate the crankcase halves, it is essential to remove the pump plunger (Fig. 33) first. Failure to take this precaution will almost certainly result in damage being caused.

Note Concerning Oil Pipe Unions. The unions for the oil tank delivery and return pipes are very close to each other at the crankcase (*see* Fig. 34). When disconnecting an oil pipe be extremely careful not to allow the spanner to foul the union adjacent to the union from which the pipe is being disconnected. Carelessness in this matter can result in a *fractured crankcase*.

Removing Pump Plunger. Do not remove the oil-pump plunger unnecessarily. If you must remove it, first drain the oil tank as described on page 59. Also unscrew the union nut securing the bottom end of the oil feed pipe from the pump housing to the rocker-box. Remove both end-caps from the pump housing by undoing the hexagon-headed securing bolts.

Just below the pump housing in front of the rear cap is the all-important guide screw and pin. Remove these together (*see* Fig. 33), and push out from the front the pump plunger and withdraw it from the rear end of the pump housing.

To Replace the Plunger. First make sure that the inside of the pump housing is clean, and check that the plunger itself is clean internally and externally. Oil the plunger and gently push it into position. Its smaller end must enter the rear of the pump housing, and the guide screw must next be fitted. Before replacing the guide screw, make certain that the steel pin inside the hollow screw is fitted as indicated in Fig. 33, or serious damage may be caused to the teeth of the pump plunger.

After replacing the guide screw, and while slowly tightening it, move the pump plunger backwards and forwards until the end of the guide-screw pin is felt to engage the profiled cam-groove at the rear end of the plunger. When this happens, tighten the guide screw firmly, but on no account tighten before proper engagement is obtained, otherwise stripping of the teeth on the timing-side engine main-shaft and of the teeth on the plunger is liable to take place.

Fit the pump-housing front and rear end-caps and see that airtight joints are obtained. The two paper washers must be in perfect condition. Renew them if they are damaged in the slightest degree. Make certain when fitting the paper washer for the front end-cap that the small oil hole in the cap itself is not obstructed.

The Pump Housing End-caps. It is advisable to apply some liquid jointing compound to one side of each paper washer. This side must be fitted in contact with the end-cap. To ensure an airtight joint at each end-cap, it is essential to see that the securing bolts are tightened down evenly and firmly. Tightening should always be effected in a diagonal order. Also occasionally check the delivery and return-pipe union nuts for tightness.

Magneto Bearings. These are initially packed with grease by the makers during assembly and further greasing should not be necessary for 10,000–15,000 miles. When a general overhaul becomes necessary it is desirable to remove the magneto and return it to Joseph Lucas, Ltd. of Birmingham, 19, or to one of their service depots, for thorough servicing. No grease nipples are fitted, but the contact-breaker requires periodical oiling.

CORRECT LUBRICATION

The Contact-breaker (Face-cam Type). The cam and tappet of the face-cam type contact-breaker (Fig. 38) require lubrication approximately every 3,000 miles. To effect such lubrication, remove the complete contact-breaker as described below.

First release the spring blade and take off the contact-breaker cover. Now, referring to Figs. 38 and 39, remove the screw (E) and the spring washer retaining the spring arm (A) to the body (L) of the contact-breaker, and detach the curved backing spring (D) and the spring arm (A). Next unscrew the screw (B) carrying the lubrication wick, and remove the

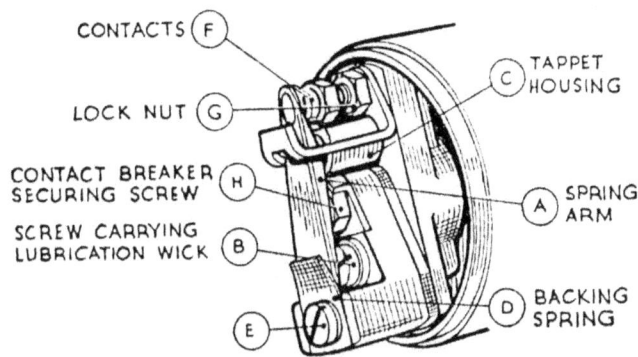

FIG. 38. FACE CAM CONTACT-BREAKER OF LUCAS ROTATING-ARMATURE MAGNETO SHOWN ASSEMBLED

This type of contact-breaker is provided on the magnetos of all 1945–53 machines and 1954 350 c.c. machines with manual ignition-control. The various parts are shown dismantled in Fig. 39. (The rotating-magnet magneto (1954 500 c.c. and 1955–7 models) is shown in Fig. 46.)

insulating bush (fibre). Straighten the tab on the locking plate (J) situated behind the head of the contact-breaker securing screw (H), and with the spanner remove screw (H). Then lever off the contact-breaker body (L) from the armature-shaft extension.

After completely removing the contact-breaker, saturate the wick, mounted in the core of the carrying screw (B), with a few drops of *thin machine oil*. Push from the contact-breaker body (L) the tappet (K) and wipe the tappet clean with a soft cloth. Smear a little thin machine-oil on the tappet and replace it in the body.

To assemble the face-cam type contact-breaker, proceed in the reverse order of dismantling. Make sure that the curved backing spring (D) is replaced so that the curved part is on the *outside*. The foregoing does not apply to rotating-magnet magnetos.

The Contact-breaker (Rotating-magnet Magneto). On 1954 500 c.c. and all later models fitted with a Lucas type SR-1 magneto having automatic ignition-control mechanism on the driving side (behind a bulge on the magneto chain-case cover), about every 3,000 miles undo the three captive screws and remove the moulded end-cover. Then apply a spot of clean engine oil to the visible end of the contact-breaker pivot pin. About every 6,000 miles loosen the nut securing the contact-breaker spring and lift off the contact-breaker lever (see Fig. 46). The spring is slotted to facilitate removal. Then smear the pivot pin with a little Mobilgrease No. 2 or a similar grease.

Cam and Contact-breaker (1958–60 Models). On the 1958–60 coil-ignition models the Lucas CAIA type contact-breaker and the automatic ignition-advance mechanism are located inside the timing-case main

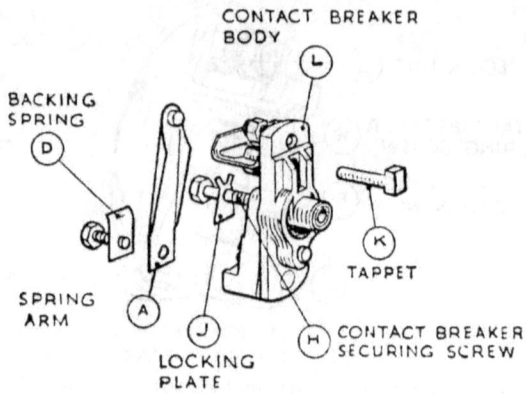

FIG. 39. FACE CAM CONTACT-BREAKER OF LUCAS ROTATING-ARMATURE MAGNETO SHOWN DISMANTLED
The same contact-breaker is shown assembled in Fig. 38.

cover. To obtain access to them, remove the two screws retaining the timing-case outer cover, and withdraw the latter (see Fig. 48).

About every 6,000 miles smear the surface of the cam very lightly with some Mobilgrease No. 2. If this is not available, use some clean *winter* grade engine oil (see page 57). Also apply a spot of clean engine oil to the contact-breaker pivot. Squeeze a little grease into the felt wick.

Remove the central fixing bolt and inject a small quantity of clean engine oil into the exposed hole. After replacing the fixing bolt and running the engine for a few minutes, centrifugal force will force out the oil over the automatic ignition-advance mechanism.

The Magneto Chain. The magneto driving-chain (enclosed in a chain case on the off-side of the engine) is not automatically lubricated like the dynamo chain. It is necessary to add some grease about every 1,000 miles. On 1945–51 models inject some Mobilgrease No. 2 or Esso Fluid Grease through the grease nipple provided on the outside of the chain-case cover.

CORRECT LUBRICATION 65

On 1952 and all 1953-7 models, the magneto chain requires occasional replenishment with one of the two above-mentioned greases. Remove the chain-case cover, and apply suitable grease generously to the chain. Also with a thin-metal strip, work some of the grease well into the automatic ignition-control mechanism (1954-7).

MOTOR-CYCLE LUBRICATION

The Dynamo Bearings. The armature bearings of the (Lucas type E3AR, 1945-50; E3-N, 1951 to 1957) dynamo, as on the magneto, are packed with grease by the makers on assembly and this should suffice for at least 10,000 miles running, or until it is necessary to make a general overhaul, when the dynamo should be removed and returned to Joseph Lucas, Ltd., or to a Lucas service depot for thorough cleaning, overhaul, and lubrication.

The Dynamo Driving Chain (1945-57). The Lucas dynamo is chain-driven from the engine shaft by a chain which is completely enclosed in the oil-bath chain case containing the primary chain. Therefore, provided the oil-bath chain case is kept properly replenished, no individual attention to the dynamo chain is necessary. The replenishment of the oil-bath is dealt with on page 68.

Gearbox Lubrication (1945-60). A.J.S. Motor Cycles advise the use of summer grade engine oil (*see* page 57) for the four-speed heavyweight gearbox on the 1948-60 models. On 1945-7 machines, however, light grease is recommended for gearbox lubrication. On no account must *thick* grease be used. Suitable greases for 1945-7 gearboxes, and for lubricating 1945 and later motor-cycle parts by means of the grease nipples provided, are as follows—

(1) Castrolease Heavy (Medium for 1945-7 gearbox).
(2) Mobilgrease No. 4 (No. 2 for 1945-7 gearbox).
(3) Shell Retinax Grease C.D. or A.
(4) B.P. Energrease C3.
(5) Esso (pressure gun) Grease.

Do not completely fill up the gearbox with engine oil or light grease. Under normal conditions it is sufficient to top up the lubricant every 1,000 miles with 2 fluid oz. of light grease or with a little summer-grade engine oil (1948-57 models) via the grease nipple on the kick-starter case or through the filler-cap orifice on the top edge of the kick-starter case cover respectively. Excessive filling will result in leakage.

All 1952-6 Burman gearboxes and the 1957-60 A.M.C. gearboxes have

66 THE BOOK OF THE A.J.S.

FIG. 40. WHEN AND WHERE TO LUBRICATE (1945 ONWARDS)

The above lubrication chart (showing a 1957 Model 18S) applies to all 1945 and later O.H.V. singles, but note the following points: on 1945–51 models the chain-driven magneto is mounted behind the cylinder and the chain-case has a grease nipple; on 1945–55 models a different type oil tank (*see* Fig. 35) with fabric-type main filter is specified. On 1958–60 models no magneto is fitted. (For key *see* opposite.)

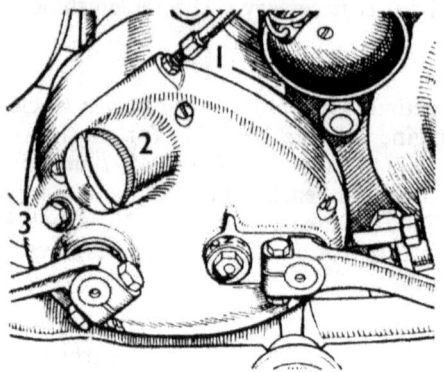

FIG. 41. THE 1952–6 BURMAN GEARBOX
(*By courtesy of "The Motor Cycle"—London*)

KEY TO FIG. 41
1. Clutch-cable adjuster.   2. Filler cap.   3. Oil-level plug.

an oil-level plug (3, Fig. 41) located close to the kick-starter spindle; to top-up the gearbox to the maximum permissible level (content: 1 pt.), it is only necessary to pour in engine oil through the filler-cap orifice until it begins to trickle from the level-plug hole. On the 1952-6 Burman four-speed gearboxes the filler cap comprises a slotted and threaded circular-cap,

CORRECT LUBRICATION

KEY TO FIG. 40

Item No.	Description of Item	Lubrication Required	Page Ref.
1	Oil tank	Before each run check oil circulation and level. Top-up as required. Every 5,000 miles change the oil and clean the filter(s). Also drain oil sump.	58, 59
2	Inlet-valve stem	If necessary, adjust the oil supply.	
3	Lucas magneto	Every 3,000 miles apply a few drops of thin oil to the contact-breaker wick and tappet (face-cam C.B.), or smear a little grease on the lever pivot-pin (rotating-magnet magneto).	63
4	Magneto chain	Every 1,000 miles inject a little grease (1945–51 models) with the grease gun, or occasionally repack the chain with grease (1952–7 models).	64
5	Gearbox	Every 1,000 miles inject 2 fluid ounces of light grease (1945–7), or top up with summer grade engine oil (1948 onwards) to the correct level. Every 5,000 miles change the lubricant.	65–8
6	Primary chain	Every 500 miles check level in oil-bath and top up if necessary to filler-cap orifice.	68
7	Secondary chain	Every 500 miles apply some engine oil if dry. In wet weather, remove, clean, and grease every 1,000 miles.	68
8	Front and rear hubs	Every 1,000 miles apply the grease gun to the hub nipples.	69
9	The brakes	Every 1,000 miles apply the grease gun to the expander-bush nipples. Weekly oil the brake linkage. Also every 3,000 miles grease the rear-brake pedal shaft.	69
10	Steering head	Every 1,000 miles grease both bearings with the grease gun.	69
11	Front-brake cable	Weekly oil the exposed end.	69
12	Rear-brake pedal	Every 3,000 miles apply the grease gun to the heel nipple.	69
13	Speedometer	Every 3,000 miles inject grease through the nipple on top of the speedometer gearbox.	70
14	Handlebar levers	Weekly apply a little oil to all moving parts. Inject some oil into the cables (where nipples are provided).	70
15	Stands	Occasionally oil fulcrum bolts.	70
16	Front forks	Every 5,000 miles (3,000 miles, 1945–7) check the hydraulic fluid content of both "Teledraulic legs," and top up if necessary.	71–4
17	Spring frame	If really necessary, replenish the rear-suspension units. Occasionally grease 1957–60 Girling cam-ring adjusters.	74

but on the 1957–60 A.M.C. gearboxes the filler cap is replaced by a circular cover secured by two small screws. Removal of the circular cover, incidentally, gives access to the clutch thrust-mechanism.

Changing the Gearbox Oil. After the first 500 miles and thereafter about every 5,000 miles change the lubricant in the gearbox. The light grease or engine oil (1948–60 models) should be drained completely, the A.J.S. gearbox flushed out with a suitable flushing oil and afterwards replenished with 1 lb. 14 oz. of grease (1945–7 boxes), or with 1 pint of engine oil (1948 onwards).

The screwed drain-plug is located low down at the rear of the gearbox shell. Where a non-fluid lubricant (light grease) is used, it may be found somewhat difficult to drain the gearbox thoroughly by removing the drain plug only. The best plan here is to remove the foot-change cover and the kick-starter case. Before replenishing the gearbox make sure that the drain plug is replaced and firmly tightened.

Primary Chain Lubrication. Remove the inspection cap from the oil-bath chain case about every 500 miles and observe the level of oil. On no account must the oil level be permitted to fall below $\frac{3}{16}$ in. from the bottom edge of the inspection-cap orifice, with the machine standing vertically on level ground. The correct amount of oil is present when its surface is level with the orifice.

If the oil level is too low, some harshness in the primary transmission generally develops, except on 1957–60 models where a sliding oil-seal in the form of two steel discs surrounds the gearbox mainshaft. Top up the oil-bath chain case as required and when necessary, using one of the brands of the summer-grade oils mentioned on page 57. Lubrication must not be neglected, for the oil-bath is responsible for lubricating: (*a*) the primary chain, (*b*) the dynamo chain, and (*c*) the engine shaft shock-absorber. (*b*) and (*c*) are omitted on 1958–60 models.

Oil-bath Inspection Cap Removal (1945–57). To remove the cap, unscrew the knurled screw approximately *four turns*. Then slide the cap sideways until it is possible to slip the back plate through the orifice and remove the complete cap assembly.

To prevent the risk of the filler cap, or inspection cap, being lost while riding, it is important to centralize the cork washer before firmly tightening the knurled retaining screw. Do not forget this when replacing the inspection cap.

Oil-bath Inspection Cap Removal (1958–60). On 1958–60 models with an aluminium oil-bath chain case, to remove the inspection cap apply the appropriate spanner (Part No. 018178) to the slot machined in the screwed cap.

Secondary Chain Lubrication. About every 500 miles examine the condition of the secondary chain. If the chain is in a dry state, turn the rear wheel by hand and apply some engine oil with a brush or oil-can. About every 1,000 miles in wet weather, it is advisable to remove the chain from the sprockets and clean and lubricate it in the following manner—

(1) Clean the chain thoroughly with paraffin.

CORRECT LUBRICATION

(2) Hang up the chain and allow to dry.

(3) Immerse the chain for at least *ten minutes* in a suitable receptacle containing Mobilgrease No. 2, B.P. Energol A.O., Esso Fluid Grease, or Castrolease Grease Graphited. The grease should be heated until just fluid and maintained in this state during the period of chain immersion.

Having lubricated the chain, fit it to the gearbox and rear-wheel sprockets. It is permissible to lubricate the chain, using engine oil instead of one of the greases mentioned, but this substitute is not so good. Allow the chain to soak for at least *an hour* where engine oil is used.

Filling Grease Gun. The grease gun (Part No. 017246) provided with the tool kit must be applied periodically to all grease nipples provided on the machine.

Suitable greases to use for various motor-cycle parts are those recommended on page 65. The grease gun must be charged so that the grease is on the *top* side of the piston. Special grease canisters are available with loose collars provided with holes. To charge the grease gun from one of these canisters, place the barrel of the gun over the hole in the central floating plate and press downwards firmly. Turn the grease gun and at the same time remove it from the floating plate. This should charge the grease gun so that the grease is flush with the top of the barrel. Having charged the grease gun, replace its screwed top-cap. If no grease canister of the type referred to is available, charge the grease gun by hand, using a suitable lath or similar implement.

The Wheel Hubs. On new machines the hubs of both wheels are packed with grease. To prevent mud and water entering the hubs, and to ensure correct lubrication, inject some grease through the nipple (accessible through the hole in the hub disc (1955 onwards)) of each hub about every 1,000 miles. Avoid excessive lubrication, or some of the grease may get on to the brake linings and impair the efficiency of the brakes.

Steering Head Lubrication. Apply the grease gun sparingly to the grease nipple in the head lug of the frame about every 1,000 miles. Also grease the nipple on the right-hand side of the handlebar lug at the same time.

The Front and Rear Brakes. Inject a little grease about every 1,000 miles through a grease nipple provided on each brake cover-plate for the expander bush. About every 3,000 miles apply the grease gun to the nipple in the heel of the rear-brake pedal (shown at (2) in Fig. 62).

Smear a few drops of engine oil *weekly* on the yoke-end pins at the front and rear ends of the rear-brake rod. Do not forget the threaded portion of the rod to which the hand adjuster is fitted. Also remember the exposed end of the front-brake cable.

The Rear Brake-drum Bearing (1955–60 Spring-frame Models). On the "springers" with full-width light-alloy rear hubs, the ball-bearing supporting the brake drum is packed with grease during initial assembly. No further lubrication should be required until it is necessary to undertake a general overhaul. The bearing should then be dismantled and repacked with fresh grease (*see* page 65).

Speedometer-Gearbox Lubrication. To ensure smooth and efficient running, grease the speedometer gearbox every 3,000 miles. The gearbox is attached to the rear-wheel spindle and the grease nipple is located on top of the speedometer gearbox as shown in Fig. 79. No further lubrication is required beyond the above-mentioned attention.

The Throttle Twist-grip. Stiffness sometimes develops and this spoils sensitive control of the throttle. To rectify stiffness is quite simple, and the following procedure should be adopted—

(1) Remove both the screws which retain the halves of the twist-grip clip.

(2) Withdraw the twist-grip from the end of the handlebars.

(3) Smear some grease on the off-side part of the handlebars over which the twist-grip fits.

(4) Smear some grease on the friction spring, and also on the drum on which the internal wire is wound.

(5) Replace the twist-grip on the end of the handlebars.

(6) Fit the two screws retaining the halves of the twist-grip clip and firmly tighten the screws.

The Handlebar Levers. It is advisable to apply a little engine oil *weekly* to all the moving parts of the handlebar levers. This will reduce friction and keep the controls responsive and easy to operate.

On 1954, 1955–7 models the control cables for the throttle slide and clutch lever have a conveniently situated nipple for the injection of engine oil by means of a grease gun. Some engine oil should be injected at the first indication of jerky or stiff action. When using the gun, hold it as nearly vertical as possible, with the nozzle facing *downward*.

The Dipper Switch. Every 5,000 miles lubricate the moving parts with a little thin machine oil.

The Stands. Occasionally lubricate the stand fulcrum-bolts; apply some engine oil to them with an oil-can. There are several small parts on the machine where only a little movement occurs. All such parts should be similarly lubricated. This will facilitate free movement and prevent rusting.

CORRECT LUBRICATION

The main parts of the A.J.S. requiring attention are indicated in the lubrication chart on page 66.

Sidecar Chassis. Do not forget to lubricate the sidecar chassis. Several grease nipples are provided for the purpose.

Hydraulic Fluids for "Teledraulic" Front Forks. The 1945–7 "Teledraulic" front forks and 1948–60 type, modified and simplified internally, require no actual lubrication. It is necessary, however, occasionally to check the hydraulic fluid content of each fork leg ($6\frac{1}{2}$ fluid oz. on 1945–7 forks, 10 oz. for 1948–50, $6\frac{1}{2}$ oz. for 1951 onwards); top up if necessary, as described in later paragraphs of this chapter. Below are specified suitable types of fluid for the A.J.S. hydraulic dampers—
 (1) Wakefield's "Castrolite."
 (2) Mobiloil "Arctic."
 (3) Shell X-100 20.
 (4) B.P. Energol SAE 20.
 (5) Essolube "20."

Level of Fluid (1945–7 "Teledraulic" Front Forks). It is desirable to check the fluid level every 3,000 miles. Position your A.J.S. so that it is resting on both wheels and is quite vertical. To maintain it in this position, insert packing beneath both footrests. Unscrew the two hexagon plugs shown at (*A*) in Fig. 2. Pull each plug (*A*) upwards to its maximum extent and thereby expose the fork damping-rod attached to the plug.

By "pumping" action eject any hydraulic fluid trapped in the tubes above the damper valves. Work each plug and damping rod up and down several times. Pause for *two minutes* to permit ejected fluid to drain down to the main supply of damping fluid.

Remove the two fluid-level plugs and their fibre washers from the fork slides. The plugs are situated just beneath the securing bolts for the front mudguard-bridge. Some hydraulic fluid should just ooze from the holes of the fluid-level plugs if the hydraulic fluid content of the forks is correct. Should no fluid be seen to ooze out from the holes, it is necessary to top up each fork leg as described in the next paragraph.

Topping up (1945–7 "Teledraulic" Front Forks). It is assumed that the two fluid-level plugs are still removed. To top up each leg of the "Teledraulic" front forks, the following procedure is required—
 (1) Pour about two tablespoonfuls (equivalent to *one fluid ounce*) of hydraulic fluid down each fork-leg inner-tube from the top end.
 (2) Work the top plug and attached damper rod up and down several times.
 (3) Wait for *two minutes* to allow hydraulic fluid to ooze from the fluid-level hole.

(4) If no excess hydraulic fluid oozes from the fluid-level hole, pour another fluid ounce of this medium down the inner tube of the fork leg.

(5) Having added further fluid, work the top plug and attached damper rod up and down several times, as previously. During all such "pumping" action, use the fingers only and make the upward strokes as sharply as possible.

(6) If still no fluid oozes from the fluid-level plug hole, investigate the reason carefully and rectify any defect responsible.

(7) As soon as hydraulic fluid is observed to ooze out of the level-plug hole, this indicates that the fluid content of the fork leg is correct, and the plugs can be replaced as referred to below.

(8) Replace the fluid-level plug on the inner side of the fork-leg slider. Do not forget to fit the fibre washer before tightening the plug with a screwdriver.

(9) Fit the plug to the top of the fork-leg inner-tube and firmly tighten with a spanner.

Hydraulic Fluid Content (1948–60 "Teledraulic" Front Forks). It is wise every 5,000 miles to check the hydraulic-fluid content of each front fork-leg. Before beginning this check, it is necessary to see that your A.J.S. is quite vertical, with the front wheel raised clear of the ground (weight on both wheels, 1951–60 models). Place a suitable box beneath each footrest. Remove the two hexagon-headed plugs, shown at (*A*) in Fig. 2, from the tops of the fork-leg inner tubes, after levering off (1955) the snap-on dome caps, or removing the rubber grommets (1956–60).

To determine the fluid content of each fork leg, remove the drain plug from the base of the fork-leg slider and permit the hydraulic fluid to drain off into a graduated measuring jug or other vessel having a capacity of at least 10 fluid ounces. Most of the fluid will drain off, but not all of it will do so.

Replace the drain plug in the base of the fork-leg slider, and on 1948–50 models work the forks up and down several times. On 1951–7 front forks the damper rod is attached to the hexagon-headed plug at the top of each fork leg and it is necessary to work each damper rod (instead of the forks) up and down, employing a pumping action. Hold the top plug with the fingers only, and make very sharp *upward* strokes. Wait two minutes and then remove the drain plug a second time and catch any further hydraulic fluid which may drain off into the graduated vessel already containing most of the fluid.

It may be necessary to repeat the 1948–57 draining procedure (including working the forks or top plugs up and down) several times to ensure that the maximum quantity of hydraulic fluid is drained off into the graduated vessel. Note the total amount of fluid extracted. It is not possible to extract in this manner the whole content of each leg (10 fluid ounces,

CORRECT LUBRICATION

1948–50; 6½ fluid ounces, 1951–60), but the amount drained off and measured should total 9½ fluid ounces or 6 fluid ounces respectively.

Topping up (1948–60 "Teledraulic" Front Forks). The checking of the hydraulic-fluid content and the topping up of each fork leg should be effected in one continuous operation. Deal with each fork leg individually.

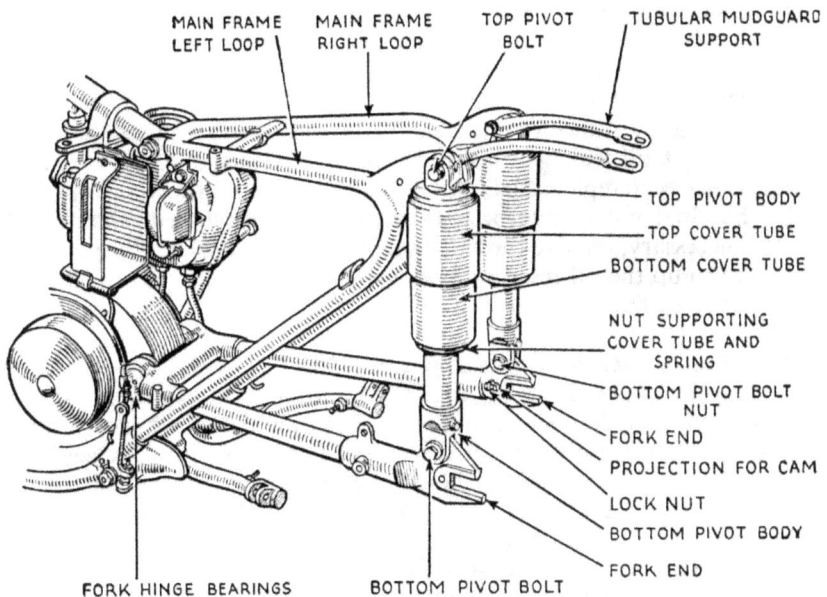

Fig. 42. Showing Details of the A.J.S. Spring Frame

"Swinging arm" type rear-suspension was first introduced in 1949 and is specified on all 1949–60 models. The rear-suspension units rarely need any attention.

It is assumed that the fluid content of the leg has already been determined. Then top up as follows—

(1) If the total amount of hydraulic fluid extracted from the fork leg measured exactly 9½ fluid ounces (1948–50) or 6 fluid ounces (1951–60), no topping up is necessary. If the amount is less than the appropriate quantity just stated, add hydraulic fluid (of the type already in use) to the graduated vessel until the total amount of fluid measures exactly 9½ fluid ounces or 6 fluid ounces, as the case may be.

(2) Replace the drain plug in the base of the fork slider.

(3) Pour the 9½ or 6 fluid ounces contained in the graduated vessel into the top of the fork inner-tube.

(4) On 1948–50 models, verify that the fork leg is fully extended.

(5) Replace the hexagon-headed top plug (and rubber washer), and firmly tighten the plug. Also replace the snap-on dome cap (1955) or rubber grommet (1956–60).

It is important to note that where 1948–57 "Teledraulic" front forks have been completely stripped down (necessarily incurring the removal of *all* hydraulic fluid), it is essential after assembly to top up each fork leg with the full 10 fluid ounces (1948–50) or $6\frac{1}{2}$ fluid ounces (1951–7), not the quantities ($\frac{1}{2}$ fluid ounce less) just quoted for topping up.

The "Swinging Arm." The "swinging arm" assembly in whose rear end the rear wheel is mounted is hinged just behind the gearbox, and the "swinging arm" fork-hinge plain bearings (*see* Fig. 42) are automatically lubricated from a reservoir containing $1\frac{1}{2}$ fluid ounces (42·6 c.c.) of engine oil.* This should suffice to lubricate the bearings for an almost indefinite period. Slight oil leakage may occur on a new machine (or where the reservoir has been replenished), but this is of no significance and stops after a few hundred miles have been covered. If replenishment should ever become necessary, remove the small screw from the off-side hinge bearing-cap and top up the oil reservoir with engine oil (*see* page 57) to the level of the screw orifice.

"Teledraulic" Rear-Suspension Units (1949–56). The rear-suspension units have hydraulic damping springs of almost identical design to that used for the "Teledraulic" front forks. But only if leakage of hydraulic fluid occurs (most unlikely) is it necessary to replenish the fork legs with the correct amount of fluid. Should the leg action become excessively lively, it is possible that some loss of damping fluid is responsible, but unless you are in serious doubt as to the correct functioning of the spring frame, you are advised to leave well alone.

The hydraulic fluid (oil) content of each "Teledraulic" rear leg can be checked in accordance with the instructions given in the maker's instruction book. The correct fluids to use are those specified on page 71. For the spring frame on all 1949–50 models each fork leg should contain exactly $1\frac{3}{4}$ fluid ounces (50 c.c.), but on the 1951 and later spring frames the recommended quantity is 85 c.c. or a little below 3 fluid ounces. On no account must the oil content exceed 90 c.c.

Girling Rear-Suspension Units (1957–60). These proprietary units are sealed by the makers and do not require to be topped up. During initial assembly their springs are lubricated and sufficient hydraulic fluid inserted in the damper units to last until the Girling units require to be renewed.

Occasionally clean and grease the cam-ring adjusters provided to give three different spring tensions. If the movement of the telescopic legs is accompanied by a rubbing noise or squeaking, remove the two half circlips securing each top cover-tube, remove the tube, and apply some grease to the outside diameter of the spring.

* Heavy gear oil (SAE 140) is recommended by the makers for 1952 and later models.

CHAPTER V

GENERAL MAINTENANCE

THIS chapter contains full maintenance instructions for all 1945-60 touring singles. Some instructions, however, have already been included in Chapters II-IV. Appropriate cross-references to these earlier chapters are therefore also included.

A.J.S. Repairs and Spares. When you have occasion to forward or deliver parts to the manufacturers* (either for repair or as patterns) always attach to *each* part a label on which is written clearly your full name and address. To ensure quick attention, all correspondence concerning spares and technical advice should be written on separate sheets, each bearing your name and address.

Always quote the *complete* engine number or frame number, according to the nature of the part involved. The frame number will be found marked on the off-side of the saddle lug (*see* page 1). The engine number (with letter prefix) will be found on the near-side of the crankcase.

There are numerous firms in the United Kingdom who can supply A.J.S. spares over the counter, and many who specialize in the repair of engines and gearboxes. Useful addresses may be found in the advertisement pages of *The Motor Cycle* and *Motor Cycling*. If taking a machine to Plumstead, first make an appointment (Woolwich 1223).

Some London Accessory Firms. Among reputable London firms (some of which have provincial branches) handling motor-cycle accessories, equipment spares, tools, clothing, etc. may be mentioned: Whitbys of Acton, Ltd.; Claude Rye, Ltd.; E. S. Motors; The Halford Cycle Co., Ltd.; Turner's Stores; James Grose, Ltd.; Marble Arch Motor Supplies, Ltd.; Pride & Clarke, Ltd.; and George Grose, Ltd.

ENGINE MAINTENANCE

Items for Maintenance. For engine maintenance there are certain items which you *must* have handy in the lock-up or garage. These include: a can of paraffin for cleaning purposes; a stiff brush for scouring dirt off the crankcase; a tin of suitable engine oil (*see* page 57); a canister of grease;

* The A.J.S. Service and Repair Dept. is in Burrage Grove, Plumstead, London, S.E.18.

a small oil-can containing some engine oil; a receptacle for oil when draining the oil tank and oil sump; a pail or some jars for washing engine parts in; some non-fluffy rags; valve-grinding paste such as Richford's (coarse and fine); some fine emery cloth; a set of engine gaskets (*see* illustrated Spares List); some jointing compound; a pair of new gudgeon-pin circlips; and some good hand cleanser, such as "Gre-solvent."

Tools Required. The A.J.S. tool kit is adequate for any normal stripping down and assembly job and should prove sufficient for routine maintenance and overhaul. It is also necessary for maintenance to obtain a suitable feeler gauge for checking the sparking plug gap (*see* page 80), an A.J.S. valve-spring compressor (for 1949 and subsequent engines with hairpin valve springs), and a valve holder for grinding-in the valves. The Part Nos. are 018276 and 017482 respectively. It is also desirable to obtain a wire-brush for cleaning sparking plugs.

Should you decide to undertake as much repair work as possible in addition to routine maintenance, stripping-down, and assembly, it is desirable to rig up a suitable bench, complete with vice, and to purchase some extra tools (various A.J.S. service tools are available).

To begin, it is a good plan to buy a medium-weight hammer, a hand-drill and an assortment of twist-drills, a hacksaw, some large and small (smooth and rough) files, and a good soldering outfit for the repair of control cables. Repair work is beyond the scope of this handbook, and you are not advised to tackle such work unless you have fair technical knowledge and skill in handling tools.

Engine Lubrication. Detailed instructions on lubricating the A.J.S. engine are given in Chapter IV. Attend to lubrication points 1 to 4 indicated in the Lubrication Chart on page 66.

The Amal Carburettor. For comprehensive advice on how to maintain correct carburation, refer to the instructions given in Chapter II.

Keep your Engine Clean. Keep your engine clean externally as well as internally. By so doing you enhance pride of ownership and obtain other advantages. Dirt is apt to mask defects and can accidentally enter the engine when it is being stripped down. It will also make rusting more likely. Rusted cylinder and cylinder head fins, besides being an eyesore, are detrimental to efficient dispersion of heat by radiation. They should be clean and black. On the A.J.S. they are stove enamelled black (except 1951–60 light-alloy cylinder heads).

To clean the cylinder and cylinder-head fins, use a stiff brush dipped in paraffin. If the stove-enamelling has worn away, paint the fins with a good proprietary cylinder black. Clean the aluminium alloy and bright surfaces with rags and paraffin, assisted by brushes where necessary, and scour off

GENERAL MAINTENANCE

the filth from the lower part of the crankcase by means of stiff brushes and paraffin. Thorough cleaning may take some time, but it is well worth while.

Check Nuts for Tightness Occasionally. On a new A.J.S. where some initial bedding-down occurs, it is advisable to check all external nuts and bolts for tightness fairly frequently. After the running-in period is completed it is a good habit to check the external nuts regularly every 3,000 miles. Pay special attention to the cylinder nuts, the nuts on the engine plates, and the union nuts for the pipe connexions.

SPARKING PLUGS, CONTACT-BREAKER, ETC.

The ignition system comprises: a 14 mm sparking plug; a Lucas rotating-armature type magneto (1945–53 models), with manual ignition control; or a Lucas rotating-magnet type magneto (1954–7 models), with automatic ignition-control mechanism on the driving side; or a Lucas type CA1A contact-breaker unit with automatic timing control (1958 onwards). The contact-breaker unit and timing control are both housed in the timing case of the 1958 and later coil-ignition models. They are operated from the inlet camshaft, and a coil is clipped to the frame top tube underneath the petrol tank. Current is taken from the battery through the contact-breaker unit to the ignition coil (unless the ignition key is in the "EMG" position).

Suitable Sparking Plugs. To obtain maximum engine performance throughout the throttle range, plus easy starting, it is essential always to run on a suitable type of sparking plug. Three reliable makes of sparking plugs are the K.L.G., the Lodge, and the Champion. Suitable types are—

K.L.G.—Fit a three-point, detachable type F80, or FE80 (1951 onwards), or else the appropriate watertight version.

LODGE—Fit a three-point, detachable type HN or a type HLN on all 1951 and later models.

CHAMPION—Fit a non-detachable type L-10 (1945–6 350 c.c.), L-10S (1945–6 500 c.c., all 1947–9 models), or type NA-8 (all 1950 and later models).

For regular bad-weather riding it is advisable to fit a weather-proof terminal cover to the plug, or else to use a watertight plug corresponding to the appropriate non-watertight plugs recommended above. If your A.J.S. was registered prior to 2nd July, 1953, it is according to law (but hardly enforceable!) necessary to fit an ignition-suppression type plug, or a terminal cover with built-in suppressor, so as not to annoy users of wireless and television sets. Note that ignition-suppression type plugs have longer-wearing electrodes.

The Sparking Plug Gap. It is advisable to check the gap between the electrodes of the sparking plug about every 3,000 miles. The correct gap is 0·020–0·022 in., and it is advisable to re-gap the plug if burning of the points has increased the gap to over 0·022 in. When re-gapping a plug it is desirable for obvious reasons to set its gap at or near the *bottom* limit.

Check the gap with a suitable feeler gauge (a wire gauge if the points are not very accessible). The gauge should be a nice sliding fit. When adjusting the gap, never attempt to bend or tap the centre electrode. Use a plug re-gapping tool (*see* Fig. 43), a small pair of snipe-nose pliers, or a small screwdriver to bend the outside (earth) electrode(s). Tapping the outer electrode(s) inwards to reduce the gap is permissible, if the plug is held in a vice and a light hammer and copper drift are used. When the plug has to be thoroughly cleaned, this should be done as described below, and the plug re-gapped *afterwards*.

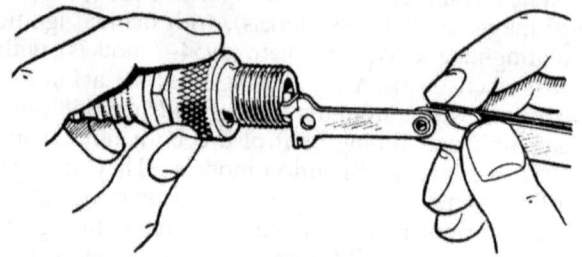

FIG. 43. THE BEST WAY TO RE-GAP A PLUG

Cleaning the Sparking plug. If carburation is quite satisfactory and excessive oil is not entering the combustion chamber, it should not be necessary to dismantle and clean the sparking plug thoroughly more often than once about every 3,000 miles. When running-in a new or rebored engine, however, it is advisable to remove and check the plug for cleanliness at intervals of about 500 miles.

Quick cleaning of a plug can be done by brushing the points and lightly rubbing their firing sides with some smooth emery-cloth. Thorough cleaning (internal and external), however, is not possible without dismantling the plug (*see* below).

To Clean K.L.G. and Lodge Plugs. Fig. 44 shows a typical detachable type (K.L.G.) sparking plug dismantled for thorough cleaning. To dismantle a detachable-type plug, grip the smaller hexagon on the gland nut (*B*) in a vice, with the plug upside down. Be most careful not to exert any pressure on the hexagon faces. Then with the plug box-spanner, or a suitable ring spanner, unscrew the large hexagon (*E*) on the plug body. Alternatively use two spanners to unscrew the gland nut from the plug body. The centre electrode (*F*) with its insulation, comprising the insulated electrode assembly (*A*), can now be detached from the gland nut. Take care not to lose the internal sealing washer (*H*).

GENERAL MAINTENANCE

To clean the insulation, wipe it clean with a cloth soaked in petrol or paraffin. If the insulation is coated with hard carbon deposits, remove these with some fairly coarse glass-paper and wash again, but make no attempt to scrape off the deposits. The internal sealing washer (H) and the surfaces on the insulator, and in the metal body on which this washer rests, are very important as they prevent gas-leakage through the plug. Therefore wipe them only with a rag soaked in petrol or paraffin. Any damage caused while dismantling will render the plug unserviceable.

To clean the metal parts (plug body and gland nut), wipe them clean with petrol, or, if necessary, scrape off the deposits with a small knife, or use a wire brush. Afterwards rinse the parts in petrol. The gland nut seldom gets very fouled, but the inside of the plug body may be very dirty, and the same may apply to the external threads of the plug. Clean and polish the points (see Fig. 44) of the centre and outside (earth) electrodes (F) and (G) with some fine emery-cloth.

See that there is no dirt or grit lodged between the body of the plug and the insulation, and particularly on the internal sealing-washer and all contacting faces. Smear a little thin oil on the internal washer and make sure that it seats properly. When assembling the sparking plug, see that the centre electrode and insulation are positioned centrally in the body bore. If not, remove, re-position by rotating the centre a quarter of a turn, and re-assemble. Do not attempt to force into position or bend.

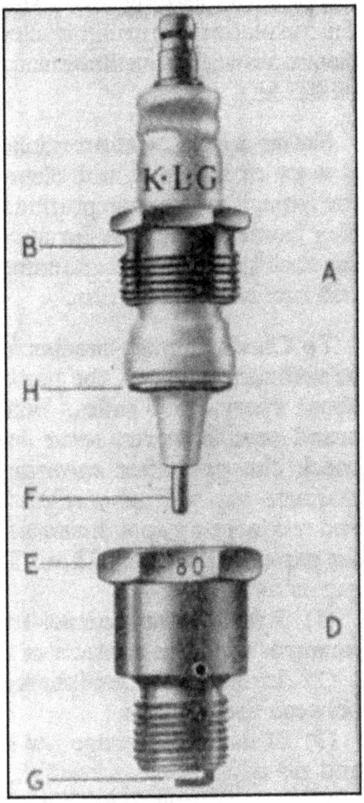

FIG. 44. DETACHABLE TYPE SPARKING PLUG (K.L.G.) DISMANTLED FOR THOROUGH CLEANING

The gland nut B and the internal washer H are shown still in position on the insulation.

Tighten the gland nut into the plug body just sufficiently to give a gas-tight joint. Do not use an open-ended spanner. Finally verify that the plug gap is correct.

To Clean Champion Plugs. A Champion non-detachable plug such as the L-10S cannot be dismantled and cleaned like the detachable-type Lodge and K.L.G. plugs. Quick cleaning is of course done in the same manner (*see* page 78). The best method of cleaning a Champion plug thoroughly is to take it to a nearby garage having an "air-blast" unit. In a matter of a few minutes the plug can be thoroughly cleaned of all deposits, washed, and tested for sparking at a pressure exceeding 100 lb. per sq. in.

To assist cleaning, use a small wire brush. Wipe the tip and outside of the insulation thoroughly clean. After removing all carbon, polish the electrodes with some fine emery-cloth. Finally, check the plug gap (0·020 in. –0·022 in.).

Fitting a Plug. Before replacing the plug, renew the copper washer if it is worn or flattened, and clean the plug threads. It is a good plan to coat the threads with some graphite paste before replacing the plug. Screw the plug home by hand as far as possible, and always use the plug spanner in the tool kit for final tightening. The use of excessive force is undesirable and can cause distortion.

To Check Contact-breaker Gap (1945–53 Models). Normally it should be sufficient to check the gap between the contacts of the contact-breaker about every 2,500 miles. Where the magneto or the contact-breaker is brand-new, however, some bedding-down occurs, and it is advisable to check the gap after covering approximately 500 miles. An incorrect magneto gap will adversely affect the functioning of the ignition system, and too large a gap will also advance the ignition timing. Always maintain the gap at 0·010 in.–0·012 in. The procedure for checking and adjusting the gap is as follows—

(1) Remove the contact-breaker cover and rotate the engine slowly forwards until the contacts of the contact-breaker are wide open.

(2) Insert the blade of the feeler gauge (attached to the magneto spanner) between the contacts.

(3) If the feeler gauge *just* slides in without friction, the gap is correct and no adjustment is needed. If the gauge is a slack fit or the contacts have to be sprung to enable it to enter, adjust the gap as below.

4) With the magneto spanner loosen the nut which secures the inner-contact screw (*see* Fig. 45) and then adjust this screw by means of its hexagon head until the correct gap is obtained between the fixed (outer) and adjustable (inner) contacts.

(5) Retighten the contact screw lock-nut and again check the gap. If correct, replace the contact-breaker cover.

From the foregoing it will be observed that checking the contact-breaker gap does not necessitate complete removal of the contact-breaker from the magneto. The same applies where cleaning is concerned.

To Check Contact-breaker Gap (1954–7 Models). On 1954 500 c.c. and all 1955 and subsequent models it is advisable after the first 500 miles to remove the moulded cover from the Lucas type S.R.-1 rotating-magnet

GENERAL MAINTENANCE

magneto and check the gap between the contacts of the contact-breaker. It is subsequently sufficient to check the gap at intervals of about 3,000 miles. Actual adjustment is seldom needed. The correct contact-breaker gap is the same as for the rotating-armature type magneto, namely 0·010 in.–0·012 in.

The correct procedure for checking the contact-breaker gap is as described for the magneto on 1945–53 models, described in sub-paragraph (1) to (3) on page 80.

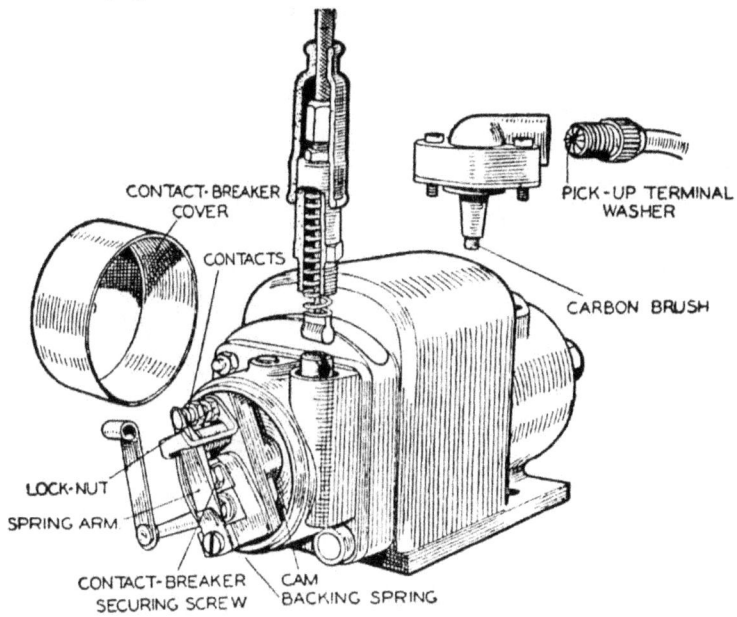

FIG. 45. SHOWING DETAILS OF LUCAS ROTATING-ARMATURE TYPE MAGNETO (1945–53)

In Fig. 39 is shown a view of the contact-breaker dismantled.

Should an adjustment of the contact-breaker gap be necessary, slacken the two securing screws (*see* Fig. 46) holding the fixed contact plate and move the plate as required until the gap is correct. Having made the required adjustment, firmly tighten the two securing-screws, again check the gap, and finally replace the moulded cover. Tighten its three fixing-screws firmly.

To Check Contact-breaker Gap (1958 Onwards). On the 1958 and later models check the contact-breaker gap after covering 500 miles on a new machine, and thereafter regularly about every 3,000 miles.

To check the contact-breaker gap, first remove the two screws securing the outer cover to the timing case, and remove the cover. Next turn the engine over slowly until the contacts are fully open. Then insert a suitable feeler gauge between the contacts and check the gap which should be 0·14 in.–0·16 in. If the correct size feeler gauge just slides in without friction, the gap is correct and no adjustment is needed. If an adjustment is required, make it as described below.

With the engine still in the position where the maximum contact gap is obtained, loosen the two screws which secure the contact plate (*see* Fig. 47). Then adjust the position of the plate as required until the gap between the contacts is correct. Afterwards fully tighten the two plate-securing screws.

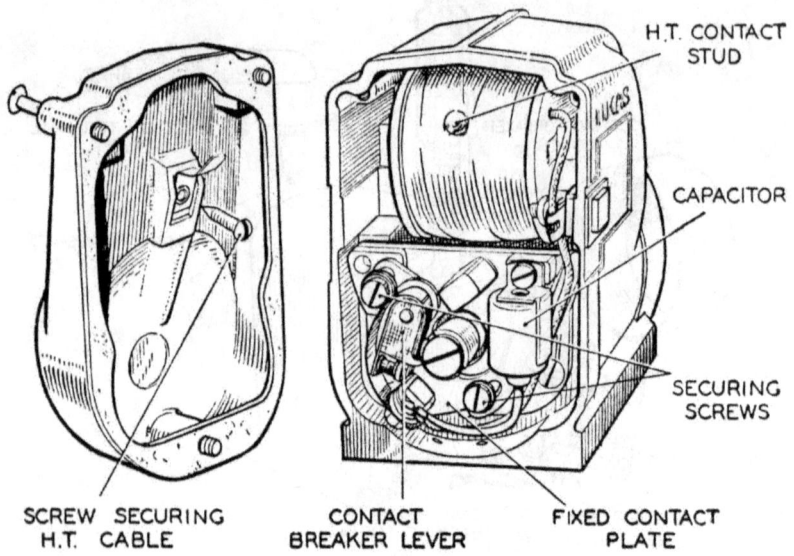

FIG. 46. CONTACT-BREAKER END OF LUCAS ROTATING-MAGNET MAGNETO (1954–7)

This magneto (not fitted to 1954 350 c.c. models) has automatic ignition-control mechanism on the driving side.

Cleaning the Contact-breaker. The contact-breaker, especially the contacts themselves, must *never* be permitted to get dirty or oily; otherwise ignition trouble will inevitably ensue, and the contacts will become burned and pitted. When checking the gap of the contact-breaker, *always* inspect the contacts closely and, if they need cleaning, do this *before* finally adjusting the gap.

If the contacts have a *grey, frosted* appearance, it can be reasonably assumed that they are fairly healthy. Should they be only slightly discoloured, clean both contacts with a cloth moistened with petrol. Where the contacts are pitted or blackened, they must be thoroughly cleaned with a fine carborundum stone or, if one is not available, *very fine* emery-cloth.

Afterwards all metallic dust and dirt must be completely removed with a petrol-moistened cloth.

When cleaning and dressing the contacts, it is essential to remove the minimum amount of contact metal necessary to ensure: (*a*) brightness of the contacts, (*b*) parallelism of the contacts, (*c*) perfect smoothness and truth of contact faces. To ensure this it is advisable to withdraw the moving contact.

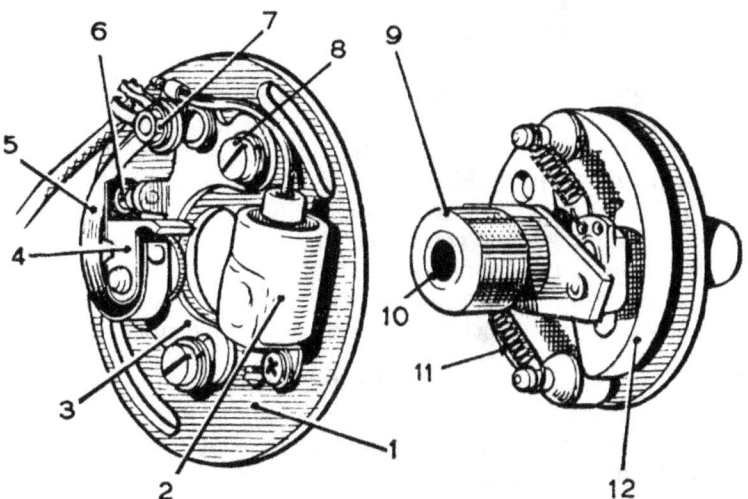

FIG. 47. THE CONTACT-BREAKER (LEFT) AND AUTOMATIC IGNITION-TIMING CONTROL (RIGHT) UNITS REMOVED FROM THE TIMING-CASE COVER AND INLET CAMSHAFT OF A COIL-IGNITION MODEL (1958–60)

1. Contact-breaker plate.
2. Capacitor.
3. Contact plate (adjustable).
4. Contact-breaker lever.
5. Spring for 4.
6. Contacts.
7. Terminal nut.
8. Securing screw (one of two) for 1.
9. Cam operating contact-breaker.
10. Hole for bolt securing timing-control unit.
11. Spring (one of two) controlling bob weight
12. Bob weight (one of two).

To Withdraw Moving Contact (1945–57). On 1945–53 models with a rotating-armature type magneto, remove the spring arm (*see* Fig. 45), carrying the moving contact, by removing the fixing screw and spring washer. When replacing the spring arm be sure to fit the small backing spring correctly. The curved portion must face *outwards*. Remove any rust from the spring. On 1954–7 models with a rotating-magnet type magneto, to remove the contact-breaker lever (*see* Fig. 46) carrying the moving contact, remove the nut securing the end of the contact-breaker spring. The spring is slotted to permit of easy withdrawal of the lever.

To Withdraw Moving Contact (1958–60). To withdraw the moving contact on 1958 and later models having coil ignition, unscrew the nut which secures the end of the spring (*see* Fig. 47) and remove the nut, spring washer, and bush. Then lift the contact-breaker lever carrying the moving contact off its pivot.

To Renew Ignition-Control Cable (1945–53). As may be seen in Fig. 45, slackness in the cable for advancing and retarding the spark can be rectified by means of the cable stop after pushing the rubber protector upwards and slackening the lock-nut. If, however, the cable frays, breaks or stretches unduly, it is necessary to renew the cable in the following manner.

Do not attempt to remove the cam itself from its housing. Remove the cable casing at the magneto by unscrewing the hexagon nut at its base. Draw fully upwards the control cable and the attached plunger. This will cause the nipple into which the cable-end is soldered to rise above the top of the boss on the cam-cage housing. Slip the nipple sideways out of the hole in the plunger and completely detach the cable. Now thread the new cable through the casing and solder the nipple on to its end. Then slip the nipple sideways into the hole in the plunger and screw the casing home. Finally, make the necessary adjustment by means of the cable stop.

Cleaning the Slip-ring (1945–53 Models). Misfiring and some difficult starting are sometimes caused by moisture, oil, or dirt collecting on the slip-ring. About every 2,500–3,000 miles remove the h.t. pick-up (*see* Fig. 45) from the magneto and thoroughly clean the track and flanges of the slip-ring. The best way of doing this is to cover a pencil with a soft cloth and press this against the slip ring while slowly rotating the engine.

The h.t. Pick-up (1945–53 Models). When cleaning the magneto slip-ring, also wipe the pick-up moulding and polish it with a fine, dry, cloth. Inspect the moulding for cracks and examine the carbon brush (*see* Fig. 45) and spring, but be careful not to stretch the spring. If the carbon brush is badly worn, renew it.

Before replacing the h.t. pick-up on the magneto, see that the carbon brush moves freely in its holder and beds down properly on the slip-ring. Good electrical contact is important.

To Renew h.t. Cable (1945–53 Models). Always use 7 mm. rubber-covered ignition cable. Referring to Fig. 45, bare the end of the cable for about $\frac{1}{4}$ in. and thread the cable through the moulded terminal. Pass the wire through the bronze washer and then bend back the cable strands as illustrated. Finally, screw the moulded terminal into the magneto pick-up.

To Renew h.t. Cable (1954–57 Models). Where a Lucas rotating-magnet type SR-1 magneto is fitted, 7 mm. rubber-covered ignition cable is also required for renewal purposes. To connect to the magneto, first remove the moulded cover from the contact-breaker side, and unscrew the pointed screw (*see* Fig. 46) from the back of the cover. Pull out the old ignition cable and push the new cable right home. Then secure the cable by tightening the pointed screw. Its point will penetrate the insulation and ensure good electrical contact with the core of the cable.

Testing the h.t. Cable. If the engine is running well, obviously the cable is sound but, if the engine refuses to start, it is desirable to ascertain whether the h.t. current is reaching the plug end of the cable. Place the the steel blade of a *wooden-handled* screwdriver in contact with the plug terminal and almost in contact with one of the cylinder fins. Kick the engine over smartly and note whether a "fat" spark occurs. If it does, the cable is sound, but if it does not the cable or magneto is at fault.

To Re-tension Magneto Chain (1945–57 Models). About every 3,000 miles remove the cover from the magneto chain-case and inspect the chain for tension. Some stretching occurs, especially on a new chain, and where this is excessive it may spoil the exact ignition-timing and accelerate wear of the chain and sprockets. Press the magneto chain-run up and down (in its *tautest* position) midway between the magneto and camshaft sprockets. If the tension is correct, the *total* deflection should not exceed approximately ¼ in. If it is appreciably more or less, re-tension the chain as described below. Over-tensioning may damage the magneto.

(1) Loosen the nuts on both bolts (nut on rear bolt only, 1954–7) which support and secure the adjustable magneto-platform.
(2) Insert the blade of a screwdriver beneath the front (rear, 1954 onwards) end of the magneto platform and prise it upwards until the correct chain tension is obtained.
(3) Tighten firmly both nuts on the magneto-platform securing bolts. On 1954 and later models tighten the single nut on the rear bolt.
(4) Again check the tension of the driving chain.
(5) Grease the chain if necessary (*see* page 58) and fit the cover to the chain-case. Do not use jointing compound. Tighten the various cover securing-screws evenly.

Automatic Ignition-control Mechanism (1954–7). The control mechanism on the driving side of the Lucas type SR-1 rotating magnet magneto requires no adjustment, but the mechanism should be greased (*see* page 65) when greasing the magneto chain.

Automatic Ignition-control Unit Removal (1958–60). Normally the unit requires no attention other than occasional lubrication (*see* page 64). Removal is therefore unlikely to be necessary unless the renewal of some part is required after an extremely big mileage. Removal is necessary, however, as a preliminary to retiming the ignition on coil-ignition models. The following is the correct procedure.

First remove the outer cover from the timing case after removing the two securing screws. Next remove the two securing screws which pass through slotted holes in the fixed contact-breaker plate (*see* Fig. 47) and remove the plate. Then remove the central bolt which secures the timing control unit to a taper on the inlet camshaft. Fit a withdrawal bolt (Part No. 024328) in place of the bolt removed, and tighten slightly. Now direct a sharp tap on the end of the withdrawal bolt. This will free the ignition-control unit from the inlet camshaft extension and enable it to be withdrawn.

Do not interfere with the detachable contact-breaker cam which is rotated by two pegs engaged in the plates for the control springs. Should for some reason the cam be removed, note its position prior to removal.

TIMING THE MAGNETO (1945–57 MODELS)

The Correct Magneto-timing. Incorrect magneto-timing can have a most detrimental effect on the engine, besides reducing its performance. A late timing will result in a "woolly" engine and a hot and noisy exhaust, with considerable overheating and inability to develop full power. An early timing, on the other hand, may result in the engine being powerful on the larger throttle openings, but it will have a nasty tendency to kick-back when being started and it will "knock" readily under slight provocation. Worst of all, the engine will be subjected to some fuel detonation and stresses for which it is *not* designed.

Never attempt to improve on the maker's timing, which is such that *the contact-breaker contacts begin to open with the piston $\frac{7}{16}$ in. before T.D.C. ($\frac{1}{2}$ in. 1949–57) on the compression stroke*. Sometimes it is necessary for some reason to remove the magneto or its driving chain. Where this is done, the magneto must be retimed. For this purpose it is desirable to have available the following two items—

(*a*) A stout screwdriver, or an old-type tyre lever with the end turned up.

(*b*) A small rod or stout wheel spoke about $5\frac{1}{2}$ in. long.

1. Timing the Magneto—Preliminaries. Remove the covers from (*a*) the contact-breaker, (*b*) the off-side of the rocker-box, and (*c*) the magneto chain-case. Also remove the plug. Check that the gap at the contact-breaker is correct (0·010 in.–0·012 in.) as described on pages 80 and 81. It is also advisable to check that the magneto chain is correctly tensioned. The contact-breaker gap *must* be correct, as this affects the timing appreciably.

Loosen by several turns the nut which secures the magneto-driving sprocket to the camshaft, but do not take the nut right off. Then, with the stout screwdriver or the tyre lever referred to above, placed behind the sprocket, lever the latter off the taper on the camshaft. Rotate the engine forwards slowly until the piston is at true T.D.C. with *both valves closed*, as described below.

2. **Finding the Exact Piston Position.** Slip the $5\frac{1}{2}$ in. length of rod through the hole for the sparking plug. Rotate the engine *forwards* slowly until it is felt that the piston is exactly at the top of its stroke. In this position no movement is imparted to the rod. Without moving the piston, mark the rod flush with the top face of the sparking-plug hole. Remove the rod and scratch another mark $\frac{7}{16}$ in. ($\frac{1}{2}$ in., 1949–57) above the first. Again insert the rod through the sparking-plug hole and slowly turn the engine *backwards* by means of the rear wheel (with top gear engaged) until the upper of the two marks on the rod is flush with the top of the sparking-plug hole; $\frac{7}{16}$ in. and $\frac{1}{2}$ in. equal 36 deg. and 39 deg. respectively before T.D.C.

3. **Timing the Contact "Break."** With the piston still at $\frac{7}{16}$ in. or $\frac{1}{2}$ in. before T.D.C., advance the ignition-control lever (all 1945–53, and 1954 350 c.c. models with manual control) on the handlebars *fully* by pushing it *outwards* to its maximum extent. Where automatic ignition-control is provided (on 1954 500 c.c. and all 1955 and later models) turn (with the finger and thumb) *to the maximum extent possible* the front plate of the automatic ignition-control mechanism. This is its fully advanced position. Lock the control in this position by inserting a small wooden wedge. Without moving the piston, rotate the sprocket secured to the magneto armature-shaft (and the driving chain) *anti-clockwise*, viewed from the driving side, until the contacts of the contact-breaker are just beginning to open.

To determine the exact moment of the "break," insert a thin cellophane slip between the contacts and exert a gentle pull on the paper when the magneto sprocket is being slowly turned.

When the exact position of the "break" has been found, secure the sprocket to the camshaft, being most careful not to permit the camshaft and/or armature to move while tightening the camshaft nut.

Finally check over the magneto timing again, verify the chain tension, grease the chain (*see* page 64) if necessary, and replace the covers for the contact-breaker, rocker-box and magneto chain-case. Before replacing the magneto chain-case cover do not forget to remove the wooden wedge previously used to lock the automatic ignition-control mechanism in the fully advanced position. Fit the sparking plug and you should be "all set."

TIMING THE IGNITION (1958–60)

The maker's recommended ignition timing for 1958 and later coil-ignition models should *never* be altered. *The timing is correct if the contact-breaker* *contacts begin to open with the piston $\frac{1}{2}$ in. before T.D.C.* (top dead centre), with the automatic timing control in the fully advanced position. Note that the timing is also correct if the contacts begin to open with the piston $\frac{1}{8}$ in. before T.D.C., with the automatic timing-control in the fully *retarded* position. The ignition can therefore be retimed, using one of two methods.

In the event of the automatic timing-control unit being removed from the taper on the inlet camshaft extension, retiming is, of course, necessary. It is also necessary when occasion is had to remove the main cover from the timing case (housing the two camwheels and the engine pinion). The following items are required when retiming the ignition—

(a) A small rod or portion of a stiff wheel spoke (about $5\frac{1}{2}$ in. long).

(b) An automatic timing-control unit withdrawal tool (Part No. 024328).

1. Before Timing the Ignition. Remove: (a) the sparking plug and its h.t. cable; (b) the cover from the off-side of the rocker-box; and (c) the contact-breaker plate and the automatic timing-control unit. Remove the ignition timing-control unit from the inlet camshaft extension as described on page 85. Before removing the plate, on which the contact-breaker and capacitor are assembled, and behind which the ignition-timing control unit is fitted, check that the contact-breaker gap is correct (*see* page 81). This is important because the gap appreciably affects the ignition timing.

2. Identifying Piston Position. Rotate the engine *forwards* slowly until the piston is at or near top dead centre on the compression stroke (inlet valve opens and then closes), with both valves fully closed. Engage fourth gear and insert the timing rod or portion of spoke through the sparking plug hole. Then rock the engine gently backwards and forwards until *no movement* is felt on the rod which should be held as vertically as possible. When the rod remains dead still, with both valves fully closed, the piston is at the extreme top of its stroke, i.e. in the top dead centre (T.D.C.) position.

Scratch a mark on the timing rod flush with the top face of the sparking plug hole, and remove the rod. Then scratch another mark $\frac{1}{2}$ in. or $\frac{1}{8}$ in. *above* the T.D.C. mark, according to whether you decide to retime with the automatic ignition timing-control fully advanced or fully retarded respectively.

3. Timing the Ignition. With the piston at true T.D.C., fit the automatic ignition timing-control unit to the inlet camshaft extension, with the gap formed by the two bob-weights (*see* Fig. 49) in line with the two tapped holes for the contact-breaker plate securing screws (shown at 4 in Fig. 48). When correctly positioned the peak of the cam (i.e. its narrowest part) is approximately at 12 o'clock. Press the ignition timing-control unit firmly on to the tapered camshaft extension and deliver a sharp tap on the cam before replacing and tightening the central securing bolt. If the *fully*

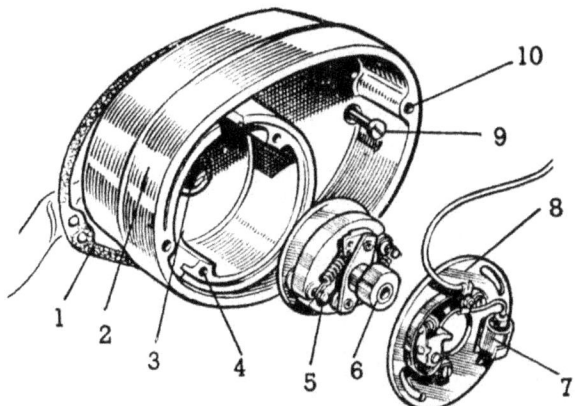

Fig. 48. The Timing Case Main Cover, Automatic Ignition Timing-control Unit and Contact-breaker Plate Shown Removed

1. Washer (between engine timing case and 2).
2. Timing-case main cover.
3. Bush for inlet camshaft extension.
4. Hole (one of two) for screws securing 8.
5. Automatic ignition timing-control unit.
6. Cam (operating contact-breaker).
7. Capacitor.
8. Contact-breaker plate with elongated holes for timing.
9. Screw (one of five) securing 2 to timing case.
10. Hole (one of two) for screws securing timing-case outer cover.

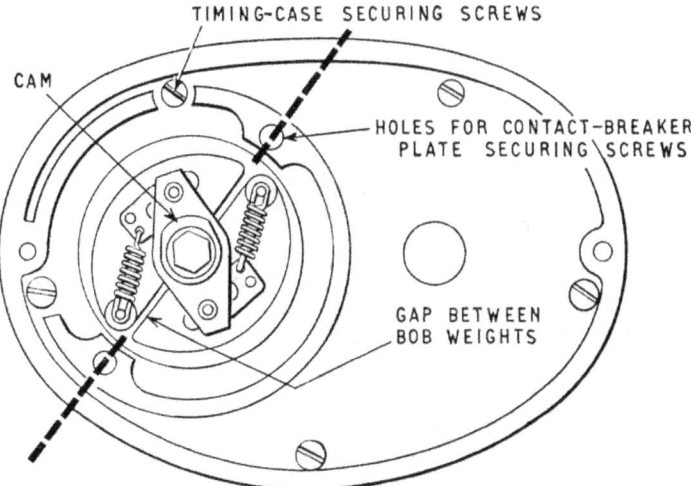

Fig. 49. Correct Alignment when Fitting the Automatic Ignition Timing-control Unit

Note the cam position and the dotted alignment line.

advanced method of timing is to be used, insert a wooden wedge between the bob-weights to fully separate them.

Replace the marked timing rod through the sparking plug hole, and with fourth gear still engaged, turn the engine slowly *backwards* until the *highest* of the two marks scratched on the rod is flush with the top face of the sparking plug hole. Position the contact-breaker plate in its housing (*see* Fig. 48) with the capacitor at 3 o'clock and *lightly* tighten the two screws securing the contact-breaker plate.

To determine the exact moment when the contacts commence to open, insert a thin cellophane slip between the contacts and exert a gentle pull on the slip when the contact-breaker plate is moved slowly in a *clockwise* direction. When the correct plate position for contact opening is obtained, tighten the two contact-breaker plate securing-screws (if using the fully *retarded* method of ignition timing).

If a wooden wedge is used to *fully advance* the ignition timing, scribe a pencil line on the contact-breaker plate, and a similar line on the plate housing, with both lines in register. Withdraw the contact-breaker plate, remove the wedge, replace the contact-breaker plate with the two scribed lines in register. Afterwards fully tighten the two contact-breaker plate securing-screws. Before replacing the sparking plug, h.t. lead, and rocker-box cover, again check the ignition timing.

TAPPET ADJUSTMENT

Check and, if necessary, rectify the tappet adjustment every 3,000 miles. It is generally necessary to adjust both tappets after every 5,000 miles. The adjustment must always be checked after decarbonizing the engine and grinding-in the valves. The need for tappet adjustment more frequently than about once every 5,000 miles is generally due to some fault which should be investigated. It is of vital importance to keep the adjustment correct to prevent damage to the valves and to maintain high engine performance.

The Clearance. On 350 c.c., 500 c.c. models the correct tappet clearance is *nil* with both valves closed and the engine *cold* (warm, not hot, on all 1953–7 models). A clearance of *nil* implies that the push-rods are free to rotate without any appreciable up-and-down play.

Detach the cover from the off-side of the rocker-box after removing the three retaining nuts and fibre washers. This exposes the inlet and exhaust tappet adjustment. As may be seen in Figs. 50 and 51, each push-rod has an adjustable head *A* secured by a lock-nut *B* to the push-rod sleeve *C*.*

* Note that a new sleeve cannot be fitted to an existing light-alloy push-rod. the sleeve and the rod being simultaneously threaded (internally) for the adjustable head, during manufacture.

GENERAL MAINTENANCE

1. Compression Plate Omitted (1949 to 1960). Turn the engine (350 c.c. or 500 c.c.) over slowly until the piston is at T.D.C. on the compression stroke, with both valves closed. See that the exhaust-valve lifter is not preventing the exhaust valve from seating fully. Then check the tappet clearance for both tappets (*see* above). Referring to Fig. 50, if an adjustment of either or both tappets is required, hold the push-rod sleeve *C* with one spanner, and with another loosen the lock-nut *B*. Then screw the adjustable head *A* up or down until a tappet clearance of *nil* is obtained. Afterwards tighten the lock-nut (*B*) (without moving head (*A*)) and again check the clearance.

2. Compression Plate Fitted. On 1945–8 500 c.c. engines having a compression plate, to adjust the tappet clearance, first rotate the engine until the exhaust valve lifts off its seat. Referring to Fig. 50, first slacken the lock-nut (*B*) on the exhaust push-rod (*C*). Next rotate the engine until the inlet valve is lifted off its seat. Loosen the locknut (*B*) on the inlet push-rod (*C*). Then screw the adjustable head (*A*) of the exhaust push-rod up or down as required to obtain a clearance of *nil*. Further rotate the engine until the exhaust valve is lifted off its seat. Now tighten the lock-nut (*B*) on the exhaust push-rod. Afterwards screw up or down as required the adjustable head (*A*) on the inlet push-rod (*C*) until tappet clearance is *nil*. Again rotate the engine until the inlet valve is raised, and tighten the lock nut on the inlet push-rod.

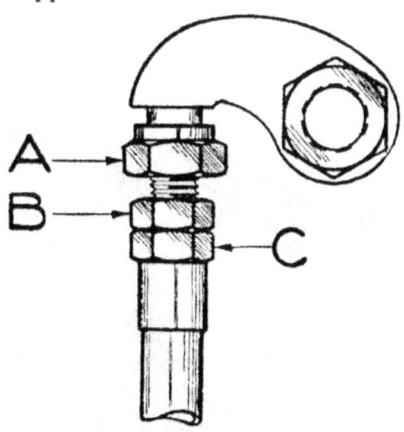

FIG. 50. TAPPET ADJUSTMENT ON 350 c.c., 500 c.c. O.H.V. ENGINES
(*see also* Fig. 51)

3. After Tappet Adjustment. Turn the engine over until both valves are closed. Check that the push-rods are free to rotate without appreciable up-and-down movement. Fit the cover to the off-side of the rocker-box and replace the three retaining nuts. Make sure that the three fibre washers are also replaced beneath the nuts. When tightening the nuts avoid using excessive pressure on the spanner. Such pressure is quite unnecessary, because a rubber fillet is incorporated at the rocker-box cover joint. Moderate pressure with the spanner will suffice to prevent oil leakage. Tighten the three nuts evenly.

DECARBONIZING AND VALVE GRINDING

The exact time at which the removal of carbon deposits becomes necessary depends to some extent on (*a*) quality of the fuel used and (*b*) the driving conditions. Under normal circumstances it is advisable to remove the cylinder head, decarbonize and, *if necessary*, grind-in the valves *when* the performance declines. If the engine develops a tendency to "knock" when

FIG. 51. PREPARING FOR ROCKER-BOX REMOVAL

The petrol tank, the oil-feed pipe to the rocker-box, and the rocker-box cover have been removed. The next operation is to remove the engine-steady bracket connecting the rocker-box to the frame top-tube, and then remove the rocker-box securing bolts.

accelerating quickly or hill-climbing, this confirms that the time for decarbonizing is due.

Do *not* remove the cylinder barrel unless you have *good* reason to inspect the piston and rings, and perhaps the bore of the cylinder. Remove the barrel, however, if any stiffness of the piston occurs, or if loss of compression (not caused by bad valve seating) develops. Decarbonizing and grinding-in the valves is quite simple if you follow the correct procedure (Sections 1–23).

1. Remove Petrol Tank. It is necessary to remove the petrol tank before detaching the rocker-box and cylinder head prior to decarbonizing, also when undertaking any major engine overhaul work. To remove the tank, turn both petrol taps to the "Off" position. Disconnect the petrol pipe from *both taps*, using *two* spanners (hold the taps when unscrewing the union nuts or cap-nuts (1955-60). Then sever the locking wires securing the four tank-fixing bolts (*see* Figs. 56-8). Now unscrew the four fixing bolts and ease the tank clear of the frame.

NOTE: The makers advise removal of the dualseat on 1954 "springer" models before attempting to remove the petrol tank. On 1953 "springer" models they recommend removing the handlebars (secured by three Allen screws) and resting the bars on the handlebar lug forward of the steering head adjuster-nut.

2. **Remove Rocker-box (1945-60).** After tank removal, the next step towards cylinder-head removal is to take off the rocker-box and push-rods. First remove the three nuts retaining the cover to the off-side of the rocker-box. Also remove the three fibre washers beneath the nuts. Then take off the rocker-box end-cover as shown in Fig. 51. Disconnect the upper union of the oil-feed pipe from the pump to the rocker-box. Now rotate the engine slowly until both inlet and exhaust valves are closed. On 1945-53 500 c.c. and all later engines, detach the engine-steady bracket (*see* Fig. 51) between the rocker-box and frame top-tube. To do this, remove the nuts and washers from the rocker-box bolt extensions and also the bolt from the frame clip.

With a spanner, remove the seven bolts (nine, 1949-60) securing the rocker-box to the cylinder head. Disconnect the exhaust valve-lifter cable. Grip the rocker-box, tilt up its right-hand side and withdraw both push-rods. These should not be interchanged, and for this reason should be marked or placed so that they can subsequently be identified. Now carefully lift the rocker-box clear of the cylinder head. On 1945-8 engines raise the front end of the rocker-box, so as to clear the exhaust-valve assembly, and swing it round anti-clockwise to clear the frame tube. The rocker-box may now be lifted clear of the inlet-valve assembly and removed from the engine. Be careful not to lose the hardened-steel caps on the ends of the valve stems (1945-8 engines). These caps are most important.

3. **Remove Cylinder Head.** Having removed the fuel tank and rocker-box as previously described, unscrew the sparking plug.* Then proceed to remove, or partially remove, the exhaust system. Before this can be done (1945-6 350 c.c. engines) remove the right-hand side of the footrest rod. Remove the nut and washer on the right-hand side of the footrest rod and partially withdraw the footrest rod from the left-hand side. Now prise off the right-hand side footrest-arm.

* Should the sparking plug be difficult to unscrew, do not apply excessive force with the box spanner. Brush some paraffin round the plug body and allow to soak prior to further use of the spanner.

To remove the exhaust system, first remove the nuts and washers which secure the exhaust pipe and silencer to their stays. Then pull the exhaust pipe and silencer away from the stays, and pull the pipe downwards from the port in the cylinder head.

Remove the Amal carburettor by unscrewing the venturi air-intake (1945–8 models) and the two nuts securing the carburettor flange to the cylinder head. The carburettor may be allowed to rest on the saddle or on the platform above the dynamo (1951–7), as shown in Fig. 54; it is not necessary to remove the throttle and air slides from the carburettor.

Next remove the four bolts which retain the cylinder head to the cylinder barrel. If these are stiff, brush paraffin round their heads and allow to penetrate before again using the spanner. Lift the cylinder head from the cylinder barrel and simultaneously remove the push-rod cover tubes which come away with the cylinder head.

4. To Remove Cylinder Barrel. Rotate the engine so that the piston is near B.D.C. Next remove the four nuts which secure the cylinder barrel to the crankcase, and then gently draw the barrel off the piston. Steady the latter with one hand as the barrel is withdrawn, and take great care not to allow the piston to fall sharply against the connecting rod. After removing the cylinder barrel, cover the mouth of the crankcase with a clean rag.

5. Piston Removal. To remove the fully-floating gudgeon-pin, it is only necessary to extract *one* circlip with the snipe-nosed pliers provided in the tool kit. Push the gudgeon-pin out from the opposite side and remove the piston. The gudgeon-pin is an easy sliding fit in the piston bosses and the small-end bush. If the piston is not of the split-skirt type, scratch an "F" on the inside to indicate which is the front.

Condition of Piston. A piston will run well for very many thousands of miles; but eventually loss of compression and/or piston slap occurs due to wear of the piston, rings, and cylinder bore, especially the last-mentioned. Examine the cylinder bore occasionally for longitudinal scores and circumferential ridges. Also inspect the piston for blackening of the skirt, scores, smearing, and other possible damage, particularly near the ring lands. The normal front to rear clearance for standard size 1953 and later pistons (new) is 0·001 in. plus or minus 0·0005 in.

Cylinder Rebores. After a very considerable mileage (when wear at the top of the bore reaches 0·008 in.) it is usually essential to have a rebore and fit an oversize piston and rings to restore the compression and performance of the engine to normal. The makers provide for rebores 0·020 in. and 0·040 oversize, and can supply 0·020 in. and 0·040 in. oversize pistons and rings to suit. Running-in is, of course, necessary after a rebore.

6. Removing Piston Rings. The piston rings should not be disturbed more frequently than once every *alternate* decarbonizing, provided that engine compression remains good. The rings can be removed by "peeling off" with a small knife, but it is preferable to remove them with the aid of three strips of thin sheet-metal (about $\frac{1}{4}$ in. wide) inserted beneath each ring as shown in Fig. 52. The rings, being made of cast iron, cannot safely be sprung out wider than the piston-crown diameter. If the rings are stuck with carbon, apply some paraffin. If this fails, use a proprietary ring-removal tool.

7. Examining Piston Rings. Inspect the two compression rings and the scraper ring very carefully. To ensure good engine compression the piston rings must have good springiness, be free, but not slack in their grooves, have a polished surface all round, and have their gaps equally spaced and of the correct size. If inspection reveals that the ring surfaces are bright all round, they are obviously making good circumferential contact with the cylinder bore and can be regarded as serviceable. If, on the other hand, the surfaces are discoloured or scorched at some points, contact is poor and it is desirable to reject the rings and fit new ones. The same applies where the rings are vertically slack in their grooves.

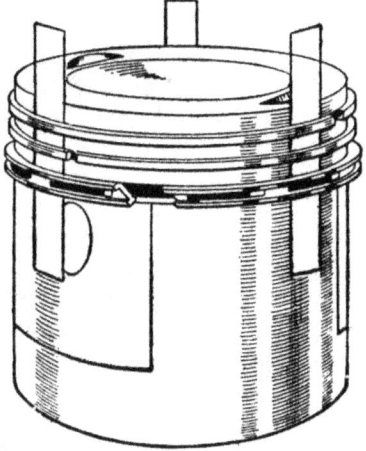

FIG. 52. THE SAFEST METHOD OF REMOVING AND FITTING PISTON RINGS

Clean the rings thoroughly on their inside faces, also the ends of the rings, and the slots in the scraper ring (*see* Fig. 52). Piston rings are made to very precise dimensions, and it is not generally practicable to fit oversize rings unless the piston is renewed also. Always fit genuine A.J.S. rings which are dimensionally correct. To reduce cylinder-bore wear, a chromium-plated top compression ring is fitted to 1953 and later engines.

8. Piston Ring Dimensions. The widths of the compression rings and the slotted scraper-ring on all engines are $\frac{1}{16}$ in. and $\frac{1}{8}$ in. respectively. The normal ring gap is 0·006 in. to 0·008 in. and rings should be renewed when the gap exceeds 0·030 in. The normal clearance of each ring in its groove is 0·003 in. (0·002 in. on 1950–60 engines).

After a considerable mileage, or if loss of compression occurs with the valves in good condition, check the gap of each piston ring. The best method of checking the gap is to push the ring squarely into the bore of the cylinder barrel with the aid of the piston and then check the gap between the ends of the ring with a feeler gauge. If the gap proves excessive, fit new A.J.S. rings (already "gapped"); if the gap is insufficient, remove some metal from *one* end of the ring to increase the gap to 0·006 in.

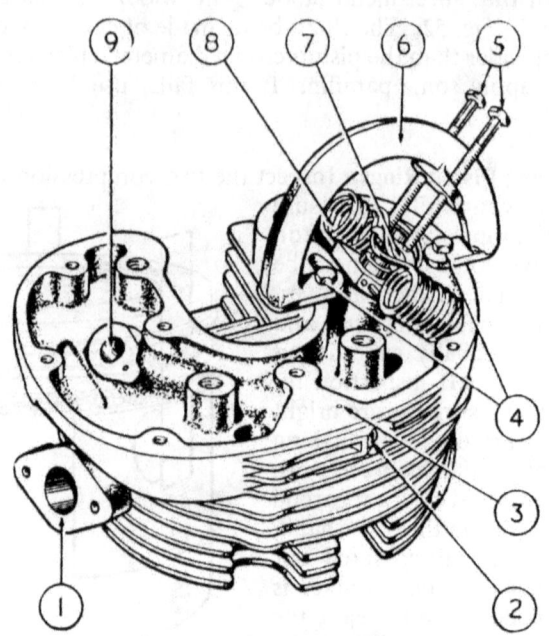

FIG. 53. VALVE-SPRING COMPRESSOR (PART NO. 014605) FOR ENGINES WITH HAIRSPRING VALVE-SPRINGS (1949–51)

KEY TO FIG. 50

1. Inlet port.
2. Hole for screw controlling oil feed to the inlet-valve stem.
3. Oil duct from rocker-box to inlet-valve guide.
4. Compressor-attachment bolts (Part No. 010795).
5. Long (operating) bolts.
6. Compressor body.
7. Valve-spring collar.
8. Hairpin valve-springs.
9. Hole for inlet-valve guide.

9. To Remove Valves (1945–8). A valve-spring compressor is not essential. Lay the removed cylinder head on the bench or table and rest each valve head in turn on a small wooden block. Then compress the duplex valve-springs by exerting pressure on the *outer* collar until the split collet can be removed from the valve stem. It may be necessary to tap each collar sharply to free the split collet, as the latter is a taper fit in the collar. On the 500 c.c. engine the inlet and exhaust valves are of identical size, unlike those on the 350 c.c. engine, but valves must not be interchanged.

To Remove Valves (1949–51). Hairpin springs are fitted to all 1949 and later 350 c.c. and 500 c.c. O.H.V. single-cylinder engines, and to remove the valves it is necessary to use the special A.J.S. valve-spring compressor illustrated in Fig. 53. This tool is not included in the tool kit, but is obtainable for a small sum from an A.J.S. dealer or the manufacturers.

After removing the cylinder head (*see* page 93) attach the flat ends of the A.J.S. valve spring compressor to the cylinder head by means of the two short attachment bolts as shown in Fig. 53. Then compress the hairpin valve-springs provided for each valve by screwing in *evenly* the two long bolts of the compressor. The countersunk depressions on the valve spring top-cap engage the reduced-diameter ends of the two long bolts.

When the hairpin valve springs are sufficiently compressed, withdraw the split collet from the valve stem which has no detachable valve-stem end cap. Then withdraw the valve from the combustion chamber. When the valve has been withdrawn, remove the valve-spring compressor from the cylinder head by slackening each of the two long bolts evenly and gradually until these two bolts are clear of the valve-spring top cap. Afterwards remove the complete hairpin valve-spring assembly. Deal with each valve and spring assembly in the manner described above. Remember that the valves are *not* interchangeable. It is advisable to put each valve assembly into separate boxes after dismantling to avoid any possibility of error when reassembling.

To Remove Valves (1952 Onwards). On all 1952 and later engines a modified and improved hairpin valve-spring assembly renders it unnecessary to employ a valve-spring compressor to remove the valves though a compressor (*see* Fig. 55) is needed for replacing them. To remove each hairpin valve-spring, insert a finger in the spring coil and pull the coil sharply upward. You can then take off the valve-spring collar and split collet, and withdraw the valve. If the tapered split collet is stuck, deliver a sharp tap on the collar to free it.

Note that the modified seat for the valve-spring has a raised impression on its under-side; this registers with a hole drilled in the valve-guide boss to ensure proper location. Note also that, as hitherto, the valves are not interchangeable and must be identified for correct replacement.

10. Removing Carbon Deposits. The best tool to use for scraping off the carbon deposits is an old (blunted) screwdriver, or a proprietary scraper (obtainable from most accessory dealers). For cleaning piston-ring grooves a suitable scraper can be made up by fitting a handle to a piece of broken piston-ring, or better still a proprietary tool can be obtained for the purpose. It is worth while decarbonizing *thoroughly*, as carbon deposits form less rapidly on smooth surfaces. Where head deposits are found to be very hard, the application of paraffin will facilitate their removal.

If the cylinder barrel has not been removed, scrape off all carbon from the piston crown, but *on no account use any abrasive*. Should this get between the piston and cylinder (as it probably would) your A.J.S. would rapidly go into a decline! Be very careful not to make any deep scratch marks on the comparatively soft surface of the light-alloy piston. Scrape off all carbon from the inside of the combustion chamber. Do not forget to chip off and completely remove all carbon from the valve ports,* the vicinity of the valves, the valve heads and the sparking-plug hole. It is permissible to use some *fine* emery-cloth to polish up the combustion chamber surface, but if this is done the cylinder head must afterwards be very

FIG. 54. SCRAPING THE CARBON OFF THE PISTON WITH A BLUNT SCREWDRIVER

The piston should first be positioned at T.D.C. When chipping off the carbon, hold the screwdriver in the manner shown. Note the carburettor laid beside the electric horn for convenience.

thoroughly cleaned and all trace of abrasive particles removed. Use a rag damped with paraffin. Do not touch the cylinder bore.

If the cylinder barrel *and* piston have been removed, it may be advisable to scrape carbon off the inside of the piston but, unless the deposits are thick, this should not be done. Remove all carbon from the piston crown, but *do not touch the skirt.* Any attempt to scrape the piston skirt may have disastrous results. The piston-ring grooves, however, need attention. Clean these up thoroughly, but be very careful not to damage the actual metal comprising the sides of the grooves. Make sure that the holes in the groove for the scraper ring (*see* Fig. 52) are unobstructed.

* If close inspection reveals any roughness of the metal surfaces inside the inlet or exhaust port, it is beneficial to smooth out such irregularities with a curved rifler.

GENERAL MAINTENANCE

The cleaning of piston rings is referred to on page 95. After decarbonizing is complete, clean all parts thoroughly with suitable clean rags and paraffin.

11. Grinding-in the Valves. Although the engine manufacturers recommend that the valves be inspected every time the engine is decarbonized, it should be understood that excessive valve grinding is not advisable as this is liable to cause the valves to become "pocketed," with a resultant loss of engine efficiency. If the valves *are* seating perfectly, leave them alone; otherwise grind-in both valves.

After removing the valves for grinding-in, clean both valve heads thoroughly and polish the valve stems with some worn *fine* emery-cloth, using an up-and-down motion with the emery-cloth held between the forefinger and thumb. Then proceed to grind-in each valve as described below, using a good grinding paste such as Richford's (tins contain two grades, coarse and fine).

To grind-in a valve, first smear the bevelled face of the valve with a *thin* layer of grinding paste. If the valve face and seat are only slightly pitted, it should be sufficient to use a *fine* grade of paste only. Serious pitting may necessitate the preliminary application of a coarse grade and, if the pitting is very severe, it may be necessary to have the valve seats refaced at a garage with a cutter having a cutting angle of 45 degrees.

Insert the valve in its seat and oscillate the valve about a quarter of a turn backwards and forwards by means of a suitable valve holder. Maintain a slight pressure between the valve and its seat and lift the valve occasionally (when the abrasive ceases to bite) and turn it to a new position. Continue to grind-in the valve until a continuous matt ring is present on both the valve seat and the valve. Generally one application of grinding paste is sufficient for the inlet valve, but the exhaust valve may require several applications to obtain good results. The part number of the A.J.S. valve holder is 017482. The valve-holder (a suction-rubber type) will suit the valve stems of all engines.

12. After Grinding-in. See that every trace of grinding paste is eradicated by cleaning the valves and the two seats with petrol and a clean rag. To ensure that the valve guides are free from damaging abrasive, it is advisable to draw a piece of clean rag through both guides.

13. To Check Valve Spring Length (1945–60). After much use the hard-pressed valve springs may weaken under the influence of heat, and thereby spoil the quick and positive action of the valves, which is so vital to high engine efficiency. The condition of the valve springs is reflected in their free length, which should be checked very occasionally with a small rule. On 1945–7 350 c.c., and 500 c.c. O.H.V. engines, the free length of inner and outer coil springs is $1\frac{13}{16}$ in. and $2\frac{1}{16}$ in. respectively.* Renew immediately any valve springs whose free length is found to be more than about $\frac{7}{32}$ in. below the free-length dimensions quoted above.

All 1949–60 single-cylinder O.H.V. engines have hairpin instead of coil-type valve-springs. Renew any hairpin valve spring whose free length is $\frac{3}{16}$ in.-$\frac{1}{4}$ in. less than its normal free length: 2 in. (between the centre of wire).

14. To Replace Valves (1945–8). Clean the insides of both valve guides; smear some engine oil on the valve stems. Then fit the inlet and exhaust valves in their respective guides. On the 350 c.c. engine the inlet valve can immediately be recognized, as it has a head of larger diameter than the exhaust valve. On the 500 c.c. engine, however, the dimensions of both valves are identical, though the material differs. In this case, before fitting the valves, note the markings "IN" and "EX" on top of the inlet and exhaust-valve stems respectively, above the grooves for the split collets.

Rest each valve head in turn on a small wooden block, and fit the duplex valve springs and collars. Compress the valve springs and then fit the split collet. A distance sleeve must be fitted next to the cylinder head under the lower collar for the exhaust-valve springs, but this does not apply to the inlet valve. Make quite sure that both split collets are properly located. The two grooves machined in the bore of each split collet must *both* register with the corresponding rings on the valve stem; otherwise damage may result. Finally replace the hardened caps on the ends of the valve stems. Under no circumstances must these caps be omitted. Failure to replace them will cause wear and possibly actual damage through fouling of the oil lug on the rocker-box by the tappet adjuster-head.

To Replace Valves (1949–51). With engines fitted with hairpin-type springs, clean both valve-guide bores with a clean rag and smear some engine oil on each valve stem. Next replace both valves in their guides. Note the remarks (*see* page 97) regarding their correct identification. Place some packing beneath each valve head with the cylinder head resting upright on the bench.

Replace each hairpin valve-spring assembly. See that the dowel pin on the valve-spring block (to which the prong ends of the hairpin valve-springs are attached) beds into the hole in the valve-guide boss.

If for some reason the valve springs are detached from their fixing block, it is essential to make sure that on assembly the spring with the narrow spaced prongs is entered into the block from the *chamfered* end.

Compress the hairpin valve-springs by fitting the A.J.S. spring compressor tool as shown in Fig. 55 and then tightening the two long bolts *evenly*. Now replace each split collet on the valve stem. Be sure that it is

---

* On 1948 engines the free length of the inner and outer valve springs is 2 in. and $2\frac{11}{64}$ in. respectively. 1949–57 engines have hairpin valve-springs.

GENERAL MAINTENANCE 101

correctly located. The split collet has two grooves machined in the bore and these must register with the *two* rings on the valve stem. Damage will probably be caused if the split collet is fitted so that only one groove engages one valve-stem ring. Finally remove the valve-spring compressor by loosening the two long bolts and lifting it off the cylinder head.

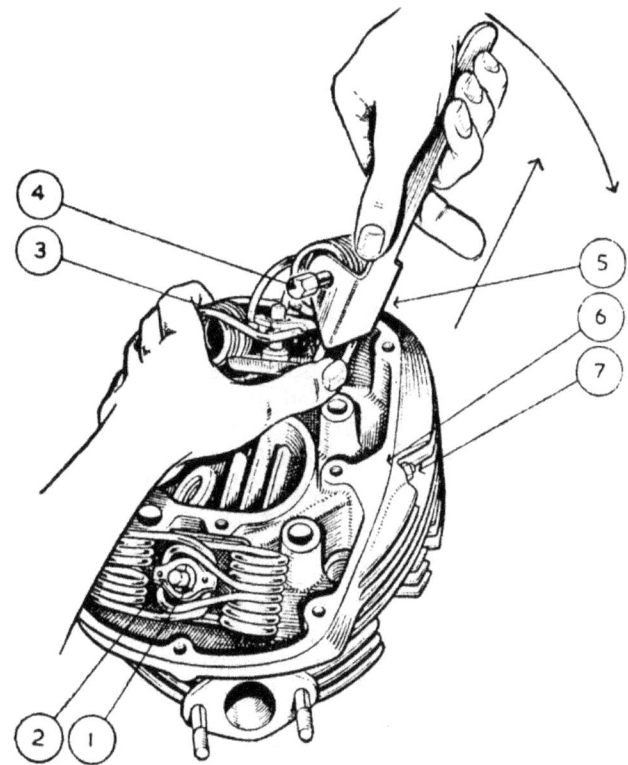

FIG. 55. VALVE-SPRING COMPRESSOR (PART NO. 018276) FOR ENGINES WITH HAIRPIN VALVE-SPRINGS (1952 ONWARDS)

KEY TO FIG. 55

1. Split collet.
2. Valve-spring collar.
3. Valve-spring collar.
4. Rocker-box bolt.
5. Valve-spring compressor.
6. Oil duct from rocker-box to inlet-valve guide.
7. Screw controlling oil feed to inlet-valve stem.

To Replace Valves (1952 Onwards). Thoroughly clean the bores of both valve guides and smear a film of engine oil on the stems of the valves. Replace the latter in their correct guides. On 350 c.c. engines wrong replacement is impossible, but on 500 c.c. engines the inlet and exhaust valves must be identified (*see* page 100). Insert suitable packing beneath each valve head and place the cylinder head in its normal position on the bench. Then fit each hairpin valve-spring as described below.

Fit the valve-spring top collar and the split collet.* Then position the hairpin valve-springs and proceed to compress each spring with the special A.J.S. valve-spring compressor shown in Fig. 55. The standard tool kit does not include this compressor, but it can be obtained from the makers or an A.J.S. dealer. To use the compressor, apply the upper end of the valve-spring to the groove in the top cap; insert a short rod (e.g. a rocker-box securing bolt) through the holes in the compressor (and the valve-spring coils) and pull upward and outward until the ends of the spring prong can be rested on the seat. Then with the fingers, press down.

Remove the rod (or rocker-box bolt) as soon as the compressor lies against the cylinder head, but maintain finger pressure until you have removed the rod (or bolt) and the compressor tool. Finally push the spring down until it locates properly. Its prong ends must lie flat on the seat.

15. Fitting Piston Rings. If these have been removed, fit them in their grooves, which should first be oiled. The safest method of fitting the piston rings is to use three strips of thin sheet-metal, as illustrated in Fig. 52. Fit the (bottom) scraper ring first, and then the two compression rings. Space the ring gaps evenly, that is, at 120 degrees to each other. It is assumed that the ring gaps are within the permissible limits (*see* page 95). If new rings are fitted, these are correctly "gapped" by the makers and are ready for immediate use.

On 1951-2 500 c.c. and all subsequent engines the top compression ring is chromium plated and one edge is marked TOP. See that this ring is replaced accordingly. Note that after a considerable mileage the word TOP may become unreadable, but for a very considerable period the correct assembly position for the chromium-plated ring can be determined by the extra brightness of the edge which makes contact with the cylinder bore. The bright edge must be at the *bottom*. When eventually the ring becomes bright over its full width (indicating full contact with the bore), it is permissible to replace the top compression ring either way round.

16. Replacing Piston. It is assumed that all parts are thoroughly clean and that the piston rings have been refitted. Smear some engine oil on the gudgeon-pin and then offer up the piston to the small-end of the connecting-rod. The piston must be replaced in *exactly* the same position as before. If it is of the split-skirt type, the split itself must face to the *front* of the machine. This is essential.

Next insert the gudgeon-pin from the side from which the circlip has been removed. Centralize the gudgeon-pin, and with the small snipe-nose pliers in the tool kit replace the circlip, using a rotary movement to ensure

* Make quite sure that the two machined grooves on the bore of the split collet register with the corresponding rings on the valve stem.

GENERAL MAINTENANCE

that it beds snugly into its groove. Perfect fitting of the circlip is essential to prevent damage. If the condition of the old circlip is suspect, renew the circlip immediately.

17. To Replace Cylinder Barrel. A *new* washer must be fitted to the cylinder base,* and its cylinder barrel side should be coated with liquid jointing-compound. Make sure that none of the compound chokes any of the oil holes and that the holes register properly. Now smear some engine oil on the piston and cylinder bore, and then turn the engine so that the piston is at or near B.D.C. Verify that the piston-ring gaps are spaced at 120 degrees and remove the rag from the mouth of the crankcase.

Ease the cylinder barrel carefully over the piston, compressing each ring as it enters the bore mouth, to enable the barrel to slide over the piston without friction. Finally replace the four cylinder-barrel retaining nuts. Tighten the four nuts, first finger-tight, and then firmly in a diagonal order, turning each nut about one-quarter of a turn at a time.

18. Fit the Cylinder Head. Wipe the bottom face of the cylinder head and the top edge of the cylinder barrel absolutely clean. Then fit the push-rod cover tubes to the cylinder head. See that the rubber gaskets are in good condition, and fitted between the top ends of the cover tubes and cylinder head. If the push-rod cover tubes were pulled away from the cylinder head during stripping down, it would probably be found that the rubber gaskets have remained located in the cylinder head. Also check that the metal washers are interposed between the top edges of the rubber gaskets and the recesses in the cylinder head (*see* Section 19).

Fit the cylinder head gasket on the top edge of the cylinder barrel. If the gasket is not in perfect condition, renew it. Whether you fit a new gasket or use the old one, it is advisable to anneal it just before placing it on the cylinder barrel. To anneal the gasket, heat it to a "blood red" colour and plunge into cold clean water. Place the two rubber glands round the inlet and exhaust tappet guides. Then replace the cylinder head on the barrel, complete with push-rod cover tubes, and fit the four cylinder head retaining bolts. Each bolt must be fitted with a plain steel-washer. Tighten each bolt a few turns and then gradually tighten all four, using a diagonal sequence to ensure an even pressure being exerted on the cylinder head.

19. Fit Correct Push-rod Cover Tube Washers. It is essential that the correct metal washers are fitted to each push-rod cover tube. There are *two thicknesses* of metal washers for fitting above the rubbers in the cylinder head, and also a conical washer for fitting on top of each cover tube beneath the rubber; the correct combination must be used according to the year and the particular model of machine. To avoid damage, this

* On a 1945-8 500 c.c. engine with a compression plate, a paper washer should be fitted on each side of it.

is important. Fit the correct type of metal washer above each top rubber gasket. The latter is a push fit in the cylinder-head recess.

20. Fit the Rocker-box (1945–8). Wipe the lower face of the box and the upper face of the cylinder head absolutely clean. Verify that the hardened-steel caps are fitted to the ends of the inlet and exhaust-valve stems. Then rotate the engine so that the piston is at or near T.D.C. on the compression stroke, with both tappets right down.

Place the special-composition washer on the cylinder-head face for the rocker-box, but before doing this inspect it carefully. Renew this washer if there is the slightest sign of damage. When fitting the composition washer make sure that its small lip is concentric with the small hole in the cylinder head through which oil is fed to the stem of the inlet valve.

Now place the rear end of the rocker-box over the inlet-valve assembly and swing it clockwise over the exhaust-valve assembly until it is in the normal position. Next raise the offside of the rocker-box slightly and insert the two push-rods down the push-rod covers, being careful not to interchange the inlet and exhaust rods. Make certain that the push-rod ends engage the tops of the flat-base tappets and the overhead rocker-arm ends.

Push the rocker-box right home and fit the seven rocker-box retaining bolts and plain steel washers. See that the bolt having a short head is fitted in the centre, right-hand position. On the 500 c.c. engine (Model 18) be careful to replace the bolt with the threaded extension (for the engine steady-stay) in its correct position. Tighten all seven bolts lightly and then, using a diagonal sequence starting near the centre, firmly tighten them all, turning each nut a little at a time.

Connect the engine steady-stay (500 c.c. only) to the rocker-box bolt with threaded extension, and fit the washer and nut. Bolt the other end of the steady to the clip on the frame down-tube. Rotate the engine a few turns to enable all parts to bed home. Then with the appropriate spanner, check that all rocker-box retaining bolts are firmly tightened. Having done this, reconnect the exhaust-valve lifter cable, and check the tappet clearances and adjust, if necessary (*see* page 90).

Fit the Rocker-box (1949 Onwards). Clean the lower face of the rocker-box and the upper face of the cylinder head. Next slowly turn the engine until the piston is at T.D.C. with both tappets right down. Inspect the cylinder-head composition washer (renew if not perfect), and lay the washer on the cylinder head.

Position the rocker-box and then raise slightly the off-side of the box to permit the two long push-rods to be inserted in their original positions. Now fit the *nine* rocker-box securing bolts. Note that the bolt with the short head goes in the centre right-hand position, while on 1949–53 500 c.c. and all later engines the bolts having the threaded extensions go one on each side of the central short-headed bolt. Tighten in a diagonal order and evenly all nine rocker-box securing bolts.

On 1949–53 500 c.c. and all later engines fit the engine steady-stay and then rotate the engine a few times so as to be sure that the various parts bed right down. Now reconnect the exhaust-valve lifter control and check the tappet clearances (*see* page 90).

21. Fit Oil Pipe and Rocker-box Cover. Reconnect the oil-feed pipe from the pump to the rocker-box. Use two spanners when tightening the upper union, to prevent the union (screwed into the rocker-box) from turning. Fit a new rubber fillet to the rocker-box side cover if examination of the fillet shows deterioration. Then fit the rocker-box side cover to the rocker-box, and replace the three fibre washers and securing nuts. Tighten these nuts evenly, but not too tightly. The provision of a rubber fillet renders excessive tightening quite unnecessary.

22. Final Engine Assembly. Final reassembly, after decarbonizing, is completed by replacing the Amal carburettor, the sparking plug, exhaust system, and footrests (1945–6). When fitting the Amal carburettor, it is important to obtain an absolutely air-tight joint at the attachment flange. Renew the washer if not perfect, also the copper washer for the sparking plug. Smear some graphite paste on the plug threads. Check the tappet clearances and adjust it if necessary.

23. Replace Petrol Tank (1945–8). The petrol tank is secured by its four fixing-bolts and a number of rubber pads and metal washers. Details of a fixing-bolt assembly are shown in Fig. 56, and the correct assembly order should be carefully noted.

To replace the tank, first lay a metal washer on each of the four tank support-brackets. Next place a *thick* rubber pad on top of each metal washer and position the fuel tank. It will be noted that one of the four fixing-bolts has a hexagon head. Fit a metal washer to this bolt and screw the latter into the rear tank-location on the left-hand side. Fit *thin* rubber pads over the other three fixing-bolts and fit the bolts.

Having fitted all four fixing-bolts, screw the bolts home evenly until the rubber pads are slightly compressed. Do not screw the bolts right home, otherwise the tank will not be effectively insulated. Finally wire-lock the fixing bolts in pairs with 22 gauge wire, and replace the fuel pipe. When tightening the union nuts at the upper end of this pipe, hold the body of each tap with the adjustable spanner provided in the tool kit.

Replace Petrol Tank (1949). On 1949 models the arrangement of the fixing-bolt washers (*see* Fig. 57) is somewhat different from the arrangement employed on 1945–8 machines which is illustrated in Fig. 56. Referring to Fig. 57, to replace the petrol tank, use the following procedure—

(1) Lay one of the twelve metal washers (*B*) on the end of each fuel-tank support bracket.

(2) Lay one of the four thick rubber pads (*A*) on top of each metal washer.

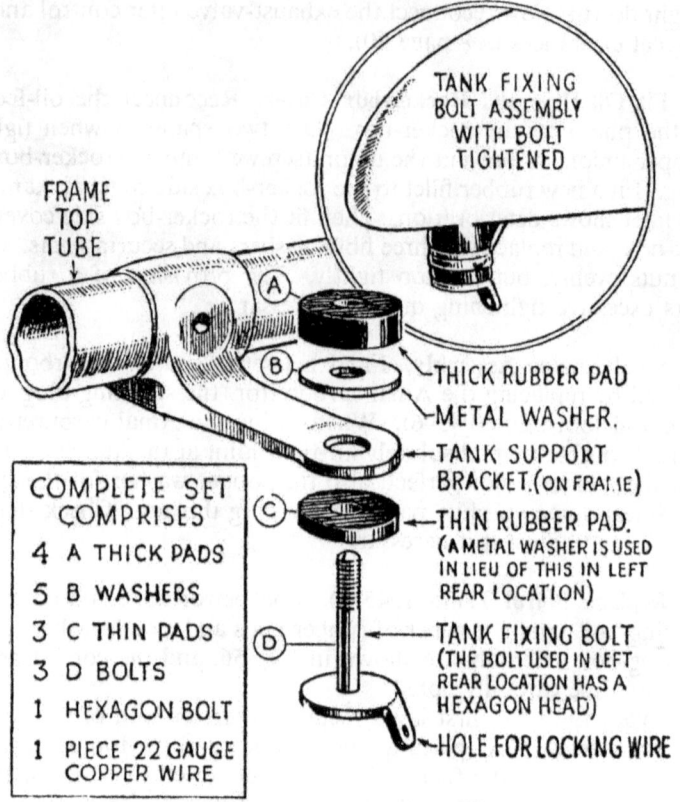

FIG. 56. PETROL-TANK MOUNTING (1945–8)

The fixing bolt at the rear of the tank on the near-side has a hexagon head, and a metal washer is used instead of a thin rubber pad.

(3) Place a metal washer (*B*) on top of each thick rubber pad.

(4) Carefully position the fuel tank.

(5) Slip one of the four thin rubber pads (*C*) over each of the four tank-fixing bolts (*D*). Then slip a metal washer (*B*) over each bolt.

(6) Insert all four tank-fixing bolts, complete with thin rubber pads and metal washers.

(7) Tighten *evenly* all four tank-fixing bolts until the rubber pads are just *slightly* compressed. Do *not* fully tighten the bolts.

(8) Wire-lock the four tank-fixing bolts. It is convenient to interlace them in pairs, using 22 gauge copper-wire.

(9) Reconnect the petrol pipes, and use *two* spanners when tightening the union nuts.

Replace Petrol Tank (1950 to 1959). The arrangement of the tank-fixing bolts and washers on 1950–9 models is shown in Fig. 58. As may be

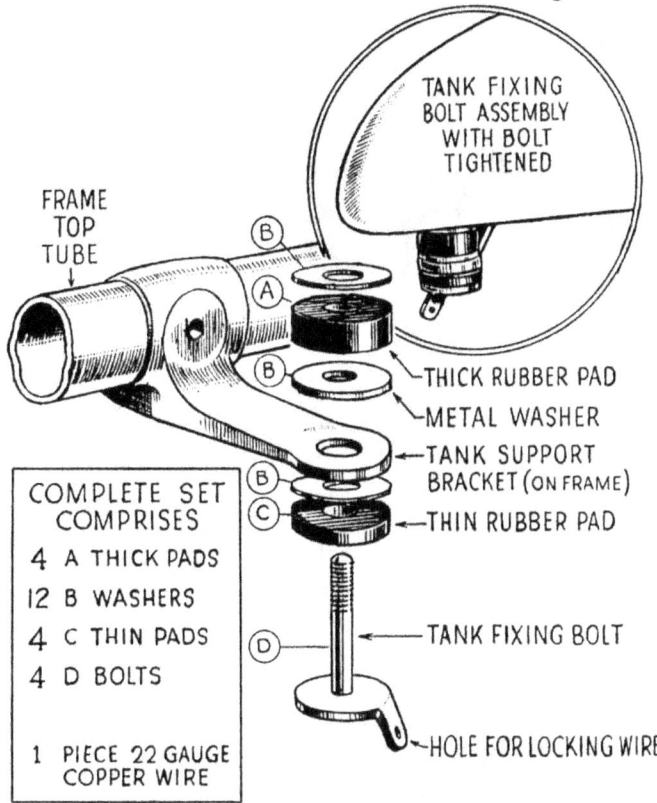

Fig. 57. Petrol-tank Mounting (1949)

Note that you must fit a metal washer above and below each tank support-bracket, and also between each thick rubber-pad and the base of the tank.

seen, an identical arrangment is provided for each of the four mounting brackets. Metal sleeves (*shown* at (*E*)) are included to enable the fixing bolts to be *fully* tightened without over-compressing the rubber pads. To replace the petrol tank, proceed as follows—

(1) Insert one of the four sleeves (*E*) in each of the four thick rubber pads (*B*), so that the top of the sleeve is flush with the top of the pad.

(2) Lay the four thick rubber pads (*B*) on the ends of the four petrol-tank support-brackets, complete with sleeves (*E*) protruding through the bracket holes.

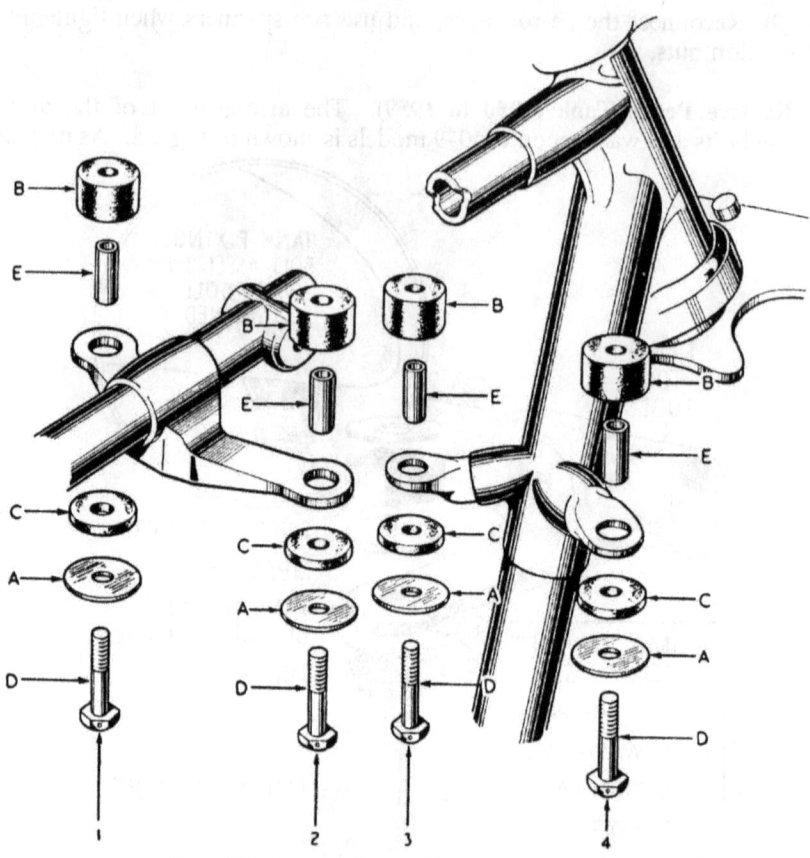

FIG. 58. PETROL-TANK MOUNTING (1950–9)

With the arrangement shown, which includes four sleeves, the tank-fixing bolts can and must be fully tightened on assembly. On the 1960 models two bolts secure the front of the tank, and one bolt the rear. The front rubbers and spacers are thick and the rear are thin. The steel washers are also different.

KEY TO FIG. 58

A. Metal washer.
B. Thick rubber-pad.
C. Thin rubber pad.
D. Petrol tank fixing-bolt.
E. Metal sleeve for fixing bolt *D*.

(3) Correctly position the petrol tank.

(4) Slide one of the four-metal washers (*A*) over each of the four tank-fixing bolts (*D*). Afterwards slip a thin rubber pad (*C*) over each tank-fixing bolt.

(5) Insert all four tank-fixing bolts, complete with rubber pads and metal washers.

(6) Tighten *firmly* the four tank-fixing bolts.

(7) Interlace the four tank-fixing bolts in pairs, using 22 gauge copper wire.

(8) Reconnect both petrol pipes, and with a spanner hold the taps when firmly tightening the union nuts or cap-nuts (1955 onwards).

VALVE TIMING

The valve timing used on A.J.S. engines is the result of most careful calculation, experiment and design. Foolish indeed is the motor-cyclist

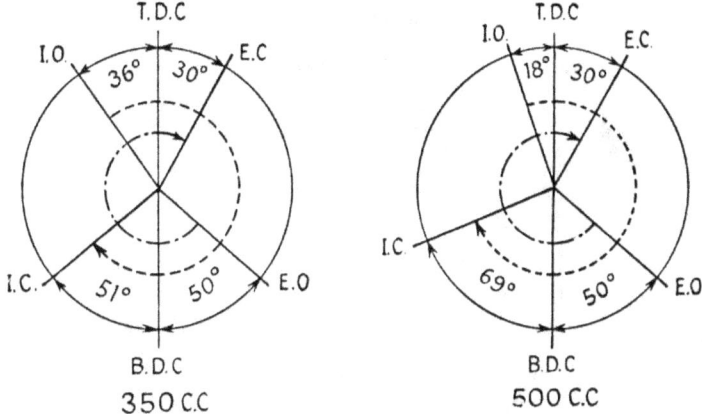

FIG. 59. VALVE TIMING DIAGRAM FOR 1954–60 TOURING-TYPE ENGINES

The above timings assume the valves to be 0·001 in. off their seats. When checking the valve timings on all engines, set both tappet clearances at 0·016 in. to ensure that the tappets are well clear of the quietening curves.

who imagines that he can improve on this setting, which is shown in degrees of crankshaft rotation in Figs. 59, 60.

After dismantling the timing gears it is necessary to re-time the valves, but this does not require actual checking of the timing by attaching a degree disc to the crankshaft and measuring in degrees of crankshaft rotation the exact periods when the inlet valve opens and the exhaust valve closes. The timing gears have a line or dot system of identification which makes correct replacement of the timing gears a simple operation.

To Dismantle the Timing Gears (1945–57). First remove the foot gear-change pedal to render accessible the timing-case. Then remove the cover from the magneto chain-case by unscrewing the six securing-screws. Also remove the rocker-box cover after removing the three fixing-nuts and fibre washers. Slacken the magneto driving-chain if it is tight.

Unscrew the nut (R.H. thread) that secures the sprocket to the magneto armature-spindle and remove this nut and the washer behind it. With a suitable tool, lever the sprocket off the spindle taper. Should the sprocket be stiff, use a suitable sprocket-drawer. Remove the magneto driving-chain and withdraw the sprocket from the camshaft in the same manner employed to withdraw the other sprocket. The securing nut for this sprocket also has a R.H. thread. Next turn the engine so that *both valves are closed*.

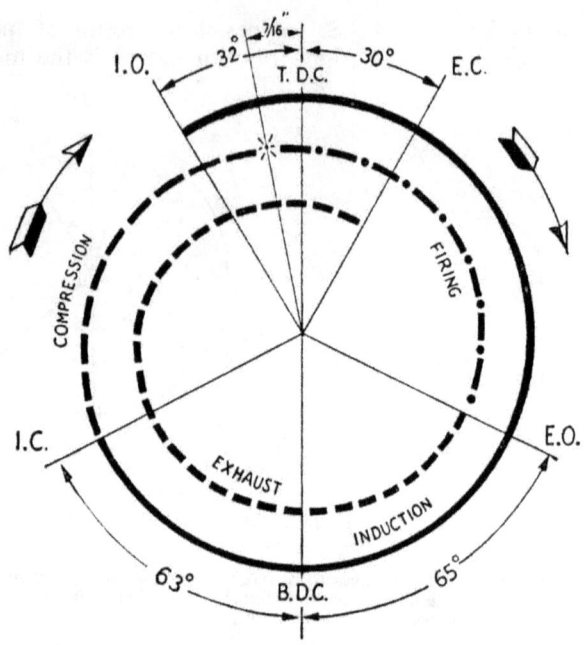

FIG. 60. VALVE TIMING DIAGRAM (1945–53 ENGINES)

This diagram is applicable to all 1945–53 350 c.c. and 500 c.c. engines. The ignition timing (full advance) is also shown ($\frac{1}{2}$ in. B.T.D.C. for 1949–53).

With a screwdriver, remove the five screws that secure the combined magneto chain-case and timing cover to the timing-case. The timing gear is then exposed. Before completely removing the timing-case cover, hold the two camwheels in position in case they should come adrift when the cover is lifted clear. The two camwheels may then be removed by pulling the camshafts from their bearings.

Generally it is unnecessary to remove the small engine pinion, but if for some reason you decide to extract the pinion, you should undo the nut (L.H. thread) and with a suitable extractor pull the pinion off the crankshaft taper to which it is keyed (one key). To assemble the timing gears, use the procedure for dismantling in the reverse order.

GENERAL MAINTENANCE   111

To Dismantle Timing Gears (1958–60). Remove the foot gear-change pedal and then remove the outer cover from the timing case after removing its two securing screws. Next remove the contact-breaker plate and the automatic ignition-control unit as described on page 85. Then remove the five screws which retain the timing-case main cover (*see* Fig. 48) and pull away the cover. This exposes the twin-camwheel timing gear shown in Fig. 62. If the washer (shown at 1 in Fig. 48) is damaged, this must be renewed. While removing the timing-case main cover, hold both camwheels in position in case they should come away during the withdrawal

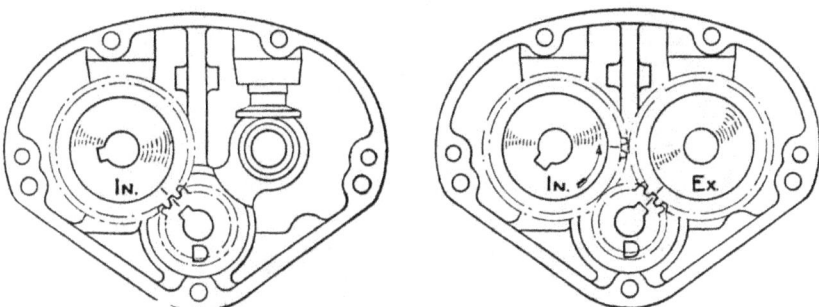

FIG. 61. HOW TO ALIGN THE TIMING GEAR MARKS (1945–9)
Fit the inlet camwheel as shown in the left-hand sketch. Then turn engine forwards, and then fit the exhaust camwheel as shown in the right-hand sketch.

of the cover. Now pull the inlet and exhaust camshafts from their bearings.

The small engine pinion is a taper fit and is keyed on to the timing-side shaft. The mark on the pinion is central with the keyway. Removal of the pinion is rarely required. To remove the pinion undo the retaining nut (left-hand thread) and with a suitable extractor pull the pinion off the tapered timing-side shaft. Use the dismantling procedure in the reverse order for assembling, and retime the ignition (*see* page 87).

Retiming the Valves (1945–9). To ensure that the valve timing is correct, it is necessary to use the following procedure when assembling the timing gears—

(1) Turn the engine slowly until the line mark on the small engine pinion (shown at (*D*) in Fig. 61) is in line with the centre of the bush for the inlet camshaft. The bush concerned is the *rear* one.

(2) Fit the inlet camshaft so that the line mark on the camwheel registers with the line mark on the small engine pinion (*D*) as shown in the left-hand illustration.

(3) Turn the engine slowly *forward* until the line mark on the small engine pinion (*D*) is in line with the centre of the bush for the exhaust camshaft (the front bush).

(4) Fit the exhaust camshaft so that the line mark on the camwheel registers with the line mark on the engine pinion as shown in the right-hand illustration.

If both camwheels are aligned in accordance with the above procedure, the valve timing *must* be correct, provided the timing-gear teeth have not

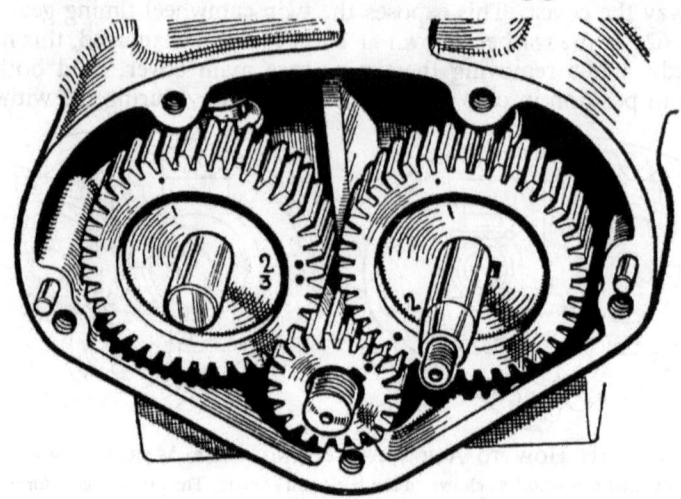

FIG. 62. THE (1950–60) TWIN CAMWHEEL TIMING GEAR WITH DOT SYSTEM OF TIMING MARKS

Note the following: the nut securing the small engine pinion (which has *one* dot) is shown removed; the inlet camshaft shown has no tapered extension which is provided on 1958–60 coil-ignition models to secure the automatic ignition-control unit. The dot system of marking the timing gears varies: 1950–3: both camwheels have 2 dot marks; 1954–5: as illustrated; 1956–60: both camwheels have 3 dot marks. Dot marks 2, 3 are always close together, and the correct inlet camwheel dot must always be aligned *first*.

become excessively worn, in which case it is time that the engine and machine are completely overhauled. It is advisable after assembling the timing gears to check that the tappet adjustment (*see* page 90) is correct, as this affects the valve timing to a small extent. Also check the magneto-chain tension (*see* page 85) and magneto timing.

On 1950–51 Engines. The 1945–9 procedure applies, but it is important to note that each camwheel has *two* timing marks (dots), marked 1 and 2. Always use the No. 1 marks and disregard the No. 2 marks for timing purposes.

On 1952–3 Engines. The procedure just described also applies, and as on the 1950–51 engines each camwheel has *two* timing dots marked 1 and 2. Disregard the dots marked 1 and always use those marked 2 for aligning with the single dot on the engine pinion.

GENERAL MAINTENANCE

On 1954–5 Engines. For these engines also the procedure previously outlined for the 1945–9 engines applies. But note that the inlet camwheel has *three* timing dots marked 1, 2, 3; the exhaust camwheel (1954–5) has two dots marked 1 and 2. On 350 c.c. touring engines align the dot marked 3 on the inlet camwheel with the single dot on the engine pinion. On 500 c.c. touring engines align the timing dot marked 2 on the inlet camwheel with the dot on the engine pinion. The dot marked 2 must also always be used for the exhaust camwheel on all 1954–5 350 c.c. and 500 c.c. engines.

On 1956–60 Engines. The 1945–9 procedure also applies, but on 1958–60 engines disregard the last remark on page 112 concerning magneto chain tension and magneto timing. After replacing the timing-case cover on coil-ignition models the ignition must be retimed (*see* page 87) when fitting the automatic ignition-control unit and the contact-breaker plate.

When fitting the inlet camwheel on 350 c.c. and 500 c.c. engines, align the dot marked 3 or 2 respectively with the dot mark on the engine pinion. When fitting the exhaust camwheel, align the dot marked 1 with the dot on the engine pinion, and disregard dots marked 2, 3.

Checking Timing by Degree Method. If for any reason you make an actual check on the valve timing by attaching a degree disc to the crankshaft, it is essential *before* starting to check the timing to adjust both tappet clearances to 0·016 in. with the piston at T.D.C. on the compression stroke.

MOTOR-CYCLE MAINTENANCE

Although engine maintenance is vital, do not neglect the tyres and the lighting system, and pay due regard to the correct lubrication and adjustment of the motor-cycle parts.

Items Necessary for Maintenance. It is desirable to have the following items available: a can of paraffin, a stiff brush, a tin of *summer grade* engine oil, a canister of light grease (*see* pages 57 and 65), a tin of hydraulic fluid and a flask graduated in fluid oz. (*see* pages 71–4), a tyre-pressure gauge, a Lucas hydrometer and battery filler, a tyre repair outfit, and a receptacle for draining the gearbox.

For cleaning purposes the following are also needed: some jars or a pail, some non-fluffy rags, two chamois leathers, a sponge and pail (if no hose is available), some soft dusters, and a tin of wax or other polish for the enamelled parts.

Tools Required. The A.J.S. tool kit is sufficient for all routine maintenance, stripping down and assembly, but it is desirable to buy a chain-rivet extractor and a box of spare chain-links. If you are in the mood to tackle repair work as well as maintenance, consider the extra tools suggested on page 76.

The Lighting System. Keep the lights bright by attending to lamp, battery, and dynamo maintenance as described in Chapter III.

Lubrication of Motor-cycle. This is fully explained in Chapter IV. Attend to the lubrication points indicated at 5 to 17 in the Lubrication Chart on page 66.

Keeping Machine Clean. If the enamelled and chromium-plated parts are neglected, the machine will soon become shabby-looking, and serious rusting may occur. On no account leave your A.J.S. soaking wet overnight. If you have not time for thorough cleaning in wet weather, grease the machine all over before using it. When cleaning the machine, use a stiff brush and paraffin for removing filth from the lower part of the gearbox.

The Enamelled Parts. Never try to remove caked mud by attempting to brush or rub it off when dry. Instead, carefully soak it off by means of a hose. When doing this, be careful not to direct the stream of water on to vital and vulnerable components such as the carburettor, dynamo, and magneto. If no hose is available, soak off the mud with a pail of water and a sponge. After removing all mud and dirt, dry the enamelled parts with a chamois leather, and afterwards polish the surfaces with soft dusters and a proprietary wax or other polish.

Cleaning Chromium. On no account use ordinary liquid metal-polish or paste to clean any of the chromium-plated parts. Such cleaners generally contain oleic acid which attacks the chromium. It is permissible, however, to clean the surfaces occasionally with some special chromium-cleaning compound. To remove tarnish (salt deposits), it is advisable to clean the surfaces regularly with a damp chamois leather and afterwards polish them with a soft duster.

To Reduce Tarnishing in Winter. It is a good plan to apply with a soft cloth to all chromium-plated surfaces one or other of the preparations on the market that help to render chromium-plate impervious to moisture—and so reduce tarnishing.

A.J.S. Motor Cycles recommend using "Tekall," a product of 20th Century Finishes, Ltd., of 175–177 Kirkgate, Wakefield. This effective preparation is obtainable in $\frac{1}{2}$ pt. and 1 pt. tins at most garages. A soft rag soaked in "Tekall" should be wiped over the chromium-plated parts. This will leave an almost invisible film which is impervious to moisture.

GENERAL MAINTENANCE

Nuts and Bolts. Occasionally (say, once a month) check over all external nuts and bolts for tightness (*see* page 77). Pay special attention to all drain plugs, the nuts securing the exhaust system, all control-lever clip bolts, the wheel-spindle nuts, the nuts at the base of the fork sliders, the brake-cam spindle nuts, the footrest-hanger nuts, the nuts or screws (1955 onwards) securing the handlebars, the mudguard-securing nuts, the battery-strap securing bolt (pre-1946), and the small screw securing the headlamp front (1949 onwards). Also keep a watchful eye on the rear chain spring-link, and the caps for the tyre-inflation valves.

TYRE PRESSURES, WHEEL ALIGNMENT

Tyre Inflation Pressures. Even the best quality rubber is not entirely impervious to air leakage, and tyre-inflation pressures slowly but surely decline in spite of the fact that the tyres and valves are in perfect condition. Therefore check the inflation pressures of both tyres *weekly*, not by "thumbing" the covers or kicking them, but by using a suitable pressure gauge such as the Dunlop pencil-type No. 6, the Schrader No. 7750, the Romac, or the Holdtite. By maintaining the inflation pressures correct, tyre deflection is reduced to the minimum, and maximum comfort, tyre life, and freedom from skidding are assured. Avoid fierce braking and excessive acceleration. Also keep oil off the treads, and maintain the wheels in true alignment.

Correct Pressures. If you ride solo and are of normal weight, you should maintain the inflation pressures of the front and rear tyres at 18 lb. per sq. in. and 22 lb. per sq. in., respectively. If you are not of normal weight,

MINIMUM TYRE INFLATION PRESSURES
(Showing load per tyre and recommended pressure
in lb. per sq. in.)

Load	Pressure	Load	Pressure
200 lb.	16 lb.	350 lb.	24 lb.
240 lb.	18 lb.	400 lb.	28 lb.
280 lb.	20 lb.	440 lb.	32 lb.

carry heavy equipment, or a pillion passenger, it is necessary to adjust the inflation pressures accordingly. Above are tabulated the correct minimum inflation pressures for specified loads per tyre.

The most satisfactory method of determining the correct inflation pressures required is to ride or take the machine to the nearest weighbridge and check individually the fully-laden weight on the front and rear tyres. Then consult the above table for the front and rear correct minimum inflation-pressures. A suitable weighbridge is to be found at most large railway stations and other transport depots. The rider and pillion rider (if carried) must, of course, be seated.

Wheel Alignment (Solo). To check the alignment on a solo A.J.S., a straight-edge or a plain board (with one edge planed perfectly straight and square) about 5 ft. long is required. Alternatively use a taut piece of string tied to an anchorage post.

Jack up the A.J.S. on its stand, with the front and rear wheels parallel to each other. Then check the wheel alignment by holding the straight-edge, board, or string in contact with both tyres (about 4 in. above the ground and parallel with it). It should contact the front and rear of each tyre if the wheels are correctly aligned. This applies, of course, only to models having identical-section front and rear tyres. Where a front tyre of smaller section is fitted, check that the gaps between the straight-edge (or string) and the tyre sides are equal, front and rear. If the wheels are out of alignment, rectify matters by means of the adjusters screwed into the rear-fork ends (*see* pages 125–8). Always check the wheel alignment (except on 1949–54 spring-frame models) after adjusting the secondary chain or altering the position of the rear wheel.

Wheel Alignment (Sidecar). Two plain boards about 5 ft. long are required. Each board must have one true edge. In addition, a third board of similar type, but about 4 ft. long, is needed.

Before checking the wheel alignment of a sidecar outfit, place the outfit on a smooth floor, preferably a concrete surface. Referring to Fig. 63, to check that all three wheels of the A.J.S. are running in track, place one of the long boards alongside the front and rear tyres of the motor-cycle and verify that the board contacts the front and rear of each tyre, as when checking alignment on a solo machine. Move the handlebars until the best contact is obtained.

Without disturbing the board placed alongside the motor-cycle tyres place the second long board so that its true edge contacts the sidecar tyre, as illustrated in Fig. 63. Then, with a steel measuring-tape, check dimensions (*A*) and (*B*), with the tape as close to the tyres as practicable. To obtain the best results, dimension (*A*) should be about $\frac{1}{2}$ in. less than dimension (*B*). If the motor-cycle and sidecar wheels are dead parallel, there is a tendency for the sidecar outfit to pull towards the left. Some "toe-in" is necessary.

Having checked the three wheels for alignment, see whether the motor-cycle itself is quite *vertical*. Referring to Fig. 63, take the 4 ft. board and rest it at a given point against the upper part of the "Teledraulic" front forks. Mark the floor where the edge of the board touches it. Then rest the board on the opposite side of the forks with its upper end in exactly the corresponding position and again mark the floor where the lower edge of the board touches. With the steel measuring-tape, check dimensions (*C*) and (*D*). If the machine is truly vertical, these two dimensions are quite equal. If you have good binocular vision you should be able to verify if the machine is vertical by visual inspection, but it is safer to make a dimensional check. Most riders prefer the motor-cycle leaning

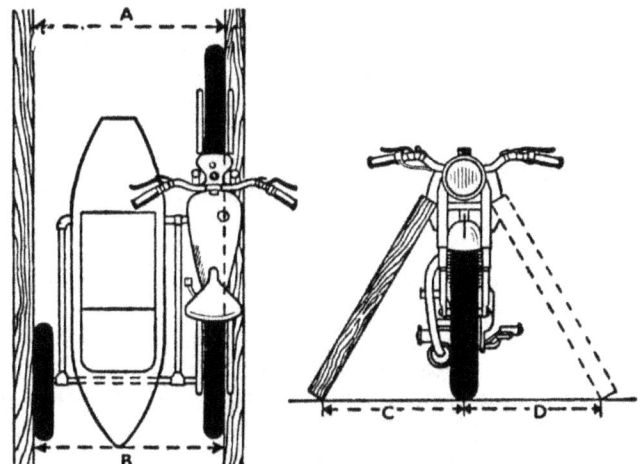

FIG. 63. CHECKING WHEEL ALIGNMENT ON A SIDECAR OUTFIT
If alignment is correct, dimension *A* is about ½ in. less than dimension *B* and dimension *C* slightly more than dimension *D*.

slightly *outwards*. Follow exactly the sidecar maker's advice. This applies also to the "toe-in" dimension.

The sidecar chassis fittings on a new A.J.S. outfit sometimes take a permanent "set," causing the motor-cycle to lean slightly towards the sidecar. This must be rectified by adjusting the attachment arms.

Tyre Treads. It is a good plan occasionally to jack-up both wheels and carefully inspect the tyre treads for small stones or flints, which should be removed.

BRAKES

Three Brake Adjustments. On A.J.S. models it is easy to keep the brakes highly efficient, because three types of adjustment are provided. It is possible to—

(1) Adjust the position of the rear-brake pedal to suit individual requirements.

(2) Make a minor hand-adjustment of both brakes.

(3) Effect a major adjustment of both brakes by means of the brake shoes.

To Adjust Brake Pedal Position (1945–55). If the existing position of the rear-brake pedal on your A.J.S. does not suit you it is possible to vary the pedal position within narrow limits (*see* Fig. 64) by means of the adjuster bolt (4) screwed into the heel of the pedal and secured by the lock-nut (5).

If it is desired to raise somewhat the rear-brake pedal (1), *unscrew* the adjuster bolt (4) after first loosening the lock-nut (5). The best adjustment for normal purposes is to set the adjuster bolt so that, with the foot clear of the pedal, the arm of the brake pedal just clears the underside of the footrest arm.

Altering the position of the brake pedal necessarily moves the rear-brake rod (3) and therefore makes it necessary to check and if necessary alter the adjustment of the rear brake as described below.

To Adjust Brake Pedal (1956–60). On the 1956–60 models the rear-brake pedal is located by a spring-loaded sprag which is positioned between the stop on the pedal and the leg of the spring which is of the hairpin type and fitted to the inner side of the pedal boss (*see* Fig. 65).

To adjust the position of the brake pedal, first loosen the nut on the off-side of the pedal spindle. Then move the pedal to the best position (normally such that the pedal just clears the footrest rubber when the brake is off). Afterwards retighten securely the nut on the off-side of the spindle, and check the adjustment of the rear brake.

Adjustment of Rear Brake. It is advisable to check the rear brake adjustment occasionally. Unless considerable wear of the brake-shoe linings has taken place, it is generally found that only a minor brake adjustment is called for. The adjustment is correct when the brake-shoe linings are almost in contact with the rear-brake drum when the pedal is in the "Off" position.

To make a minor (1945–55) adjustment, jack the A.J.S. up on its rear or centre stand. Then on 1945–55 models to eliminate "lost motion," screw the hand adjuster (2) at the rear of the brake rod (*see* Fig. 70) farther on to the rod until slight friction is felt between the brake linings and the brake drum when the rear wheel is spun with the gear-change lever in "neutral." Having obtained contact between the linings and drum, *unscrew* the self-locking adjuster nut *two complete turns*.

On 1956–60 "swinging arm" models the rear-brake adjustment is similar to that just described for the 1945–55 models, but on the later models the hand-type adjuster is on the front end of the brake rod (*see* Fig. 66). It is advisable after tightening the adjuster so that the brake linings just contact the drum, to *unscrew* the self-locking adjuster nut *five complete turns*.

Where it is not possible to adjust the rear brake by means of the hand

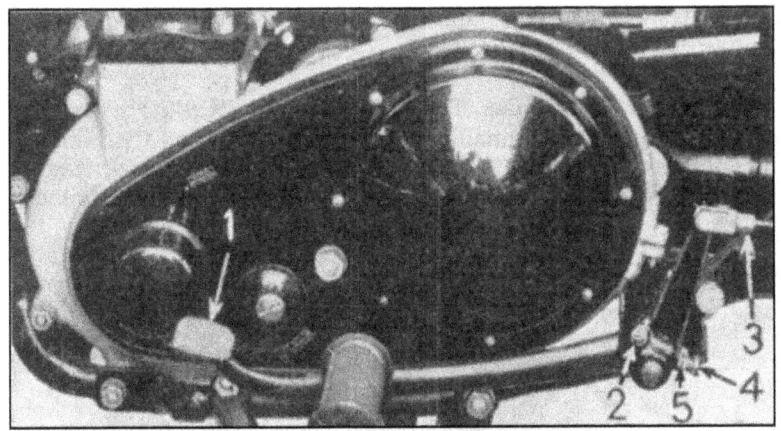

Fig. 64. Adjustment for Rear-brake Pedal (1945–55)
On 1945–54 models the adjuster bolt (4) on the heel of the pedal is located almost vertically. Note the detachable domed clutch-cover fitted to 1954–7 models.

KEY TO FIG. 64

1. Rear-brake pedal.
2. Grease nipple.
3. Rod to shoe expander-lever.
4. Pedal adjuster-bolt.
5. Lock-nut for item 4.

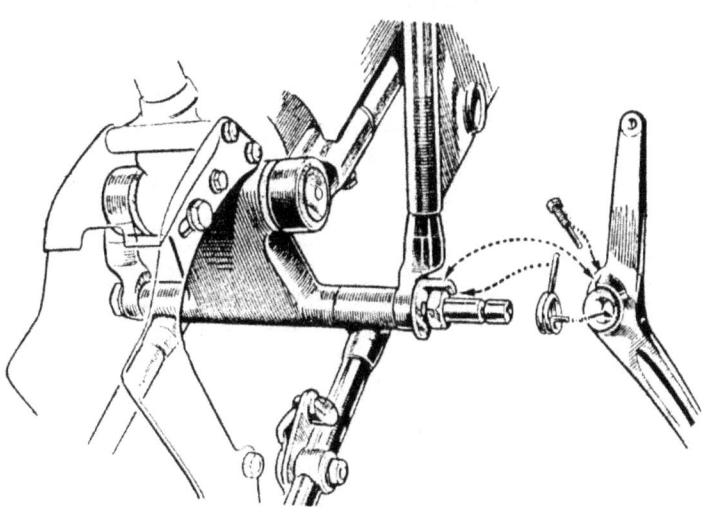

Fig. 65. Adjustment for Rear-brake Pedal (1956–60)

adjustment, owing to a poor angle between the brake expander lever and rod, recourse must be had to a major adjustment (by means of the brake shoes) as described on pages 121–2.

Adjustment of Front Brake. This adjustment, like that of the rear brake, should be checked occasionally. It is satisfactory when the brake-shoe linings are nearly in contact with the front-brake drum when the handlebar lever is not operated. Unless considerable wear of the brake linings, or

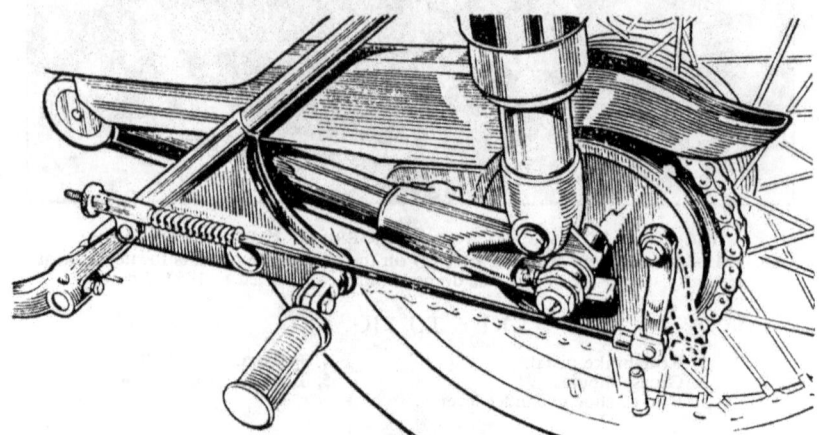

FIG. 66. REAR BRAKE ADJUSTMENT ON "SWINGING ARM" MODELS (1956 ONWARDS)

Where the brake-rod adjustment is exhausted as shown, a brake-shoe adjustment is needed.

of the cable control (or of both) develops, a minor hand-adjustment should be sufficient. This is effected in the following manner—

The adjustment for the front brake is provided on the near-side of the telescopic-fork assembly. First jack up the A.J.S. on both its stands (centre stand, 1956 onwards). Then slacken the knurled lock-nut. Now take up "lost motion" by unscrewing the knurled cable-adjuster nut until the brake-shoe linings just contact the brake drum when the front wheel is spun by hand. Finally, screw down the knurled adjuster *two complete turns* and tighten the lock-nut securely.

If hand adjustment of the front brake is no longer possible owing to the poor angle between the brake expander-lever and the cable, a major adjustment must be made by means of the brake shoes.

Brake Shoe Adjustment (1945–7 Models). To rectify loss of braking efficiency which cannot be rectified by the hand-type adjuster it is necessary to effect a major adjustment of the thrust collar fitted to the tongue of each brake shoe. The adjustment is the same for the front and rear brakes, and details of the adjustable thrust-collar are shown in Fig. 67. As may be seen, each thrust collar (7) has machined slots (5), (6), (8), of different depth.

Referring to Fig. 67, to effect a major brake-adjustment it is necessary to remove each thrust collar from the tongue of its shoe and turn the collar so that the slot next less in depth engages the brake shoe (3) on replacing the shoe. Where the brake linings are badly worn, the two shallow slots (5) are suitable. If no wear of the brake linings has occurred, use the two deep

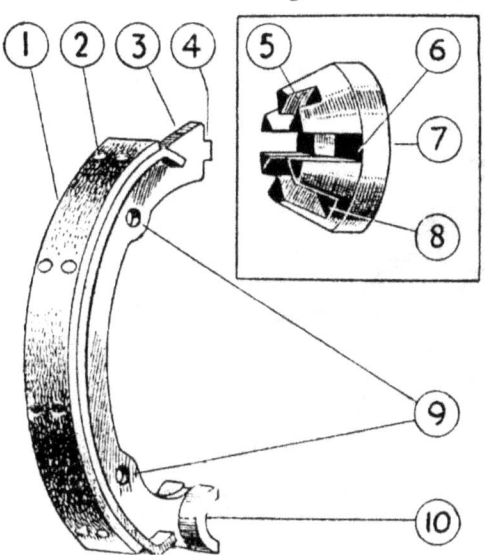

FIG. 67. SHOWING 1945–7 BRAKE SHOE WITH THRUST-COLLAR ADJUSTMENT

KEY TO FIG. 67

1. Brake-shoe lining.
2. Rivet (8 per set) for securing lining.
3. Brake shoe.
4. Brake-shoe tongue.
5. One of two shallow slots.
6. One of two deep slots.
7. Adjustable thrust-collar.
8. One of two medium-depth slots.
9. Holes for shoe springs.
10. Heel of brake shoe.

slots (6). If only moderate wear of the linings is present, it is advisable to make use of the two medium-depth slots (8). It should be noted that the tongue (4) enters the centre of the thrust collar (7).

Both brake shoes belonging to the *same* pair must be matched and it is essential to use the same depth slot when fitting each collar to the tongue of the shoe before fitting the shoes to the front or rear brake cover-plate.

Having effected a major brake-adjustment (to offset loss of leverage or because further hand-adjustment is impossible), slacken off the hand adjuster and make a minor brake-adjustment as described on page 120.

Brake Shoe Adjustment (1948–60 Models). Fig. 68 shows the improved peep-section brake shoe provided for the front and rear brakes on 1948–60 models. It will be observed that the thrust collar formerly provided has been replaced by a hardened thrust pin. This renders a major brake adjustment very simple. It is effected in the following manner.

Referring to Fig. 68, it is necessary only to remove the thrust pin (1) from the brake shoe (3) and then fit a shim washer (2) beneath the hardened thrust-pin. Eight shim washers (Part No. 000174) are contained in the tool kit of each new A.J.S. to permit adjustment if and when necessary.

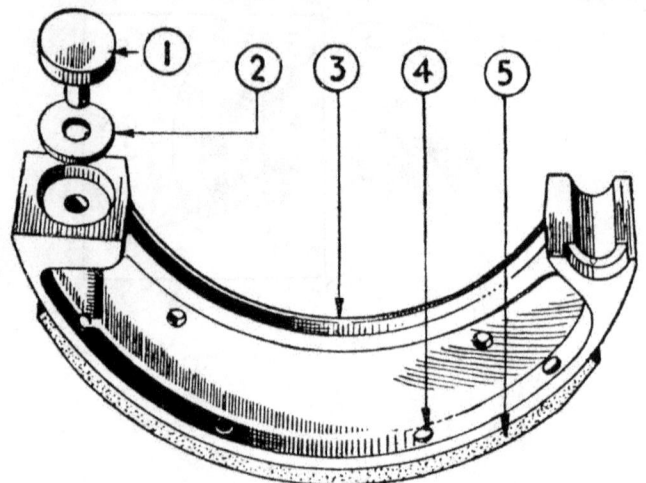

FIG. 68.   SHOWING 1948–60 BRAKE SHOE WITH THRUST-PIN ADJUSTMENT
KEY TO FIG. 68
1. Hardened thrust-pin.
2. Shim washer.
3. Brake shoe.
4. Rivet (8 per set) for securing lining.
5. Brake-shoe lining.

Having effected a major brake-adjustment, slacken off the hand adjuster and make a minor brake-adjustment as described on page 120. See that the adjustment is not too close. The wheel must be able to turn without any friction.

Brake Shoe Interchangeability.   Although it is permissible to fit the rear-brake shoes and associated parts to the front-brake cover plate, this is not desirable without good reason. The brake shoes on the *same* cover-plate are *not* interchangeable.

Positioning of Front-Brake Cover Plate.   The front-brake cover plate is secured to the front-wheel spindle with an internal and external nut. A locating washer is fitted between the cover plate and the internal nut (1945–54 models).

If the front wheel has been removed (*see* page 143), it is important, before replacing it in the "Teledraulic" front forks, to position the internal nut correctly. When the locating washer is fitted adjacent to it, the locating-washer outer face (1945–53 models) must stand proud of the outer edge of the brake drum to the extent of $\frac{1}{16}$ in. A dimensional check should be made. Place a suitable straight-edge across the outer edge of the brake drum and then measure vertically the distance between the edge and the outer face of the locating washer. If the distance is less or greater than $\frac{1}{16}$ in., adjust the internal nut accordingly.

On 1954–60 models position the internal nut so that, when the locating washer (1954 models) is fitted next to it, and the cover plate is applied, the outer face of the plate is flush with the edge of the wheel-hub shell.

Fit the external nut so that its hexagonal side abuts the front-brake cover-plate.

Centralizing Brake Shoes. Where a front- or rear-brake cover-plate has been removed and the shoe assembly dismantled or disturbed, it is advisable to centralize the two shoes in the brake drum during assembly. This ensures that equal pressure is exerted on the drum by *both* linings. Lack of centralizing is often accompanied by an irritating squeak occurring during brake application.

Centralize the brake shoes before replacing the front wheel, or, where the rear wheel is concerned, after replacing the rear wheel.

To effect centralizing, first loosen the nut securing the brake cover-plate to the spindle of the wheel. Also (on 1953 and subsequent models) loosen slightly the nut on the fulcrum stud for the front wheel. Next increase the leverage of the shoe expander operating-lever by slipping a box spanner over the lever. Exert pressure on the spanner to expand the shoes to their full extent and simultaneously tighten the nut on the spindle so as to secure the brake cover-plate to the spindle. Also tighten (1953 onwards) the nut on the fulcrum stud for the front wheel.

The Rear Brake Drum. Transmission harshness, and even wheel-spoke fracture, may result from slackness of the nuts and bolts securing the brake drum and integral rear-wheel sprocket to the hub of the wheel.

Removal of the rear-brake drum and sprocket is seldom necessary, but when occasion is had to remove and dismantle a rear wheel, the securing bolts and nuts should be checked for tightness. On 1945–50 models the rear-brake drum and integral sprocket are secured to the wheel hub by six bolts, nuts, and tab-washers. On 1951–6 models five bolts, nuts, and tab-washers are fitted, but on 1955–60 machines with spring frames and quickly-detachable rear wheels, bolts and nuts are not used, the back face of the brake drum engaging five studs projecting from the hub face. It is most important that all tab-washers (where fitted) are sound and properly locked.

The Front Brake Drum. On all 1945–7 A.J.S. machines the front-brake drum is secured to the wheel hub by means of eight countersunk screws.

On 1948–53 models ten countersunk screws are provided. During the assembly of a wheel, check that these screws are done up firmly. On 1954 and later machines the brake drum of the front wheel is a shrunk-in fit in the shell of the hub. Five screws provide additional security. On 1958–60 models the brake drum is cast in the hub shell.

THE TRANSMISSION

The Four-speed Gearbox. Apart from attending to lubrication as described on page 65 in Chapter IV, the gearbox itself needs no attention for thousands of miles. After a very big mileage it may need stripping-down and thoroughly overhauling. The gearbox is best returned to the makers or an authorized repairer for this work.

All 1945–56 A.J.S. models have a four-speed Burman gearbox and multi-plate clutch. The general arrangement of the gear train, etc., is similar on the two types of Burman gearboxes used. On 1957 A.J.S. models a new gearbox, designed and made by Associated Motor Cycles, Ltd., is fitted. This compact unit incorporates some well-proved Norton features, and the clutch centre embodies a transmission shock-absorber of the rubber-block and vane type.

Checking Tension of Primary Chain (1945–60). The tension of the primary chain (*see* Fig. 125) should be checked occasionally and, then if necessary, adjusted. Adjustment of the primary chain must always be effected *before* that of the secondary chain, as it alters the tension of the secondary chain automatically.

To check the adjustment, place the machine on the rear or the centre stand and remove the inspection cap from the oil-bath chain case (*see* page 68). Then with the fingers check the chain whip (total up-and-down movement) mid-way between the two sprockets, with the chain in its tightest position. The whip should be approximately $\frac{3}{8}$ in.

Adjusting Primary Chain (1945–55). If an adjustment is needed, slacken the nut on the right-hand side of the gearbox upper fixing-bolt, and (1945–51) the nut on the right-hand side of the gearbox lower fixing-bolt. Also loosen a few (2–3) turns the front nut on the gearbox adjuster eye-bolt. Then screw up the rear nut on the adjuster eye-bolt until the chain is felt to be quite taut, as checked with the fingers inserted through the inspection-cap orifice. Now loosen the rear nut on the adjuster eye-bolt and carefully tighten the front nut until the chain tension is found to be correct. Tighten the rear nut to lock the assembly. Afterwards tighten the nut on the gearbox top fixing-bolt and (1945–51) that on the gearbox bottom fixing-bolt. Replace the inspection cap on the oil-bath chain case, and check the tension of the secondary chain.

GENERAL MAINTENANCE

Primary Chain Adjustment (1956–60). On all 1956–60 models a snap-on cover between the rear engine-plates gives instant access to a redesigned adjustment. Referring to Fig. 69, if a primary chain adjustment is called for, first loosen the nut on bolt (5) and slacken lock-nut (3). Now screw the adjuster bolt (1) *into* the crosshead (2) to take up primary-chain slackness. Then pull on the secondary chain to move the Burman gearbox and tighten the primary chain until it is correctly tensioned (⅜ in. whip), as checked with the fingers through the inspection-cap hole on the oil-bath chain

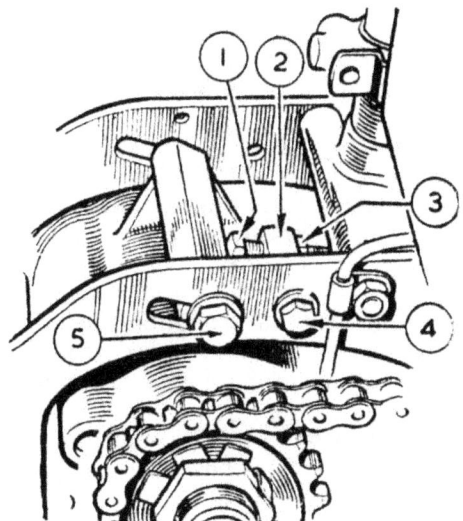

FIG. 69. PRIMARY CHAIN ADJUSTMENT ON 1956–60 MODELS
The snap-on cover has been removed to show the adjustment.

case. If the chain is over-tightened, screw the adjuster bolt (1) *out of* the crosshead.

After correctly retensioning the primary chain, retighten lock-nut (3) and also the nut on bolt (5). Finally replace the inspection cap on the oil-bath chain case, replace the snap-on cover over the engine plates, and check the tension of the secondary chain.

To Adjust Secondary Chain (Rigid-frame Models). Check and, if necessary, adjust the tension of the secondary chain occasionally, but, before making a chain adjustment, attend to the primary chain as previously described. It should be noted that secondary-chain adjustment, involving sliding the rear wheel bodily in the slotted fork-ends, generally necessitates an adjustment of the rear brake being made, and care must be taken not to upset wheel alignment. Chain adjustment is correct when the chain, in its most taut position, has a total whip of ⅜ in. to ½ in. at the centre of the bottom chain-run.

To tighten the secondary chain, first jack up the machine on the stand. Then loosen both the nuts on the rear-wheel spindle. Loosen the nearside nut first. Also slacken 2–3 turns the nuts on the two chain adjuster-bolts which are screwed into the front of the fork-ends. Then progressively and *uniformly* screw both adjuster bolts farther into the fork-ends until the tension of the chain is correct. It is vitally important to screw both adjuster bolts into the fork-ends exactly the same amount, otherwise wheel alignment (*see* page 116) will be spoiled; this will necessitate a further adjustment being made. Having obtained the correct chain tension without upsetting wheel alignment, tighten the nuts on the rear-wheel spindle and again verify the chain tension. Finally tighten the lock-nuts on the chain adjusters and ascertain whether the rear brake is in need of adjustment (*see* page 120).

To Adjust Secondary Chain (1949–54 Spring-frame Models). Check the secondary chain tension occasionally. If an adjustment is called for, first verify that the tension of the primary chain is correct, because an adjustment of this chain necessarily alters the tension of the secondary chain. The secondary chain is correctly tensioned when the chain, in its tightest position, has a total up-and-down movement (obtained by finger pressure) of $1\frac{1}{8}$ in. in the centre of the bottom chain-run.

Note that the total whip of $1\frac{1}{8}$ in. is reduced to about $\frac{1}{2}$ in. (the normal running adjustment) when the machine is off its centre stand and you are astride the saddle.

Secondary-chain adjustment (as on rigid-frame models) entails moving the rear wheel bodily in the rear fork-ends which are open-ended and slotted. Two cams are attached to the rear-wheel spindle, and these cams (which turn together) are in contact with two projections in the slotted ends of the rear forks. The projection on the off-side fork-end is set by the makers, and its position is locked by a lock-nut. This ensures the maintenance of perfect and permanent front- and rear-wheel alignment.

To retension the secondary chain, with the machine on its centre stand, loosen the nut to the right of the speedometer gearbox, and slacken the external nut on the near-side end of the rear-wheel spindle. Now push the rear wheel forward so that both the rear-wheel spindle cams contact the projections on the rear fork-ends. Then with an adjustable spanner applied to the hexagon body of the near-side cam (and while keeping a forward pressure on the rear wheel), turn the near-side cam until a total chain whip of $1\frac{1}{8}$ in. is obtained. Hold the rear wheel in this position; firmly retighten the external nut on the near-side end of the rear-wheel spindle. Finally retighten firmly the nut to the right of the speedometer gearbox after first making sure that the gearbox is positioned so that no stress is imposed on its driving cable.

To Adjust Secondary Chain (1955–60 Spring-frame Models). Occasionally check that the tension of the secondary chain is correct. With the machine on its centre stand there should be 1⅛ in. total up-and-down movement at the centre of the lower chain-run, with the chain in its tightest position. As on 1949-54 spring-frame models, this whip is reduced to about ½ in. when the rider is seated and the wheels are resting on the ground.

Before making an adjustment of the secondary chain, always check and if necessary adjust the tension of the primary chain (*see* page 124). After

FIG. 70. REAR BRAKE ADJUSTMENT (1945-55) AND SECONDARY CHAIN ADJUSTMENT (1955-60) ON SPRING-FRAME MODELS

KEY TO FIG. 70

1. Grease nipple for brake expander bush.
2. Hand adjuster for rear brake (*see also* Fig. 66).
3. Spindle-end nut.
4. Lock-nut (brake cover-plate).
5. Chain adjuster-screw.
6. Lock-nut for screw 5.

adjusting the secondary chain always check the rear-brake adjustment (*see* page 120).

On 1955 and later models an adjuster screw and lock-nut (*see* Fig. 70) are provided on the front side of each rear fork-end. To make a secondary chain adjustment (with the machine on its centre stand), loosen the spindle-end nut (3) on the near side; slacken the adjacent lock-nut (4) for the brake cover-plate. Now loosen the lock-nut (6), on each side of the hub, and screw *out* the chain adjuster-screw (5) as required to tighten the chain correctly. Note that it is essential to unscrew both chain adjuster-screws *the same amount*, and before tightening the lock-nuts and spindle-end nut it is desirable to check the alignment of the wheels (*see* page 116).

Removing Secondary Chain (1955-60). On 1955 and later spring-frame models the guard for the secondary chain shrouds the chain very closely and the procedure outlined below is recommended if you wish to remove the chain without first removing the chain guard.

Position the motor-cycle on its centre stand and rotate the rear wheel until the connecting-link on the chain is close to the rear-wheel sprocket. Remove the link. Now pass a piece of string (about 10 ft. long) through the centre hole of the end link of the top run. Draw both ends of the string together and tie them together. Keeping the string taut at the rear end with one hand, with the other hand pull the bottom run of the chain backwards. When the end of the top run of the chain leaves the gearbox sprocket the string will be left attached, one strand lying on each side of the sprocket teeth. When the chain is finally clear, cut the string on one side at a position approximately 1 ft from where it is looped through the chain link. Pending the replacement of the secondary chain, leave the string in position.

Replacing Secondary Chain (1955–60). Push the longer cut-end of the above-mentioned string through the hole in the centre of the chain end-link and tie both the lower ends of the string together. Pull the string from the rear end, while guiding the chain up on to the gearbox sprocket teeth. Keep pulling until the chain encircles the rear-wheel sprocket. Afterwards remove the string and replace the chain connecting-link. Be careful when doing this to fit the spring link correctly (*see* Fig. 77).

The Dynamo Chain. The tension of the chain which drives the dynamo (*see* Fig. 75) should be checked *monthly* and adjusted if necessary in accordance with the instructions given on page 41 of Chapter III. It is not necessary to remove the oil-bath chain case cover as shown in Fig. 75.

Harsh Transmission (1945–56). If harshness in the transmission develops, immediately check the level of oil in the oil-bath chain case. Provided the oil level is maintained correctly, proper lubrication of the faces of the two cams of the shock absorber (*see* Fig. 75) fitted to the engine shaft is ensured. Top up the oil level, using engine oil, as required (*see* page 57). If harshness continues, remove the outer half of the oil-bath chain case and dismantle and lubricate the components of the shock-absorber.

The Engine Shaft Shock-absorber (1945–56). When assembling the engine shaft shock-absorber, fit the components in this order: (*a*) the spacing collar, which is a sliding fit on the driving-side flywheel main-shaft and lies between the bearing of this shaft and the engine sprocket; (*b*) the engine sprocket, which is integral with the dynamo driving-sprocket; (*c*) the shock-absorber cam which overrides the engine sprocket cam under the influence of the engine impulses; (*d*) the shock-absorber spring; (*e*) the cap washer, which retains the shock-absorber spring; (*f*) the sleeve lock-nut, which must be firmly tightened against the driving-side flywheel main-shaft.

GENERAL MAINTENANCE

The Clutch Shock-absorber (1957–60 Models). The 1957–60 engines do not incorporate an engine shaft shock-absorber, but instead a transmission shock-absorber embodied in the clutch centre. As may be seen in Fig. 71, the clutch shock-absorber has six rubber blocks. After a very considerable mileage it may become necessary to remove and renew these.

To remove the six rubber blocks, first remove the domed clutch-cover (1957 models) from the oil-bath chain case or the oil-bath chain case cover (1958–60 models). Also remove the clutch spring pressure-plate (*see* Fig. 71), the springs, and the spring cups. Next remove the three

 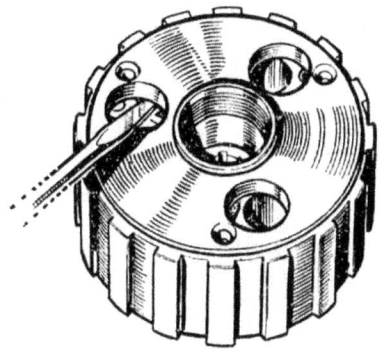

FIG. 71. SHOWING (LEFT) VIEW INSIDE THE CLUTCH SHOCK-ABSORBER COMPARTMENT AFTER REMOVING THREE SCREWS AND PRISING OFF THE STEEL COVER-PLATE AS SHOWN (RIGHT).

securing-screws and prise off the steel cover-plate from the clutch shock-absorber compartment. Then remove the rubber blocks.

To compress the thick rubbers while extracting the thinner ones, a useful tool is a "C"-shaped spanner (engaging two slots in the clutch centre), having an extension handle fitted to it. To use this tool, engage fourth gear, apply the rear brake, position the tool, and pull the handle upwards (opposite to the direction of clutch rotation). Then with a short piece of hub spoke (pointed at the end), prise out the thin rubber blocks, followed by the thicker ones. Fit new rubber blocks in the reverse order of removal. Note that, where the clutch centre is removed, it is necessary to use a tool such as a gearbox main-shaft to hold the clutch centre while extracting the rubber blocks.

Clutch Slip. This must be avoided at all costs, as it causes damage and overheating, and spoils performance. Sometimes it is due to incorrect adjustment of the clutch springs (*see* page 134), but generally it is due to insufficient free movement in the clutch operating-mechanism, which can be felt at the handlebar clutch-lever. A method of testing for clutch slip is to place the machine on its stand, start up the engine, engage top gear, and then apply the rear brake. It should be possible to pull up the engine, even on full throttle, without the occurrence of clutch slip.

1945–51 Burman Clutch (Minor Adjustment). If wear of the inserts is such that only a minor adjustment is called for, loosen the locking nut

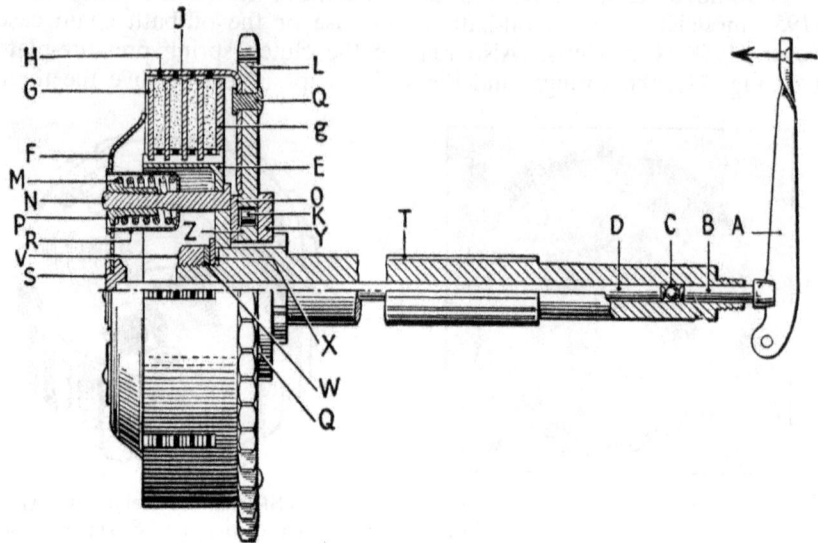

Fig. 72. Details of Burman Multi-plate Clutch and Operating Mechanism (1945–51 Models)

KEY TO FIG. 72

A. Clutch operating-lever.
B. Short steel plunger.
C. Steel ball.
D. Long thrust-rod.
E. Clutch centre.
F. Spring pressure-plate.
G,g. Steel plain-plates.
H. Friction plates (five, 500 c.c.)
J. Clutch case.
K. Roller-bearing rollers (24).
L. Clutch sprocket.
M. Clutch spring (four or five).
N. Stud for spring-adjustment nut.
O. Washer (thin) retaining roller-bearing.
P. Spring-adjustment nut.
Q. Rivet.
R. Spring cup (one of four).
S. Pressure-plate boss.
T. Gearbox mainshaft.
V. Nut retaining clutch-centre.
W. Locking plate.
X. Plain washer.
Y. Washer (thick) retaining roller-bearing.
Z. Roller-bearing ring.

on the control-cable adjuster, which is screwed into the rear of the kick-starter housing. Then unscrew or screw up a few turns the cable adjuster, according to whether it is desired to decrease or increase respectively the effective length of the control cable. Decreasing the effective length of the cable does, of course, reduce the clearance (*see* Fig. 72) between the short steel plunger (*B*) and the nose of the operating lever (*C*). After making the required adjustment, retighten the locking nut on the cable adjuster.

1945-51 Burman Clutch (Major Adjustment). If wear of the Burman clutch inserts is such that it is impossible to obtain correct adjustment of the clutch operating-mechanism by means of the minor (cable) adjustment just described, a major adjustment is called for. This entails altering the effective position of the fulcrum pin (for the clutch-operating lever) in the kick-starter case.

Referring to Fig. 73, to effect a major adjustment, first remove the two screws (H) with a suitable screwdriver, and detach the cap (G). Then proceed

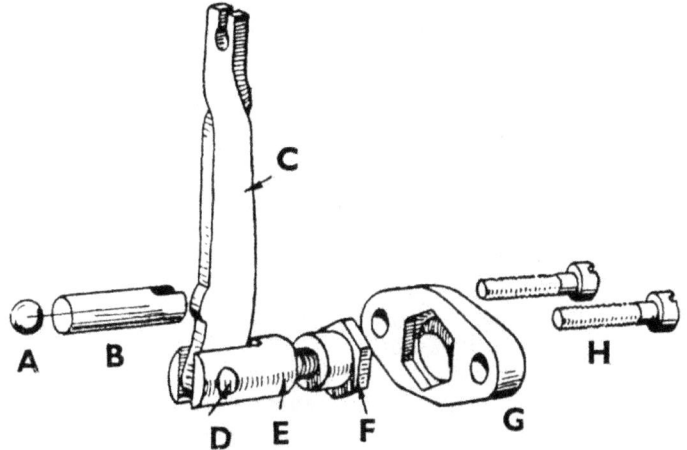

FIG. 73. CLUTCH OPERATING-LEVER ADJUSTMENT (1945-51 MODELS)
The operating-lever fork (E) slides in the kick-starter cover case, and its position is determined by the sleeve nut (F) locked by the cap (G) secured to the outside of the cover by two screws (H).

KEY TO FIG. 73

A. Steel ball.
B. Short steel plunger.
C. Operating lever.
D. Fulcrum pin.

E. Fork for operating lever.
F. Sleeve nut.
G. Cap for sleeve nut.
H. Cap securing-screws.

to adjust the sleeve nut (F) with an open-ended spanner until there is a clearance of about $\frac{1}{32}$ in. between the short steel plunger (B) and the nose of the operating lever (C). To increase or decrease the clearance, turn the sleeve nut (F) clockwise or anti-clockwise respectively. Normally a sleeve-nut adjustment of one or two turns suffices to obtain the correct clearance. Finally, lock the sleeve nut by replacing the cap (G) and the two securing screws (H).

1952-6 Burman Clutch Adjustment. The clutch adjustment on the Burman type B52 four-speed gearbox fitted to 1952-6 models differs from that provided on the 1945-51 models. With the clutch correctly adjusted there should be $\frac{1}{8}$ in.-$\frac{3}{16}$ in. free movement of the clutch operating-cable.

To check this free movement, lift the outer casing of the cable at the point where it enters the adjuster screw on the kick-starter casing cover, and see if you can move the casing freely with the fingers up and down the above amount. Also check the backlash at the handlebar lever.

Should there be excessive free movement of the clutch control-cable (resulting in clutch drag and noisy gear-changing), adjust the clutch control in the following manner. First slacken the lock-nut on the clutch cable adjuster-screw ((1), Fig. 41) and screw in the adjuster screw (by turning its hexagon) as far as possible to ensure that the internal operating-lever is in its normal position. Next remove the domed clutch-cover (1954–6) which is secured by eight screws. On 1952–3 models remove the oil-bath chain case cover. Now with the plug spanner, slacken the large central lock-nut, and with a screwdriver gently screw in the thrust cup to which the lock-nut is fitted, until contact with the thrust rod (inside the gearbox mainshaft) can be felt. Then unscrew the thrust cup *exactly one-half turn*. Afterwards firmly retighten the central lock-nut. When doing this be careful not to allow the thrust cup to turn. Replace the domed clutch-cover (1954–6) and effect the final clutch adjustment by unscrewing the external cable adjuster-screw until the correct amount of free movement of the clutch cable-casing (*see* above) is obtained. Finally secure the adjuster screw by tightening the lock-nut.

If insufficient free movement of the clutch cable (caused by wear of the friction inserts) is present, clutch-slip results and an immediate adjustment must be made. Slacken off the external cable-adjuster, remove the domed clutch-cover, loosen the large central lock-nut, and then unscrew the thrust cup (to which the nut is fitted) a turn or two. Afterwards screw in the thrust cup until, as previously mentioned, the cup makes contact with the thrust rod inside the gearbox mainshaft. Then unscrew the thrust cup *exactly one-half turn*, and retighten the lock-nut. Finally replace the domed clutch-cover and make a control-cable adjustment by means of the external adjuster screw and lock-nut until the required free movement of $\frac{1}{8}$ in.–$\frac{3}{16}$ in. is obtained.

1957–60 A.M.C. Clutch Adjustment. All 1957–60 A.J.S. models have a four-speed gearbox and multi-plate clutch made by Associated Motor Cycles, Ltd. Details of the multi-plate clutch and the clutch operating-mechanism are shown in Fig. 74. To avoid clutch-slip or drag (caused by insufficient or excessive free movement of the cable), it is essential to maintain $\frac{1}{8}$ in. – $\frac{3}{16}$ in. free movement of the clutch operating-cable.

Note that *insufficient* free movement will quickly ruin the clutch inserts and can generate sufficient heat to soften the clutch springs. Should clutch slip occur, make an *immediate* check on the free movement. *Excessive* free movement of the cable, besides causing clutch drag, also causes noisy gear-changing. Both are objectionable.

GENERAL MAINTENANCE 133

To check for the correct free movement of the clutch operating-cable, lift the outer casing where it enters the adjustable cable-stop on the cover of the kick-starter casing. Total up-and-down movement should be as stated in the previous paragraph.

To rectify *insufficient* free movement of the operating cable (caused by

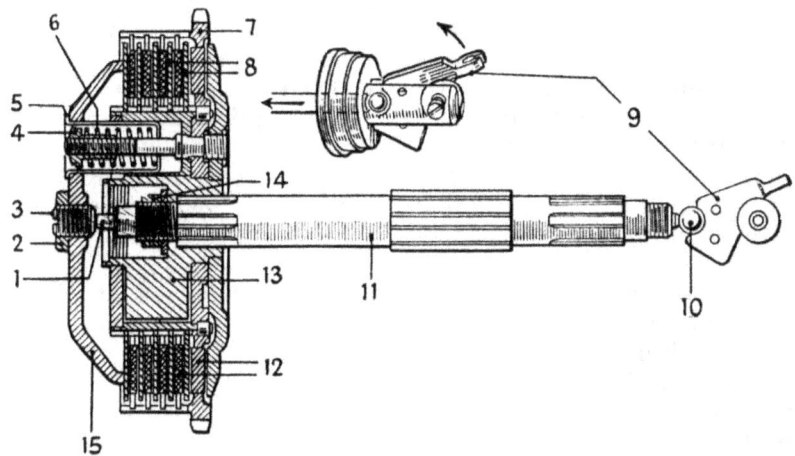

FIG. 74. DETAILS OF A.M.C. MULTI-PLATE CLUTCH AND OPERATING MECHANISM (1957–60 MODELS)

KEY TO FIG. 74

1. Long thrust-rod.
2. Lock-nut for 3.
3. Thrust cup.
4. Spring adjustment-nut.
5. Clutch-spring cup.
6. Clutch spring (three).
7. Clutch sprocket.
8. Steel plain-plates.
9. Clutch operating-lever.
10. Steel ball.
11. Gearbox mainshaft.
12. Friction-insert plates.
13. Clutch centre.
14. Nut securing 13.
15. Spring pressure-plate.

wear of the friction inserts causing the plates to close up), first loosen the lock-nut and slacken off the adjustable cable-stop on the cover of the kick-starter casing. Next remove (1957 models) the domed cover (secured by eight screws) from the oil-bath chain case (Fig. 64). On 1958 and later models remove the screwed cap from the oil-bath chain case cover. Referring to Fig. 74, with the sparking-plug spanner provided in the tool kit, loosen the lock-nut (2). Then with a screwdriver *unscrew* the thrust cup (3) a turn or two, and afterwards carefully screw it in until you feel it contacts the end of the long thrust-rod (1). Having done this, *unscrew* the thrust cup (3) *exactly one-half turn*, retighten the lock-nut (2),* and screw home firmly the domed clutch-cover (1957) or the screwed cap

* See footnote on page 134.

(1958–60). Finally adjust the cable-stop until the required free movement ($\frac{1}{8}$ in.–$\frac{3}{16}$ in.) of the operating cable is obtained, and retighten the cable stop lock-nut. Check for backlash at the clutch lever on the handlebars.

To rectify *excessive* free movement of the clutch operating-cable, loosen the lock-nut on the adjustable cable-stop and, referring to Fig. 74, screw in the stop as far as possible to ensure that the operating lever (9) is in its normal position. Next slacken the lock-nut (2). With a screwdriver gently *screw in* the thrust cup (3) until you feel that it contacts the end of the long thrust rod (1). Then *unscrew* the thrust cup *exactly one-half turn* and finally retighten the lock-nut (2).* Refit the domed clutch-cover on the oil-bath chain case, and make the final adjustment by means of the adjustable cable-stop. When these operations have been carried out, and the clutch adjustment is found to be correct, the cable-stop lock-nut should then be retightened.

To Adjust Clutch Springs (1945–56 Models). A spring adjustment may be necessary if clutch-slip persists in spite of the free movement of the clutch cable being correct (*see* pages 130–1). On 1945–53 models first remove the outer half of the oil-bath chain case (*see* page 135). On 1954–6 models remove the domed cover (secured by eight screws) from the oil-bath chain case (*see* Fig. 64). This gives access to the clutch-spring adjuster nuts shown at *P* in Fig. 72.

A suitable tool for tightening the adjuster nuts on 1945–51 models is an old and broad screwdriver, slotted on the engaging edge. To make an adjustment on 1952–6 models, use the slotted screwdriver provided on one of the spanners in the tool kit. *Screw in fully each adjuster nut and then unscrew it exactly four turns.* Then check (*see* page 129) whether clutch slip still exists. Further tightening is undesirable, especially as this causes the clutch to be rather heavy to operate. Should tightening beyond the recommended amount be necessary in order to cure clutch slip, this indicates that: (*a*) the springs have lost their proper tension; or (*b*) the clutch inserts are worn so badly that they need renewal; or (*c*) the inserts have become impregnated with oil.

Should oil on the clutch plates be the cause of slip, soak the plates in petrol and afterwards allow to dry. Roughen glazed inserts with some sand-paper. After adjusting the clutch springs, or checking the adjustment, replace the outer half of the oil-bath chain case (1945–53) or the domed cover (1954–6).

To Adjust Clutch Springs (1957–60). As on 1945–56 models, an adjustment may be required if clutch-slip continues in spite of the adjustment of the control cable being correct (*see* page 132). To obtain access to the

* When retightening the lock-nut (2, Fig. 74) be careful to see that the adjustable thrust cup does not also rotate.

clutch-spring adjuster nuts, on 1957 models, remove the domed cover (secured by eight screws) from the oil-bath chain case. On 1958–60 models remove the outer half of the oil-bath chain case. Care must be taken when doing this.

Referring to Fig. 74, remove the spring adjusting nuts (4), withdraw the three springs (6), and the spring cups (5). Then check that the spring cups do *not* contact the holes machined in the steel plate for the clutch shock-absorber assembly (*see* Fig. 71). Contact is indicated by burrs formed on the cups. Remove any burrs with a fine file and apply a little graphite grease on the cups before replacing them.

Check the free length of the clutch springs which should be $1\frac{7}{8}$ in. If the free length is found to be $\frac{3}{16}$ in.–$\frac{3}{4}$ in. below the correct length, replace the clutch springs. After replacing the spring cups and springs, *screw in the adjuster nuts until their heads are flush with the spring cups*. Finally replace the domed cover (1957) or the outer half of the oil-bath chain case (1958–60).

Removing Outer Half of Oil-bath Chain Case (1945–57). Place a suitable receptacle beneath the oil-bath to receive the oil as it runs out. Next disconnect the front connexion of the rear-brake rod. Also unscrew the battery clamping screw and remove the battery from its carrier. This applies to 1945–9 models. On 1950 and subsequent models it is not necessary to disturb the battery and rear-brake rod. Remove the near-side footrest arm.

The next step is to remove the screw which binds the metal band at the rear of the oil-bath chain case, and detach the band. Take off the rubber oil-sealing band, and remove the nut and plain washer from the bolt projecting from the centre of the chain case. Finally withdraw the outer half of the chain case. This exposes the primary chain, clutch, dynamo chain, and engine shaft shock-absorber (*see* Fig. 75).

Removing Outer Half of Oil-bath Chain Case (1958–60). A very strong polished aluminium oil-bath chain case is fitted to the coil-ignition models. As may be seen in Fig. 76, the rotor of the Lucas RM15 alternator is secured to the engine shaft and the stator is bolted to the outer half of the chain case. Attached to the stator is an important cable which passes through the inner half of the chain case. Care must be taken not to damage this cable.

Remove the snap-on cover between the rear engine plates and disconnect the three snap connectors. Also remove the near-side footrest. Unscrew the knurled adjuster nut from the rod operating the rear brake. To catch engine oil which will drain from the chain case when the outer half is removed, lay a suitable drip tray beneath the chain case. Now remove the drain plug and allow all the oil (12 ounces) in the chain case to drain off. Also unscrew the oil-bath inspection cap (*see* page 68), and remove the nut located in the centre of the outer half of the chain case. Then remove the 14 screws which secure the outer half of the chain case.

With the rear brake pedal depressed, withdraw the outer half of the chain case *squarely* so as to prevent damaging the stator windings. Also *be most careful not to impose any strain on the stator cable.* Thread each connector through the rubber grummet in the oil-bath chain case, one at a time.

FIG. 75. OIL-BATH CHAIN CASE WITH OUTER-HALF REMOVED (1945–56)
This view shows the engine shaft shock-absorber, the primary chain, the clutch, and the dynamo driving chain. The engine shaft shock-absorber is omitted on 1958–60 models (*see* Fig. 76).

Replacing Outer Half of Oil-bath Chain Case (1945–50). First make quite sure that the faces of both halves of the chain case are quite clean and undamaged. The face of the outer half must be smeared with some liquid jointing-compound. Remove the knurled adjusting nut from the rear-brake rod and depress the pedal to its full extent. Then replace the outer half of the chain case.

Replace the plain washer and nut on the centre fixing-bolt and tighten the nut with a suitable spanner. Make quite sure that both halves of the chain case *exactly register* before the nut is firmly tightened. Check that the metal and rubber bands are undamaged and quite clean. Then apply some liquid jointing-compound to the edge of the oil-bath chain case.

Press the rubber band in place so that the free ends abut at the rear of the chain case. Now replace the metal band. Begin at the front end of the chain case and draw the two free ends together by hand and replace the binding screw. Tighten this screw firmly, and then replace parts removed to facilitate dismantling.

Permit the jointing-compound to set one hour, and afterwards remove the inspection cap from the chain case and replenish with engine oil (*see* page 57) to the correct level. Finally replace the inspection cap.

Replacing Outer Half of Oil-bath Chain Case (1951–2). First check that the faces of both halves of the chain case are clean. Remove the knurled adjusting nut from the rear-brake rod. Verify that the rubber

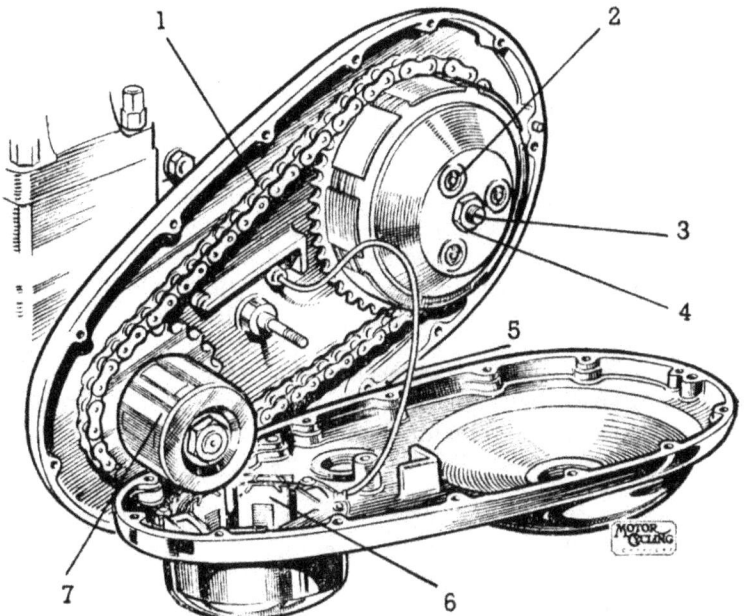

FIG. 76. OIL-BATH CHAIN CASE WITH OUTER HALF REMOVED (1958–60)
No engine shaft shock-absorber is included, the transmission shock-absorber being included in the clutch.

1. Primary chain.
2. Spring adjustment nuts.
3. Adjustable thrust cup.
4. Lock-nut for 3.
5. Stator lead.
6. Stator.
7. Rotor.

(*By courtesy of "Motor Cycling"*)

and metal bands are undamaged and clean. Note that the "T" section rubber band is not symmetrical and its wider edge must be *outwards*. Fit the rubber band by placing its narrow edge on the rear portion of the chain case, such that the join in the band is positioned just to the rear of the battery carrier. Apply the rubber band first to the extreme forward edge of the chain case.

Depress the rear-brake pedal fully and then position the outer half of the chain case. Move it as required to ensure that its outer edges snap under the exposed portion of the rubber band. Then fit the plain washer and nut to the centre fixing bolt. Tighten the nut firmly. Replace the metal band; start at the forward end of the chain case and draw together the two free ends of the band with one hand, while replacing the binding screw with the other. Firmly retighten the binding screw and fit the footrest arm. Finally remove the inspection cap from the chain case, pour in engine oil (*see* page 57) to the proper level (page 68), and replace the inspection cap.

Replacing Outer Half of Oil-bath Chain Case (1953–7). Check that the faces of both halves of the chain case are clean and that the rubber and metal bands are both clean and undamaged. The rubber band is of the endless type and of larger section than the earlier version. Position the outer half of the chain case so that its exterior edge coincides exactly with that of the back half, and then fit the endless rubber-band. Next fit the metal band. Begin at the front end of the chain case and draw together the two free ends of the band with one hand, while inserting the binding screw with the other hand. When tightening the binding screw, apply light blows (with a rubber mallet) all round the exterior of the band. This will cause the metal band to creep on the rubber band and enable the binding screw to be fully tightened down. Replace the nut and washer on the centre fixing bolt, replace the footrest arm and finally remove the inspection cap from the oil-bath chain case, pour in engine oil (page 57) to the correct level (page 68), and replace the inspection cap.

Leakage from Oil-bath (1945–57). If leakage be detected after replacing and replenishing the oil-bath chain case, this may be due to one or both faces of the case being damaged or distorted. Both faces should fit closely to a surface plate and, if there is any suspicion of distortion due to accidental impact prior to assembly, a check with a surface plate should be made. Another possible cause of oil leakage is imperfect registering of the two joint faces during assembly. Great care must be taken to ensure *exact* registering of the halves, without which an oil-tight oil-bath is unobtainable. It is also essential to see that the rubber band is correctly positioned, and that the contacting faces are scrupulously clean.

Replacing Outer Half of Oil-bath Chain Case (1958 Onwards). First check that the paper washer is undamaged. Offer up the outer half of the chain case and gently take up the slack of the stator lead (*see* Fig. 76) by pulling gently on the lead from the back of the inner half of the chain case. Locate the outer half of the case with the central nut and tighten the nut lightly.

Replace the 14 securing screws and tighten them first in a diagonal order, and then all round the case. Now tighten firmly the central fixing nut, and replenish the oil-bath chain case with suitable engine oil to the correct level (*see* page 68). Finally replace the screwed inspection cap (*see* page 60), fit the rear-brake adjuster nut, and the near-side footrest, connect up the three snap connectors, and replace the snap-on cover between the rear engine plates.

Clutch Cable Removal (1945–9). Should complete removal of the clutch cable be necessary, first remove the oil filler-cap from the cover of the kick-starter case. Next screw fully home the clutch cable adjuster on the back of the case (on top of the case, 1952 onwards). Now disconnect the clutch cable from the operating lever. This can be done through the oil filler-cap orifice.

To Replace Clutch Cable. Proceed in the reverse order of removal, and finally check and, if necessary, adjust the clutch operation as described on pages 130–8.

To Remove Primary Chain and Clutch Assembly (1945–56). The outer half of the oil-bath chain case must first be removed, as described on page 135. Referring to Fig. 72, remove by unscrewing uniformly (with end of spanner Part No. 017254) the four spring adjustment-nuts (P) and withdraw the clutch spring pressure-plate (F), complete with the four springs (M) and spring cups (R). Now remove the spring link from the primary chain and take the chain off the sprockets.

With top gear still engaged, again apply the rear brake and, after flattening the turned-up part of the locking plate W located beneath the large central nut, unscrew the nut V retaining the clutch centre E to the sleeve on the gearbox mainshaft T. Remove the locking plate W and the plain washer X situated on the mainshaft behind the retaining nut. The entire clutch assembly may now be removed.

Withdraw the clutch assembly bodily by pulling it away from the gearbox mainshaft. The use of an extractor is generally quite unnecessary, as the clutch centre is a sliding fit on the mainshaft, but avoid losing any of the twenty-four clutch-bearing rollers which become free to move end-wise when the clutch centre and sprocket assembly (including the roller bearing retaining-washers) is withdrawn from the mainshaft.

To Remove Primary Chain and Clutch Assembly (1957–60). First remove the outer half of the oil-bath chain case (*see* page 135). Referring to Fig. 74, remove by unscrewing uniformly (with the end of spanner Part No. 017254) the spring adjustment-nuts (4), and take away the spring pressure-plate (15), complete with the three clutch springs (6) and the clutch-spring cups (5). Disconnect the primary chain by removing the spring link, and remove the chain. Engage fourth gear and apply the rear brake. Then with a suitable box-spanner unscrew the nut (14) which secures the clutch centre (13) to the gearbox mainshaft (11). Now pull away the complete clutch assembly from the mainshaft. An extractor is available if required.

Replacing Clutch Centre, Clutch Sprocket, and Primary Chain (1945-56).
Referring to Fig. 72, fit the roller bearing retaining-washer (*Y*) on the gearbox mainshaft splined-sleeve. This is the thicker of the two retaining washers. Next replace the roller-bearing ring (*Z*) on the splined sleeve of the mainshaft and with thick grease position the twenty-four rollers (*K*) on the bearing ring. Replace the clutch sprocket (*L*) over the rollers.

Next fit to the gearbox mainshaft splined-sleeve the washer (*O*) retaining the roller bearing. This is the thinner of the two retaining washers. Then fit the clutch centre (*E*) to the splined sleeve of the mainshaft and push home. Afterwards replace in this order: the plain washer (*X*); the

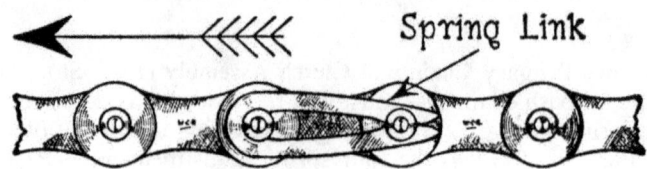

FIG. 77. BE CAREFUL TO REPLACE A CHAIN SPRING-LINK CORRECTLY
The closed end must always face the direction of chain movement.

locking plate (*W*), and the nut (*V*) retaining the clutch centre. This nut cannot be fully tightened until the primary chain is fitted.

Replace the primary chain on the two sprockets, being careful that the spring link is correctly fitted (*see* Fig. 77). Now tighten very firmly the nut (*V*) which retains the clutch centre (*E*) to the mainshaft splined-sleeve. When tightening this nut, engage fourth gear and apply the rear brake to prevent the mainshaft turning. Turn up the edge of the locking plate (*W*) against a flat on the nut (*V*) retaining the clutch centre (*E*).

Fitting Clutch Plates and Springs (1945-56). Referring to Fig. 72, slide into position in the clutch case (*J*) attached to the clutch sprocket (*L*) a steel plain-plate (*g*) (*on* 1945-51 models the thickest of the steel plain plates). Make certain that the recessed part of this steel plate faces *towards* the clutch centre (*E*) and overhangs its flange (350 c.c. models).

Next slide into position one of the clutch friction-insert plates (*H*). Then fit a steel plain-plate, followed by another friction-insert plate, and so on, alternately, until the complete set of plates has been fitted. It should be noted that Models 16M, 16MS have five steel plain-plates and four friction-insert plates, whereas on Models 18, 18S the number is six and five respectively.

Now insert the four spring cups (*R*) into the spring pressure-plate (*F*) and offer up the pressure plate to the assembly. Fit the clutch springs (*M*) and retain the springs in place by screwing the four adjustment nuts

GENERAL MAINTENANCE 141

(*P*) on to the studs (*N*). Tighten each nut a few turns as fitted, and then fully tighten in a uniform manner all four nuts. Afterwards slacken back each adjustment nut *four complete turns*. This is the standard spring-adjustment.

Finally check the adjustment of the primary chain and replace the outer half of the oil-bath chain case (*see* pages 124 and 136). Also verify that there is sufficient free movement in the clutch control (*see* page 130).

Replacing Clutch Centre, Clutch Assembly, and Primary Chain (1957–60). Referring to Fig. 76, apply a little anti-centrifuge grease to the clutch-sprocket bearing, and position the complete clutch-assembly* over the bearing rollers. Then fit the spring washer and the nut (13) securing the clutch centre (14) to the gearbox mainshaft (11). Tighten this nut lightly. Replace the primary chain, being careful to see that its spring link is correctly fitted (see Fig. 78). Engage fourth gear, apply the rear brake, and then tighten firmly the nut (13) securing the clutch centre (14), to the mainshaft. Position the spring pressure-plate (15) and fit in this order: the clutch-spring cups (5), the three clutch springs (6), and the spring adjustment-nuts (4). With the end of the appropriate spanner (Part No. 017254), screw home the adjustment-nuts until they are *just flush with the spring cups*. Finally check the primary chain adjustment (*see* page 125), and the clutch control adjustment (*see* page 132). Replace the outer half of the oil-bath chain case (*see* page 138).

To Remove Clutch Bearing (1957 Onwards). The clutch centre is secured to the clutch back-plate by the three clutch studs and lock-nuts. The bearing can be removed after separating the clutch centre from the back plate. Before assembling, apply a little anti-centrifuge oil.

THE FRAME, ETC.

The Saddle Adjustment. On pre–1949 models an adjustment is incorporated at the bottom ends of the saddle-mounting springs. It is worth experimenting with the nut adjustment until the most comfortable saddle position is obtained.

On the later rigid, spring-frame A.J.S. singles an adjustment for the saddle is provided at the rear and front. You are advised to experiment until you obtain the best adjustment to suit your own particular physique.

To make an adjustment at the rear of the saddle, alter the position of the lower spring fixing-nuts on the screwed studs to which the springs are attached. To make an adjustment at the front, remove the fuel tank and

---

* Note that if the clutch assembly has been removed from the clutch centre, fit first the clutch sprocket, and then alternately steel plain-plates and friction insert plates.

experiment with the three evenly-spaced positions for the hinge bolt. Where a dualseat is fitted there is no adjustment.

Handlebar Adjustment. The handlebars on all 1945–60 A.J.S. models are adjustable for angle to suit individual requirements. On 1945–7 models loosen the two nuts which secure the handlebars to the "Teledraulic" front forks and then adjust handlebars as required. On 1948–53 models loosen the four nuts on the studs of the box-type clamp provided at the rear of the aluminium-alloy head lug, and then adjust the bars for angle. After making the adjustment, be sure to retighten firmly the two or four securing nuts. Three securing screws are used on 1954–60 models.

The Steering Head Bearings (1945–60). On a new machine some initial bedding occurs during the first 100 miles' running, and the adjustment of the steering head should be checked when this mileage has been completed. Subsequently it is only necessary to check the steering-head adjustment about every 3,000 miles.

The ball-bearing races of the steering head have spherical seats and are of the self-aligning type. Thus they are not designed to fit tightly in the steering-head lug.

Checking Steering Head Adjustment. Jack up the front of the machine by placing a box beneath each footrest to take all the weight off the front wheel. Then exert hand pressure upwards from the extreme ends of the handlebars. There should be no appreciable shake present and the steering head must be quite free to turn. If some shake is detected, adjust the steering head forthwith as described below.

To Adjust the Steering Head. The following is the correct procedure for adjusting the steering head. It is assumed that the front wheel is quite clear of the ground. Loosen the two pinch-screws located in the fork crown. On 1948–52 models slacken the nuts on the fork-crown studs (slacken pinch-bolts, 1945–7). Next slacken the domed lock-nut at the top of the steering column. Having slackened the lock-nut, screw down very gradually the lower adjusting nut for the steering head. This adjusting nut is located immediately below the lock-nut. While tightening the lower adjusting nut, test for steering-head slackness by placing the fingers over the gap between the frame top-lug and the handlebar lug, while simultaneously exerting upward pressure on the front edge of the front mudguard.

Tighten the adjusting nut until the steering head is free to turn without perceptible up-and-down play. Afterwards tighten the domed lock-nut and the two pinch-screws in the fork crown (tighten stud nuts on 1948–52 models). Finally withdraw the boxes or other packing from beneath the footrests.

GENERAL MAINTENANCE

The "Teledraulic" Front Forks (1945–60). Apart from checking the level of the hydraulic fluid occasionally (pages 71–4) and topping up if necessary, no attention is called for. No adjustment is necessary and all working parts are automatically lubricated by means of the hydraulic damping fluid. Unless damage has been accidentally sustained, the "Teledraulic" front forks should normally not require to be dismantled. However, after a very big mileage (say 30,000 miles) the oil seals and washers may require attention.

Having regard to the negligible attention normally required in respect of the "Teledraulic" front forks, the author has not included in this handbook detailed instructions for their stripping down and subsequent assembly. Those who on rare occasions require such information should refer to the appropriate instructions given in the instruction book issued with each new A.J.S. machine, or else contact the manufacturers.

"Swinging-Arm" Rear Suspension. As regards lubrication (*see* page 74), no attention should normally be required, except perhaps very occasionally on 1945–56 models with A.J.S. "Teledraulic" rear-suspension units, and then only if the telescopic legs become excessively lively.

On 1957–60 models (with Girling rear-suspension units) in the event of the legs becoming noisy in action, grease the outside of each spring as described on page 74. The springs on the Girling units are adjustable for loading. If you are above average weight, carry a pillion passenger, or regularly negotiate rough terrain, raise the base of each spring as required by turning with a "C" spanner *clockwise* the cam ring provided at the base of each telescopic lower member. Three positions are obtainable, and the highest gives the maximum stiffness of springing. The application of a little thin oil to the cam ring facilitates an adjustment. Should you fit a sidecar to your machine, it is advisable to change the suspension-unit springs, as stronger springs are generally desirable.

WHEEL REMOVAL

Removing Front Wheel (1945 Onwards). Jack the machine up on both the stands.* Disconnect the yoke end of the front-brake cable from the brake-expander lever by removing the split-pin and retaining pin. Slacken (1945–7), but do not remove, the nut which secures the front brake coverplate to the left-hand fork slider. The split-pin securing the nut need not be disturbed. On 1948–9 models, slacken both anchorage bolts instead.

---

* Never attempt to use a front stand without first supporting the machine on the rear stand (rigid-frame models) or the centre stand (spring-frame models). On 1945–50 spring-frame models (16MS, 18S) the makers advise the insertion of a wood batten ($\frac{7}{8}$ in. thick) beneath the centre stand to avoid lack of balance when applying pressure to the front wheel during removal.

On 1950–60 models remove the bolt securing the brake anchor-stay to the brake cover-plate. Next loosen the nut on the left-hand side of the front-wheel spindle.

Remove the four nuts which clamp the fork-slider caps to the "Teledraulic" fork sliders. Detach both caps and place them aside separately, so that they may later be replaced exactly as before removal. These caps must *not* be interchanged. Then disengage the front brake cover-plate from the anchorage stud fitted to the left-hand fork slider on 1945–7 models. Apply pressure to the front wheel so as to reduce the effective height of the wheel spindle, and withdraw the wheel towards the front.

To Replace Front Wheel (1945 Onwards). Hold the left-hand fork-slider cap under the location on the front-wheel spindle, and offer up the front wheel assembly and cap so as to engage the cap with its two retaining studs. Simultaneously engage the slot in the front brake cover-plate with the anchorage stud in the left-hand fork slider (1945–7). On 1948–9 models engage with two anchorage bolts. On 1950–60 models bolt lightly the brake anchor-stay to the cover plate. When replacing the front wheel remember to flatten the tyre so as to get the wheel spindle between the forward studs securing the slider caps. Fit the two nuts securing the left-hand fork-slider cap (and wheel spindle) and tighten the nuts lightly. Then fit the right-hand fork-slider cap and tighten lightly the cap securing-nuts. Make sure that the caps have not been interchanged and are fitted exactly as before. On 1950–60 models bolt firmly the brake anchor-stay and replace the yoke-end pin.

Tighten lightly the nut on the left-hand side of the front-wheel spindle. Then firmly and evenly tighten the two nuts which secure the near-side fork-slider cap (and wheel spindle). Verify that the gaps, fore and aft, between the cap and the end of the fork slider are *exactly* equal. Ensuring that these gaps are equal is most important. Now firmly tighten the nut on the left-hand side of the front-wheel spindle, also the nuts securing the offside slider cap. Finally replace and tighten the nut on the brake anchorage stud (1945–7), and split-pin the nut. On 1948–9 models tighten firmly the two anchorage bolts (the bolt securing the anchor stay on 1960–60 models). Replace the yoke-end pin.

After Fitting Front Wheel (1945 Onwards). If any stiffness in the action of the telescopic front-forks is noticed after replacing the front wheel, slacken the nuts securing the off-side slider cap, operate the forks sharply up and down, and retighten the slider cap securing-nuts. This should cure the stiffness.

Removing Rear Wheel (Rigid-frame, 1945–55). Put the machine on the rear stand. Disconnect the lead for the rear lamp at the connexion

GENERAL MAINTENANCE

close to the rear-wheel spindle. Next unscrew the gland nut on the speedometer driving-cable. Also detach the spring link on the secondary chain, separate the ends and allow the chain to hang clear of the rear-wheel sprocket, but engaging with the small sprocket on the gearbox mainshaft. Remove the knurled adjusting nut from the rear-brake rod.

Next detach the rear portion of the rear mudguard. To do this, first remove the two nuts (bolts, 1953 onwards) which secure the rear portion to the front portion. Also loosen the nut and washer from the bolt securing the mudguard side-bridge and tool-box stay to the tubular stay. Next slacken about four turns the two nuts which secure the rear mudguard side-stays to their studs. Then remove the rear portion of the rear mudguard, complete with stays. To disengage the top fixing-bolt, it is advisable to spring the tool-box outwards (on 1945-8 models) as required.

Now slacken the nuts on both sides of the rear-wheel solid spindle and carefully remove the rear-wheel assembly from the fork-ends. To enable the assembly to clear the brake cover-plate anchor bolt, tilt the wheel slightly and then withdraw to the rear.

To Replace Rear Wheel (Rigid-frame Models). Replace the rear wheel assembly, using the reverse order employed for removal. Note that it is important, before finally tightening the nuts on the ends of the wheel spindle, to position the speedometer gearbox correctly. Positioning must be such as to permit the gearbox driving-cable being properly fitted.

The replacement of the rear wheel is facilitated thus: position the wheel in the fork-ends (with the brake cover-plate hanging free); then, while holding the wheel on its nearside as far forward in the fork-end as is possible, swing the offside backwards; lift up the free cover-plate so that its slot engages the square-headed anchor bolt, and then swing the offside end of the spindle forward until engagement is completed.

After replacing the rear wheel, make sure that the slotted end of the brake cover-plate is correctly located on its anchoring bolt (*see* Fig. 78). Finally check the adjustment of the secondary chain (*see* page 125), the alignment of the wheels (*see* page 116), and the adjustment of the rear brake (*see* page 110).

Removing Rear Wheel (1949-54 Spring-frame Models). Jack the machine up on its *centre* stand, with (1949-50 models) a piece of wood $\frac{7}{8}$ in. thick interposed between the centre stand and the ground. Disconnect the Lucas snap connector fitted in the lead of the rear lamp. Also disconnect the rear-brake expander lever. To do this, remove the split pin and the yoke-end pin. On 1951-4 models it is only necessary to remove the adjuster nut from the rear-brake rod. Loosen the four securing-bolts on 1953-4 models and remove the detachable rear portion of the rear mudguard. On 1949-52 models raise the hinged portion of the mudguard. Detach the spring link from the secondary chain and partially remove the chain in such a manner that it is completely off the rear-wheel sprocket, but hanging on the gearbox sprocket. Engage a gear to keep the sprocket stationary.

Unscrew the cable gland-nut and disconnect the speedometer cable from the speedometer gearbox. Loosen the nut (on the rear-wheel spindle) which positions the speedometer gearbox. Also loosen *three complete turns* the two exterior nuts on the rear-wheel spindle.

With an adjustable spanner applied to the hexagon on the spindle nearside cam (Fig. 79), turn the cam until the wheel is as far forward as possible

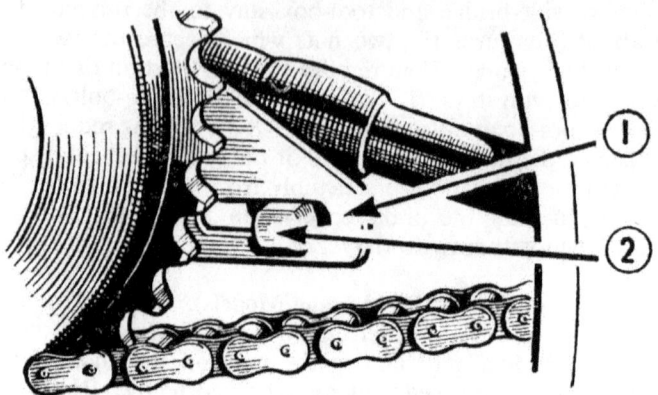

FIG. 78. SHOWING CORRECT REAR BRAKE COVER-PLATE ANCHORAGE (ALL 1945-54 MODELS)
1. Rear brake cover-plate.   2. Bolt anchoring cover-plate to frame.

when pushed to front. Press the nearside of the wheel firmly forward against the cam stop and pull the offside of the wheel backward until the brake cover-plate disengages the square-headed anchor bolt. Finally withdraw the rear wheel from the fork-ends.

To Replace Rear Wheel (1949-54 Spring-frame Models). Reverse the previously described procedure for removal. Check that the speedometer-drive dogs are engaged but do not tighten the nut which locates the speedometer gearbox until *after* you have reconnected the speedometer cable and tightened the external spindle nuts. Note that replacement of the rear wheel in the fork-ends is facilitated by using the following procedure.

While allowing the brake anchor-plate to hang free, hold the wheel on its nearside as far forward as possible in the fork-end, swing the offside backward, raise the free cover-plate so that its slot engages the square-headed anchor bolt, and then swing the offside end of the spindle forward until engagement is complete. Having replaced the rear wheel, check the secondary-chain adjustment (page 126), also the rear-brake adjustment (page 110). Also check that the brake cover-plate anchorage is correct (*see* Fig. 78).

GENERAL MAINTENANCE

Removing Quickly-detachable Rear Wheel (1955–60 Spring-frame Models). First place the motor-cycle on its centre stand. Slacken (1955–8) the bolt located at the rear on each tubular member to which the detachable rear-portion of the mudguard is attached. Also loosen the two bolts

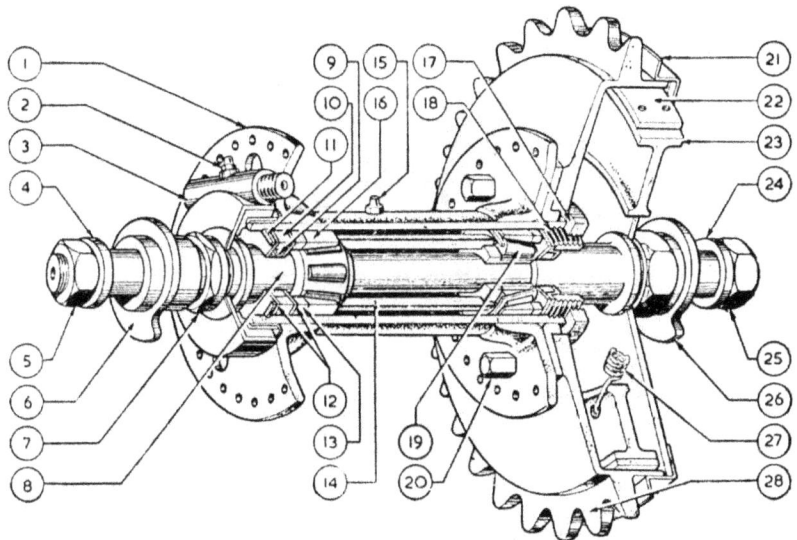

FIG. 79. DETAILS OF REAR-HUB ASSEMBLY ON 1949–54 SPRING-FRAME MODELS

KEY TO FIG. 79

1. Offside hub-flange.
2. Speedometer-gearbox grease nipple.
3. Speedometer gearbox.
4. Spigot bush for offside fork-end.
5. Nut on solid spindle.
6. Offside cam.
7. Nut locking speedometer gearbox in position.
8. Spacer between speedometer gearbox and offside bearing.
9. Oil seal.
10. Collar encircling oil seal.
11. Circlip locating roller bearing.
12. Washer retaining oil seal (one each side of seal).
13. Spacer between oil-seal inner washer and bearing.
14. Spacer between the roller bearings.
15. Hub grease nipple.
16. Roller-bearing outer race.
17. Lock-nut (bearing adjusting ring).
18. Bearing adjusting ring.
19. Taper roller.
20. Bolt securing brake drum and sprocket to hub.
21. Rear brake cover-plate.
22. Brake lining.
23. Brake shoe.
24. Spigot bush for nearside fork-end.
25. Nut on solid spindle.
26. Nearside cam.
27. Brake-shoe spring.
28. Brake drum and sprocket.

holding the two portions of the mudguard together. Disconnect the snap connector provided in the lead to the stop-tail lamp. Now remove the detachable rear-portion of the rear mudguard.

On 1959–60 models a deep section one-piece rear mudguard is fitted. To facilitate rear wheel removal it is desirable to lay some suitable packing (e.g. wood blocks) beneath the centre stand so as to lift the rear wheel a greater distance from the ground.

Referring to Fig. 80, disconnect the speedometer drive by unscrewing the cable gland-nut (5) and withdrawing the end of the driving cable from the speedometer-drive gearbox (4). Next remove the nut (11) and washer

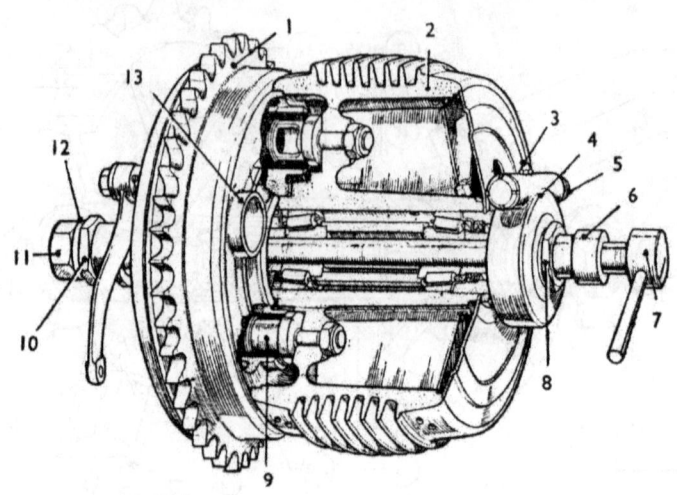

FIG. 80. DETAILS OF LIGHT-ALLOY HUB ASSEMBLY USED ON 1955–60 SPRING-FRAME MODELS WITH QUICKLY-DETACHABLE REAR WHEEL

On 1955–6 models the brake-drum wall has drilled holes instead of the tubular bosses shown; these bosses engage rubber-sleeved pins on the light-alloy hub.

(*By courtesy of "The Motor Cycle"—London*)

KEY TO FIG. 80

1. Brake drum and sprocket.
2. Full-width light-alloy hub.
3. Grease nipple for 4.
4. Speedometer-drive gearbox.
5. Gland nut for speedometer-drive cable.
6. Distance collar.
7. Hub spindle.
8. Nut locating 4.
9. Rubber-sleeved driving pins on 2.
10. Nut securing brake cover-plate.
11. Nut on spindle end.
12. Washer for 11.
13. Tubular bosses to engage pins 9.

(12) from the near-side of the hub spindle (7). Do not disturb the nut (8) which secures the speedometer gearbox (4). Withdraw the hub spindle (7), by means of its short tommy-bar, together with the distance collar (6), which will fall away as the spindle is withdrawn. Then ease the hub sideways from the drilled holes on the brake-drum wall (1955–6 models), or ease the rubber-sleeved pins on the hub from the tubular bosses on the brake-drum wall (1957–60 models). The rear wheel is then free to be withdrawn from the machine which should be leaned at an angle (1959–60 models).

GENERAL MAINTENANCE

To Replace Quickly-detachable Rear Wheel (1955–7 Spring-frame Models). Follow the removal procedure in reverse. Referring to Fig. 80, offer up, the quickly-detachable wheel, insert the hub spindle (7) *without* the distance collar (6); engage the holes or tubular bosses in the brake-drum wall, with the hub driving-pins; hold the wheel in its normal position; withdraw the hub spindle. Then insert the distance collar and replace the hub spindle. When tightening the nut on the nearside of the spindle, make sure

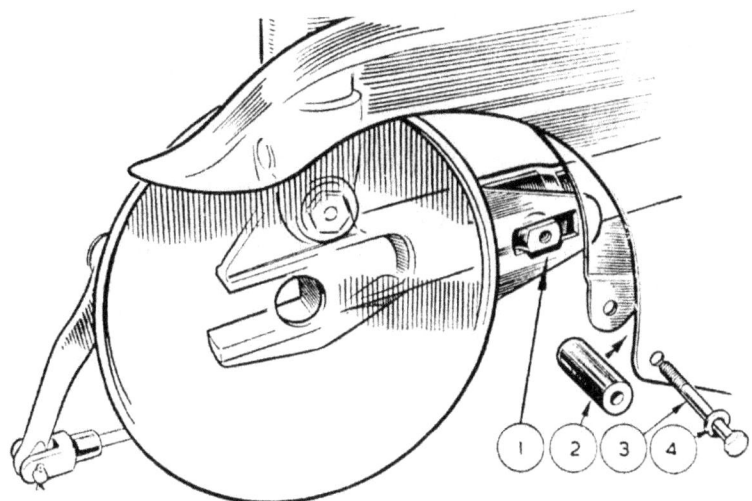

FIG. 81. THE REAR BRAKE COVER-PLATE ANCHORAGE (1955–60 SPRING-FRAME MODELS)

KEY TO FIG. 81
1. Brake-anchorage boss.
2. Distance sleeve.
3. Anchorage bolt.
4. Washer.

that the opposite end of the spindle contacts the secondary chain adjuster-screw, to ensure correct wheel alignment. This should be correct if the chain adjuster-screws have not been disturbed. If in any doubt, check the wheel alignment (*see* page 116); also check the adjustment of the rear brake; (*see* page 118).

When replacing the rear wheel, make sure that the speedometer-drive dogs engage properly before tightening the cable gland-nut (5). Defer tightening the nut (8) locating the speedometer-drive gearbox (4) until the driving cable has been connected up, and the hub-spindle nut (11) has been tightened. Also make sure that the brake cover-plate anchorage is correct (*see* Fig. 81).

Wheel Bearing Adjustment. It is advisable very occasionally to check the adjustment of the wheel bearings and rectify it if necessary. The roller bearings of both wheels should be adjusted so that a slight amount of end-play (approximately 0·002 in.) can be felt. Should no end-play be present, there is an appreciable risk of the roller bearings becoming damaged during running; 0·002 in. bearing end-play represents a just perceptible end-play as felt at the rim. See that there is not more than $\frac{1}{64}$ in. rock.

Adjusting the Roller Bearings. To adjust the rear-wheel bearings, it is necessary to remove the wheel from the machine (*see* pages 144–7), but with a 1945–54 front wheel its removal is not necessary. Bearing adjustment (1945–54) is on the near-side or off-side, according to whether the wheel concerned is rear or front respectively. On 1955–60 models the adjustment for both wheels is on the off-side.

To adjust the roller bearings of a front or rear wheel, loosen the lock-nut for the bearing adjusting-ring. Next tighten the bearing adjusting-ring until *all* play has been eliminated. Then slacken off the adjusting-ring exactly *one-half turn*. This should give about 0·002 in. end-play. Finally retighten the lock-nut, taking care to see that the adjusting-ring does not move in the process, and see that the hub cover-plate (1955–60) is positioned to allow the grease gun to be applied to the grease nipple.

INDEX

AIR filter, 23-4
Alignment—
  headlamp, 25
  wheel, 116
Amal carburettor details, 12-16
Ammeter readings, 28, 34
Automatic ignition-control, 85

BATTERY, maintenance, 35-8
Brake—
  adjustment, 117-22
  drums, 123
  lubrication, 69
  shoes, 120-3
Brakes, use of, 9
Brushes, commutator, 39
Bulb renewal, 26-7, 33-4

CARBON deposits, removing, 91
Carburettor—
  cleaning, 21
  principles, 12-16
  settings, 17
Chain—
  dynamo, 41, 65, 128
  magneto, 64, 85
  primary, 68, 124
  secondary, 68, 125-8
Changing engine oil, 59
Cleaning—
  carburettor, 21
  chromium, 114
  contact-breaker, 82
  enamelled parts, 114
  engine, 76, 91-2
  lamps, 28, 35
  sparking plugs, 78
Clutch—
  adjustment, 130-4
  assembly, 139
  cable, 139
  plates sticking, 6
  shock-absorber, 129
  slip, 129

Commutator brushes, 39
Compression plate, 91
Connexions, battery, 38, 47
Contact-breaker—
  gap, 80-2
  lubrication, 63-4
Controls, 2-3
Crankcase—
  filter, 60
  splitting, 61
C.V.C. unit, 37, 41, 42, 52
Cylinder—
  barrel removal, 94, 103
  head removal, 93, 103

DECARBONIZING, valve grinding, 91-109
Drain plug, crankcase, 59
Driving licence, 2
Dynamo—
  bearings, 65
  chain, 41, 44, 65, 128
  maintenance, 39-44
  removing, 41

ELECTROLYTE level, 36-8
Engine—
  lubrication, 53-65
  oils, suitable, 57
  shaft shock-absorber, 128
Exhaust-valve stem lubrication, 59

FELT element, removing, 60
Filters—
  carburettors, 23-4
  oil, 60-1
Focusing headlamps, 25-6, 29
Front forks, "Teledraulic," 71-4, 143
Front-wheel removal, 143-4
Fuel consumption, excessive, 19

GAP—
  contact-breaker, 80-1
  sparking plug, 77
Gauze filters, oil tank, 61

Gear—
  change indicator, 6, 7
  changing, 6-8
Gearbox lubrication, 65-7
Grease gun, use of, 69
Grinding-in valves, 91-4, 99

HANDLEBAR—
  adjustment, 142
  controls, 3, 70
Harsh transmission, 128
Headlamps, 26-32
Hills, negotiating, 9
Horn adjustment, 46
H.T. cable, 84-5

IGNITION timing, 86-90
Illumination, correct, 25
Inlet-valve stem lubrication, 59
Insurance, 1

JET-NEEDLE wear, 22

KICK-STARTER, use of, 4

LIGHT-UNIT, removing, 33
Lighting switch, 25
Lubrication—
  chart, 66, 67
  engine, 53-65
  motor-cycle, 65-74

MAGNETIC crankcase-filter, 60
Magneto—
  bearings, 62
  chain, 64, 85
  timing, 86-7
"Monobloc" carburettor, 14-23

NUTS and bolts, 115

OIL—
  circulation, 55, 58
  level, 58
  pump, 53-5, 58, 61-2
  tank, 56
Oil-bath—
  chain case, removing, 135
  inspection cap, 68

PETROL tank, 4, 92, 105-9
Pick-up cable, 84
Pilot-jet obstruction, 18
Piston—
  removal, 94, 102
  rings, 95-6, 102
Preliminaries, 1
Primary chain, 68, 124
Push-rod cover-tube washers, 103

QUICKLY-DETACHABLE rear wheel, 147-9

REAR lamps, 35
Rear suspension, 74, 143
Rear-wheel removal, 145-6
Reflector, removing, 27
Registration licence, 1
Repairs and spares, 75
Rocker-box removal, 93, 104
Running-in advice, 10

SADDLE adjustment, 141
Secondary-chain, 68, 125-8
Shock-absorbers, 128
Sidecar alignment, 116
Slip-ring, cleaning, 84
Slipping clutch, 129
Slow-running adjustment, 18
Sparking plugs, 77-80
Specific gravity of electrolyte, 38
Speedometer-gearbox lubrication, 70
Standard-type carburettor, 12-14, 16-22
Stands, 70
Starting engine, 2-4
Steering head, 69, 142
Sticking clutch-plates, 6
Stop-tail lamps, 35
Stopping procedure, 9
Switch panel, lighting, 29, 34

TANK filters, 56, 60-1
Tappet adjustment, 90-1
Taps, petrol, 4
"Tekall," 114
"Teledraulic" front forks, 143
Terminals, battery, 42
Throttle twist-grip stiff, 70

INDEX

Timing—
  coil, 87–90
  magneto, 86–7
Tools, 76, 113
Topping-up battery, 35
Tuning Amal carburettor, 16–20
Twist-grip adjustment, 19
Tyre pressures, 115–16

VALVE springs, 96
Valve timing, 109–13
Valves, grinding-in, 91–4, 99

Vent plugs, battery, 36
Voltage control, 41

WARMING-UP engine, 5
Wheel—
  alignment, 116
  bearing adjustment, 149–50
  hub lubrication, 69
  removal, 143–50
Wiring—
  diagrams, 48–51
  system, 47

AUTOBOOKS WORKSHOP MANUALS

ALFA ROMEO GIULIA 1300, 1600, 1750, 2000 1962-1978 WSM
AUSTIN HEALEY SPRITE, MG MIDGET 1958-1980 WSM
BMW 1600 1966-1973 WSM
BMW 2000 & 2002 1966-1976 WSM
BMW 2500, 2800, 3.0 & 3.3 1968-1977 WSM
BMW 316, 320, 320i 1975-1977 WSM
BMW 518, 520, 520i 1973-1981 WSM
FIAT 1100, 1100D, 1100R & 1200 1957-1969 WSM
FIAT 124 1966-1974 WSM
FIAT 124 SPORT 1966-1975 WSM
FIAT 125 & 125 SPECIAL 1967-1973 WSM
FIAT 126, 126L, 126 DV, 126/650 & 126/650 DV 1972-1982 WSM
FIAT 127 SALOON, SPECIAL & SPORT, 900, 1050 1971-1981 WSM
FIAT 128 1969-1982 WSM
FIAT 1300, 1500 1961-1967 WSM
FIAT 131 MIRAFIORI 1975-1982 WSM
FIAT 132 1972-1982 WSM
FIAT 500 1957-1973 WSM
FIAT 600, 600D & MULTIPLA 1955-1969 WSM
FIAT 850 1964-1972 WSM
JAGUAR E-TYPE 1961-1972 WSM
JAGUAR MK 1, 2 1955-1969 WSM
JAGUAR S TYPE, 420 1963-1968 WSM
JAGUAR XK 120, 140, 150 MK 7, 8, 9 1948-1961 WSM
LAND ROVER 1, 2 1948-1961 WSM
MERCEDES-BENZ 190 1959-1968 WSM
MERCEDES-BENZ 220/8 1968-1972 WSM
MERCEDES-BENZ 220B 1959-1965 WSM
MERCEDES-BENZ 230 1963-1968 WSM
MERCEDES-BENZ 250 1968-1972 WSM
MERCEDES-BENZ 280 1968-1972 WSM
MG MIDGET TA-TF 1936-1955 WSM
MINI 1959-1980 WSM
MORRIS MINOR 1952-1971 WSM
PEUGEOT 404 1960-1975 WSM
PORSCHE 911 1964-1973 WSM
PORSCHE 911 1970-1977 WSM
RENAULT 16 1965-1979 WSM
RENAULT 8, 10, 1100 1962-1971 WSM
ROVER 3500, 3500S 1968-1976 WSM
SUNBEAM RAPIER, ALPINE 1955-1965 WSM
TRIUMPH SPITFIRE, GT6, VITESSE 1962-1968 WSM
TRIUMPH TR2, TR3, TR3A 1952-1962 WSM
TRIUMPH TR4, TR4A 1961-1967 WSM
VOLKSWAGEN BEETLE 1968-1977 WSM

VELOCEPRESS AUTOMOBILE BOOKS & MANUALS

ABARTH BUYERS GUIDE
AUSTIN-HEALEY 6-CYLINDER WSM
BMW 600 LIMOUSINE FACTORY WSM
BMW 600 LIMOUSINE OWNERS HAND BOOK & SERVICE MANUAL
BMW ISETTA FACTORY WSM
BOOK OF THE CARRERA PANAMERICANA - MEXICAN ROAD RACE
COMPLETE CATALOG OF JAPANESE MOTOR VEHICLES
DIALED IN - THE JAN OPPERMAN STORY
FERRARI 250/GT SERVICE AND MAINTENANCE
FERRARI 308 SERIES BUYER'S AND OWNER'S GUIDE
FERRARI BERLINETTA LUSSO
FERRARI BROCHURES AND SALES LITERATURE 1946-1967
FERRARI BROCHURES AND SALES LITERATURE 1968-1989
FERRARI GUIDE TO PERFORMANCE
FERRARI OPP, MAINTENANCE & SERVICE H/BOOKS 1948-1963
FERRARI OWNER'S HANDBOOK
FERRARI SERIAL NUMBERS PART I - ODD NUMBERS TO 21399
FERRARI SERIAL NUMBERS PART II - EVEN NUMBERS TO 1050
FERRARI SPYDER CALIFORNIA
FERRARI TUNING TIPS & MAINTENANCE TECHNIQUES
HENRY'S FABULOUS MODEL "A" FORD
HOW TO BUILD A FIBERGLASS CAR
HOW TO BUILD A RACING CAR
HOW TO RESTORE THE MODEL 'A' FORD
IF HEMINGWAY HAD WRITTEN A RACING NOVEL
JAGUAR E-TYPE 3.8 & 4.2 WSM
LE MANS 24 (THE BOOK THAT THE FILM WAS BASED ON)
MASERATI BROCHURES AND SALES LITERATURE
MASERATI OWNER'S HANDBOOK
METROPOLITAN FACTORY WSM
MGA & MGB OWNERS HANDBOOK & WSM
OBERT'S FIAT GUIDE
PERFORMANCE TUNING THE SUNBEAM TIGER
PORSCHE 356 1948-1965 WSM
PORSCHE 912 WSM
SOUPING THE VOLKSWAGEN
TRIUMPH TR2, TR3, TR4 1953-1965 WSM
VEDA ORR'S NEW REVISED HOT ROD PICTORIAL
VOLKSWAGEN TRANSPORTER, TRUCKS, STATION WAGONS WSM
VOLVO 1944-1968 ALL MODELS WSM

BROOKLANDS BOOKS & ROAD TEST PORTFOLIOS (RTP)

AC CARS 1904-2009
ALFA ROMEO 1920-1933 ROAD TEST PORTFOLIO
ALFA ROMEO 1934-1940 ROAD TEST PORTFOLIO
BRABHAM RALT HONDA THE RON TAURANAC STORY
BUGATTI TYPE 10 TO TYPE 40 ROAD TEST PORTFOLIO
BUGATTI TYPE 10 TO TYPE 251 ROAD TEST PORTFOLIO
BUGATTI TYPE 41 TO TYPE 55 ROAD TEST PORTFOLIO
BUGATTI TYPE 57 TO TYPE 251 ROAD TEST PORTFOLIO
DELAHAYE ROAD TEST PORTFOLIO
FERRARI ROAD CARS 1946-1956 ROAD TEST PORTFOLIO
FIAT 500 1936-1972 ROAD TEST PORTFOLIO
FIAT DINO ROAD TEST PORTFOLIO
HISPANO SUIZA ROAD TEST PORTFOLIO
HONDA ST1100/ST1300 PAN EUROPEAN 1990-2002 RTP
JAGUAR MK1 & MK2 ROAD TEST PORTFOLIO
LOTUS CORTINA ROAD TEST PORTFOLIO
MV AGUSTA F4 750 & 1000 1997-2007 ROAD TEST PORTFOLIO
TATRA CARS ROAD TEST PORTFOLIO

VELOCEPRESS MOTORCYCLE BOOKS & MANUALS

AJS SINGLES 1955-65 350cc & 500cc (BOOK OF)
AJS SINGLES 1945-60 350cc & 500cc MODELS 16 & 18 (BOOK OF)
ARIEL 1939-1960 4 STROKE SINGLES (BOOK OF)
ARIEL LEADER & ARROW 1958-1964 (BOOK OF)
ARIEL MOTORCYCLES 1933-1951 WSM
ARIEL PREWAR MODELS 1932-1939 (BOOK OF)
BMW M/CYCLES R26 R27 (1956-1967) FACTORY WSM
BMW M/CYCLES R50 R50S R60 R69S (1955-1969) FACTORY WSM
BSA BANTAM (BOOK OF)
BSA ALL FOUR-STROKE SINGLES & V-TWINS 1936-1952 (BOOK OF)
BSA OHV & SV SINGLES - 250cc 1954-1970 (BOOK OF)
BSA OHV & SV SINGLES 1945-54 250-600cc (BOOK OF)
BSA OHV SINGLES 350 & 500cc 1955-1967 (BOOK OF)
BSA PRE-WAR MODELS TO 1939 (BOOK OF)
BSA TWINS 1948-1962 (BOOK OF)
BSA TWINS 1962-1969 (SECOND BOOK OF)
CATALOG OF BRITISH MOTORCYCLES (1951 MODELS)
DOUGLAS PRE-WAR ALL MODELS 1929-1939 (BOOK OF)
DOUGLAS POST-WAR ALL MODELS 1948-1957 FACTORY WSM
DUCATI 160cc, 250cc & 350cc OHC MODELS FACTORY WSM
HONDA 50 ALL MODELS UP TO 1970 INC MONKEY & TRAIL (BOOK OF)
HONDA 90 ALL MODELS UP TO 1966 (BOOK OF)
HONDA MOTORCYCLES 125-150 TWINS C/CS/CB/CA WSM
HONDA MOTORCYCLES 250-305 TWINS C/CS/CB WSM
HONDA MOTORCYCLES C100 SUPER CUB WSM
HONDA MOTORCYCLES C110 SPORT CUB 1962-1969 WSM
HONDA TWINS & SINGLES 50cc TO 305cc 1960-1966 (BOOK OF)
HONDA TWINS ALL MODELS 125cc THRU 450cc UP TO 1968 (BOOK OF)
INDIAN PONYBIKE, BOY RACER & PAPOOSE ILL PARTS LIST & SALES LIT
LAMBRETTA ALL 125 & 150cc MODELS 1947-1957 (BOOK OF)
LAMBRETTA LI & TV MODELS 1957-1970 (SECOND BOOK OF)
MATCHLESS 350 & 500cc SINGLES 1945-1956 (BOOK OF)
MATCHLESS 350 & 500cc SINGLES 1955-1966 (BOOK OF)
NORTON 1938-1956 (BOOK OF)
NORTON DOMINATOR TWINS 1955-1965 (BOOK OF)
NORTON MODELS 19, 50 & ES2 1955-1963 (BOOK OF)
NORTON MOTORCYCLES 1957-1970 FACTORY WSM
NORTON PREWAR MODELS 1932-1939 (BOOK OF)
ROYAL ENFIELD SINGLES & V TWINS 1937-1953 (BOOK OF)
ROYAL ENFIELD 736cc INTERCEPTOR FACTORY WSM
ROYAL ENFIELD 250cc & 350cc SINGLES 1958-1966 (SECOND BOOK OF)
SUZUKI 50cc & 80cc UP TO 1966 (BOOK OF)
SUZUKI T10 1963-1967 FACTORY WSM
SUZUKI T20 & T200 1965-1969 FACTORY WSM
TRIUMPH PRE-WAR MOTORCYCLE 1935-1939 (BOOK OF)
TRIUMPH MOTORCYCLES 1937-1951 WSM
TRIUMPH MOTORCYCLES 1945-1955 FACTORY WSM
TRIUMPH TWINS 1956-1969 (BOOK OF)
VELOCETTE ALL SINGLES & TWINS 1925-1970 (BOOK OF)
VESPA 1951-1961 (BOOK OF)
VESPA 125 & 150cc & GS MODELS 1955-1963 (SECOND BOOK OF)
VESPA 90, 125 & 150cc 1963-1972 (THIRD BOOK OF)
VESPA GS & SS 1955-1968 (BOOK OF)
VINCENT MOTORCYCLES 1935-1955 WSM

PLEASE VISIT OUR WEBSITE
www.VelocePress.com
FOR A DETAILED DESCRIPTION
OF ANY OF THESE TITLES

www.ingramcontent.com/pod-product-compliance
Lightning Source LLC
Chambersburg PA
CBHW070550170426
43201CB00012B/1793

INTRODUCTION

Welcome to the world of digital publishing ~ the book you now hold in your hand, while unchanged from the original edition, was printed using the latest state of the art digital technology. The advent of print-on-demand has forever changed the publishing process, never has information been so accessible and it is our hope that this book serves your informational needs for years to come. If this is your first exposure to digital publishing, we hope that you are pleased with the results. Many more titles of interest to the classic automobile and motorcycle enthusiast, collector and restorer are available via our website at www.VelocePress.com. We hope that you find this title as interesting as we do.

NOTE FROM THE PUBLISHER

The information presented is true and complete to the best of our knowledge. All recommendations are made without any guarantees on the part of the author or the publisher, who also disclaim all liability incurred with the use of this information.

TRADEMARKS

We recognize that some words, model names and designations, for example, mentioned herein are the property of the trademark holder. We use them for identification purposes only. This is not an official publication.

INFORMATION ON THE USE OF THIS PUBLICATION

This manual is an invaluable resource for the classic motorcycle enthusiast and a "must have" for owners interested in performing their own maintenance. However, in today's information age we are constantly subject to changes in common practice, new technology, availability of improved materials and increased awareness of chemical toxicity. As such, it is advised that the user consult with an experienced professional prior to undertaking any procedure described herein. While every care has been taken to ensure correctness of information, it is obviously not possible to guarantee complete freedom from errors or omissions or to accept liability arising from such errors or omissions. Therefore, any individual that uses the information contained within, or elects to perform or participate in do-it-yourself repairs or modifications acknowledges that there is a risk factor involved and that the publisher or its associates cannot be held responsible for personal injury or property damage resulting from the use of the information or the outcome of such procedures.

WARNING!

One final word of advice, this publication is intended to be used as a reference guide, and when in doubt the reader should consult with a qualified technician.

PREFACE

IN this book I have dealt, as far as possible, with those points which are likely to be of assistance to the owner or prospective owner of a Morgan Three Wheeler.

The recent introduction, the four-cylinder model, is dealt with thoroughly. Many useful photographs have been obtained and these should be of great assistance when decarbonizing and general maintenance items are under consideration.

The book also covers the J.A.P. and Matchless engines, and it is hoped that it will be of benefit to all owners of one of these delightful three wheelers.

Finally, I would thank the Morgan Motor Co., Ltd., for supplying certain blocks and much useful information.

1935

H. J.

CONTENTS

CHAP.		PAGE
	PREFACE	
I.	THE RANGE OF MORGAN MODELS	1
II.	PRELIMINARIES	10
III.	DRIVING AND RUNNING-IN	17
IV.	ENGINE MAINTENANCE AND OVERHAULING	28
V.	THE TRANSMISSION	69
VI.	THE FRONT WHEELS AND BRAKES	81
VII.	THE LIGHTING AND STARTING EQUIPMENT	90
VIII.	TOURING	105
IX.	COMPETITIONS	109
X.	BUYING AND SELLING	112
XI.	THE WATER-COOLED MODELS AND WINTER PRECAUTIONS	116
XII.	LEGAL MATTERS	118
	APPENDIX	122
	INDEX	129

MORGAN

OFFICIALLY RECOMMEND
LUBRICATION BY SHELL

Specific grades shown in manufacturer's instruction book

THE BOOK OF THE MORGAN

CHAPTER I

THE RANGE OF MORGAN MODELS

THE Morgan Runabout was first produced in 1909, and the machine as at present manufactured is the outcome of twenty-six years experience of one type of vehicle. The reliability is, and has been for many years, unquestioned, and it admirably fulfils the purpose for which it was first intended, i.e. to meet the requirements of those whose ambition was the possession of a light car, but whose means permitted nothing more expensive than a motor-cycle combination. The Morgan provides car comfort, sociability and weather protection, and an entire absence of fatigue after a lengthy journey, coupled with utility, speed, and ease of control; and last, but by no means least, economy equal to the average high-powered sidecar outfit.

The initial outlay is also far less than that called for when buying a light car, in addition to which the annual tax amounts to only £4, and the cost of maintaining the vehicle is proportionately low.

Since the previous edition of this book an entirely new departure is offered in the form of a three wheeler fitted with a four-cylinder water-cooled unit. This model has been produced only after several years of patient and careful experimental work. The engine is made for the Morgan Motor Co., Ltd., by a firm of world-wide repute, has a total capacity of 933 cc. and a R.A.C. rating of 7·95 h.p. It is of very simple design, the number of working parts being reduced to the absolute minimum. The power output and smoothness in running are notable features of the four-cylinder engine. Ignition is automatically controlled and the whole of the electric fittings are carried out by Lucas in an up-to-date manner. The carburettor is the latest Zenith downdraught type, while the pistons are of a special aluminium alloy and the crankshaft is balanced and runs in three bearings. The chassis is of a special design, particularly suitable for a three wheeler, and is made from steel channel of a very deep section, with a large centre tube connecting engine and gearbox. The transmission is by enclosed propellor shaft through a three-speed and reverse gearbox containing a bronze worm wheel and steel worm, the final drive is by $\frac{3}{4}$ in. chain, whilst the springs, steering, etc., follow standard and proved Morgan practice. The body, which is an occasional four, has a low sporting appearance, is nicely built, and is fitted with all-weather equipment and adjustable seats for both driver and passenger, thus providing ample leg room with easy access to the rear seats. The comfort of the driver in particular is looked after by providing a spring steering wheel and all controls in a handy and convenient position. The general appearance of the car is exceptionally smart and the lamps, radiator, and windscreen frame are chromium plated, whilst an attractive stone guard of modern type is fitted in front of the radiator. The performance is exceptionally good, the car being capable of approximately 70 m.p.h. with a petrol consumption of between 45 and 50 m.p.g. The wheel base is 8 ft. 3 in. with a track of 4 ft. 2 in. The brakes are operated by a simple system giving efficient braking on all wheels from the foot pedal, while the hand lever operates the rear brake only and is fitted with a ratchet for parking purposes. An accelerator pedal is fitted to the right of the brake pedal and works in conjunction with a control lever on the steering wheel. The radiator is chromium plated and of the honeycomb type. The price complete is £120.

The foregoing does not in any way displace the twin-engine models that for twenty-six years have made the Morgan Motor Co. famous. A full range of these models will be continued and various engines are offered. Many improvements have been made during the last two seasons, and all models have proved themselves so satisfactory that there has been no need for other than detail alterations to bodywork and finish. A few of the improvements that have been made from time to time are a new type of flexible clutch centre to the engine, the totally enclosing of the valve gear and the filtering of all lubricating oil, thus prolonging considerably the life of this unit. The 1935 models are all fitted with lamps having a dip and switch arrangement, an accurate needle type of speedometer, whilst the general finish has received special attention, with a view to providing a better appearance. The new side-valve water-cooled engine made specially for the Morgan by the Matchless Motor Cycles (Colliers), Ltd., and introduced during the 1933 season, was greeted with the immediate approval of both dealers and public. This unit is exceptionally well balanced, quiet,

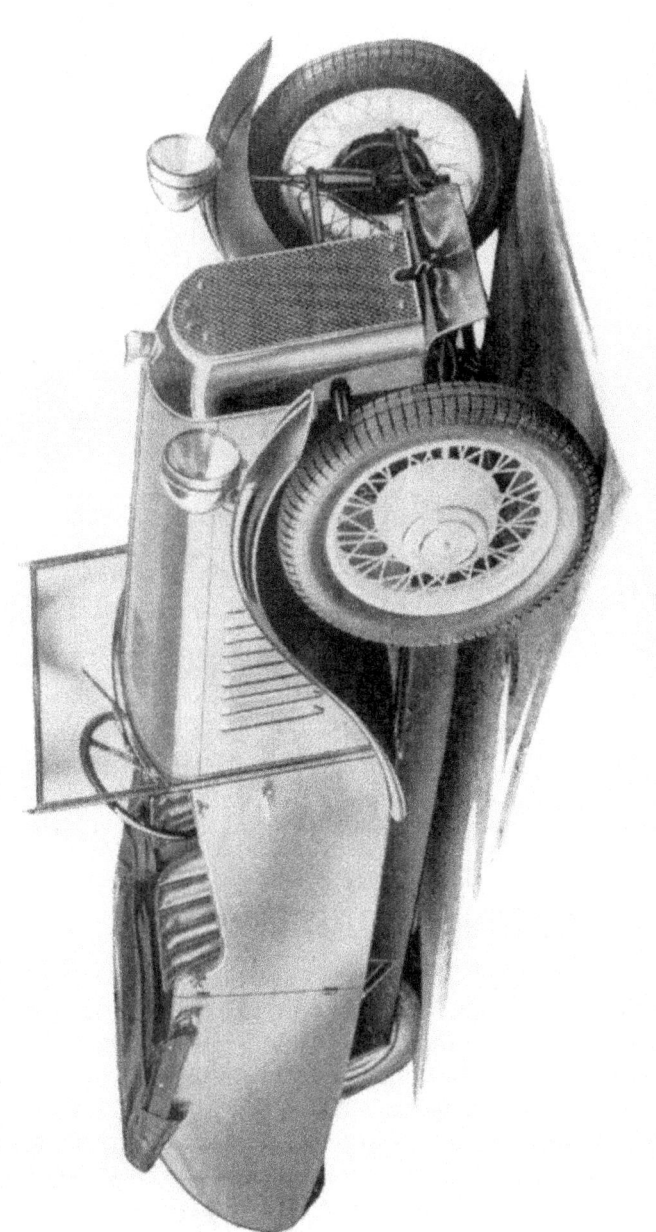

FIG. 1. THE FOUR-CYLINDER MODEL.

(*From "The Motor Cycle"*)

and smooth, coupled with a really good performance. The maximum speed is equal to 60 m.p.h., climbing powers are good, there being few hills on main roads which cannot be taken quite easily on top gear. In addition to this unit a special 10/35 h.p. O.H.V. air-cooled engine has been designed for fitting to the sports models. Up to date, beautifully constructed, it has a genuine sports performance

FIG. 2. THE FAMILY MODEL

but at the same time retains those characteristics associated with the side-valve edition—smooth, quiet, and well-balanced. Although air-cooled it will not overheat, due to the detailed attention that has been paid to finning and cylinder-head design. Its maximum speed is over 70 m.p.h. and hills do not worry it at all.

THE RANGE OF 1935 ENGINES

MATCHLESS ENGINES

S.V. Water-cooled. Bore 85·5 mm. Stroke 85·5 mm. Capacity 990 cc. Compression 5·6. Car type detachable cylinder heads. Controlled water circulation, maximum water flow round valve seats. Turbulent type combustion chambers allowing high power output with smooth running. Valve springs and tappets totally enclosed by quickly detachable covers. Birmal Lo-ex pistons. Full floating gudgeon pins. Roller big end bearings. Starting gear operating direct on crankshaft.

O.H.V. Air-cooled. Capacity 990 cc. Compression ratio 6 to 1. It has a striking appearance with an excellent performance, being

THE RANGE OF MORGAN MODELS

smooth and sweet-running as well as powerful. The vertical ribs of the cylinder head are set in line of travel to obtain the best cooling and the enclosed O.H.V. rocker gear is mechanically lubricated throughout. There is also an adjustable oil feed to the inlet valve guide. The crankcase is similar to that used for the S.V. W.C. engine, with the exception of the cams and rockers. The latter are

FIG. 3. THE SPORTS-FAMILY MODEL

provided with steel rollers and have been strengthened considerably to withstand the extra load of the stronger valve springs.

O.H.V. Water-cooled 10/40 h.p. As above specification, but with water-cooled heads and cylinder barrels (Fig. 4), and a rather better performance.

BODYWORK AND GENERAL FINISH

The coachwork for all 1935 models has been greatly improved, all fittings are now chromium plated, and an extra coat of varnish is given to prolong that new appearance.

Ample room is provided in all bodies, which are upholstered in best quality leather-cloth and Moseley "Float-on-Air" cushions are supplied. Windscreens are glazed with safety glass and a screen wiper is fitted. V-shaped screens are supplied for the sports models, but in the case of the Sports Two-seater a flat fixed screen is an optional fitting. The **Family Models** have rigid but easily detachable side screens.

THE BOOK OF THE MORGAN

GENERAL SPECIFICATION

The following general specification applies to all models except the **Four-cylinder Model F** which is described in detail on page 1.

Clutch. Single dry plate, fitted with Borg & Beck flexible centre, very smooth in action, needing little attention.

Gearbox. Three-speed and reverse. Ratios: O.H.V. Models: 1st, 12·4; 2nd, 7·5; top, 4·58; reverse, 16·5. S.V. Models: 1st, 13·1; 2nd, 8; top, 4·85; reverse, 17·5.

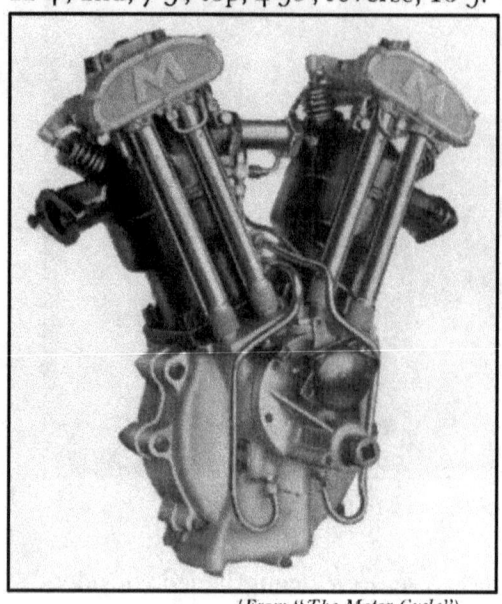

(From "The Motor Cycle")
FIG. 4. THE O.H.V. MATCHLESS WATER-COOLED ENGINE

Transmission. Shaft from flywheel through centre bearing (obviating shaft whip) to gearbox, thence to worm and wheel; final drive taken by single chain of $\frac{3}{4}$ in. pitch, which, being short and running at low speeds, gives no trouble.

Brakes. Large internal expanding on all wheels. Rear operated by pedal, front by hand lever with ratchet.

Steering. Improved geared, very much lighter than hitherto, giving easy manipulation with absolute control.

Body. Coach-built from seasoned wood and sheet metal. Entirely separate from chassis and easily detachable, fitted with Moseley Float-on-Air cushions.

Wheels. 18 × 3 Dunlop Magna detachable and interchangeable.

Tyres. 26 × 4 in. Dunlop.

Chassis. Special patented design made from steel tubes; light and immensely strong.

Tanks. Capacity approximately 4 gal. petrol, 1 gal. oil.

Lubrication. Dry sump (Wakefield Patent Castrol XL for engines and Castrol D for the gearbox are recommended).

Electrical Equipment. Lucas 6-volt head and side lights combined, with dipping device. Electric starter and horn.

Ignition. Battery and coil.

THE RANGE OF MORGAN MODELS

Finish. Standard colours: black with choice of red, green, or cream wheels, except on **Super Sports Model** (see page 8). Special colours £3 10s. extra.

Overall Dimensions. Family and Sports Two-seater, 10 ft. 6 in. × 4 ft. 11 in. **Super Sports,** 10 ft. 4 in. × 4 ft. 11 in. **Sports Family,** 10 ft. 10 in. × 4 ft. 11 in.

Track. All models 4 ft. 2 in.

Wheelbase. All models, 7 ft. 3 in., except **Sports Family,** which is 4 in. longer.

Equipment. Includes full kit of tools with jack, tyre inflator,

FIG. 5. THE SPORTS TWO-SEATER

grease gun, spare wheel and tyre, suction screen wiper, Cooper-Stewart speedometer, side-screens to **Family Model,** and number plates.

THE FAMILY MODEL

Body. Two-door coach-built body, with all-weather equipment. Front seats adjustable for driver and passenger, giving ample leg room and comfort with access to rear seats. Sloping single panel windshield fitted with safety glass.

Upholstery. Seats covered in best quality leatherette, body trimmed to match. Foot mat in front compartment.

Hood and Cushions. Quickly adjusted hood, covered in best quality black twill with detachable rigid celluloid side screens, providing complete protection when in position. Hood envelope provided.

Fitted with S.V. water-cooled engine, £95 complete.

THE SPORTS-FAMILY MODEL

A roomy Sports Four-seater coach-built body with two doors, ample room and weather protection. Ideal for the family man who requires real sports performance and appearance with extra accommodation. Choice of three engines as specification detailed on previous pages. With 10 h.p. S.V. water-cooled engine, £115. With

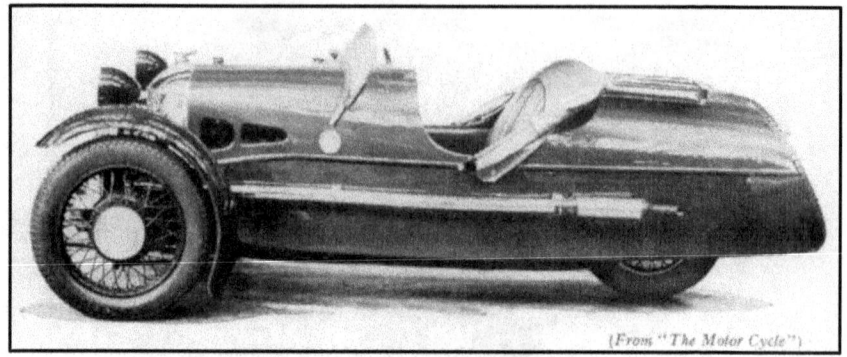

Fig. 6. The Super Sports Model

10 h.p. O.H.V. air-cooled engine, £120. With 10 h.p. O.H.V. water-cooled engine, £125.

THE SPORTS TWO-SEATER

Exceptionally smart two-door coach-built body, giving maximum leg room and comfortable seating.

Luggage can be carried in the locker provided behind the seat squab.

Fitted with either a Vee or Flat Single Panel Screen. With its low centre of gravity it will hold the road at any speed. This machine is ideal for week-end runs or long tours at high average speeds.

With S.V. water-cooled engine, £110; with O.H.V. air-cooled engine, £115; with O.H.V. water-cooled engine, £120.

THE SUPER SPORTS MODEL

Long low lines characterize this popular Morgan production. Its very appearance is that of speed, but apart from appearance it

THE RANGE OF MORGAN MODELS

has speed, remarkable acceleration, road-holding and ease of control. Fitted with front shock-absorbers, special twin-float carburettor, Brooklands type chromium plated exhausts, spring steering wheel and Fort Dunlop tyres, it meets with the immediate approval of those who appreciate a thoroughbred. The standard colour schemes are—

Body and chassis black with wheels and wings a choice of red green and cream, or all black with aluminium wheels.

Body and chassis light blue, wheels and wings cream.

Body red and cream; chassis and wings Red; wheels cream.

Body British racing green; wings, wheels and chassis darker green.

CHAPTER II

PRELIMINARIES

THE object of this chapter is for the man who, having selected the model which he considers most suitable for his requirements, is faced with the sundry formalities in connection with the legal side of motoring, and also getting the car covered under an insurance policy before venturing on to the road.

THE DRIVING LICENCE.

This costs 5/- per annum and expires twelve months after the date on which it was taken out. Every driver of a mechanically-propelled vehicle must be in possession of a driving licence whilst driving such a vehicle. Seventeen is the minimum age for a licence to drive a motor-car and 16 for a motor-cycle. It should be specially noted here that under this section of the law a Morgan is classed as a motor-cycle combination and a boy or girl of 16 years of age is therefore permitted to drive a Morgan. After the age of 17 years has been reached the holder of the licence is allowed to drive any type of mechanically-propelled vehicle, regardless of the number of wheels with which it is fitted. Application for a licence to drive must be made to the offices of the Town or County Council in which the owner resides. These Municipal authorities will provide the appropriate form of application, which must be completed and returned to the Council with the necessary fee of 5/-. The possession of a driving licence is no proof of driving ability—indeed, it is compulsory that one takes out the licence before receiving any tuition in the driving of the vehicle. A driving test is to be given to holders of a new driving licence. This does not apply to the person who held a driving licence before 1st April, 1934. Licences issued before the test are marked " provisional," and the holders are liable to be called upon to pass the specified test any time after 1st April, 1935. A declaration as to physical fitness must be made by every applicant for a driving licence. This declaration must be in the form prescribed by the authorities, and it must state whether or not the applicant is suffering from any disease or physical disability specified in the form or from any other disease or disability which would be likely to render it dangerous to drive.

A licence is non-transferable and the authorities do not notify

PRELIMINARIES

the driver when his licence is due for renewal, the onus of taking out a renewal licence resting entirely with the licensee.

A police officer may at any time stop a motorist and ask to see his or her driving licence without giving any reason for so doing. Failure to produce the licence whilst in charge of the car is a punishable offence, but many police authorities do not take action on this count, providing the licence is not expired and can be produced at the station of the police officer within five days from the time of the request. The police officer is not allowed to take note of any endorsements which may have been entered in the licence on the back pages. These endorsements, if any, are a record of any motoring offence of which the motorist has been convicted. In some cases, although the motorist may have been found guilty by the magistrates, no order is made by them that the licence shall be endorsed.

In the police court itself, no reference may be made to any endorsements in respect of previous offences until the magistrates have decided whether the defendant is guilty or otherwise. This is so that the magistrates shall not be influenced by any past offences, but, should they decide to convict, they may then request the defendant to produce his licence so that they may consider his past history before inflicting the fine or other penalty. Should the motorist fall foul of the police, the licence may be suspended for a period or cancelled altogether, whereupon he is, of course, prohibited from driving. The latter penalty is rarely enforced, but the former procedure is now fairly frequent.

RENEWING THE DRIVING LICENCE.

Upon the expiry of the licence at the end of twelve months, it will be necessary to complete a Form for the Application of Renewal of Driving Licence and send this, together with the licence fee of 5/- to the appropriate Local Council Offices from which the licence was originally obtained. Strictly speaking, one is then not allowed to drive owing to his not being in possession of the licence, and the position is really somewhat ambiguous. It will usually be found, however, that if some proof is carried, such as a copy of any letter which may have been sent to the Council requesting a renewal of the licence, or the counterfoil of the postal order if payment was made in this manner, it will satisfy the police should they desire to see the driver's licence. In order to further safeguard one's self, it is a good plan to apply for renewal a week or so before the actual date of expiry of the licence. This difficulty will not exist at all, of course, if the driver calls in person at the Council Offices with his licence, when a renewal will be issued without delay.

It should be remembered that the driving licence must be signed before driving any vehicle on the public road.

REGISTRATION OF THE VEHICLE.

Before the purchaser takes the car on a public highway it must be taxed, registered, and fitted with registration number plates, one at the front and the other at the back. Tax, in the initial instance, is payable at the same time and to the same Municipal authority as the registration is effected, and in the case of a Morgan is £4 per annum commencing on the 1st January and expiring on 31st December. If desired, a quarterly tax may be obtained at a cost of £1 2s. for each quarter, the quarter days being 24th March, 30th June, 30th September, and 31st December.

Alternatively, the vehicle may be taxed from any day the owner wishes, the tax in this case to run until the end of the year. The table given hereunder shows the amount of duty payable from the date of issue of the tax until 31st December, if taken out on or after—

1st Feb.	1st Mar.	25th Mar	1st May	1st June	1st July	1st Aug.	1st Sep.
£ s. d.	£ s. d.	£ s. d.	£ s. d.	£ s. d.	£ s. d.	£ s. d.	£ s. d.
3 17 0	3 10 0	3 3 0	2 16 0	2 9 0	2 2 0	1 15 0	1 8 0

Before a new car can be registered, the authorities will require some proof that the vehicle is *ipso facto* new, and production of the Manufacturer's or Agent's Sales Delivery Note, or the Agent's Invoice, either of which should bear the engine and any other numbers by which the car can be proved not to have been previously registered. These, and other details which the authorities will ask for, must be supplied on the appropriate form of application for a licence. In return for this form and the amount of the tax, the owner will receive a registration book and the licence. This latter must always be carried on the machine in a licence holder fitted to the near side of the vehicle. There is no necessity to carry the registration book, but the owner will be well advised to read carefully the instructions printed thereon. Upon the expiration of the licence, a different form (obtainable from the Council offices) must be completed and sent to the Council, together with the registration book and the amount of the tax. If the registration book is lost a new one can be obtained on payment of a fee of 5/-.

NUMBER PLATES.

Although a Morgan is rated as a motor-cycle for duty purposes, strangely enough the number plates carrying the registration numbers must be the same size as those on a four-wheeled car. The numbers must be painted on, or the plates may be cast in aluminium complete with the appropriate numbers—in any case it is, strictly speaking, illegal for plates to be fitted with numbers which are detachable, as, for instance, in the case of numbers

FIG. 7. NUMBER PLATE DIMENSIONS

which are riveted on. Each letter or figure must be 3½ in. high and with the exception of figure 1, must be 2½ in. wide. The actual lettering or figuring must be ⅝ in. broad and there must be a half-inch space between each letter and figure, a half-inch margin along the top and bottom, and an inch margin each side. (See Fig. 10.)

INSURANCE.

Before venturing on the public road with his car every motorist is now compelled to take out a third party insurance policy. In addition to the usual policy, or cover note, the insurance company will hand to the owner a certificate of insurance in the prescribed form and when applying for his car licence, the applicant must—by production of the insurance certificate or otherwise—satisfy the Licensing Authority that the necessary cover against third party risks will be in force at the time the car licence becomes operative.

The driver of a vehicle must, when requested by the police, give his name and address, and produce the insurance certificate. If it cannot be produced immediately, it must be shown within five days at any police station.

There are a very large number of insurance companies in Great Britain, and almost all of them cater for the motorist. Insurance companies are divided broadly into two classes, Tariff and non-Tariff. There are many excellent non-tariff companies, but their charges vary considerably, and, since it is impossible to quote more than one case, the Tariff prices are taken. The following details are therefore those which apply to an ordinary Tariff policy.

A COMPREHENSIVE POLICY.

This type of policy covers the following contingencies—

Loss of or Damage to Car. This covers transit by sea between any ports in Great Britain, Ireland, the Isle of Man, or the Channel Islands. The exceptions are: loss of use, depreciation, wear and tear, mechanical or electrical breakdowns, failures or breakages, damage to tyres by application of brakes or by road punctures, cuts or bursts.

The insurance company bears the reasonable cost of removing the car from the scene of the accident to the nearest repairers, and similarly the cost of delivery to the owner after repairs. Repairs, up to a reasonable amount, may be executed without the consent of the company, provided that a detailed estimate is previously obtained.

Liability to the Public. Claims by the public, including passengers, for personal injury or damage to property, including animals, caused by the car. The policy also indemnifies under this section: the insured whilst driving a private car or motor-cycle not belonging to him; relatives or friends not entitled to indemnity under any other policy whilst driving the insured car with the owner's knowledge and consent.

Injury to Owner. Personal injuries sustained in direct connection with the insured car or whilst travelling in any other private car: death, £1,000; loss of two limbs or sight of both eyes, £500; loss of one limb or one eye £250.

Medical Expenses. Where compensation is paid under the provisions of compulsory insurance, and where to the knowledge of the insurer a third party has received hospital treatment, the insurer shall also pay to the hospital a sum not exceeding £25 for each person so treated. This obligation does not apply where a charge has already been made by the hospital.

PRELIMINARIES 15

The cost of a comprehensive policy at tariff rate for a Morgan is £11 5s. With the exception of obtaining a driving licence which form of application must be completed and signed by the applicant in person, the agent supplying the car will, if so requested, attend to all the foregoing details without making any charge for his service in this connection.

LIGHTING REGULATIONS.

During the hours of darkness every car must carry at least two forward white lamps and one red rear light. Each of the forward lights must be not more than four inches from the extreme outside point of the width of the car, which regulation is complied with in the case of the Morgan where the headlamps are fitted near the top of the mudguards. Each of these lamps is fitted with what is termed a double filament bulb, one filament showing a bright light and the other, consuming as it does less current, merely shows a small light. This small light takes the place of the usual sidelamps on a car having two head and two small lamps. One of the number plates must also be illuminated at night, and the usual practice is to make the tail lamp perform the double duty of showing a red light to the rear and a white light on to the back number plate, which method is adopted on the Morgan. "Hours of darkness" are defined by the Ministry of Transport as being from one hour after sunset to one hour before sunrise during official " summer time," and from half an hour after sunset to half an hour before sunrise during the remainder of the year.

AUDIBLE WARNING OF APPROACH.

The law compels all mechanically-propelled vehicles to possess a means by which warning of approach may be given. This, of course, usually takes the form of a horn of some description, but it is as well to point out here that whatever type of instrument is adopted, it must be attached to the vehicle firmly—it is not sufficient, say, for the driver to have a bulb hooter lying loose on the seat by his side. Furthermore, it is now an offence to sound a horn whilst the vehicle is stationary, in just the same manner as it is against the law to use the warning device unnecessarily whilst the car is in motion. It is also an offence to sound the horn between the hours of 11.30 p.m. and 7 a.m. on any road on which there is provided a system of street lighting, furnished by means of lamps placed not more than 200 yards apart. The Morgan is fitted with an electric horn as part of its standard equipment, and this will be found to be both efficient and reliable.

HIRE-PURCHASE BUYING.

This system of purchasing a motor vehicle is to-day approved and practised by many people, and, indeed, it has much in its favour and very little against it. If desired, the agent will arrange all details, and the usual procedure is for the purchaser to deposit one-quarter the price of the car and any accessories, the amount of the tax and insurance premium being added to this sum. The remaining balance is then discharged in a series of monthly instalments extending over a period of twelve, eighteen, or in some cases, twenty-four months. Interest at the rate of 5 per cent per annum is usually charged on the balance after deducting the deposit.

CHAPTER III

DRIVING AND RUNNING-IN

No apology is needed for introducing this chapter, as although a person may be an accomplished car driver or motor-cyclist, he will very possibly feel a little "at sea" on taking over a Morgan, as the control and general "feel" is altogether different from other types of motor vehicles. Nevertheless, so simple is the Morgan that one can almost unhesitatingly state that it is possible to learn to start, drive, control, and stop the machine in well under an hour even if he be a complete novice to the machine, providing the tuition is undertaken on a road which is comparatively free from traffic. Choose a secondary road for preference where the pupil can give his mind entirely to the job in hand without having his attention distracted by lines of passing traffic.

To become a really proficient driver depends to a great extent upon the pupil, but after four hours' driving it should be possible to negotiate the thickest of traffic in any city—the golden rule is to keep calm and avoid getting worried. Do not be over-anxious but pull in to the left-hand side of the road occasionally, stop the engine, and rest for a while.

As previously stated, if you are a holder of a new driving licence you will have to pass a driving test after 1st April, 1935, so it behoves you to become really proficient in the art of driving.

THE CONTROLS.

As with any form of motor vehicle, the driver is called upon to use both hands and both feet. In ordinary straightforward driving, however, it is only necessary to keep the steering straight and observe the courtesy of the road. It is under these latter circumstances that riding in a Morgan can be enjoyed to the full. The controls are clearly shown in Fig. 8, those on the steering wheel being the throttle and air levers which deal with the quantity and strength of petrol mixture reaching the engine and therefore control the speed. The ignition control lever is seldom used except when actually starting up, when it is fully retarded. (This is automatic on the four-cylinder model.) The carburettor and ignition controls are on precisely the same lines as those on most motor-cycles. The front wheel brake lever is centrally situated and is operated by the driver's left hand. The gear lever is next to the brake lever and is the shorter of the two levers (see Figs. 10 and 11). The left and right foot pedals control the clutch and rear wheel brake respectively. The exhaust valve lifter is situated on the near-side of the dash-board, and, except for starting the engine, may be ignored.

Before learning to drive it is advisable to become well versed in the method of starting the engine. Once one has learned how to

(*From "The Motor Cycle"*)

FIG. 8. THE MORGAN "CONTROLS"
(TWO-CYLINDER MODELS)
The Selector Mechanism is at the base of the Gear Lever on the Three-speed Reverse Morgans

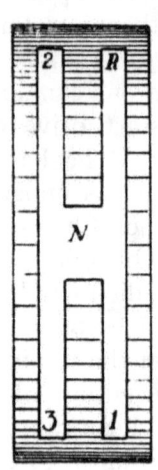

FIG. 9

do this—and the procedure is quite simple—it seems to impart a feeling of confidence with regard to acquiring the art of driving. Electric self-starters are employed on the three-speed models, but it is just as advisable to learn how to swing the engine, in case the starter should fail to work. Ascertain before starting off that there is sufficient petrol and oil in the tanks, and if the engine is of the water-cooled type, see that the radiator is filled to within an inch or two of overflowing.

STARTING THE ENGINE.

Self starters are fitted standard to all three-speed models and will be found quite efficient under normal conditions. The following is the procedure for starting with the handle.

DRIVING AND RUNNING-IN

Before preparing to start up pull the front wheel brake lever back a few notches until a resistance is felt on the lever, indicating that the brakes are on. Next see that the gear lever is resting between the two small projections on the gear gate, or, in the case of the three-speed models, where marked N in Fig. 9. This is termed "neutral," and while the gears are in this position it will be impossible for the engine to propel the car. See that the petrol is on. Now open the throttle lever slightly. Keep the air lever closed, and fully retard the ignition. These carburettor and ignition

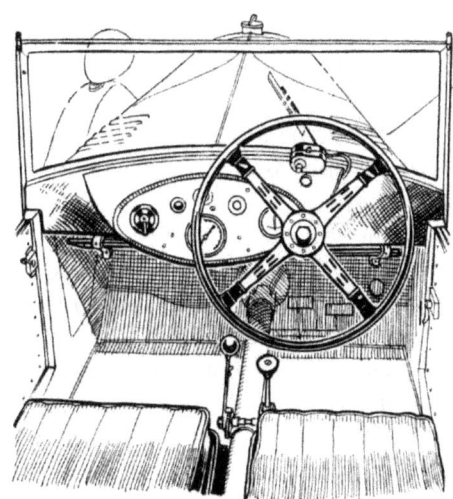

(From "The Motor Cycle")

FIG. 10. THE CONTROLS OF THE FOUR-CYLINDER MODEL.

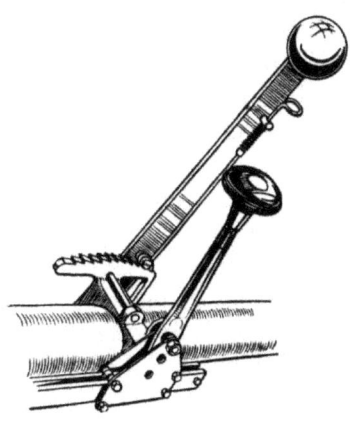

(From "The Motor Cycle")

FIG. 11. THE BRAKE AND GEAR LEVERS.

levers are respectively open and advanced when the lever is moved away from the point where the wire cable and casing enters the control lever body. The carburettor must now be flooded by depressing the tickler in the centre of the float chamber cover. Do not impatiently press this up and down in quick succession—merely keep it down until petrol is seen to drip from the base of the carburettor or from the top of the float chamber. The choke on the four-cylinder model should be in operation before starting a cold engine.

Now insert the starting handle, grasp firmly with the right hand, and make a point of wrapping the thumb round the handle in the same direction as the four fingers. This point is important, as, by its adoption, there is no possibility of receiving a sprained wrist or dislocated thumb should the engine backfire. Do not attempt to "swing" the engine. The coil ignition makes it only necessary to pull sharply over compression for the engine to start. Once the engine is running, advance the ignition control fully, open the air lever, and regulate the speed by means of the throttle lever so that the engine does not "race" at high speed. In addition to serving no useful purpose, it is very bad for the engine to allow it to run fast whilst the car is stationary.

LUBRICATION SYSTEM.

The term " dry sump " indicates that oil is drawn from the tank to the engine by means of an oil pump, and is returned from the engine sump to the tank by means of another pump, thus ensuring a constant circulation of oil in the engine, whilst maintaining a " dry sump."

The level of oil in the tank should never be allowed to fall below the half-full mark. The integral oil pump is of the single plunger, double acting type, the one end of the plunger being used for exhausting the crankcase sump and the other end for delivering oil to all the essential parts of the engine interior, from whence it drains in to the sump to be returned to the tank. No oil " tell-tale " is fitted, but it is important to observe occasionally if the oil is circulating. A practice should be made at the commencement of each run of removing the filler cap from the oil tank and, if correctly circulating, oil will be seen issuing from the pipe immediately under the cap. This check should be made preferably upon starting up the engine from cold, as, owing to the fact that, when stationary, oil from all parts of the engine interior drains back into the sump and until the surplus is cleared the return is very positive, whereas normally it is somewhat spasmodic and mixed with air bubbles, due partly to the fact that the return oil plunger has a greater pumping capacity than that delivering fresh oil and partly to the variations in the amount of oil in suspense in the crankcase, according to engine speed. For example, upon a sudden acceleration the return flow may cease entirely for a time only, of course to resume at a greater rate than normal upon deceleration. No provision is made for external adjustment of the oil supply, the correct delivery to each part of the engine being arranged internally, by suitably dimensioned passages. It might here be explained that, in the case of the " Matchless " type engine, oil is forced direct to the timing gear chamber, which, after filling same to a pre-determined level, overflows into the flywheel chamber and so drains away to the sump. Oil is also forced into the timing gear side flywheel axle bearing, and thence through a drilled passage in the flywheel to the

DRIVING AND RUNNING-IN

big end bearings, the splash from which passes up into the cylinder interiors. In addition to this splash, the cylinders are provided with direct oil passages, ensuring an adequate supply under all conditions for these, the most vital parts of the engine. In the case of the J.A.P. engine, oil is fed by gravity to one end of a double acting pump, whence it is forced through the centre of the timing spindle shaft, the main shaft, a passage drilled in the flywheel, and then through the centre of the crank pin to the big end bearing itself.

(*From "The Motor Cycle"*)
FIG. 12. SHOWING THE ADJUSTABLE OIL FEED TO THE INLET VALVE GUIDES ON THE TWIN-CYLINDER MODELS

(*From "The Motor Cycle"*)
FIG. 13. THE GEAR BOX FILLER PLUG IS BETWEEN THE REAR SEATS ON FOUR-SEATER MODELS

From the big end bearing oil escapes into the interior of the crankcase, and by splash system lubricates No. 1 cylinder wall and piston. No. 2 cylinder is lubricated by a by-pass from the pressure side of the pump connected to the cylinder wall.

The driving and timing spindle bearings are lubricated by oil collecting upon the crankcase walls and draining through specially prepared pockets of oil holes in the bearings. All oil eventually drains back into the sump, from whence it is forced by the other end of the double-acting pump plunger back into the oil tank.

The crankcases of both engines are maintained under a partial vacuum. Thus, oil vapour or mist, which condenses to the bottom of the box situated beneath the timing case, is drawn back into the engine via a $\frac{3}{16}$ in. diameter pipe. This pipe leads from the bottom of the box to the underside of the timing side main bearing.

No attention to this oiling system is required other than observing the return of oil to the tank prior to a run, and the continual replenishment of the supply tank, the level of oil in which, as mentioned above, must be above the half-full mark and must not be filled when the engine is cold to a level higher than 1 in. below the return pipe outlet.

The entire system is simplicity itself, only one moving part being employed, viz. the double diameter plunger. This plunger is rotated by the engine shaft, and moves backward and forward while rotating under the influence of the small guide screw which engages with the profiled annular groove cut in the plunger end. As the plunger moves in its housing in one direction, the large end draws oil from the sump, while at the same time the smaller end is delivering fresh oil to the various channels provided. Upon the reverse movement of the plunger the large end returns to the tank the oil already drawn from the sump, while the smaller end draws a fresh charge of oil from the tank in readiness for delivery to the engine upon the following movement of the plunger. This action, of course, goes on all the while the engine is revolving, and since the exhausting plunger is the larger one the engine sump is always kept clear of oil, hence the term "dry sump," while at the same time a large quantity of clean, cool oil is being forced under pressure to all working parts. A filter for the oil is provided and will be found on the side of the tank. This filter consists of a cartridge through which the oil is compelled to pass before returning to the tank. This cartridge filter can be removed after unscrewing the hexagon-headed cap. It should be removed and cleaned in petrol at least once every 2,000 miles, while once each season or not less frequently than once every 5,000 miles the tank should be thoroughly washed out with petrol and afterwards filled to correct level with fresh, clean oil. To avoid undue waste it is permissible to arrange for this clean-out when the oil is at the lowest recommended level, although it must be pointed out that normally it is highly desirable to add fresh oil frequently in small quantities in preference to allowing the supply to become almost exhausted before refilling, the reason for this being that the more oil there is in the tank, the cooler it will keep in circulation.

FOUR-CYLINDER LUBRICATION SYSTEM.

Fig. 14 shows the details of the lubrication system. All parts of the engine are lubricated from the oil reservoir in the sump, by gear

DRIVING AND RUNNING-IN

pump to all crankshaft main bearings, connecting rod big end bearings, and camshaft bearings, and by splash to the remainder of the engine.

Engine	Summer	Winter
J.A.P. . . .	Patent Castrol XL Triple Shell	Patent Castrol XL Triple Shell
Matchless . . .	Patent Castrol XL Triple Shell	Patent Castrol XL Triple Shell
Ford	Patent Castrol XL Triple Shell	Patent Castrol AA Triple Shell

DRIVING OFF.

Having seated yourself comfortably at the steering wheel, depress the clutch pedal (the one on the left) and engage low gear by pushing the gear lever forward (or backward in the case of the three-speed models) so that it passes the foremost of the small projections on the gear gate (two-speed models). If the gear lever will not pass this point do not attempt to force it, but return it to neutral and remove the foot from the clutch pedal momentarily. Then again push the clutch down and make another attempt to engage the gears. Having engaged low gear, release the hand brake lever, open the throttle a little, and, keeping a careful eye on the direction of travel, very gently release the foot pressure from the clutch pedal, when the car will commence to glide forward. If the clutch pedal is released too suddenly either the engine will stop or alternatively the car will lurch forward with a jerk. To stop, all that is necessary is to press both foot pedals down simultaneously. Before removing the feet from the pedals bring the gear lever to neutral and pull the hand brake on. It is excellent practice to go through all this procedure several times in order to become familiar with the steering and general " feel " of the controls. Having thus far made satisfactory progress, there only remains the changing of the gear, from " first " to " second " and " second " to " top."

The gears are changed when the machine has attained a speed of about ten to fifteen miles an hour, and the procedure is as follows. Having attained the necessary speed in low gear, depress the clutch pedal and close the throttle almost fully. Then pull the gear lever back as far as it will go, which will be just beyond the rearmost

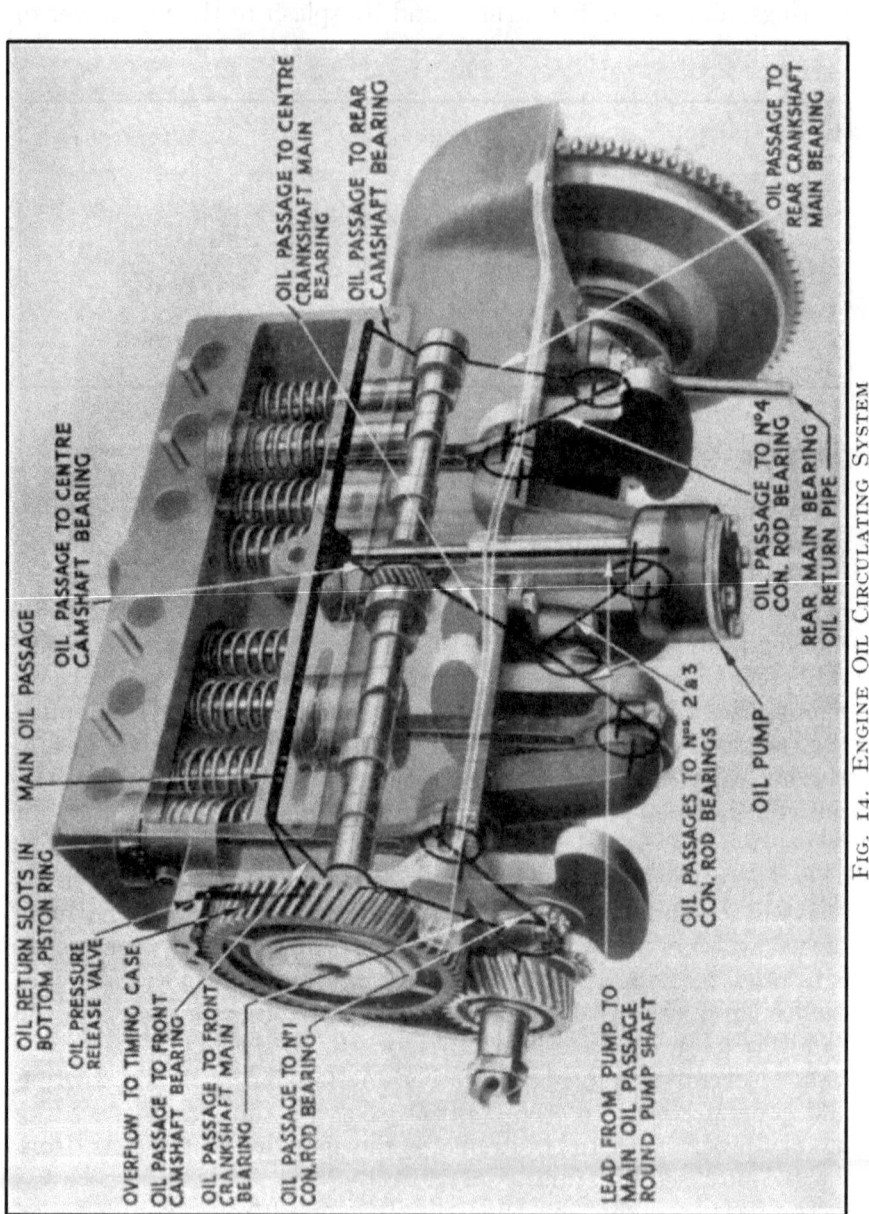

Fig. 14. Engine Oil Circulating System

DRIVING AND RUNNING-IN

projection on the gear gate. On the three-speed models the gear lever should be moved forward, which is the second gear, until sufficient speed has been obtained, when the lever should then be moved to the left through neutral and again forward. (See Fig. 9.) Now remove the foot from the clutch pedal (there is no need to do this slowly this time) and open the throttle again. The speed of the car is now controlled entirely by the throttle, clutch, and brakes.

It should be borne in mind, however, that a good driver prides himself on using the brakes as little as possible when on the open road or approaching traffic or corners. When actually in traffic, or driving in town, matters are somewhat different, and the brakes are then used very frequently, as is also the clutch of course, the latter when slowing down to a standstill or to change gear.

CHANGING DOWN.

Changing from top to a lower gear is quite a simple matter. Moreover, owing to the remarkable pulling powers of the Morgan, it is seldom necessary to change to the lowest ratio. Almost any hill one is likely to encounter may be climbed " on top " with ease, but should the car be slowed down to seven or eight miles an hour owing to traffic or other circumstances, it is advisable to change to a lower gear in order to accelerate smartly and without stressing the engine. The best method of effecting a downward change is that of " double de-clutching," and the procedure is as follows. First de-clutch and slip the gear lever into neutral. Then release the clutch pedal, and slightly accelerate the engine speed by the hand throttle. Now, whilst the engine is still running fairly fast owing to its being disconnected from the driving wheel, by reason of the gears being in neutral, again depress the clutch-pedal, at the same time pushing the gear lever into second or first gear position, when the clutch may be gently released and the speed of the car again controlled by the throttle, and, if necessary, the brakes. If the road speed of the car is very low at the time it is desired to change down, it will be unnecessary to speed up the engine whilst the gears are in neutral, but the double de-clutching process as above explained is well worth carrying out for all changes of this nature. The rule when changing down is: the higher the road speed, the higher must the engine speed be, and it will be found that if, for any reason, one has to make a change to low when travelling at, say, 15 m.p.h., quite a liberal throttle opening will be necessary in order to avoid a bad change, which will give evidence by giving forth an unpleasant mechanical grating noise; and, indeed, if a really clumsy change is made some damage may result.

When driving, exercise all possible care, keep a look-out for cyclists or other vehicles suddenly emerging from side roads, or for pedestrians suddenly stepping off the pavement or dashing from behind stationary trams and buses. Use the front-wheel brakes as much as the rear, especially if the road surface is wet or greasy, and give consideration to other road users.

RUNNING-IN.

The first hundred miles or so will have a very big effect on the performance of the car, and more particularly the engine, in its later life, and it is whilst this small distance is being covered that extreme care in handling is called for. The following two hundred miles should also see no hard driving if the best results are hoped for, and in reality it is an accepted fact that as many as 500 miles is necessary before an engine can be safely passed as be ng run in. It is difficult to give any speed above which it might be undesirable to indulge in, but a rough guide would be to say, " Do not exceed 30 m.p.h. for the first 500 miles." A better method is to refrain from opening the throttle more than one-third of its full range for this distance, and if the engine shows signs of labouring or pulling hard on a hill or when travelling slowly in traffic, do not hesitate to change to the lower gear. The idea is to keep the engine as cool as possible, and owing to its newness it will probably be somewhat stiff with regard to some of its bearings—particularly so where the pistons are concerned, as these are now made of an alloy of aluminium on all Morgan engines, and this alloy has the property of expanding when heated more than iron or steel. The result might be that one or both pistons would, if allowed to overheat or run short of oil, become too tight a fit in its cylinder bore, thereby setting up a seized piston. Keep the chains, clutch, sliding axles, and the brake gear and operating joints well greased, and give an eye to the quantity of grease in the bevel box occasionally; this should be kept absolutely full with a good grade of lubricant of about the consistency of butter—i.e. a heavy bodied grease. (Wakefield's " Gear Ease " is recommended.)

The correct grade of oil to be used in the three-speed gear boxes is Patent Castrol " D." A heavier grade, such as "Wormease," may be used during the summer months, but starting may then be difficult, owing to the drag of the oil on the gears. Oil should be maintained at such a level that the mainshaft is half covered with lubricant when the gears are stationary. The capacity is $2\frac{1}{2}$ pints.

TYRE PRESSURES

Front	Rear
19 lb. per sq. in.	25 lb. per sq. in.

CHAPTER IV

ENGINE MAINTENANCE AND OVERHAULING

WE now come to the question of keeping the engine in good running order, as, like all things mechanical, the engine calls for a certain amount of attention from time to time in order to get the best and most economical results. The engines as fitted to the Morgan are all well-tried products and have been on the market for a number of years, so the prospective purchaser may select whichever type he thinks will best suit his purpose, knowing that he cannot possibly pick one which has not passed through the experimental stages.

In view of the very big differences in construction, etc., the maintenance of the four-cylinder model is dealt with separately at the end of this chapter.

DECARBONIZING TWO-CYLINDER MODELS.

After a period of running, every internal combustion engine forms a deposit of carbon in the combustion chambers, i.e. the cylinder heads, piston heads, round the valve ports and guides, behind the piston rings, and underneath the heads of the pistons. This deposit is formed chiefly of burnt oil, road matter which is drawn into the engine via the carburettor, and is also the product of the combustion of the petrol. This deposit is very detrimental to the running of the engine if allowed to form in excessive quantities, giving cause, as it does, to overheating, heavy petrol consumption, harsh running, and "knocking" or "pinking," the latter effects having a disastrous effect on the life of the engine bearings. Benzol mixture in lieu of petrol will lessen the tendency to knock, and if it is not convenient to decarbonize the engine at the time, this substitute may be adopted, but it is only a temporary palliative and the carbon should be removed at the first opportunity.

The task should take about four hours, although this depends in a great measure upon the skill and appliances to hand. No special tools are required other than those supplied with the standard tool-kit, and the job, though a dirty one, is interesting, and most owners prefer to carry out the work themselves. In this case, if one is a novice, it is as well to have the assistance of an expert on the first occasion. Alternatively, a garage will

ENGINE MAINTENANCE AND OVERHAULING

undertake the job at a cost of, roughly, a pound or twenty-five shillings. Decarbonizing should be carried out in the first thousand miles of running in the case of a new machine, thereafter every 4,000 to 5,000 miles should be sufficient—the period depends, to a great extent, upon the quantity and quality of the oil used.

DISMANTLING.

The procedure, in the case of water-cooled models, is first to drain the radiator, turn off the petrol tap and undo the union nuts at each end of the petrol pipe, when this will be free. Unscrew the union nuts at each end of the induction pipe where it is attached to the cylinders when the carburettor will merely be attached to the car by the control wires. It is as well at this point to tie this member loosely to the radiator spout in order to avoid kinking the Bowden wires. Disconnect the exhaust pipes at the cylinder exhaust ports, taking care of the copper-asbestos flange washers or rings which are there to make a gas-tight joint, so ensuring quiet running.

Remove the aluminium valve covers in the case of the overhead valve J.A.P. engine, take

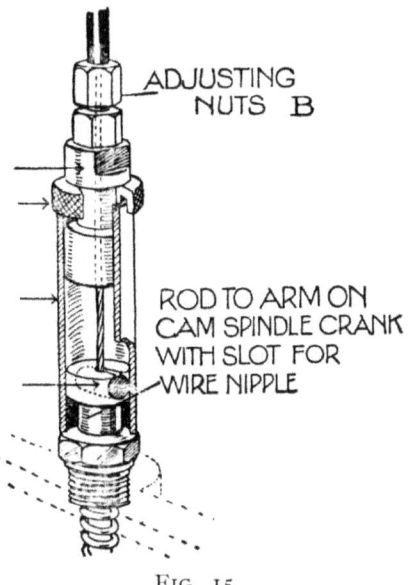

FIG. 15

out the sparking plugs, compression taps (if any), and also, in the case of side-valve engines, the valve caps. Disconnect the exhaust lifter wire where it is attached on the top of the crankcase—this can be easily done if the Bowden adjuster is first screwed down as far as possible, taking care to first run the lock-nut up to the top of its threads, Fig. 15. It is a good plan to have two boxes, one relating to each cylinder, into which all small parts, such as sparking plugs, washers, etc., can be placed. There is then very little risk of any small part becoming mislaid, and the system of having a box for each cylinder ensures that when re-assembling, each cylinder will receive the part with which it was originally fitted. On the side-valve water-cooled engines the water pipes must be disconnected at the four points where they meet the cylinders.

On over-head valve engines it is only necessary to disconnect the two top pipes.

Now, in the case of over-head valve engines which have detachable cylinder heads, each head is held down on to its cylinder barrel by four bolts having hexagon heads. If the heads are stuck down, it is usually possible to free them by alternately lifting with a fairly sharp jerk at the exhaust and inlet ports alternately. In passing, it may be pointed out that all threads are of the right-hand type as in normal practice—that is to say, looking end-on at the nut or bolt, whichever it is desired to undo, it should be turned in an anti-clockwise direction.

REMOVING OVERHEAD VALVES.

The cylinder heads having been removed, place one head on the bench, or large strong box if no bench is available, and remove the valves. To do this it will be necessary to first remove the valve cotters, so releasing the springs. To do this, place a small block of wood under the valve heads. Then, having removed the hardened steel caps fitted loosely on the end of the valve stem, depress the valve springs and valve spring collars and remove the split collars which encircle the valve stems. The springs are rather strong, and it is advisable to enlist the services of a friend for this operation. Special valve spring compressing tools can be obtained from the makers of the engine and these simplify the task considerably. The valves will now slide through their guides, and, if they are not marked on their head to show which is the inlet and which the exhaust, care must be taken to ensure that they are replaced correctly.

The actual process of decarbonizing may now be carried out, and cleaning in turn the piston top, cylinder head and valve ports, and cleaning the valves and polishing with very fine emery cloth. The utmost care should be taken to ensure that every trace of carbon is removed from all parts by means of a blunt knife or an old screw-driver. Take care not to damage the piston heads, as these are made of aluminium which, owing to its comparative softness, is easily scratched. The cylinder heads are cast iron and cannot be hurt by scraping, but the two narrow rings whereon the valve heads seat must be avoided in the scraping process—only a very slight scratch across either of these seatings may result in a loss of compression, unless the scratch can be removed in the course of grinding the valves.

The engine may be rotated to get the pistons to the top of their

ENGINE MAINTENANCE AND OVERHAULING

stroke when it is desired to clean the piston tops, but before commencing this it is advisable to remove the gasket in order to avoid damaging it during the decarbonizing. The same gaskets may be used again providing they have suffered no damage in the course of dismantling the cylinder heads.

VALVE GRINDING.

Some owners do not believe in grinding-in the valves each time the engine is decarbonized, but it will be found that if this item is overlooked on some occasions the seatings will be in a rather bad state and may call for a considerable amount of grinding before

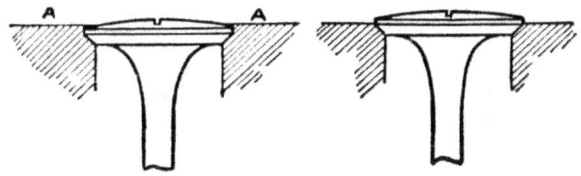

FIG. 16. DIAGRAM ILLUSTRATING HOW VALVES BECOME POCKETED AFTER FREQUENT REGRINDING

they can be restored to perfection. On the other hand, if the work is done every time the engine is decarbonized, very little time need be spent before good results are obtained, and one has the satisfaction of knowing that a thorough job has been made when the machine is restored to running order.

To grind a valve, the chamfered face must first of all be smeared lightly with a mixture of emery paste and oil. The addition of a little paraffin will lessen the tendency for the oil to dry up during the grinding-in. The valve must be replaced in the valve guide and rotated in a back and forward manner so that the chamfered face rubs with the seating in the cylinder head. After about half a dozen rubs move the valve round so that its face makes contact with a different portion of the valve seat. Repeat this operation several times, occasionally supplying a little grinding paste to the faces. The valve may be considered to be properly ground-in when its face and seating present a perfectly bright ring. Avoid the tendency merely to rotate the valve on its seating in a continuous direction, do not use a coarse abrasive, and be very careful not to overdo the grinding-in which, if indulged in too frequently or for too long at a time will result in the valves becoming "pocketed" owing to the metal forming the seating having been ground away. (Fig. 16.) The side-valve engines have valves with a slot across the head, which permits the grinding-in to be carried out with a screw-driver, but the over-head valve types, owing to the absence of this slot, call for a special grinding tool which may be obtained from the manufacturers concerned. Before replacing the valves every precaution must be taken to remove all traces of the grinding compound from the valves and cylinder head. This is best done by washing in paraffin. Smear the valve stems with a composition of powdered graphite and oil which may be purchased ready mixed from most garages, and replace in their guides, assembling with the springs, etc.

REPLACING CYLINDER HEADS.

When replacing the cylinder heads, everything must be scrupulously clean, particularly the faces on the head and cylinder barrel. The four bolt holes must be cleaned out unless one had the forethought to loosely screw in the cylinder-head bolts before cleaning the piston heads. Both sides on the gasket should be scrubbed with a wire brush, and the gasket may then be covered on each side with a thin coating of one of the proprietary jointing compounds. The cylinder-head bolts, should be tightened down equally in turn so as to ensure that the head is evenly pulled down on to the gasket. Before inserting the cylinder-head bolts it is a good tip to smear their threads with graphite, which will ensure their easy removal next time.

REMOVING CYLINDERS.

Should it be desired to inspect the pistons or main bearings, or to remove the carbon from beneath the piston crowns, the cylinder barrels must be removed, and this is best done before the cylinder heads are replaced. Also, in the case of J.A.P. side-valve engines, the following notes apply without exception, as, as previously stated, this type of engine has fixed cylinder heads, consequently the barrel must of necessity be removed when the time for decarbonizing arrives. The four nuts at each cylinder base must be removed, and, in the case of those nuts at the rear of the cylinders, it will be found that these are rather inaccessible. True, they can be got at without disturbing the crankcase, but by far the best method is to disconnect the engine from the chassis and slide it forward an inch or two. The procedure is as follows. Unscrew the four set-bolts holding the crankcase into the chassis, remove the pivot pin holding the clutch withdrawal fork in position just behind the flywheel, and disconnect the Bowden ignition wire operating the ignition advance

ENGINE MAINTENANCE AND OVERHAULING

and retard. The engine may now be drawn forward, or if desired, removed entirely from the chassis. When lifting the cylinders, get a friend to steady the piston as it leaves the cylinder mouth in order to prevent its becoming damaged.

The gudgeon pins are a floating fit and it is only necessary to push these out in order to free the pistons from the connecting rods, bearing in mind the fact that these components should be replaced in the same order. Wrap clean cloths round the connecting rods so as to keep any dirt from falling into the crankcase. It is advisable to remove the piston rings so that the carbon in their grooves may be removed, but it must be borne in mind that these rings are cast iron and are exceedingly brittle (Fig. 17). The safest way is to insert three or four narrow strips of thin sheet tin under the ring at regular intervals round the circumference in order to hold the ring out of its slot, when it will be easy to slip the ring from off the piston, laying each one down in such a manner that it may be replaced in its correct groove. The gudgeon pins, minus their pistons, can now be placed in the small end of the connecting rod and tested for wear in the gudgeon pin bush. They should just be a smooth fit when free from oil. If the pins themselves are worn they will give evidence of this by two small steps, each of which can be felt by lightly drawing the finger nail endways along the pin. The steps, if any, will each be found about an inch or so from the ends of the gudgeon pin.

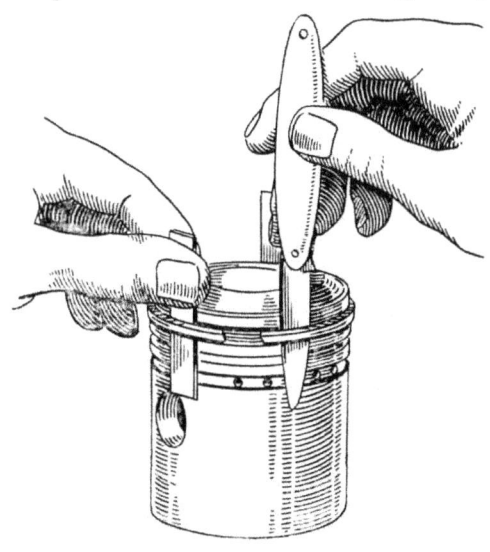

FIG. 17. REMOVING PISTON RINGS

TESTING THE BIG ENDS.

Up and down play in the big-end bearings may be looked for after the crankcase has been washed out with paraffin. The method of testing the big-end bearings is to first get the connecting rod in its topmost position by turning the flywheel and then, grasping the top of the rod, slowly pull upwards and push downwards, when any slack or wear in the bearings will be felt. A bearing in good order will not permit of the connecting rod being moved vertically at its lower extremity, although the side-play here is essential, as is also the case with regard to the piston, when fitted to the connecting rod.

FLUSHING OUT THE CRANKCASE.

Before flushing out the crankcase, remove the drain plug fitted in the base of the crankcase and allow all the oil to drain off. Then pour about a quart of light flushing oil in (after replacing the drain plug, of course), and, holding each connecting rod at the top, revolve the flywheels so as to distribute the oil and give it a chance to cleanse the bearings. When draining off, leave the plug out for ten minutes or so in order to leave as little of the oil behind as possible. Then replace the plug and pour about a quarter of a pint of engine oil into the crankcase, and see that the pistons are oiled before replacing the cylinders. Set the piston rings so that their gaps are an equal distance from each other. When replacing the induction pipe take care to tighten each nut a little at a time in order to avoid air leaks at this point. Adjust the tappets as follows: When the engine is cold the tappets should have a minimum clearance, so that they are just freed. The Matchless engines should have a clearance of ·004 for the inlet valve and ·006 for the exhaust valve. After the engine has been run for a short time and all the working parts have become warmed up, tighten all nuts again and then check the tappet clearances. The cylinder holding down nuts must be tightened down alternately, a little at a time, as otherwise the cylinder neck may be strained. In the case of over-head valve engines, it will usually be found that the cylinder-head nuts will need a considerable amount of tightening down during the first few miles after having been disturbed. If a Matchless engine is to be dismantled, the crankcase must not on any account be separated until the pump plunger has been withdrawn. To withdraw this plunger, first remove both end caps and also the guide screw, when the plunger can be pushed out large end first. When reassembling, this plunger must be inserted after the crankcase sections have been bolted together, and before refitting the end caps the guide screw must be replaced with its relieved tip engaging the profiled cam groove in the plunger. By moving the plunger to and fro while this screw is being introduced, the correct location of the groove can be easily felt, and the screw in question must be finally firmly screwed home.

ENGINE MAINTENANCE AND OVERHAULING   35

THE TIMING GEAR.

If it is necessary to inspect the cam wheels the timing gear cover must be removed, and this can only be done after the magneto or distributor has been taken off. A pan or some receptacle should be provided to catch the oil as the timing cover is being removed. This oil need not be replaced when refitting the cover as, when the engine is started, the oiling system will commence to build up the required level.

The re-timing of valves or ignition appears to most beginners to be shrouded in mystery, but in reality it is by no means difficult, although the services of one who has had previous experience of the job are worth having at the first attempt. Should such a person not be available, however, all that is necessary is a little care and thought.

RE-TIMING THE VALVES.

In re-timing an engine of the V-twin variety, always work on the "back" cylinder which is termed No 1. In the case of the Morgan, the "back" cylinder is the one nearest the driver's side. (Fig. 18.) Over-head valve engines are easier to time when the cylinder heads are off, but side-valve engines must be timed with the cylinders *in situ*. The method of timing by degrees is far more accurate than by fractions of an inch, but entails having the engine away from the chassis in order that a disc cut from cardboard may be affixed to the flywheel. This disc should be of the same diameter as the flywheel, and should be marked off in degrees, i.e. its circumference should be divided and marked off in 360 equal parts, each part of course representing one degree. The disc should now be fitted to the flywheel by the small screws which normally hold the clutch dust cover in position. Next, make up a pointer from thin sheet metal and fix this firmly to any convenient bolt on the crankcase so that the pointed end can be bent to almost touch the divisions on the cardboard disc. The flywheel must now be rotated until the piston of No. 1 cylinder is exactly at the top of the stroke, and a mark made on the disc at the exact spot at which the pointer registers. For the purpose of carrying out the timing, it must now be remembered that the engine runs in a clockwise direction when one faces the timing gear, so that to get the piston to a point "after top dead centre" (t.d.c.) the flywheel must be turned clockwise, and of course "before t.d.c." is obtained by rotating the flywheel in an anti-clockwise direction, assuming that the piston was at top dead centre at first. Bear in mind at the same time, however, that one of the cam wheels must run in an anti-clockwise direction owing to the gearing so ordaining matters, This fact is mentioned, as, to a beginner, it is likely to be somewhat confusing. The cam wheels must be inserted whilst No. 1 piston is at the points given hereafter: J.A.P. over-head valve, inlet valve just opening 15 degrees (or $\frac{3}{32}$ in. on piston) before top dead centre. Exhaust valve closes $22\frac{1}{2}$ degrees (or $\frac{5}{32}$ in. on piston) after top dead centre, i.e. when the flywheel has been rotated through $37\frac{1}{2}$ degrees

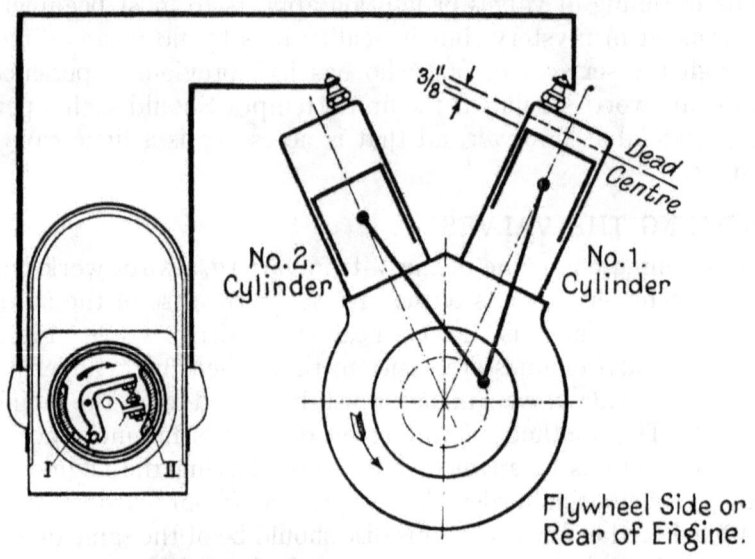

FIG. 18. VALVE TIMING DIAGRAM (J.A.P. ENGINE)

which can be found of course by referring to the timing disc. J.A.P. side-valve, inlet valve just opening 10 degrees (or $\frac{1}{32}$ in. on piston) before top dead centre. Exhaust valve just closed 20 degrees (or $\frac{1}{8}$ in. on piston) after top dead centre.

Having timed No. 1 cylinder, turn the flywheel back so that this piston is approximately at the top of the stroke, when, upon inspecting the piston of No. 2 it will be seen that this is only about two-thirds on its way from bottom dead centre. (Fig. 18.) The procedure now is to turn the flywheel in a clockwise direction until No. 2 piston is at the top of the stroke and then proceed through another complete revolution of the flywheel during which No. 2 piston will travel downwards and up again to the top. It is now at the correct top dead centre position to insert the cam wheel. The instructions for timing the valves of No. 1 cylinder now being applied to those of No. 2. In order to carry out any timing

ENGINE MAINTENANCE AND OVERHAULING

operations on side-valve engines it is desirable to remove the valve caps so that the position of the piston may be readily seen. Alternatively, removal of the compression taps will permit of a length of wire being inserted so that the piston may be felt. In this case it is a good plan to mark the wire at the point where the piston is at top dead centre.

To remove the cam wheel on the Matchless engines, gently turn the engine until the marks on both cam wheel and small pinion coincide, when, by raising the front inlet valve by means of a screwdriver or suitable lever, the cam wheel is free to be withdrawn.

When replacing the cam wheel, unless help is available to raise the inlet valve as directed above, it is necessary to hold it in a raised position by inserting a block of suitable height between the cylinder base and the lower valve spring cap. Then, holding all four cam levers up with the fingers, gently insert the cam wheel with its marked tooth gap coinciding with the marked tooth of the small pinion. After carefully cleaning the faces of the timing gear case and cover, and smearing the latter with quick-drying gold size, gently apply the cover with screw holes in correct register, when all fixing screws should be thoroughly and evenly tightened down with a good stout screwdriver.

MAGNETO TIMING.

The timing disc may also be used for timing the magneto, and in the case of J.A.P. engines the ignition control lever should be in the fully advanced position for timing purposes. Particular care must be taken when timing to see that the fibre heel of the contact breaker bell-crank lever is engaging with the correct cam. These cams are usually marked I and II (Fig. 18), which figures relate to the respective cylinders, as previously mentioned. The easiest way to decide which cam is the correct one for No. 1 cylinder is by putting the straightedge across the cams at the points where the fibre heel will first strike, No. 1 cam being that which is farthest from the point of contact of No. 2, having regard to the normal direction of rotation of the contact breaker, as shown in Fig. 18. Now, assuming the valves have been properly timed, turn the flywheel until the inlet valve on No. 1 opens, and proceed until this valve closes, when the piston will be rising on the compression stroke, which is the one on which the contact breaker points should be timed to open. When the piston is nearing the top of the compression stroke, couple up the magneto drive so that the platinum points on the contact breaker are just commencing to separate on No. 1 cam as set out for the different engines: J.A.P. over-head valve and J.A.P. side-valve 40 degrees before the piston is at top dead centre. There is no need to check the timing of No. 2 cylinder, as, contrary to the valve timing, if the magneto timing is correct for one, it must, automatically, be right for the other cylinder.

Before rotating the engine it will now be necessary to remove one of the high-tension pick-up brush holders carrying the high-tension lead and inspect the distributor ring through the orifice. If a segment of brass embedded in the vulcanite is visible, that particular wire must be led to No. 1 cylinder, but if only the vulcanite can be seen the wire must be connected to No. 2 cylinder, the remaining lead going to the other cylinder, of course.

On the models employing coil ignition the following notes will be found useful.

COIL IGNITION. (J.A.P. ENGINE.)

The combined distributor and contact breaker is usually carried in a clip attached to the timing lever. The timing can be adjusted by loosening the clamping screw on the clip, and turning the distributor housing in the desired direction. The contact breaker heel is thus moved round the cam, and so the positions of firing are altered.

Before removing the distributor from the engine for any reason it is advisable to mark the distributor housing and lever so that it can be replaced in the same position and so avoid re-timing.

The general procedure for timing or checking the timing is as follows.

Turn the engine over until No. 1 piston is at the top of its compression stroke (that is, on top dead centre). On most engines this position is indicated by a mark on the flywheel. Fully retard the ignition control.

With the engine and the control set in the above position, the timing is correct if the contacts are just commencing to separate and the metal electrode on the rotating distributor arm is pointing to the insert in the moulding connected to plug No. 1. If necessary, slacken the clamping screw on the timing lever, and turn the distributor housing until this position is found. After setting the distributor, tighten the clip.

It should be seen that the plugs are connected to the distributor in sequence according to the firing order of the engine.

If, on running the engine, the firing is found to be slightly too

ENGINE MAINTENANCE AND OVERHAULING

early, or too late, this may be corrected by again slackening the clamping screw, and turning the distributor a fraction in the required direction, afterwards tightening the clamping clip.

COIL IGNITION. (MATCHLESS ENGINE.)

Remove two screws holding the bakelite cover of the distributor and take the cover off. Then take out the small rotor arm which will be observed immediately under the cover. This is not fixed in any way and all that is necessary to remove it is a gentle pull outwards with the fingers. Next slacken off the distributor cam so that it is free to be turned in any required direction. The cam fits on to a taper and by releasing the small screw that will be seen in the centre of the cam, the latter will be drawn off its taper automatically. Rotate the engine by hand until the piston in No. 1 (R.H., or driver's side) cylinder is seven-sixteenths of an inch before the top dead centre of the compression stroke (i.e. the stroke upwards immediately after inlet has closed). Then with ignition lever in fully advanced position and the cam loose on the shaft, move the cam round until the points are just about to break. Carefully note that the cam does not move and gently tap back on to the taper and tighten up the screw. Re-check to ascertain that no alteration has taken place when tightening up cam.

Start up the engine and fully retard the ignition. With the throttle fully open the engine should run at about 1,500 to 1,600 revolutions per minute, i.e. at about the same speed as 25 to 28 miles per hour. If any considerable variation to this speed is obtained an alteration in the required direction should be made. When satisfied that the timing is correct, refix the rotor and cover.

CARE OF THE MAGNETO.

The magneto is an instrument which most motorists regard with awe. They know little about it, and in the majority of cases they do not want to know. Fortunately, however, a knowledge of its functions is by no means necessary, for practically the only parts which ever require attention, and to which, at any rate, the ordinary driver can attend himself, are the contact breaker and the pick-up. The first essential in both these departments is absolute cleanliness. The contact breaker points should only require adjustment at long intervals, but it is of the utmost importance that they should be kept clean and free from oil; otherwise difficult starting, misfiring, and loss of power will result.

If adjustment should become necessary it can be effected without removing the contact breaker. The engine should be rotated by hand until the points are seen to be fully opened. An examination will show that of the two points one is attached to the rocker arm and the other to a fixed pin which has, at its extremity, a lock nut. The lock nut should be loosened with the magneto spanner provided for the purpose, and the hexagon head which is immediately adjacent to the point should be turned with the same spanner until the correct gap is obtained. The magneto spanner has attached to it,

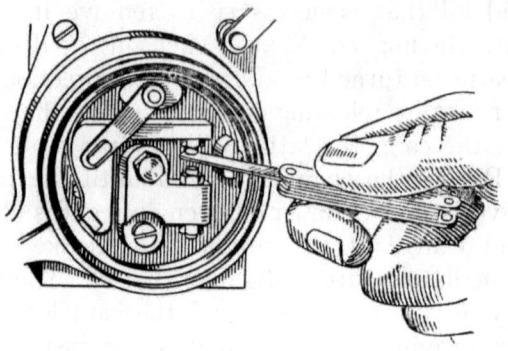

Fig. 19. Contact Breaker, showing Gap being Tested (Magneto)

incidentally, a gauge for finding the correct gap. When this gap has been obtained the lock nut should be tightened, it being noted that the pin itself does not revolve while this is being done. After tightening the lock nut it is, in any case, advisable to check the gap once more. (See Fig. 19.)

Freeing a Stuck Rocker Arm. It should be noted that the rocker arm of the magneto is not sticking open, i.e. that it is working freely on its bearing. If it is found to be stiff, the contact breaker complete should be removed. This is done by unscrewing the primary pin, of which the hexagon head may be seen in the centre of the contact breaker. The contact breaker itself may then be levered gently out of its taper, and the rocker arm bearing cleaned and polished. In order to do this the flat locating spring must be pushed to one side, when the rocker arm can be prised off its bearing. (See Fig. 20.) At the same time the points should be examined, and, if found to be burned or blackened they should be cleaned with a very fine emery cloth, or file, and afterwards washed in petrol. Great care must be taken that all metal dust or particles of dirt are wiped away before the contact breaker is reassembled.

The contact breaker cannot be replaced in a wrong position, since it is definitely located by a key and keyway. Each pick-up

ENGINE MAINTENANCE AND OVERHAULING

is held in place by two screws, which, when removed, will allow the high-tension pick-up brush to be removed complete with its holder. This should be dry and clean, and any oil or dirt should therefore be removed with a cloth moistened in petrol. If the carbon brush is oily it is probable that there is a certain amount of oil on the slip-ring in the magneto itself. To clean this, insert a corner of a cloth into the hole revealed by the removal of the pick-up and push it down with the end of a pencil. Then revolve the engine

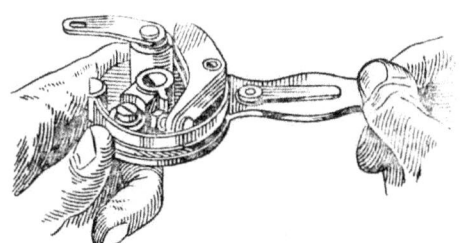

FIG. 20. REMOVING ROCKER ARM OF CONTACT BREAKER

two or three times. When the cloth is removed it will probably be found to be oily, and the operation should be carried out again until it comes out quite clean.

COIL IGNITION EQUIPMENT

Very little attention is needed to keep the coil ignition equipment in first class condition. It should be inspected occasionally, and the following instructions on lubrication, cleaning, and adjustment should be carried out. As the set also depends on the battery and dynamo, maintenance hints are given for those units on pages 90 and 104.

LUBRICATION.

Distributor Shaft. The greaser on distributor shaft should be given one turn about every 500 miles. Re-pack the greaser with a good quality high melting point grease when necessary.

Cam. About every 3,000 miles give the cam the slightest smear of vaseline.

CLEANING AND ADJUSTMENT.

Distributors and Contact Breaker. The distributor shaft carries a 2 lobe cam, and is driven at half-engine speed, so that the contacts open once each revolution of the engine. Occasionally remove the distributor moulding by pushing aside its two securing springs.

See that the electrodes are clean and free from deposit. If necessary, wipe out the distributor with a dry duster and clean the electrodes with a cloth moistened with petrol. Clean the outside of the moulding, particularly the spaces between the terminals. Next examine

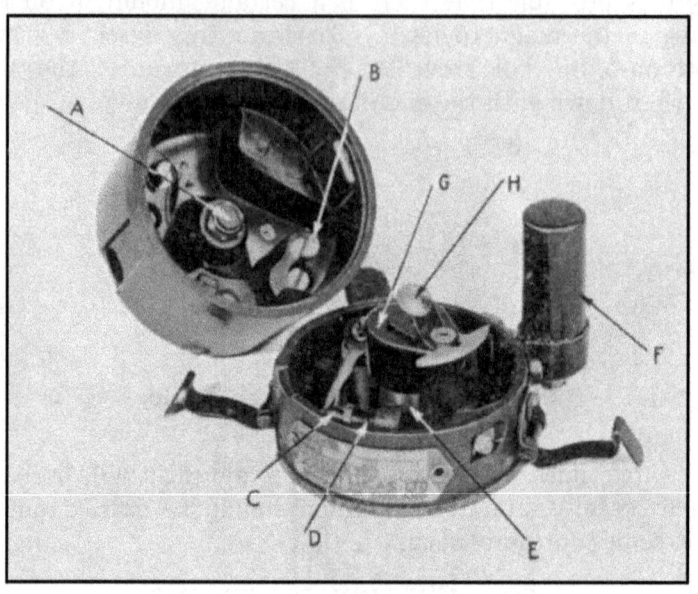

FIG. 21. DISTRIBUTOR AND CONTACT BREAKER, TYPE DJ (1932 MODEL)

A. Carbon brush
B. Electrode
C. Contacts
D. Locking nut
E. Rotating cam

F. Condenser
G. Rotating distributor arm
H. Spring contact

the contact breaker; it is important that the contacts C are kept free from any grease or oil. If they are burned or blackened, they may be cleaned with very fine emery cloth, and afterwards with a cloth moistened with petrol. Care must be taken that all particles of dirt and metal dust are wiped away. Misfiring may be caused if the contacts are not kept clean.

The contact breaker gap is carefully set before leaving the makers, and a gauge is provided on the spanner dispatched with each distributor. Provided that the cam is kept clean and that the instructions on cam lubrication given above are carried out, the wear on the fibre heel is negligible, and consequently the contact breaker gap will only need adjustment at very long intervals. If the cam is dirty, it may be cleaned with a cloth moistened with petrol, and afterwards given the slightest smear with vaseline. To

ENGINE MAINTENANCE AND OVERHAULING

test the contact breaker gap, slowly turn the engine over by hand until the contacts are seen to be fully opened. Now insert the gauge (·012-·015 in.) on the spanner into the gap; if it is correct the gauge should be a sliding fit. It is not advisable to alter the setting unless the gap varies considerably from the gauge. If adjustment is necessary, proceed as follows.

When the contacts are fully opened, slacken the locking nut *D* on the stationary contact screw, and rotate it by its hexagon head until the gap is set to the thickness of the gauge. After making the adjustment, care must be taken to tighten the locking nut.

Coil. The coil unit (Fig. 21A) is not adjustable in any way, and requires no attention beyond seeing that the terminal connections are kept tight and the moulded coil top is kept clean.

THE SPARKING PLUG.

Many drivers do not seem to appreciate the extremely important part which the sparking plug plays. A plug can be made to withstand either soot or oil,

FIG. 21A. THE COIL UNIT (1932 MODEL)

and the correct plug for any engine is the one which stands just the right combination of the two. If, therefore, a plug which is designed to withstand extreme heat is used in an engine which does not get very hot, it will at once oil up. Vice versa, an oil-resisting plug will soon burn out on an engine in which the flame heat is high. Special heat-resisting plugs cost more than ordinary touring types, and are only intended for use under racing conditions, and they should not be used on normal touring engines. A good racing plug will allow an engine to be run at the maximum speed and load of which it is capable without causing pre-ignition, but it will not, in itself, give extra power or speed to an engine as compared with normal plugs, except in its ability to avoid causing pre-ignition. Ordinary type sparking plugs are always best for normal engines, and should also be used on racing engines during periods of light load running.

Only plugs of a well-known make should be used. The following table shows at a glance the various types of Lodge plugs suitable for the different engines—

J.A.P. . .	.	.	O.H.V.	H 1 or H 2
J.A.P. . .	.	.	S.V.	C 3
Matchless	.	.	O.H.V.	H 1 or H 2
Matchless	.	.	S.V.	C 3
Ford .	.	.	S.V.	C 3

There are two main ways in which a sparking plug can give trouble. The first, and most usual, way is that it may become "sooted up"; the second, which fortunately is somewhat rare, is that the porcelain or mica insulation may develop a crack or other defect. If the latter occurs the plug should be scrapped, unless it is of the detachable type, when a new centre portion may be fitted.

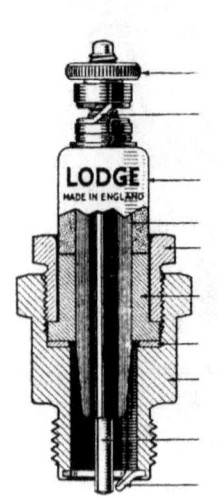

FIG. 22. THE LODGE STANDARD 18 MM. SPARKING PLUG (C 3)

FIG. 23. THE LODGE 18 MM. SPORTS SPARKING PLUG (H 1)

The broad term "sooted up" may be subdivided into at least two departments. The electrical current which passes through the plug may actually be shorted by a blob of oil on the plug points. The oil is easily washed off with petrol, and the plug will then be quite satisfactory.

Carbon deposit, however, forms on the plug points and the cavity around them in the same way as it does on the other surfaces of the combustion chamber. A plug will continue to work with a certain amount of deposit on its business end, but if this deposit

ENGINE MAINTENANCE AND OVERHAULING 45

becomes excessive the electrical current prefers to travel through it than to jump the space at the plug points; consequently, no spark appears and the engine will not fire.

Plug Testing. If a plug is suspected to be faulty the ordinary test of laying it on the cylinder head, rotating the engine, and watching for a spark does not prove anything definite. If no spark occurs it certainly does not prove that there is a fault in the electrical system, but if by the

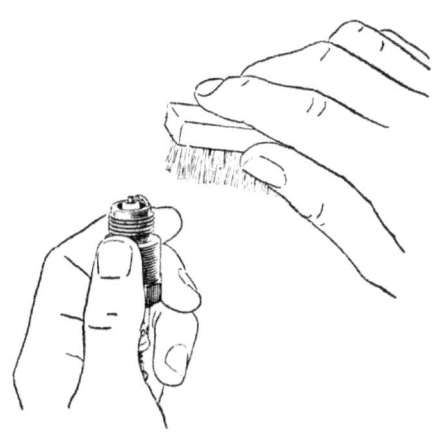

Fig. 24. How to Clean Non-detachable Plugs

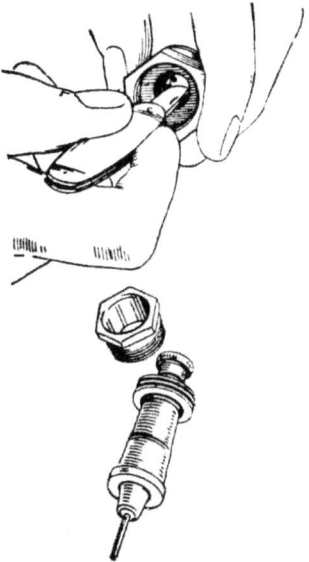

Fig. 25. Carbon may be Scraped Off Metal Parts with a Pocket Knife

same means a spark can be seen on the points of another plug, the first plug was obviously defective. Should, however, a spark be seen at the points of the plug, it cannot be assumed that a spark obtained under atmospheric pressure will spark under the compression in the engine.

It is advisable to clean the plug thoroughly, if the points and the cavity around them bear evidence of much carbon deposit. The number of drivers and even mechanics who seem to have no knowledge of how to clean a sparking plug is legion, and some detailed explanation of the methods to be followed is therefore advisable.

With a plug of the detachable type the gland nut should be undone and the centre portion of the plug removed. The body of the plug and the insulation which surrounds the centre electrode should then be scraped clean; washing it with petrol is of little use, for this will not, of course, dissolve the carbon deposit. It is quite simple to remove the carbon from the inside of the body with a penknife, but great care should be taken in removing it from the insulation, for if a knife is used roughly here the mica or porcelain may be damaged irreparably. The best thing to do is to wipe away as much deposit as possible with a rag and then to polish the insulation lightly with a strip of fine emery cloth. The points themselves should also be cleaned, either with a knife or with emery cloth, and the plug may then be reassembled.

Plug Point Gap. After long use the points of a plug will be found to have been eaten away by continual sparking which has taken

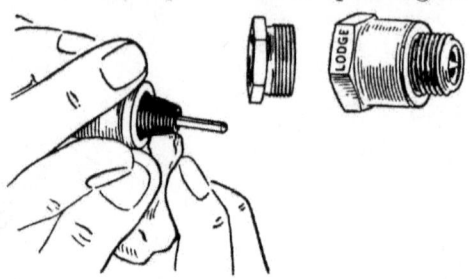

FIG. 26. CLEAN PLUG INSULATION WITH A PETROL-SOAKED RAG

place at them. This causes them to be too far apart, in effect, and if plug points are too far apart difficult starting results. The correct gap between the points is ·018 in., and this can, of course, be correctly measured with a feeler gauge. Expert drivers can usually judge the gap by eye, but if the driver cannot do this a crude way of measuring it is to insert the tip of the thumb nail between the points, and to note that it is a close fit. If the points are found to be too far apart, they should be tapped closer together, but in no case should the centre electrode be touched, the side electrode or electrodes being tapped lightly towards the centre until the required gap is obtained.

Cleaning a non-detachable plug is not so simple a matter. It is usually impossible to get into all the nooks and crannies with the blade of a knife or other sharp instrument in order to scrape away the carbon deposit, although on some plugs this can be done to a certain extent. Nowadays most non-detachable plugs are those which are specially designed to withstand great engine heat —which means that they are the more expensive plugs and are therefore worth attention. (If a cheap non-detachable plug becomes carboned up, the best thing to do is to throw it away.) The only really effective way of removing the deposit on a non-detachable plug is to burn it off, and this is an operation which is liable to cause damage to the insulation.

ENGINE MAINTENANCE AND OVERHAULING 47

Burning Off the Carbon. If a blow lamp is available proceed as follows—

First obtain a tin and half fill it with water; then fix a piece of wire round the body of the plug and balance the plug so that the high-tension terminal is immersed in the water. Then play the flame of the blow lamp on to the points and threaded parts of the plug until these become a dull red. With the high-tension terminal in water, excessive heat is conducted away from the centre electrode and little damage is likely to be done. The plug should be allowed to cool down slowly and, when cool, the points and the cavity around them will be found to be quite clean.

If no blow lamp be available, the threaded part of the plug only should be placed in the flame of a gas ring, until the same degree of heat is obtained. This, however, is rather more dangerous than the system already described, since there is nothing to conduct the heat away from the central electrode.

Apart from attention to sparking plugs, contact breaker, and pick-ups, there is little in the ignition system which will call for attention. One point, however, must be mentioned. This is as regards the high-tension cables. If either of these has been allowed to touch the cylinder, the rubber in the part affected will have been burnt away and it is probable that spasmodic firing will occur, the misfiring actually only taking place when the bare cable touches the cylinder and makes contact with it. It is also possible that misfiring, or a complete loss of spark, will occur owing to a defective connection between the wire and the terminal or the wire and the carbon brush holder. The remedy here is, of course, simple —the terminal clip and the brush holder must be detached and the actual connection examined.

THE AMAL CARBURETTOR

General Description. The design of this instrument combines the well-known features of both Amac and Brown and Barlow carburettors. The shaped adapter giving a clear gas passage of high volumetric efficiency is retained.

A constant mixture strength throughout the full range of the throttle valve is obtained by a well-known method of regulating the fuel supply by means of a suitably tapered needle adjustably attached to the throttle valve.

A metered jet is provided to regulate the maximum amount of fuel available at full throttle.

The "idling" system consists of pilot jet and by-pass, provision for adjusting the mixture being provided by the horizontal knurled screw on the mixing chamber side; the throttle stop screw providing a definite throttle opening for "idling" when the control lever is closed.

The carburettor is supplied with a souble lever control, which is cable operated.

Construction of the Amal Carburettor. Referring to the sectional diagram, Fig. 27, which shows the constructional arrangement, A is the carburettor body or mixing chamber, the upper part of which is fitted with throttle valve B, with taper needle C, attached by needle clip.

The throttle valve regulates the quantity of mixture supplied to the engine.

Passing through the throttle valve is the air valve D independently operated and serving the purpose of obstructing the main air passage for "starting" and "mixture" regulation.

Attached to the underside of the mixing chamber, by the union nut E, is the jet block F, and interposed between them a fibre washer to ensure a petrol-tight joint.

On the upper part of the jet block is the adapter body H, forming a clean through-way. Integral with the jet block is the pilot jet, supplied through the passage K.

The adjustable pilot air intake L communicates with a chamber, from which issues the pilot outlet M and the by-pass N.

An adjusting screw (T.S.) is provided on the mixing chamber wall, by which the position of the throttle valve for "idling" is regulated independent of the cable adjustment.

The needle jet O is screwed in the underside of the jet block, and carries at its bottom end the main jet P. Both these jets are removable when the jet plug Q, which bolts the mixing chamber and the float chamber together, is removed.

The float chamber, which can be supplied either top or bottom feed, consists of a cap R suitably mounted on a platform S, containing the float T and the needle valve U attached by the clip V.

The float chamber cover W has a lock screw X for security on the large float chamber only.

How the Amal Works. The petrol tap having been turned on, petrol will flow past the needle valve U, Fig. 27, until the quantity of petrol in the chamber R is sufficient to raise the float T when the needle valve U will prevent a further supply entering the float chamber.

ENGINE MAINTENANCE AND OVERHAULING

The action of the float can readily be understood, for, as the quantity of fuel in the float chamber is used, the float *T* will drop, carrying

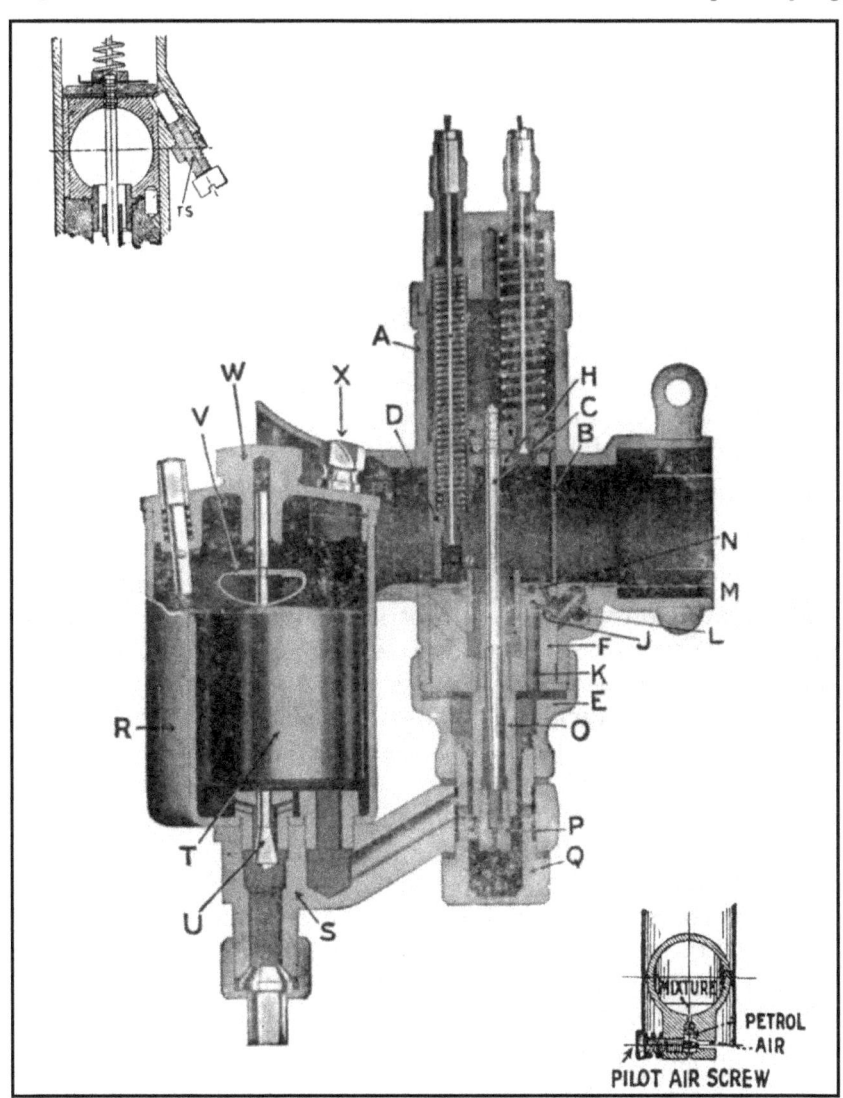

FIG. 27. THE AMAL CARBURETTOR

with it the needle *U*, and admitting a further supply. Thus automatically the petrol lever is kept constant.

In connection with the float chamber, it must be clearly understood that any alteration to the *standard level* can only have detrimental results.

The float chamber having filled to its correct level, fuel passes along the passages, through the diagonal holes in the jet plug Q, when it will be in communication with the main jet P and the pilot feed hole K; the level in these jets being, obviously, the same as that maintained in the float chamber.

Imagine the throttle valve B very slightly open, as the piston descends, a partial vacuum is created in the carburettor, causing a rush of air through the pilot air hole L, and drawing fuel from the pilot jet J. The mixture of air and fuel is admitted to the engine through the pilot outlet M.

The quantity of mixture capable of being passed by the pilot outlet M is insufficient to run the engine. This mixture also carries excess of fuel. Consequently, before a combustible mixture is admitted, throttle valve B must be slightly raised, admitting a further supply of air from the main air intake.

The farther the throttle valve is opened, the less will be the depression on the outlet M, but, in turn, a higher depression will be created on the by-pass N, and the pilot mixture will flow from this passage as well as from the outlet M.

The mixture provided by the pilot and by-pass system is supplemented at approximately $\frac{1}{8}$ throttle by fuel from the main jet system, the throttle valve cut-away governing the mixture strength from here to $\frac{1}{4}$ throttle. Proceeding up the throttle range, mixture control by the position of the needle takes place from $\frac{1}{4}$ to $\frac{3}{4}$ throttle, and thereafter the main jet is the only regulation.

The air valve D, which is cable operated on the two-lever carburettor and hand operated on the single-lever carburettor, has the effect of obstructing the main through-way and, in consequence, increasing the depression on the main jet, thus enriching the mixture.

Tuning Hints. There are four separate ways in which the quality of the mixture supplied by an Amal Carburettor can be varied, and these are given hereunder in the order in which the adjustments should be made.

1. Main jet ($\frac{3}{4}$ to full throttle).
2. Pilot air adjustment (closed to $\frac{1}{8}$ throttle).
3. Throttle valve cut-away on the air intake side ($\frac{1}{8}$ to $\frac{1}{4}$ throttle).
4. Needle position ($\frac{1}{4}$ to $\frac{3}{4}$ throttle).

The diagram seen in Fig. 28 clearly indicates the part of the throttle range over which each adjustment is effective. The carburettor having been carefully fitted, the general tuning can be carried out. The following sequence may be observed.

ENGINE MAINTENANCE AND OVERHAULING

1. Obtain main jet size.
2. Pilot adjustment.

To weaken slow running mixture screw pilot air adjuster outwards.
To enrich slow running mixture screw pilot air adjuster inwards.
Screw pilot air adjuster home in a clockwise direction.

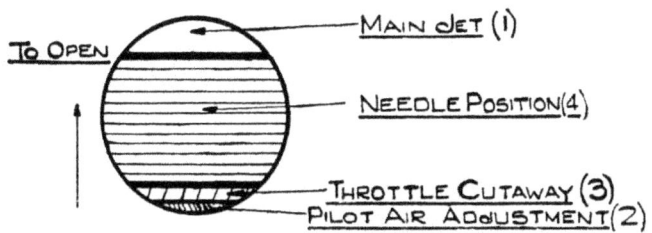

FIG. 28. RANGE AND SEQUENCE OF ADJUSTMENTS

Place gear lever in "neutral." Slightly flood float chamber by gently depressing the tickler until fuel can be observed overflowing from the mixing chamber.

Set ignition half-advance, throttle approximately $\frac{1}{8}$ open, close air lever, start the engine, and warm up.

After warming up, reduce the engine revolutions by gently closing the throttle.

The slow running mixture will prove too rich unless air leaks are present.

Very gradually unscrew the pilot air adjuster.

The engine speed will increase and must be again reduced by gently closing the throttle until, by a combination of throttle position and air adjustment, the desired "idling" is secured.

It is sometimes necessary to retard fully the ignition before good "idling" results, particularly when the magneto runs at engine speed, or when excessive valve overlap and very early ignition timing is employed.

Throttle Stop. If it is desired that the engine should continue "idling" with the throttle lever closed, the position of the throttle valve must be set by means of the throttle stop screw T.S., the throttle lever being in the "closed position" during this adjustment. Alternatively, if the screw T.S. is adjusted clear of the thottle valve, the engine will shut off in the normal way by the control lever. Do not take the throttle stop screw out completely. Failure to secure good "idling" will probably be traced to one of the following causes—

Air leaks at the junction of the carburettor and engine, or through the valve guide, due to worn inlet valve stem and guide. Faulty inlet and exhaust valve seatings. Sparking plug points too close. Try a gap ·025 in. Sparking plug oily. Too much ignition advance. Magneto contacts dirty or too close. Examine contact breaker. Examine slip ring for oil. Examine for carbon brush jamming in holder, or glazed on contact face. Examine for fractured brush holder. Examine high tension cables for shorting. Magneto insulation may be broken down, or the interior mechanism wet.

Throttle Valve Cut-away (see Fig. 28). Given satisfactory "idling" set the magneto control at half advance, air lever fully open.

Very slowly open the throttle valve, when, if the engine responds regularly up to one-quarter throttle, the valve cut-away is correct.

A *weak mixture* is indicated by spitting back through the air intake, with blue flames, hesitation in picking up, which disappears when the air lever is closed down, and this can be remedied by fitting a throttle valve with less cut-away.

A *rich mixture* is shown by black smoke from the exhaust. Engine stops, or nearly stops, when the air valve is closed. The remedy for this is a throttle valve with more cut-away.

All Amal valves are stamped with two numbers, the first indicating the Type No. of the carburettor, and the second figure the amount of cut-away on the intake side of the valve in sixteenths of an inch.

Thus: 6/4 is a type 6 valve with $\frac{4}{16}$ in. or $\frac{1}{4}$ in. cut-away. The standard valve for multi-cylinder engines is No. 4.

Needle Position. Air full open.

Open the throttle half way.

Note if the exhaust is crisp and the engine is lively.

Close air valve slightly below throttle. Exhaust note and engine speed should then remain practically unaltered.

Weak Mixture. Raise needle in throttle valve, *if*—popping back or spitting occur with blue flames from carburettor intake. Test by lowering air valve gently. Engine revolutions will rise when air valve is lowered slightly below the throttle valve.

Rich Mixture. Lower needle in throttle valve, *if*—engine speed does not increase progressively as the throttle is raised, smoky exhaust and heavy laboured running; on closing air valve slightly below throttle valve, tendency to misfire and eight stroke is present.

The normal needle setting is with the needle clip in No. 3 groove.

Having found the correct needle position, the carburettor setting is now complete, and it will be found that the driving is practically automatic once the engine is warmed up.

ENGINE MAINTENANCE AND OVERHAULING 53

For a semi-automatic setting, when extreme economy is desired, lower the needle one groove farther after carrying out this range of tests. For speed work the main jet may be increased by 10 per cent, when the air lever should be fully open when on full throttle.

THE FOUR-CYLINDER ENGINE
TAPPETS.

Adjustable tappets are not provided on the engine, so here is one adjustment which is completely eliminated. As may be seen by

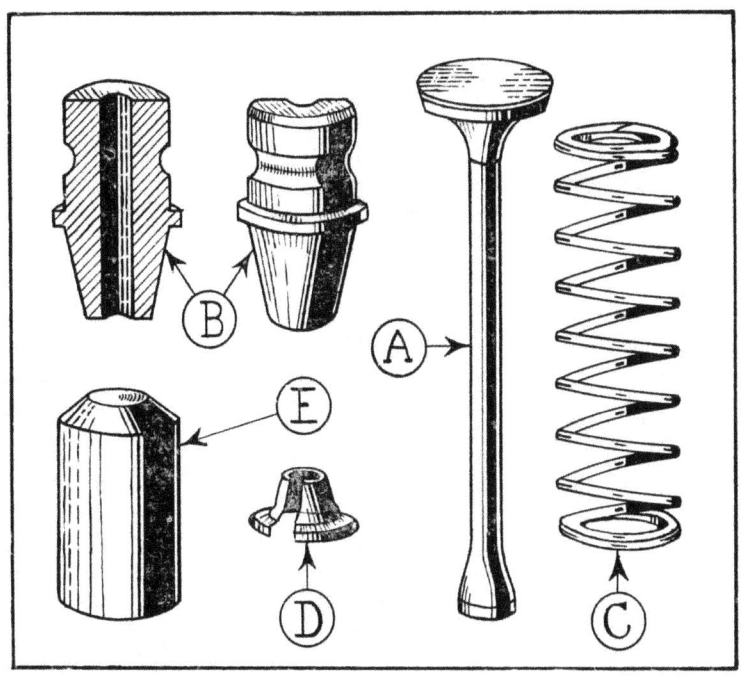

FIG. 29. THE VALVE COMPONENTS
A. Valve   D. Valve spring retainer
B. Valve guide E. Tappet (non-adjustable)
C. Valve spring

reference to Fig. 29, the special silicon-chrome steel valves have mushroom-ended stems having great wearing capacity, and these mushroom ends are in direct contact with plain hardened tappets of approximately 1 in. in diameter. It will thus be readily appreciated that wear occurs very slowly indeed, and the clearances provided (·013 in. inlet and exhaust) with the engine cold are not increased to any extent until a very big mileage has been covered. When eventually the clearances do require adjustment as shown by a feeler gauge, the valves must be ground in (see page 66) or else the feet of the valve stems ground off as required. (The latter is not a job you can do.)

VALVE TIMING.

Apart from the fact that it is a very intricate job interfering with the valve timing, it is quite unwarranted. Leave the valve timing strictly alone. It has been set with precision by engineers who know their job and any attempt to alter it is to be strongly deprecated.

THE CONTACT BREAKER.

Every 5,000 miles, or sooner if ignition trouble develops, you should, in addition to overhauling the plugs, examine the contact breaker upon whose proper functioning "fat" sparks at the plugs and correct ignition timing largely depend. To do this, press down the distributor cap clamp and remove the cap from the distributor body, allowing the cap to rest on the H.T. cables away from the contact breaker. Then prise the rotor off the distributor shaft with a screwdriver (see Fig. 31). The contact breaker is now easily accessible. Turn the engine over with the starting handle until the contact points (A, Fig. 30) are fully separated, the fibre block on the contact arm resting on the high lobe of the cam. Then with a ·018 in. feeler gauge (included in the tool kit) check the gap at the contacts as shown in Fig. 30. This gap should not require frequent actual adjustment but should be checked and the contacts examined regularly.

When the gap is found to exceed ·018 in., adjust by loosening the contact lock screw B and turn the contact screw C very slightly clockwise as required. Finally, re-tighten the lock screw and again check the gap between the contacts. With this type of contact breaker the cam is on the inside of the contact arm and thus wear of the fibre block tends to reduce the gap at the contacts which to some extent compensates for wear of the contacts themselves. It is not necessary to touch the cam although this can be prised off if desired after slackening the centre screw. I do not, however, advise this to be done.

With coil ignition the ignition switch should be turned off when the car is left standing, otherwise, besides wasting battery "juice," the contact points may become pitted and burned, due to sparking across them, assuming the contacts are nearly closed. After a considerable mileage some pitting or burning and wear of the contacts

ENGINE MAINTENANCE AND OVERHAULING

is likely to be found, and besides adjusting the gap at the contacts it is necessary to true up the contacts.

Do not true up the contacts with a file. This treatment, although satisfactory for some types of contact breakers, is not recommended in the case of the contact breaker employed on the four-cylinder engine. It is desirable to remove the contacts (i.e. the contact screw and arm) and dress them perfectly smooth with an oil stone. Do not touch the contacts if they have smooth, dull grey surfaces.

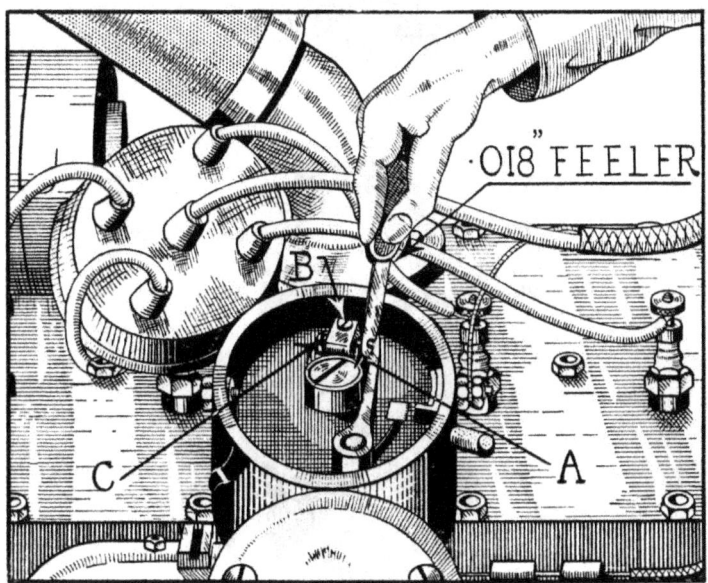

FIG. 30. CHECKING GAP AT CONTACT BREAKER POINTS
The feeler gauge should just enter without binding

Only the barest amount of metal must be removed and each face must be dead square and flat, otherwise a host of troubles will develop. After truing up and replacing the contacts, check the gap and refit the distributor rotor and cap.

CARE OF DISTRIBUTOR.

Apart from looking after the contact breaker, no attention to the distributor is necessary other than occasionally cleaning the distributor contacts and the high tension contact with a soft dry duster, and verifying that the plug cable connexions are clean and tight. The distributor shaft, however, requires periodical lubrication (see page 57).

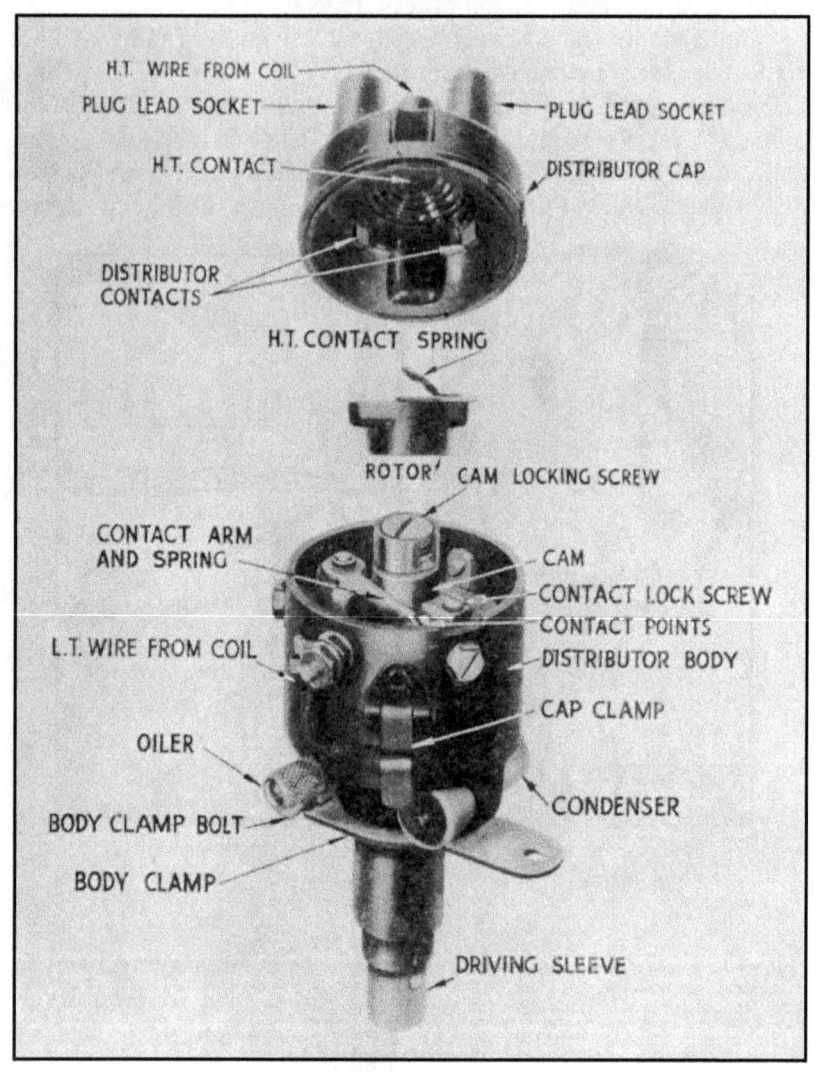

Fig. 31. Showing the Parts of the Distributor and Contact Breaker

The distributor cap and rotor have been lifted off to show the interior details

ENGINE MAINTENANCE AND OVERHAULING

THE IGNITION COIL

Keep the insulation of the coil clean and the connexions tight. No other attention is necessary.

IGNITION TIMING

A centrifugal type of governor sees to it that at low engine revolutions the spark is automatically retarded and automatically advanced in direct proportion to the increase in engine speed. The governor is very carefully adjusted to provide the ignition timing which gives the best all-round results. It is not desirable to alter this setting in the ordinary way, but the design of the distributor is such that an adjustment *can* be made.

To retard the spark beyond the standard setting, slacken the body clamp bolt at the distributor base (see Fig. 31) and move the distributor body *anti-clockwise* (i.e. in the direction of rotation). Similarly, to advance the spark, move the distributor body *clockwise* (i.e. opposite to the direction of rotation).

As removal of the distributor does not upset the timing, re-timing should only be called for in exceptional circumstances. When it becomes necessary the procedure is as follows—

Put No. 1 firing piston in the correct position at which the " break " at the contact breaker should begin to take place. The timing pin on the front of the timing gear cover must be unscrewed and the plain end inserted into the hole and pressed in while slowly revolving the engine with the handle until the pin clicks into a machined slot on the timing gear. This automatically gives the correct position for the piston. Now rotate the distributor body until the contacts are about to open (the rotor should point to No. 1 contact), and secure in this position.

LUBRICATING THE DISTRIBUTOR.

Every 1,000 miles fill the oil cup at the side of the distributor with engine oil and apply a thin film of vaseline or grease to the cam which actuates the rocker arm.

OILING GENERATOR.

Every 1,000 miles fill the two oil lever holes provided for bearing lubrication at each end of the generator with engine oil. Do not overdo it, however, because excessive oil, especially at the rear bearing, may find its way through to the commutator and cause trouble.

STARTING MOTOR LUBRICATION.

The bearings are of the oilless type and require no lubrication whatsoever.

FUEL PUMP.

The fuel pump (see Fig. 32), which is situated on the near side of the engine and operated by an eccentric on the camshaft, is, like the

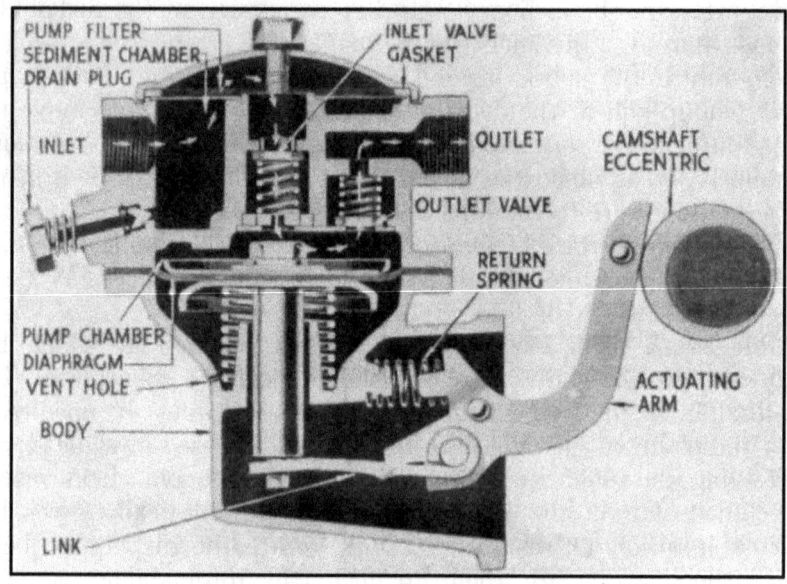

FIG. 32. SECTIONAL VIEW OF CAMSHAFT-DRIVEN FUEL PUMP

This pump is equivalent to a plunger type. As the camshaft eccentric pushes the actuating arm forward the pump diaphragm is pulled downwards and creates a vacuum above it, with the result that petrol is drawn into the diaphragm chamber past a non-return disc valve and filter. When the camshaft eccentric rotates so that the actuating arm returns towards the camshaft the diaphragm rises and ejects the petrol through the outlet valve

gauge, entirely automatic in action and requires no attention, except keeping it free from dirt and occasionally checking over the connexions for tightness.

CLEANING PUMP FILTER.

Every six months or 5,000 miles undo the screw in the centre of the pump cover (Fig. 32) and remove the cover and also the gasket, which enables the screen or filter to be removed for cleaning. Make quite sure when replacing the cover that the gasket is not fractured and that the cover is bedding down properly. Use a new gasket if in doubt.

CLEANING DRAIN PUMP TRAP.

The design of the fuel pump provides for a trap to collect impurities and also any water which may enter the pump along with the fuel. Besides cleaning the pump filter it is also advisable at fairly long intervals to unscrew the drain plug at the side of the pump

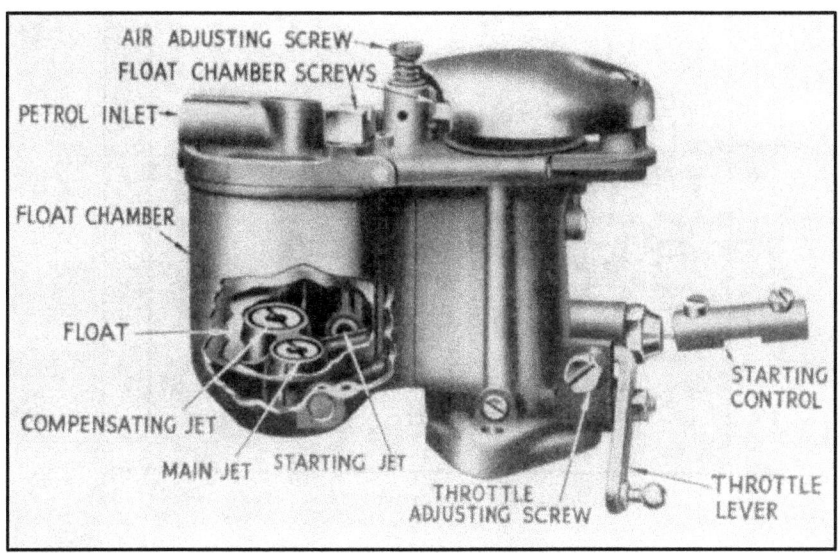

FIG. 33. PART SECTIONAL VIEW OF THE CARBURETTOR
All jets except the slow-running jet can be seen in the above illustration
Note the two slow-running adjusting screws

(Fig. 32) and drain off the trap. Before doing this, however, first loosen the inlet pipe union which is situated immediately above the plug.

THE CARBURETTOR.

This is a down-draught type with top feed to the float chamber and four jets, namely, a main jet, a starting jet, a compensating jet, and a slow running jet. It is entirely automatic in action and assures a correctly proportioned mixture at all speeds. A partly cut-away view of the instrument is shown in Fig. 33.

Adjusting for "Tick-over." Warm up the engine first and then carefully adjust (*a*) the throttle adjusting screw, and (*b*) the air adjusting screw; (*a*) should be approximately ½ to 1½ turns open after the screw touches the throttle lever and (*b*) about ½ to 1 full turn open. The two adjusting screws are clearly shown in Fig. 33.

The best adjustment for the throttle screw is ¾ turn open, but on no account screw it in more than 1½ turns.

The Automatic Air Valve. It is wise occasionally to check the action of the automatic air valve of the carburettor. But as this

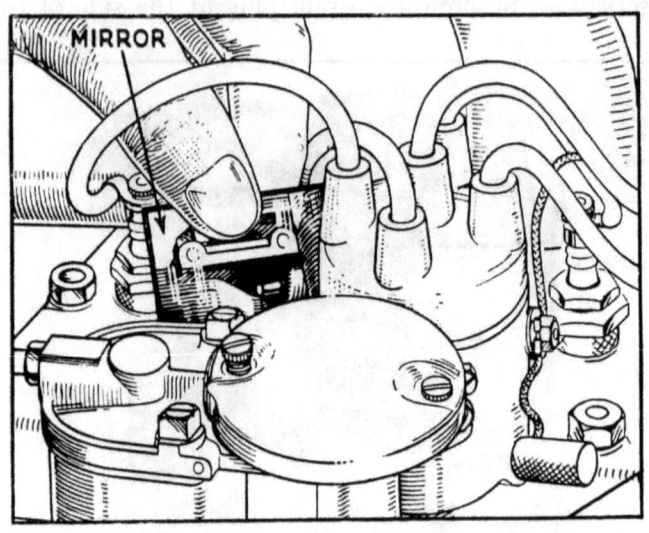

Fig. 34. Examining the Automatic Air Valve with a Mirror

valve is in rather an inaccessible position, the best way to find out whether it is functioning correctly is to hold a mirror between the cylinder head and carburettor as shown in Fig. 34. Observe whether the valve oscillates in its chamber.

The Easy Starting Device. After a considerable time, stretch in the control wire may cause the valve to open only partially and prevent the easy starting device operating. The remedy is to shorten the control wire slightly. Another possible cause of the easy starting device failing to operate is incomplete closing of the throttle, due to a faulty return spring. Inspect the throttle operating mechanism occasionally and see that it works freely.

Removing the Jets. Although ample provision for filtering the fuel is included in the fuel system, it is impossible to guarantee that no traces of water or minute dirt particles shall obtain access to the

ENGINE MAINTENANCE AND OVERHAULING

jets and cause a stoppage or partial stoppage. It is a simple matter, however, to get at the jets for cleaning purposes if this is necessary. Proceed as follows—

Undo the two square-headed screws on top of the float chamber (Fig. 33) and remove the float chamber bowl complete with the four jets. Each jet is slotted to take a screwdriver, so that it is then a simple matter to remove the jets from the float chamber bowl. The main and compensating jets are situated in the bottom of the float chamber, the slow-running or idling jet is located on the rear edge of the bowl at the top, and the starting jet on the outside of the float chamber just in front of the starting device. When removing a jet see that you employ a good-fitting screwdriver because if the jet slot is damaged removal may be very difficult.

Cleaning the Jets. It is advisable to connect the jet up to a pump with rubber and then clear the jet with a few quick strokes of the pump. Do not try and clear the jet with a pin or piece of wire, as this is more than likely to deform the accurately calibrated orifice and so spoil the efficiency of the carburettor.

You must under no circumstances whatever remove the emulsion block, as it is of supreme importance that an airtight joint exists between it and the bowl. The emulsion block is the die-cast plate held by three screws to the rear face of the float chamber. It comprises a nozzle projecting into the venturi tube.

CHECK SUMP LEVEL.

The level should be checked every 200 miles, or more frequently if you are in the habit of driving fast at every available opportunity. To check the level of oil in the sump, with the car level and the oil cold, pull out the dip-stick situated on the near side of the engine, wipe it clean with a rag and, after again inserting it, remove it and examine the mark left by the oil. If this mark reaches the point indicated " F " on the dip-stick, the sump is full and no further oil should be added. If it reaches between " F " and the point marked " L " the sump is not full but the level is not dangerously low. If it reaches below " L " the level is dangerously low and the car should not be driven in this condition, otherwise there is a considerable risk of causing serious damage. The best policy is at all times to *keep the level of oil in the sump up to or very close to the point " F " shown on the dip-stick.* Then you can rest assured that you will have no serious mechanical trouble brought about through lack of oil.

REPLENISHING ENGINE SUMP.

The oil filler is mounted high up in a readily accessible position at the front of the engine on the near side, and also functions as a breather. To replenish the sump with oil it is only necessary to remove the filler cap and pour in the oil. Partial withdrawal of the dip-stick itself will facilitate the flow of oil into the engine. After replenishing, see that the filler cap is properly replaced, and when refitting the dip-stick push it all the way down, because if it is not inserted fully into the opening some of the oil will escape.

DRAIN SUMP EVERY 1,000 MILES.

In the case of a new engine, the oil sump should be completely drained after the first 300 miles and replenished up to the correct level (see preceding paragraph) with approximately ½ gallon of engine oil of the proper quality and viscosity. After running another 700 miles, again drain and replenish. Subsequently do this every 1,000 miles. It is best to drain the engine while the engine is warm, as this enables it to be done more thoroughly, but do not flush out the engine with paraffin, for it is difficult to remove all traces from the internal oil-ways and recesses. Consequently, this causes oil dilution to some extent and may set up serious local friction.

Special proprietary brands of flushing-out oils are obtainable if you wish thoroughly to cleanse the inside of the engine.

CLEANING PUMP FILTER.

About every 5,000 miles detach the engine sump by removing the screws holding it to the crankcase and then remove the cylindrical gauze filter for cleaning. To remove the filter take out the two screws which fix the cover to the pump body, raise the cover, and slide the filter off the pump. Clean the filter with a brush, rinse in petrol, but make no attempt to clean it with a rag. Be careful on refitting the filter not to damage it, as it is a tight fit on the pump. Do not omit to clean out the sump itself thoroughly, and when refitting it to the crankcase, renew the gaskets to ensure an oil-tight joint.

DECARBONIZING

See that you have the necessary gaskets at hand. You will need a copper and asbestos cylinder head gasket and a cylinder head water outlet connexion gasket. If you intend removing the valves, you will also want a manifold gasket as well as a valve chest cover

ENGINE MAINTENANCE AND OVERHAULING

gasket. In addition to these gaskets you should also have available some sparking plug washers and a radiator rubber outlet hose, in case the old rubber is found to be perished. As regards tools, you will find that your tool outfit contains most essential items, but a good set of box type spanners will be found extremely valuable. For dealing with the valves, a spring compressor and a valve grinding tool will have to be purchased (see pages 66 and 67).

First remove the bonnet. (It is not *essential* to remove the bonnet, but the job is much simplified if this is done.)

The generator will have to be removed, and the procedure is as follows: remove the clamp, and after disconnecting the cut-out wire lift off the generator. Having put the generator in a safe place, disconnect the L.T. and H.T. wires running from the coil to the distributor at the coil. The H.T. wire, it should be noted, is held in place by spring tension and may be readily pulled out of its socket. Next, disconnect the H.T. wires at the sparking plugs, but before doing this do not forget to number them to ensure correct replacement. (No. 1 firing cylinder is nearest the radiator.) The distributor can then be removed complete with rotor and cap after first unscrewing the set screw which holds the distributor body clamp to the cylinder head. *Do not undo the body clamp bolt holding the distributor in position in the clamp*, otherwise the ignition timing will be upset. Take out all four sparking plugs and undo the two cap set screws holding on the water outlet connexion.

Removing the Cylinder Head. The removal of the cylinder head is very simple, because the detachable cast-iron head is above the level of the valves and the inlet and exhaust manifolds. All you have to do is to unscrew the thirteen nuts evenly on top of the head. To avoid the risk of distorting the cylinder head when unscrewing the retaining nuts, unscrew each nut about half a turn first and then a complete turn. Finally, unscrew all thirteen nuts completely.

Next remove the C. & A. gasket from the top of the cylinder block. Be careful always to replace the old gasket by a new one. When fitting the new gasket, make sure that you do not allow it to catch on any of the studs, because if it becomes bent even slightly, or otherwise damaged, it will no longer maintain a gas-tight seal between the cylinder block and head, and if a bad joint is permitted to exist the benefits obtained from decarbonizing are largely negatived.

Rotate the engine with the starting handle until two of the pistons are at the top of their strokes (the two other pistons being at the bottom of their strokes), and then stuff some clean rag into the remaining two cylinders to prevent carbon chippings getting into them and perhaps scoring the glass-like surfaces of the cylinders. Also stuff a piece of rag into the distributor driving shaft well and each of the water circulation holes.

Commence work on the cylinder head. Put this down in an inverted position and with a *blunt* instrument, such as an old screwdriver or chisel, thoroughly chip off and scrape all carbon deposits from the four combustion chambers. After doing your best on the head, clean up all carbon dust with a rag damped in paraffin. Do not use emery cloth unless you are satisfied that you can remove all traces of abrasive particles afterwards.

In the case of the pistons, the use of emery cloth is definitely barred, because not only are they made of a comparatively soft aluminium alloy into which abrasive particles are sure to become bedded, but, with the cylinder block *in situ*, some of the abrasive will undoubtedly get between the top piston rings and the cylinders. Chip and scrape all traces of carbon off the two pistons which you have put on T.D.C. Avoid using excessive pressure, or the piston crowns may be scratched deeply, with the result that carbon afterwards forms more quickly. Finally, clean off all carbon dust and remaining particles with a rag damped in paraffin, leaving each piston crown as smooth as possible. Now take the rags out from the cylinders whose pistons are lying at B.D.C. and shake them, crank the engine over with the handle until these pistons are on T.D.C. and deal with them as you have the other two, not forgetting to cover up the mouths of the cylinders already dealt with. It only remains now to scrape off any deposits which may have accumulated on the face of the cylinder block in the neighbourhood of the valves and on the valve heads. Some of the valves are bound to be open, and you must see that loose carbon does not fall on to the valve seats or into the ports. Really thorough decarbonizing should include removal of carbon deposits in the valve ports, but this cannot be done without taking out the valves. It is wise, therefore, to make a point of dealing with the carbon here every alternate decarbonizing when the valves are ground in.

Before replacing the cylinder head, pour a little clean engine oil on to the cylinder walls and smear it round with your finger until there is a thin film right round the walls. After scrupulously cleaning the face of the cylinder block, lower the new gasket over the block, keeping it quite parallel with the block. Do not on any account use force, but ease it down gently. Now, after seeing that

ENGINE MAINTENANCE AND OVERHAULING

the face of the cylinder head is also quite clean, lower the head over the studs, keeping it quite parallel to avoid jamming on the latter. With the head in position, tighten up the thirteen nuts, beginning with the centre one, then one at a corner, then one at the diagonally opposite corner, then two at the other corners, and then the remaining nuts in a " criss-cross " order. Screw each nut right down by hand first and then give each a half turn with a spanner, following this up with a whole turn. Finally, tighten them all up securely,

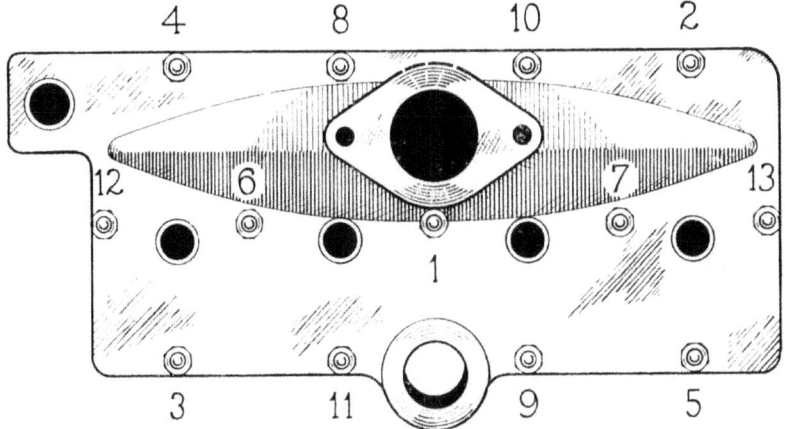

FIG. 35. ORDER FOR TIGHTENING CYLINDER HEAD NUTS
The above order need not be followed exactly, but always start at the centre and work diagonally. Loosen the nuts similiarly

but it is unnecessary and unwise to use excessive force when doing this. Replace the four sparking plugs and renew any copper washers which are damaged or carbonized.

Now replace the water outlet connexion, using a new gasket, and afterwards tighten up the two cap screws. Next refit the distributor, being careful to see that the tongue on the distributor shaft is located correctly in the slot provided in the drive shaft. As the slot is machined off centre, there is no risk of installing the distributor incorrectly, which it is presumed was previously removed complete with rotor and cap. Re-insert the set screw holding the distributor clamp to the cylinder head and then reconnect the H.T. wires to the correct sparking plugs. Also reconnect the H.T. and L.T. wires to the coil. Nothing else now remains to be done except to strap down the generator. Do not forget to reconnect the wire from the battery to the starter motor, if this has been disconnected.

After Decarbonizing. Refill the radiator, check the oil level in the sump, replace the bonnet and start up. After allowing the engine to get well warmed up, switch off, and with a spanner go over the thirteen nuts on the cylinder head. Also, watch out for any signs of water leakage. Tighten the nuts again after 300 miles of running.

GRINDING-IN THE VALVES.

With the cylinder head removed, the nine short bolts securing the cover to the timing case must be removed and the cover plate taken off in order to expose the valves. Before this can be done, however, it is necessary to disconnect the pipe from the fuel pump to the carburettor and also the choke wire and the accelerator rod, and remove the induction and exhaust manifolds separately, complete with carburettor, by taking off the securing nuts. It is not desirable and quite unnecessary to remove the carburettor, but the exhaust pipe clip must be loosened.

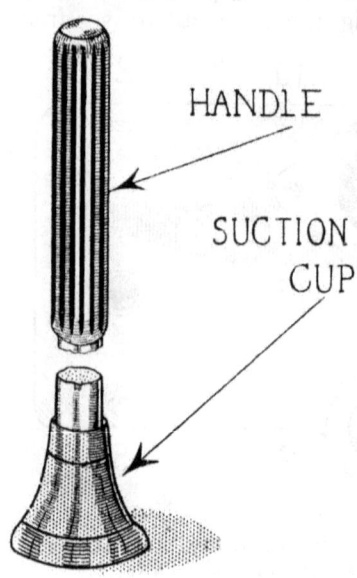

FIG. 36. SHOWING A SUCTION TYPE OF VALVE GRINDING TOOL SUITABLE FOR FORD ENGINES

This type of grinding-in tool, of which there are many proprietary makes available, must be used because the valve heads are not slotted to take a screwdriver

To remove each valve after taking off the timing cover it is necessary to proceed as follows. With a suitable valve spring compressor, slip one end under the valve spring just above the retainer (D, Fig. 29) and the other under the retainer just above the tappet guide.

Then compress the valve spring with the compressor tool until the valve spring is compressed sufficiently to enable the spring retainer to be withdrawn. The valve spring can now be slipped off. Before the valve can be removed, the valve guide must first be removed. To remove it you should push up the valve in its guide as high as possible and then with a light hammer and a suitable drift (a piece of wood is safest) tap the valve guide downwards, inserting the drift through the space between the valve and its seating. Be careful to keep the drift away from the edges of the semicircular halves of the guide. Only a few gentle taps should be necessary to free the guide from its taper and enable the two halves of the guide to be withdrawn by hand from the valve chest. Then

ENGINE MAINTENANCE AND OVERHAULING 67

draw out the valve from above. Deal with each valve guide and valve similarly.

Although the valves are numbered, it is possible, if you are not careful, to mix them up, especially if the heads of the valves on which the numbers are stamped are carbonized up. On no account must any of the valves or their guides be interchanged. The simplest method of avoiding mixing the valves is to keep the valves in the

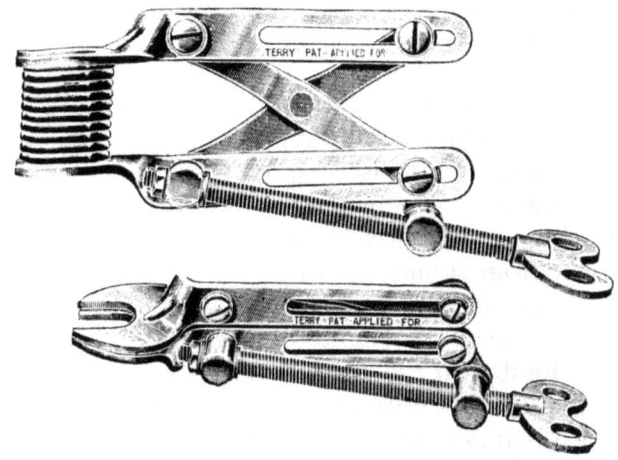

FIG. 37. SHOWING A SUITABLE TYPE OF VALVE SPRING COMPRESSOR
The tool shown is a Terry and possesses excellent features. The jaws, which are always parallel, will open to $5\frac{1}{2}$ in. and are locked at every point

head until you are ready to grind in. You should take the opportunity, when removing the valves, of cleaning the carbon deposits which cannot be got at when removing the cylinder head only.

The materials required for grinding in the valves are some fine quality grinding paste, some paraffin, and an assortment of clean fluffless rags. Working from No. 1 cylinder backwards to No. 4 cylinder, take out No. 1 exhaust valve and remove all traces of carbon. Do not scrape the stem but clean the whole valve with a rag damped in paraffin. Examine the bevelled-off circumference of the valve which beds down on the valve seat. Some pitting or little spots will be noticed. If these are very numerous and deep indentations are observed, do not proceed with valve grinding but have it refaced. If the pitting is not very extensive or deep, grind in the valve in the following manner.

With a small piece of rag, apply a thin film of grinding paste to the bevelled surface of the valve. Then lower the valve on to its seat. Now take the two halves of the valve guide, place them round the stem, and push the guide into position. If the guide is a loose fit, fit a new one and grind in with it in place. This is necessary because the valve must be kept quite central when grinding in. With a suction type grinding tool, rotate the valve backwards and forwards with a turn of the wrist. Push down on the valve lightly. Every few oscillations raise the valve off its seat and rotate it half a turn to a new position. Continue gently grinding in, and now and again adding fresh paste (when the valve gets dry it will begin to " screech ") until the bevelled surface of the valve and its seat becomes bright all round and the pitting marks on both the valve and its seat have completely disappeared.

As soon as you have finished grinding in, tap or push out the valve guide from above and withdraw the valve. Clean it in paraffin and with a rag just moistened in paraffin remove every trace of grinding paste from around the valve seat. Deal with the four inlet and four exhaust valves just described.

Replacing the valves is quite straightforward. Deal with each valve thus: First turn the engine over until the tappet concerned is down. Then lower the valve to its seat after oiling the stem and place the two halves of the valve guide around the stem and push the two-piece guide up in place. Then slip the valve spring over the valve stem and with a valve spring compressor, compress the valve spring sufficiently to enable the retainer to be slipped over the end of the valve stem. At this point it is a good plan to check the valve clearances with a feeler gauge. The correct clearance is ·013 in. If, after grinding in, you find that the clearance is greater than ·015 in., you must grind in again until the correct clearance is obtained. If the clearance is less than ·013 in., it will be necessary to have the foot of the valve stem ground off. It must be ground off dead level, otherwise a side strain may be imposed on the valve stem by the tappet.

When you have put back all eight valves and their springs, bolt on the timing case cover tightly, using a new paper washer, and refit the inlet and exhaust manifolds, fitting a new gasket (C. & A.) here also. Before fitting the manifolds, clean the inside of the exhaust manifold and the slots in the induction pipe flanges. Reconnect the fuel pump to the carburettor and also the carburettor controls, and the exhaust pipe to the exhaust manifold. The remainder of the assembly details have been given previously.

CHAPTER V

THE TRANSMISSION

THE CLUTCH (CONE TYPE)

THE Morgan clutch seldom calls for any attention beyond greasing, and in this connection no fear need be entertained that the clutch will slip through over lubrication. The outer circumference of the flywheel is fitted with two grease nipples which lead to the clutch lining. The clutch pedal should be depressed whilst grease is being injected through these nipples, and a length of wood cut to wedge in front of the seat support and hold down the pedal will be found of great assistance here. Grease may also be inserted directly into the flywheel by hand, and although this is a somewhat messy performance it ensures that the clutch thrust race is kept well lubricated. Altogether there are three ball-races in the neighbourhood of the flywheel, these being (*a*) the inner clutch thrust race, (*b*) the clutch extractor race which can be seen whilst the engine is *in situ* and is fitted to the rearmost end of the phosphor-bronze clutch cone, and (*c*) the small spigot ball-race concealed inside the centre boss of the flywheel, and into which is fitted the foremost end of the transmission shaft. Neither of these three ball-races is called upon to act as a ball-race until the clutch is disengaged. That is to say, whilst the clutch is in with the engine running, the whole of each race, together with the balls, simply rotate as a solid mass. Naturally, therefore, they do not call for a large amount of lubrication, but little and often is the best advice, as owing to the centrifugal action they are inclined to sling off the grease, whereupon the clutch will be found somewhat harsh. The clutch itself is of the cone variety lined with fabric and appears to last almost indefinitely. The adjustment of the clutch is made by the four nuts which control the spring pressure between the clutch face and the flywheel. These nuts are drilled on their hexagons, and care should be taken to ensure that they are wired up in pairs after carrying out any adjustment to prevent their unscrewing on their own accord and so upsetting the adjustment (Fig. 38). To increase the clutch pressure the nuts must be turned in a clockwise direction. This of course, can be effected on all models up to and including 1929, with the engine in the chassis, but on the 1932 models, owing to a clutch dust cover being fitted which serves to prevent the ingress of mud and grit into the clutch, it will be necessary to remove the engine in order to gain access to the adjusting nuts.

The models previous to 1930 are also fitted with a clutch dust cover, but it is of such a type that the clutch adjusting nuts are get-at-able without disturbing the engine. It is not possible to remove the clutch cone entirely without first taking out the engine.

Dismantling the clutch. With the engine away from the chassis, no difficulty will be found in taking the clutch apart, and this task

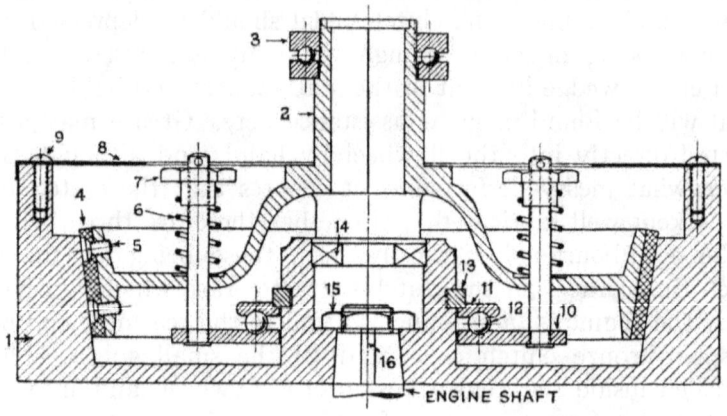

FIG. 38. MORGAN FLYWHEEL AND CLUTCH

1. Flywheel
2. Brass clutch
3. Outside thrust bearing
4. Fabric
5. Rivets or screws
6. Clutch springs
7. Adjusting nuts
8. Dust cover
9. Cover screws
10. Thrust ring (square)
11. Thrust ring (round)
12. Balls
13. Split ring
14. Ball race
15. Flywheel nut
16. Engine shaft

can be carried out in a very few moments. The dust plate which is attached to the rim of the flywheel by a number of small screws must first be removed, and the wire coupling up the clutch nuts disconnected. After removal of these nuts the clutch cone will be found to be free of the flywheel, but care must be taken of the balls which will fall out of the inner clutch thrust race after the clutch spring nuts have been removed.

This ball-race is simply held in position by a split steel ring, fitting firmly into a groove encircling the centre-boss of the flywheel. Gentle prising with a screw-driver between the ends of the ring will facilitate its removal, after which the two portions forming the inner clutch thrust race can be removed. Possible troubles here are: (1) Loose clutch fabric. This is held in position by a series of countersunk head screws. A loose lining gives rise to a fierce clutch and the best cure is a new fabric, although the old one may sometimes be used again by removing the screws, and rotating the lining a little on the cone and drilling fresh holes to take the screws. In any event, whether fitting a new or re-fitting the old fabric, see to it that only very small holes are drilled so that the screws are a tight fit into the fabric, as large holes will obviously allow the lining to shift about and no cure will have been effected. (2) The four long studs projecting from one half of the inner clutch thrust race may be loose, in which case their ends must be re-riveted, or, on the other hand, they may have steps or shoulders worn along their sides. If this is so it will set up a fierce clutch, or perhaps clutch slip, as the shoulders are apt to prevent the clutch cone from going right home, thereby preventing the fabric from coming fully into contact with the internal cone machined in the flywheel, with the result that the clutch is unable to transmit the full power to the rear wheel. The fierce clutch effect is due to the clutch cone becoming temporarily "hung up" on the steps after the foot has been removed from the clutch pedal, and then suddenly jumping past the step and so making very sudden contact with the flywheel cone. The grooves in which the balls run may be badly worn or pitted, and in this event a much sweeter clutch action will be obtained if a new race complete with balls is fitted. (3) The square hole in the phosphor-bronze clutch cone should be a very free fit on the square end of the propeller shaft along which it slides when the clutch moves into or out of engagement. See that the square is a true one—this can be checked by replacing the cone on the propeller shaft and gently rocking in a circular motion. A badly worn square will not permit the two cones to meet truly, consequently only part of the fabric will be in engagement with the flywheel, another state of affairs which may account for a slipping clutch. (4) The clutch extractor race upon which the two oblong fibre blocks bear when withdrawing or letting in the clutch is not of so much consequence, providing a full set of balls is in place between the two halves of the race. Renewals are seldom needed here, but if it should be necessary to fit any replacements, the rearmost half of the race screws off by a left-hand thread, i.e. clockwise, after the riveted-over portion of the phosphor bronze has been chiselled or filed away round its edges. A vice will almost certainly be needed in which to hold the race firmly, when the clutch cone can be unscrewed from the race. (5) There only remains the spigot ball-race fitted up inside the flywheel centre-boss. This may give some little trouble in getting out, but unless one is sure that this race is suffering from some defect it may be well left alone. It is a good plan to insert a small quantity of grease into this spigot bearing whilst the engine is out. If the small rounded portion of the propeller shaft at the extreme front end has a small groove on it, this is evidence that the shaft is not a tight fit inside the spigot race. The only sure cure is to remove the propeller shaft (a lengthy and messy job for the private owner) and to fit a new end to the propeller shaft.

Before assembling the clutch give all the parts a good wash in petrol, and use a liberal quantity of heavy grade grease. Do not forget to replace the dust cover—that is, if it is desired to continue with this fitment. Some owners habitually run without it, their contention being that it is inclined to harbour dust and any small stones which may find their way into the clutch. Having replaced the engine, always make sure that there is a small amount of lost movement on the clutch pedal, otherwise the clutch will be prevented from going right home. If necessary, adjustment of the pedal may be carried out beneath the floor boards by means of the series of holes drilled in the clutch operating rods.

Normally, the rear end of the vehicle where will be found the countershaft and bevel wheels, together with the gear dogs, etc., will need no attention beyond keeping the bevel box filled to the top with a stiff grease, and also keeping the gear selector forks, their rod, and the gear dogs, and the dog sprockets and chains, well supplied with grease. The selector forks will need renewing from time to time, but these are very inexpensive and easily replaced.

CLUTCH (PLATE TYPE)

The single dry-plate clutch is entirely different in construction and operation from the cone type described previously, and none of the maintenance instructions apply. Actually the plate clutch requires little attention. Its construction will be easily understood by referring to Fig. 39, and the only points where oil is necessary are the three toggles shown. As a result of wear in the toggles, the withdrawal lock may be observed to be running out of truth, and this will be transmitted to the pedal, setting up vibration. The remedy will be obvious, as each toggle is provided with an adjusting screw and lock-nut. Fierceness is more or less unknown with this type

of clutch. Its sweetness may on rare occasions be impaired by a
" juddering " effect, which can usually be traced to dryness of the
spline along which the spinning plate assembly travels. No provision is made for lubricating this spline, as it is imperative that
grease should not find its way to the fabric or metal faces which
come into contact with it. Should the necessity arise, the engine
should be taken out of its
frame, the splines carefully
cleaned and oiled only just
sufficiently to damp them.
While dismantling, the fabric
and metal plates should be
thoroughly washed in petrol
and all traces of dust removed. This may be present as the result of slight
wear of the fabric caused
when taking up the drive.
Only reassemble when perfectly clean and dry, and on
no account apply an abundance of grease to the ball
race located in the centre

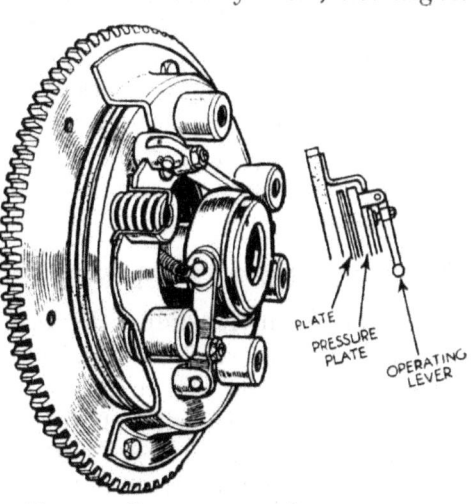

FIG. 39. SHOWING THE CONSTRUCTION OF THE PLATE TYPE CLUTCH

of the flywheel for carrying the front end of the transmission shaft
It is only necessary thinly to smear this race with the finger.

THREE-SPEED GEARBOX AND TRANSMISSION.

The gearbox is of special design and no adjustment is provided
or necessary. The main shaft is extended into a casing containing
a bronze worm wheel and a steel worm, the latter being keyed to
the main shaft. The most important question in connection with
the gearbox is that of lubrication, and in this direction it should
here be noted that oil must be maintained to the correct level.
This is indicated on a dip-stick provided with the tool kit. It is
neither necessary nor desirable to fill the box any higher than the
indicated level. The correct lubricant is Patent Castrol "D."
It will be noticed that after running a few miles the gearbox becomes
quite warm: this is natural, and no harm will result unless the
machine is used with insufficient oil in the box. See that the air
vent fitted to the gearbox cover is kept clear and also that the screws
holding the gearbox cover are tight. Leather oil seals are fitted to
the worm wheel shaft and should be renewed when it becomes

necessary to dismantle the box for any purpose. The front end of the box contains an oil seal of special design, and this likewise should be replaced if the box is dismantled. If for any reason it is desirable to remove the gearbox from the chassis, proceed as follows: jack up and support machine by suitable blocks or trestle under the main chassis members, remove rear wheel as already directed, slacken off four "U" clips that secure the channel irons to the main members, remove dowl pins holding the selector rod yokes to striker rods and remove nuts from six flange bolts. The grease nipple in the centre member should also be unscrewed as this may foul the ball race on the tail end shaft. Having proceeded thus, the gearbox and complete rear fork and springing assembly can be drawn away.

OVERHAULING THE CHANGE-SPEED GEAR.

To take down the sliding dog gear proceed as follows: Remove the starting pin which is fitted at the end of the countershaft. This pin is tapered and must obviously be driven out by striking the small end smartly with a fairly heavy hammer. Next remove the two split pins—one at each end—from the short length of round steel connecting the fork to the small right-angled steel portion known as the bell crank, remove the nut at the end of the fork shaft, when the fork can be tapped off and the dog will slide off the countershaft. On the near side there is only the nut to be removed from the fork shaft and the fork eased off the shaft. The fork shaft may now be slid through and taken out of the tube in which it normally slides. The sliding dogs should show no marks on their jaws if the gear changing has been correctly carried out during the machine's usage. If, however, the jaws are badly rounded on either of the dogs, replacements should be fitted, otherwise the gears will be liable to jump out on their own accord when on the road.

REMOVING THE DOG SPROCKETS.

Having dismounted the sliding dogs, the procedure of taking off either dog sprocket is first to remove the chain of the sprocket in question, ease off the spring circlip surrounding the countershaft by means of a screw-driver, and the sprocket may be levered off, bringing with it a small distance tube (Fig. 40). These dog sprockets are hardened and seldom call for renewal until the chains have worn their teeth "hooky" (Fig. 41)—this will not take place for many thousands of miles.

THE TRANSMISSION

DISMANTLING THE BEVELS.

This job is comparatively simple, but it must be stated at the outset that in order to get quiet running from this quarter, correct and careful assembly is most essential, and unless the owner is possessed of a little mechanical knowledge the work should be entrusted to a capable mechanic. In any event, assembly is greatly assisted by removing the body at the beginning of operations, and this in turn is best carried out by first taking out the

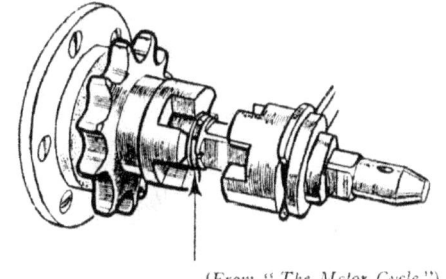

(*From "The Motor Cycle"*)

FIG. 40
TO REMOVE A SPROCKET IT IS NECESSARY TO DETACH THE OUTER DOG AND STRIKING FORK AND TO PRISE OFF A SPRING CIRCLIP

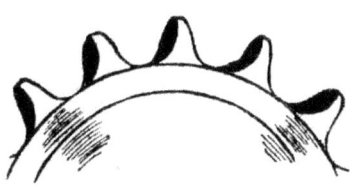

FIG. 41
THE BLACK PORTIONS SHOW HOW SPROCKET TEETH WEAR "HOOKY"

engine. If it is also proposed to extract the propeller shaft this can only be done after the power unit has been taken from the chassis, so, strictly speaking, the time spent in removing the engine cannot be looked upon as a non-productive effort.

Having removed the sliding dogs and dog sprockets, take out the six small screws holding the circular side plates on each side of the bevel box. The countershaft may now be driven out by means of a heavy hammer and stout brass punch. Assuming the body is off the chassis it is advisable to drive the shaft towards the near side, as by so doing the teeth of the bevel wheels will not be subjected to any strain. The countershaft is fitted with two keys for locating the large bevel wheel and care must be taken that neither of these is allowed to drop out when assembling again. Take care to keep the side plates, distance pieces, and oil-retaining washers in such a manner that they may be replaced in their same sides.

In order to remove the small bevel pinion it will be necessary to take out the propeller shaft, as it is seldom possible to extract the pinion whilst the shaft is in position. Having removed the countershaft and large bevel wheel, remove the rear forks by taking out the fork-securing bolt and, by means of a long brass punch, tap out each of the securing cones. These are a taper fit into the bevel box, and the near side cone can only be removed by inserting the punch through the offside cone so as to drive the near side member out of the bevel box (Fig. 42). The forks will now be free at their forward end, and there will be found at the back of the bevel box a small, thin, circular plate held in position by four

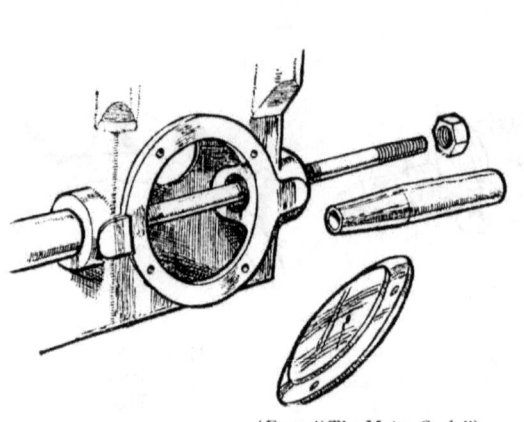

(*From "The Motor Cycle"*)
Fig. 42
The Rear Fork Pivot Pins are Held in the Gearbox by a Long Central Bolt and are Tapered into their Sockets

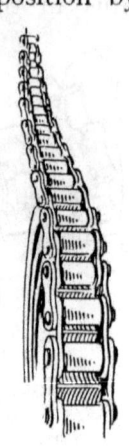

Fig. 43
An Exaggerated View of a Chain running on Sprockets which are Out of Line

screws. Upon removal of this plate, the shaft may be driven through from the front end. Before attempting to drive out the shaft, however, make sure that the short metal strip, which will be found secured by a nut just above the small bevel pinion, is clear of the ball-race. The edge of this ball-race can just be seen protruding from its housing inside the bevel box. The small bevel pinion is fitted to the propeller shaft on a taper and key, and great care must be exercised not to damage the thread at the end of the shaft when removing the pinion.

When assembling, have all parts thoroughly washed in petrol, and the bevels should be so meshed that the teeth of the small pinion bear on those of the large one for their full length, and at the same time there must be a small amount of clearance between the teeth—if the mesh is too slack, or otherwise, noisy bevels are bound to result.

The rear fork cones, if worn where the forks hinge, should be replaced with oversize cones obtainable from the manufacturers. It is, however, almost certain that the forks will need reamering out at this point to fit the larger cones, so that unless one has the necessary tools the job should be placed in the hands of a repairer. In passing, it is as well to point out that the long fork-securing bolt passing through these cones should be kept tight. Failure to do this will result in the cones wearing their tapered holes in the bevel box, which state of affairs will make it practically impossible to keep the rear forks and wheel laterally rigid.

ADJUSTING CHAINS.

This is best carried out with the machine standing on a level floor. The brake must be disconnected from its rod, and the brake clip bolt loosened. Adjustment is carried out by means of the bronze nuts on the chain adjusters, and the aim should be to have the wheel central in the forks. This can be ascertained by means of a rule and measuring the distance from the rim to the fork on either side. Do not make the mistake of having the chains too tightly adjusted, as they are inclined to tighten up a little when the machine is carrying a load. The correct tension is such that there should be about 1 in. up and down lift when the bottom run is felt at a point midway in the drive.

Having obtained correct alignment of the wheel as well as proper chain tension, tighten up the wheel spindle nuts, and run the chain adjusting nuts up so that they just meet the fork ends. Do not tighten these nuts up unduly, or the continued strain will, in time, pull the rear wheel back in the fork slots and so tighten the chains and possibly set up a binding rear brake. The brake is the last item to be attended to, and the brake clip surrounding the fork tube, having previously been slackened as before mentioned, must be driven backwards or forwards along this tube, according to whether the wheel has been moved backwards or forwards in the fork slots. Having tightened the clip, and inserted the long brake bolt to perform its duty of anchoring the brake-operating arm, connect up the brake rod. Now, before venturing on the road, just check the brake adjustment by sitting in the driving position and depressing the brake pedal. If there is very little movement on the pedal the brake is binding, whilst if the pedal can be pushed right down until it meets the floorboards, the brake band is not making contact with its drum. In either case the obvious remedy, that of adjustment, can be effected by slightly shifting the brake clip along the fork tube, and/or making use of the series of holes drilled in the brake rod.

REAR SPRINGS.

Every 10,000 miles or so, jack up the car under the bevel box and clean and grease between the leaves of the back springs. If the wheel is clear of the ground the spring leaves will each gape apart sufficiently to permit the insertion of a thin knife blade covered in grease. The spring shackle pins can also be tested for wear, and if loose in their bearings, should be renewed. The forward ends of the springs are attached to two angle pieces by U-bolts, and also ordinary bolts. The nuts on these should all be checked to see that they are tight, and the four bolts securing the angle pieces to the top of the bevel box may also need a little tightening.

ATTENTION TO CHAINS. (TWO-SPEED MODEL.)

These are protected to some degree by wooden guards over the top run of either chain, which, to some extent, shield the chains from the dripping mud and water which is flung by the wheel to the under portion of the body. The lower runs of the chain, however, are not protected in any way, and although the chains as fitted are amply large and seldom known to break, wear may be minimized to some degree by occasionally removing them, and after scrubbing in paraffin and rinsing off, immersing in a shallow bath of molten tallow and graphite. This method, though admittedly somewhat messy, will thoroughly lubricate the rollers inside, whereas the normal system of smearing on cold grease merely lubricates the outside of the chain, and the inner working surfaces are left to run dry. A badly-worn chain should not be expected to give satisfactory service on new sprockets, or vice versa, as the worn member will produce rapid wear on the new chain or sprockets as the case may be. A chain may be tested for wear by attempting to pull it away from its sprocket in the direction of the arrow in Fig. 44. Another way is to stretch the chain out fully on a flat surface when the amount of wear on the rivets may be felt by alternately compressing and stretching a portion at a time. There is no need to disturb the wheel adjustment when re-fitting the chain, as the ends can be made to meet very easily by arranging that they come together on the rear sprocket (Fig. 45). It then becomes a very easy matter to insert the connecting link, taking care to fit the spring clip so that when travelling round the upper run the open ends of the

THE TRANSMISSION

clip point rearwards (Fig. 46). A chain rivet extractor and a few inches of spare chain should be carried, together with a spare connecting link, and a double-cranked link. When purchasing a new chain see that it is of the same make as its fellow member which, presumably, is still good for service on the other pair of sprockets. The feature of this precaution is, chiefly, that the spares

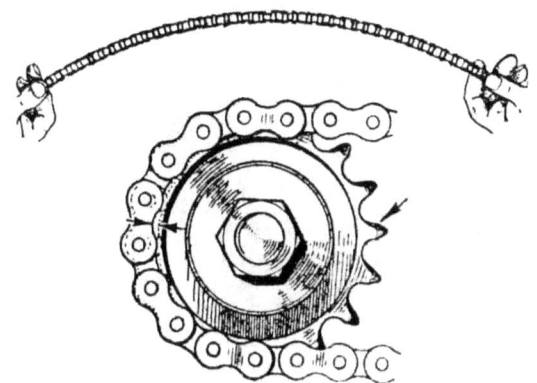

FIG. 44. METHODS OF TESTING A CHAIN FOR WEAR

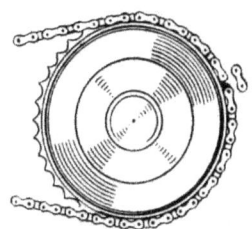

FIG. 45
THE CORRECT WAY TO
INSERT CHAIN LINKS

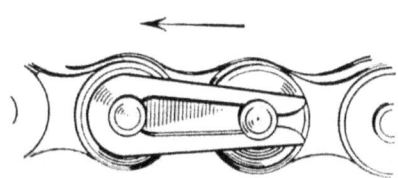

FIG. 46
The closed end of the coupling link should point in the direction of travel. The open end is trailing, as shown above

for one make of chain will not be found suitable for the same size and type of chain made by a different manufacturer.

REAR WHEEL REMOVAL. (THREE-SPEED MODEL.)

To remove the rear wheel, disconnect the tail lamp plug. Remove spare wheel from rear tail panel and take out panel after removing the four nuts that hold it in position. (In the case of the Super Sports, the top panel is hinged on models previous to 1935.) Removal of this panel allows easy access to the "knock-out" spindle nut on the left-hand side. Place the jack in centre of channel iron under the rear of the gearbox and lift the wheel just sufficiently to clear the inflated tyre. Take off the spindle nut; take brake cable nipple out of the slot in cam lever and pull or tap out the spindle (Fig. 47), when the wheel will fall out. The chain can be lifted off the sprocket without disconnecting. The wheel nut and brake come away as one unit, so that if the spare wheel is to be fitted, the change-over is carried out in the same manner as when changing a front

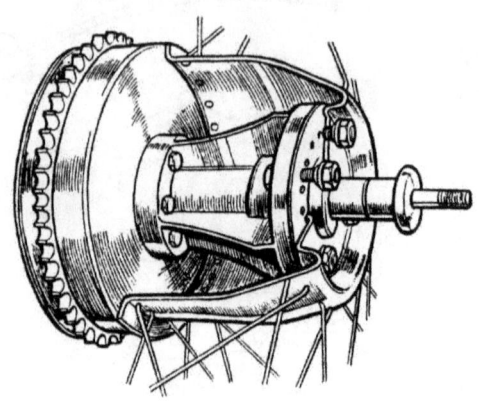

FIG. 47. SHOWING THE KNOCK-OUT SPINDLE WITH NUT REMOVED

wheel. Do not forget to replace wheel nuts with radiused ends inside.

The correct inflation pressure for the rear tyre is 25 lb. per sq. in.

REAR WHEEL SUSPENSION.

The fork carrying the rear wheel consists of two independent arms mounted on either side of the gearbox, both arms being coupled by a strong tie bar. As the rigidity of the rear wheel depends on these arms being secure, the nuts holding the tie bar and rear spindle should be checked occasionally and their *tightness* ensured. While the fork should be free to rotate on its bearings, there should be no side movement. This can only result in failure to keep the nuts, referred to above, tight, and will, if allowed to continue, cause wear. Should any side movement be observed, the wheel should be removed, the nuts holding the tie bar taken off, and the requisite number of shims removed from the latter. These shims will be found immediately between the fork arms and tie bar on either side. If through neglect wear becomes excessive, there is no other adjustment, and the gearbox and arms should be sent to the Morgan works for attention.

CHAPTER VI

THE FRONT WHEELS AND BRAKES

ALL Morgans are fitted as standard with Dunlop Cord Balloon wired-on tyres measuring 26 × 4·00, i.e. the same size as fitted to most small cars. The rims are of the well-base variety, and tyre removal is very simple, provided the valve "inside" is first removed to ensure that the tube is properly deflated. A tool called the tyre spoon is provided in the tool kit, and this is the only instrument necessary to remove or fit a tyre. Owing to the cant on the wheels, it will sometimes happen that the front tyres show an inclination to wear on one side of the tread only, whereupon it becomes advisable to change the tyres round in order to get the utmost service from each tread. When the treads begin to wear down, it is advisable to go round them at regular intervals picking out the small sharp-edged flint chippings which have a nasty habit, if left undisturbed, of working through the canvas and so causing a punctured tube. They also, of course, allow the ingress of wet which will rot the canvas foundation of the tyre and possibly cause its premature demise.

To remove the "inside" from a Schrader valve, the small dust-cap is slotted at the top, and this slotted end is inserted in the valve housing and will then engage with two pegs forming part of the "inside," which may then be unscrewed. When replacing, do not over-tighten the "inside," as, apart from this not being necessary, it is somewhat fragile and, if damaged, its removal may present some difficulty.

FRONT HUBS AND SPINDLES.

The front hubs on the earlier models are ball-bearing of the cup-and-cone type. On the later models the hubs run on journal bearings. Adjustment for wear is carried out by means of the adjustable cone, after removing the split-pin, castellated nut, and tongued lock-washer. The cone may then be screwed in, but with a bearing of this type it is essential that a little play is left after the castellated nut has been replaced and screwed up tightly. The large cone is a push-on fit on the spindle, and, if worn, may be removed by means of a hammer and punch. Both the hub caps on the earlier models are also removed in the same way. On the later models the hub caps may be removed by undoing the securing screw. The cover stud hole should be closed while lubrication is being carried out, by inserting the bolt which holds the cover in place. The hub bearings should be kept well supplied with a grade of stiff grease—a thin or semi-fluid grease is not recommended, owing to the fact that it finds its way on to the front wheel brake linings and greatly impairs their efficiency. There are no lubricators fitted to the hubs, so that the only method of greasing these bearings is to take off the hub caps, fill with grease, and replace, screwing them right home, which will force the grease through to the inner bearing.

The wheel spindle itself is held into the sliding axle by means of a large nut, which nut in turn is prevented from working loose by a washer of the "star" type, the tongues of which are flattened over on to the sides of the nut after tightening. Never, on any account, omit to fit these star washers when replacing the spindles, and, again, never use the old washers again—new ones may be obtained for a copper or so, from any Morgan service agent. Without these washers the nut will very probably work loose, and it is quite on the cards, that the vibration may cause the spindle, complete with its wheel, to come adrift from the chassis.

THE FRONT WHEEL BRAKES.

These are actuated by means of heavy Bowden cable (see Fig. 48) by a central lever fitted to the main chassis tube. This lever is very conveniently situated near the driver's left hand, and a ratchet is incorporated in the system whereby the brake may be left in the "on" position if it is desired to leave the machine when on a gradient. For all ordinary purposes of driving it is sufficient to use the front brakes only, as the braking stresses are then distributed between two of the tyres, instead of being confined to the one in the case of the rear wheel brake. Incidentally, when using the front brakes it is practically impossible to provoke a skid. Adjustment is carried out by slackening off the two setbolts holding the smaller of the two clips to the central chassis tube and sliding this clip forward—about half an inch is usually sufficient. On all three-speed models a small sleeve adjuster is provided on each of the front brake plates and for the rear brake a similar adjuster is attached to the rear wheel spindle. Both front wheels should be jacked off the ground and spun to see that the brakes are not binding when the lever is in the "off" position after any adjustment has been made. The Bowden cables should be loosely taped to some convenient portion of the chassis in the

THE FRONT WHEELS AND BRAKES

region of the flywheel to prevent their being caught in any moving part, such as the clutch. Before taping up the cables, however, put the wheels on full lock by pulling the road wheels (do not turn the steering wheel whilst the machine is stationary). We will now assume that the road wheels are set as if for taking a left-hand corner, in which case the cable leading to the off-side (i.e. the driver's side) should be secured to the chassis so that as much slack cable as possible is left between the point at which it is secured and the point where it attaches to the arm on the brake drum. Now pull the road wheels to the opposite or right-hand lock, and anchor the near-side cable in the same manner. The reason for this, as will be seen, is to ensure that the steering lock is not in any way restricted by there being insufficient slack left in the brake cables. Before taking to the road, see that the brakes may be applied easily, and that they release the wheels when the lever is "off." Any stiffness may be found traceable to the sharp angles in the Bowden cables due, perhaps, to the method in which they have been tied to the chassis.

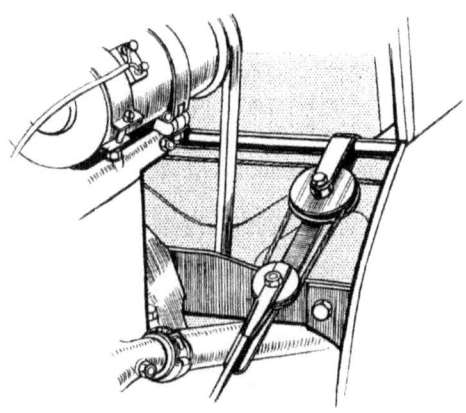

(*From "The Motor Cycle"*)

FIG. 48. THE FRONT BRAKES ARE OPERATED BY CABLES PASSING OVER PULLEYS

The brakes may be adjusted by means of the cable stops; there is one on each brake drum, at the point where the inner Bowden wire leaves its casing. These stops should always be screwed right home. If, when the front brakes are applied, the steering is pulled towards one side of the road, say the right-hand side, the trouble lies in the left-hand (or near-side) brake, and vice versa. The Bowden casing on the side in question should be carefully inspected for kinks or sharp bends, rusty cable where it enters or leaves the casing, or stiffness in the brake camshaft, or maybe binding of the brake-shoes themselves. The inner Bowden wire is, in reality, one piece reaching from one front wheel to the other via the small pulley wheel fixed to the hand lever. Consequently, there is a tendency for any stiffness in one brake or its portion of the inner wire to lag in action when the lever is pulled on, with the result, of course, that the freer side only will come into operation. To inspect the front brake linings, jack up the side in question, remove the large spindle nut and star washer, and tap the spindle from out of the sliding axle, when it will, of course, still be attached to its wheel. The Bowden cable may be disconnected, and the brake cam plate, complete with the brake shoes and operating cam will be free of the wheel. Before replacing, squirt a small amount of oil on to the cam spindle and cam faces, as well as to the pivot pin. If the linings are greasy, they should be scrubbed in petrol with a stiff brush, or better still, if time permits, they may be warmed near a fire when a large proportion of the grease will exude from the friction material.

Take care, too, to wipe the inside of the brake drums free from any congealed grease or dirt. Always keep the brakes up to concert pitch, and so soon as they call for attention see that they are put into first-class condition immediately. In reality they will call for very little attention, but any time spent in improving their action or efficiency is always worth while.

THE FRONT SPRINGING.

Each wheel is sprung independently of its fellow, and the system, although remarkably simple, has much to commend it, in so much that the shocks encountered by one wheel are not transmitted to the opposite member, thereby considerably adding to the riding comfort. The large coil spring absorbs the jolts, whilst the smaller coil at the bottom of the sliding axle takes up the rebound as the sliding axle travels downwards after hitting a bump. The sliding axle, which is made of phosphor-bronze, slides up and down on a steel tube (on later models this tube is dispensed with and the wing stay forms the bearing surface), which tube, in turn, is held in position by being clamped between the top and lower chassis front members by the long stay holding the mudguard. After seven or eight thousand miles running, the sliding axles will show signs of wear owing to the constant friction from the steel tube. To renew a worn sliding axle, proceed as follows: Jack up the front wheel, disconnect the steering and brake cable, remove the large nut holding the wheel spindle where it passes through the sliding axle, and then remove the wheel complete with its spindle. A hide-faced or lead hammer, or heavy wooden mallet will come in useful here, as these will inflict no damage to the threads on the spindle. Slack off both nuts on the chassis tie-rod, and remove the mudguard. It is not essential on the later models to remove the mudguard entirely. Just take out the top mudguard bolts and push mudguard back out of the way. Next take off the nut at the bottom of the

THE FRONT WHEELS AND BRAKES 85

wing stay—this nut is castellated and is held by a split-pin. The wing stay, or mudguard stay, may now be lifted out, and, by gently pressing down the lower chassis cross member by means of the foot, the sliding axle will come away complete with its tube and both springs. It is advisable to loosely tie both springs to the sliding axle by means of a length of wire before actually pulling the axle away, as they have a tendency to fly with some considerable force on leaving the chassis unless prevented in this manner. When assembling with the new sliding axle, fit the tube after having thoroughly greased this and the hole in the sliding axle through which it passes, slip on both springs, and, placing the lower end of the sliding axle tube in its recess in the lower chassis tube, press downwards until the top end of the sliding axle tube can be passed under the end of the top chassis tube. Gently wriggle the sliding axle until the tube drops into its recess at the end of the top chassis member and complete the assembly by inserting the mudguard stay and fitting the split-pin after the nut has been firmly tightened. The remainder of the task calls for no special hints, except that the star washer which locks on the large wheel spindle nut must not be overlooked. It is always advisable to fit a new sliding axle tube whenever a sliding axle is being replaced. The cost of this tube only amounts to a shilling or so, and the agent from whom it is purchased will ensure that it is a fairly free fit in the sliding axle (Fig. 49.) if requested to do so.

THE STEERING GEAR.

All recent Morgans are fitted with what is termed reduced or geared steering. That is to say, a form of gearbox containing toothed wheels is built into the steering layout, the purpose of this gearing being to minimize the effort called for when steering the vehicle. The same principle is used on all four-wheeled cars, and the result is that the machine may be driven for hours at a time without setting up aching arms or fatigued wrists, as is the case with steering of the direct type, as was at one time fitted to Morgans. The small toothed pinion fixed to the bottom of the upper portion of the steering column meshes with an internally toothed wheel attached to the top end of the lower half of the steering column, these two halves of the column of course being separate. The number of teeth in the larger ring is exactly twice the number of teeth on the small pinion, so it follows that when the steering wheel is turned the lower half of the column will only turn half the distance of the upper half. The steering reduction being therefore known as

2 to 1. A grease nipple is fitted to the lid of the steering gear box and the grease gun should be applied here occasionally. Beyond this, no further attention is called for, but it may be pointed out that the height of the steering wheel may be altered by simply removing the four small nuts and bolts holding the top of the steering box in position, lifting out the wheel and upper half of the column, and turning the lid of the steering box half a turn

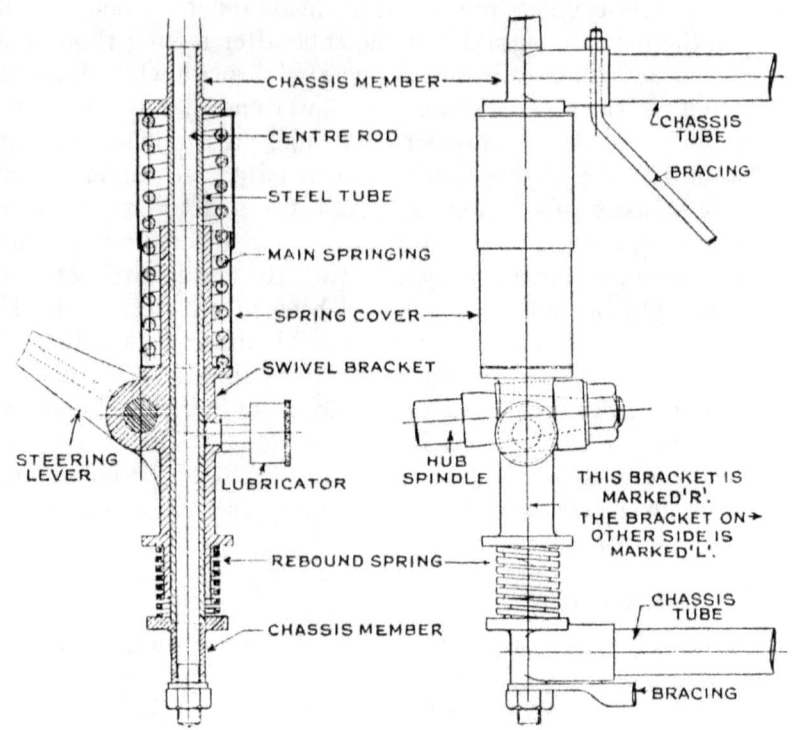

FIG. 49. SECTIONAL VIEW OF FRONT WHEEL SPRINGING AND SLIDING AXLE ASSEMBLY

before replacing the column and engaging the toothed pinions. Should an undue amount of backlash develop between the pinions (a small amount of play is essential here) adjustment is provided by removing the three small set-bolts situate round the steering column top half where it enters the steering box, and turning the boss (which is eccentric) round until some resistance is felt, when the three set-bolts may be replaced.

The extreme lower end of the steering column, which by the way is tubular, has fitted to it a solid steel square (on later models a spline is used) to which, in turn, is attached the steering drop-arm.

THE FRONT WHEELS AND BRAKES

From this arm extends the steering universal to the off-side steering arm. The track rod couples the wheels together by attachment to the steering arms of each wheel. The steering arm pins, to which is fitted the track rod, are of conical or taper formation, the object of this being to prevent steering wobble. These pins should on no account be greased or their purpose in this respect will be defeated. The track rod is pressed into contact with these taper pins by pressure of the spring, and owing to the holes in the track rod being tapered to suit the angle of the pins, a slight amount of friction is set up which will effectively damp out any tendency to wobble on the front wheels so far as this point is concerned. The front wheels have what is known as a "castor" action by reason of the wheel spindles being fitted at a point behind the sliding axles. This method of fixing tends to keep the wheels pointed in a forward direction when the machine is in motion; consequently, it is not necessary to correct continually the course of the machine on a straight road, as it will have no tendency to drag or wander from one side of the road to the other. If the steering should pull to one side all the time it may be either that the front wheel tyre pressures are unequal (for correct tyre pressure see Chapter III), or the front wheels are out of track. The track of the front wheels is adjustable by means provided on the track-rod at the near side, and when correct the wheels should "toe in" $\frac{1}{8}$ in. at the front. To check the track, place a length of rod against the inside of one front wheel at a distance from the ground, equal to the height of the hub-cap from the ground—this measurement will be found to be somewhere about 14 inches. Make a chalk mark on the inside of each rim to coincide with this measurement with the wheels set dead straight. Now bend the rod so that each end will just touch these marks. The next step is to check the wheels in a similar manner but with the chalk marks at the rear—that is to say, the car must be pushed along until the wheels have made exactly half a turn. It is advisable to measure the height of the marks to ensure that they are the same distance from the ground as before, when the rod must be threaded through and the distance between the ends of the rod and the chalk marks noted.

The wheels may be taken as being in correct adjustment when they are one-eighth of an inch wider at the back than at the front. To effect adjustment, disconnect the track rod at the near-side end, slack off the lock-nut when the end of the track rod may be turned on its threads, thereby lengthening or shortening the track rod according to which way the end is turned. If the wheels are too wide at the back it will be necessary to screw the track rod end farther on. This will have the effect of shortening the rod and will, when the rod is again coupled to the steering arm, draw the wheels closer together at the back. It may be necessary to check the distances between the wheels two or three times before the desired result is attained, but the track rod must, of course, be properly coupled up to the steering arm each time before taking measurements.

Correct wheel alignment is very vital, as, should the wheels not be in correct alignment, the life of the tyres will be seriously curtailed. Causes of mal-alignment, among other things, are: The track rod may be bent or either wheel spindle bent, which, in turn, may be brought about by striking an obstruction with some force, such as the edge of the pavement when drawing to a standstill. Also, many of the causes of steering wobble, some of which are given hereunder, may also set up bad wheel alignment.

STEERING WOBBLE. (" B " TYPE CHASSIS.)

Wobble on the front wheels when the vehicle is in motion is not likely to display itself until the machine has done some thousands of miles. If, and when it does, however, it is sometimes a little difficult to trace the cause, as this is usually due to a number of small defects, which, combining into one total, make for general slackness in some of the various points in the steering layout. Having gone over the steering from stem to stern, as it were, and found the one or more roots of the trouble, the cure is, in almost every case, obvious and simple. Look first of all for a bent rear wheel spindle, or loose nuts on this spindle, as it is not generally realized that either of these is liable to set up a wobble on the front wheels. The steering wheel itself may be loose, or the steering column where fitted to the body in the vicinity of the steering box may be loose. The bolts here sometimes enlarge the holes in the woodwork of the body unless kept up tight. The steering column tube at the lower end may be loose. This is best checked by rocking the steering to and fro when, if loose, the lower end of the steering column will be seen to move about. The steering drop arm may be loose where it fits on the square end of the column, or alternatively, the square end itself may be loose in the column. In this latter event, the column must be removed and the rivets holding the square end tightened or renewed. The rivets holding the steel blocks in the steering universal are apt to wear somewhat, but in many cases can be tightened up by removing the universal and re-riveting the old pins. The bolts and set-bolts

THE FRONT WHEELS AND BRAKES

on the track rod and universal respectively may be worn loose in their threads. The sliding axles may require renewing, or the wheel spindle nuts may have worked loose, thus setting up loose wheels, as well as allowing the steering arms to move in relation to the road wheels. The front wheel bearings may need adjustment, or the wing stay nuts may need tightening. If the steering column is removed from its tube at any time give a liberal coating of grease before replacing, as this column, being a fairly close fit over a comparatively large area, is subject to stiffness in the steering if allowed to become dry, and, in time, rust may find its way in, with the result that the steering becomes unduly heavy.

CHAPTER VII

THE LIGHTING AND STARTING EQUIPMENT

DESCRIPTION OF OPERATION OF EQUIPMENT.

THE electrical equipment used on Morgans is a self-contained system, and is, in effect, a miniature electrical power plant. The dynamo, which is driven by the engine, is the source of supply of current for the lamps, starter motor, and accessories, as well as the ignition coil. A battery is included in the equipment to act as a "reservoir" of energy to supply the current for the starter motor and the lamps when the car is stationary.

The dynamo output is controlled by what is known as the third brush method. The object of this third brush system is to regulate the output of the dynamo at high speeds and keep it steady, independent of the speed at which the dynamo is running, as it must be remembered that the dynamo speed varies as the engine speed. The dynamo is arranged so that it gives its full output or a reduced output, according to the position of the charging switch. The markings on this switch are " Summer Half Charge " and " Winter Full Charge," and it is intended that the switch is kept in the former position during the summer months, when the lamps are very little used, and in the latter position during the winter, when the lighting and starting load is heavier. It should be noted that the dynamo automatically gives its full output whenever the lamps are switched on. This charging arrangement ensures that the battery is kept in good condition without the possibility of excessive overcharging.

Connected between the dynamo and the battery is the cut-out. It is, in effect, an automatic switch, which acts as a "valve" in the dynamo charging circuit, allowing the flow of current from the dynamo to the battery only. It completes the charging circuit when the dynamo is running fast enough to generate a voltage sufficiently high to charge the battery, and disconnects it again when the speed is low. The function of the cut-out is very often misunderstood—it does not prevent overcharging of the battery. It fulfils no other object than that of preventing current from flowing from the battery through the dynamo windings when the car is stationary or when it is running very slowly.

THE LIGHTING AND STARTING EQUIPMENT 91

The starting motor is constructed with a shaft fitted with a pinion, which, on rotation, runs into engagement with the geared rim of the flywheel. Immediately the engine begins to fire, the pinion is automatically thrown out of mesh.

Now let us observe what happens in the various circuits when the equipment is in use. First, the starting switch is closed, thereby allowing a current to flow from the battery to operate the starter motor, to start the engine. When the engine is running it is driving

FIG. 50. SWITCHBOX (MAGNETO IGNITION MODELS)
A. Charging and ignition switch.   B. Lighting switch

the dynamo, but will not charge the battery until the cut-out operates. When the speed of the engine is increased, the needle of the ammeter will be seen to flicker over to the " charge " side. This means that the cut-out has closed and is allowing a small current to pass to the battery. As the car speed increases, the current will increase also, until it reaches a maximum. It will then remain nearly constant irrespective of the car speed, owing to the third brush regulating system.

At night the lighting switch will be closed by the driver, allowing the current to pass from the battery to the lamps. If the lamps are switched on when the car is stationary, i.e. the dynamo not running, all the current for lighting has to come from the battery, and the amount will be shown on the discharge side of the ammeter. If the engine is running, the ammeter will register the difference of the amount of current being discharged by the battery and the current passing into the battery from the dynamo.

Coil Ignition Warning Lamp. This lamp is incorporated in the instrument panel when coil ignition is fitted. It automatically gives a red light whenever the ignition is on and the engine is stationary, and so reminds the driver to switch off. This prevents the possibility of the battery being discharged by current flowing through the coil windings.

It will be noticed that the warning lamp also lights when the engine is running very slowly. This is because the lamp is connected across the cut-out points and will light up at speeds below the cutting-in-speed of the dynamo.

After long service, the warning lamp bulb may fuse out. This will not affect the ignition, but it should be replaced as soon as possible so as to act as a safeguard to the battery. Care must be taken that the replacement bulb is of the same size and type as the one originally fitted. The voltage and current consumption will be found stamped on the cap of the bulb.

The Battery. It is of the utmost importance that the battery should receive regular attention, as upon its good condition depend the satisfactory running of the starting motor, the illumination of the lamps, and the running of the car. The following are the most important maintenance hints—

1. Keep the acid level $\frac{3}{8}$ in. above the top of the plates.
2. Add only distilled water, never tap water.
3. Test the condition of the battery by taking readings of the specific gravity of the acid with a hydrometer (see Fig. 51).
4. The battery must never be left in a discharged condition.
5. Keep the terminals spanner tight, and smeared with vaseline. Also, with earth return sets, see that the nut securing the lead from the negative battery terminal to the chassis is tight.

Topping Up. At least once a month the vent plugs in the top of the battery should be removed, and the level of the acid solution examined. If necessary, distilled water, which can be obtained at all chemists and most garages, should be added to bring the level above the top of the plates, but well short of the bottom of the vent plugs. If, however, acid solution has been spilled, it should be replaced by a diluted sulphuric acid solution of the strength indicated on either the side or cover of the battery. It is important, when examining the cells, that naked lights should not be held near the vents, on account of the possible danger of igniting the gas coming from the plates.

THE LIGHTING AND STARTING EQUIPMENT 93

Greasing Terminals. Examine the battery terminals and see that they are quite tight. Keep them smeared with vaseline to prevent corrosion. The top of the battery should be kept clean and dry; care should be taken not to spill water on it when adjusting the level of the electrolyte or taking specific gravity readings.

Storage. If the car is not used for several months the battery must be given a small charge from a separate source of electrical

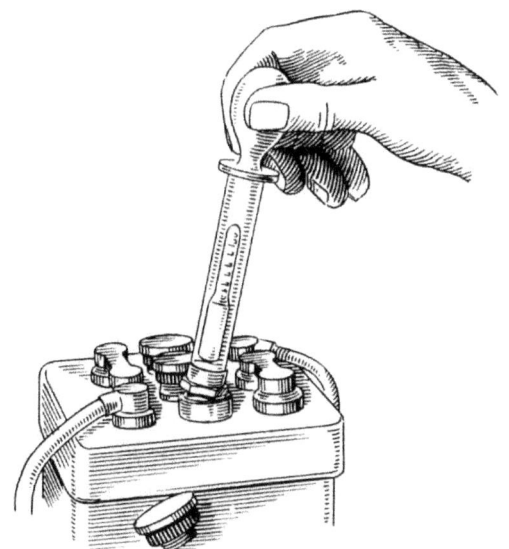

FIG. 51. USE OF HYDROMETER FOR TESTING SPECIFIC GRAVITY OF ACID

energy about once a fortnight, in order to obviate any permanent sulphation of the plates. In no circumstances must the electrolyte be removed from the battery and the plates allowed to dry, as certain changes take place which result in loss of capacity.

TESTING THE CONDITION OF BATTERY.

It is advisable to complete the inspection by measuring the specific gravity of the acid, as this gives a very good indication of the state of charge of the battery.

An instrument known as a hydrometer is employed for this purpose, and should be of the type shown in Fig. 52. Voltmeter readings of each cell do not provide a reliable indication of the condition of the battery unless special precautions are taken, which make such a test unsuitable for the average owner, and on that account we do not recommend this test.

HOW TO USE THE HYDROMETER.

Before measuring the specific gravity of the acid solution by means of the hydrometer, see that the acid is at its correct level.

Fig. 52.
A Popular Type of Hydrometer

Readings should be taken for each of the cells in turn after a run on the car, when the electrolyte is thoroughly mixed. The readings should be approximately the same. If one cell gives a reading very different from the rest, it may be that the acid has been spilled or has leaked from this particular cell, or there may be a short between the plates. In this case the battery should be returned to the makers so that they may trace the cause and prevent the trouble from developing.

With batteries for which the strength of the acid recommended is 1·225, the specific gravity of the solution when the battery is fully charged will be 1·225–1·250. When half discharged it will be about 1·200, and when fully discharged about 1·150.

For other types of batteries for which the strength of the acid is 1·285 or 1·320, the specific gravity figures are: 1·285 to 1·300 when fully charged, about 1·210 when half discharged, and 1·150 when fully discharged.

If the battery is found to be in a half discharged or lower state of charge, the charging switch should, if possible, be left in the full charge position for longer periods of running (see page 90). It should be remembered that the battery will be helped to regain its normal condition if its load is temporarily lessened, as, for instance, by using the side instead of the head lamps. If the gravity does not rise in a reasonable time, it is advisable to have the battery inspected by the makers. On the other hand, if the battery is always found to be in a fully charged condition and the acid level gets unusually low, then decrease the charging time.

The battery must never be left in a fully discharged condition, and unless some long runs are to be taken, it is advisable to have the battery charged up from an independent electrical supply.

USE OF BATTERY CHARGING SWITCH.

The battery is the "reservoir" for the energy generated by the dynamo, and once it is "full," there is no object in delivering further

THE LIGHTING AND STARTING EQUIPMENT 95

current to it. While it is always better to keep a battery overcharged rather than undercharged, it should be remembered that excessive overcharging will quickly reduce the acid level and tend to shorten the life of a battery.

Therefore, to ensure that the battery is kept in good condition, without the possibility of excessive overcharging, the dynamo on the majority of cars is arranged to give alternative outputs. In summer, when the lamps are very little used, the dynamo gives about half its full output during daytime running. During the winter, when the lighting and starting load is heavier, it is intended that the charging switch should be kept in the "full charge" position.

The charging switch should be kept in the appropriate position according to the season. For cars running under average conditions, this will ensure that the battery is kept in a fully charged state.

However, in exceptional cases, it may be advisable to use the switches out of season. For instance, if, in winter, the car is run regularly during the day with practically no night running, and the hydrometer readings are always found to be about 1·225 or 1·285 (according to the type of battery), and if the acid level gets unusually low, then it is probable that the battery is being overcharged. In these circumstances, move the charging switch to the "half-charge" position. On the other hand, if exceptional use is made of the lamps and starter in the summer, causing the battery to be in a low state of charge (hydrometer readings of 1·200 or under), then run with the switch in the "full charge" position.

The majority of sets are arranged so that when the lamps are switched on, the dynamo automatically gives its full charge. This can easily be ascertained by noting that there is no change of ammeter reading on moving the charging switch when the lamps are on and the car is running. If there is a change of reading, it follows that the dynamo is not arranged to give its full output when the lamps are switched on, and, consequently, it is important to switch to this position whenever the lamps are in use.

In equipments where the dynamo is not arranged to give a reduced output, the battery should be charged for 1 to 2 hours during the daytime running in the summer, for slightly longer than this in the winter, and whenever the lamps are in use.

While these times will serve as a rough guide for cars running under average conditions, the charging period should obviously be varied if the hydrometer readings indicate that the battery is being under- or overcharged.

THE DYNAMO.

Very little attention is necessary to ensure satisfactory running of the dynamo. Very occasionally—about every season—remove the end cover and examine the brushes and commutator.

Brushes. Inspect the three brushes and see that they press firmly on to the commutator. With some dynamos the brush is secured by a screw to a spring arm; the arms should move freely on their pivots.

Brushes should "bed" evenly on the commutator; that is, the face in contact with the commutator should present a uniformly polished appearance. Dirty brushes may be cleaned with a cloth moistened with petrol.

After cleaning or removal for any purpose, care must be taken to replace brushes in their original positions, otherwise they will not "bed" properly on the commutator. This is particularly important with control brushes (the smallest of the three brushes).

After long service, when the brushes have become worn so that they will not bear properly on the commutator, they should be replaced. It is recommended that none but genuine Lucas brushes are fitted, as these are specially made and will give the best results and the longest life.

Cleaning Commutator. The surface of the commutator should be kept clean and free from oil and brush dust, etc.; neglect of this precaution will result in the commutator becoming blackened, causing sparking to occur at the brushes, and consequently shortening the life of the commutator. The best way to clean the commutator is to insert a fine duster, held by means of a suitably shaped piece of wood, against the commutator surface, slowly rotating the armature at the same time.

Dynamo Drive. This should be examined occasionally and any excessive backlash in the teeth of the gear wheels taken up. This is best done by slacking off dynamo bracket nuts and moving the bracket in the required direction. It will be seen that bolt holes in the dynamo bracket are elongated for this purpose; 2–3/1,000ths backlash is permissible. Make sure that the bracket holding the dynamo is always tight and that the dynamo is tight in the clamp. Excessive backlash and movement only can ruin the gear teeth. Lubricate as instructed elsewhere. When fitting new gear wheels, remove dynamo from clamp and ensure that both wheels are properly tight before re-fitting; also see that the wheels mesh the whole width of teeth.

Lubrication. As the bearings are packed with grease before leaving

THE LIGHTING AND STARTING EQUIPMENT   97

the manufacturers, very little attention is needed. A few drops of oil, however, may be added through the lubricators, when provided, say every 1,000 miles. The reader is cautioned that far more trouble has been caused by excessive oiling than by too little.

After a considerable mileage, the dynamo should be dismantled for cleaning, adjustment, and re-packing the bearings with grease.

Dynamo Field Fuse. With some dynamos a fuse is provided in the field circuit to protect the machine in the event of anything being wrong in the charging circuit, e.g. a loose or broken battery connection. The fuse is of the cartridge type and is housed along with the half charge resistance in a small rectangular unit fixed on the dynamo yoke. If the dynamo fails to charge the battery at any time (indicated by no charge reading being given on the ammeter during daytime running), inspect the fuse and if it has blown, replace it with the spare fuse provided. If the new fuse blows after starting up, the cause of the trouble must be found, and the equipment should be examined by the makers.

CUT-OUT AND FUSE UNITS.

With most equipments, the cut-out is mounted together with one or more fuses as one unit, which usually also forms a junction box. This unit is generally mounted on the engine side of the dash. The terminals are identified by letters and the cable ends by coloured sleevings. With some equipments, the cut-out is mounted as a separate unit on the dynamo yoke.

The cut-out is accurately set before leaving the makers and does not require adjustment, and therefore the cover protecting it is sealed.

Replacing Fuses. Before replacing a blown fuse, inspect the equipment the fuse protects for faulty wiring, and see that all connections and terminals are tight. If the fuse blows repeatedly, and the cause cannot be traced, the equipment should be examined by the makers.

Type CF3 Unit. The fuse in this unit is in the accessories circuits and the indication that it has blown will be the failing of the horn or any other electrical accessory connected to the "+" and "E" terminals. Remove the fuse from its holder (see Fig. 53), and see whether there is a break in the fuse wire. If it has blown, replace with the spare fuse "C."

WIRING EXTRA ACCESSORIES.

When fitting extra accessories to the car they should be wired to the combined junction box, cut-out, and fuse unit, usually mounted on the engine side of the dash.

With the CF3 unit (Fig. 53), the terminals marked "+" and "E" are utilized.

When wiring up accessories to these units, the fuse should be removed while wiring is being carried out. With equipments that

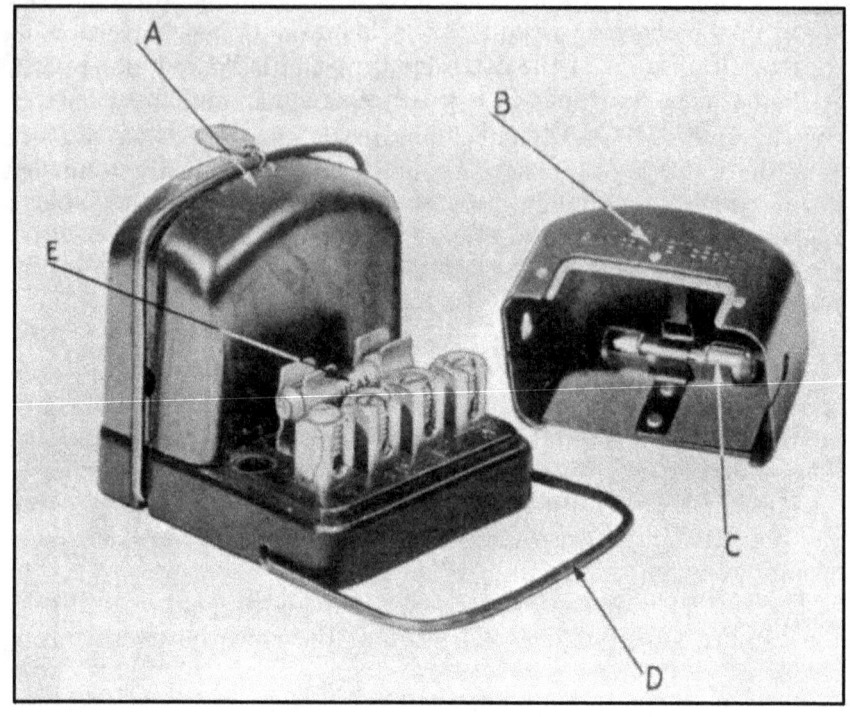

FIG. 53. CUT-OUT AND FUSE (TYPE CF3)

A. Cut-out cover
B. Fuse cover
C. Spare fuse
D. Clip for securing fuse cover
E. Fuse in auxiliary accessories circuits

do not include one of the above junction box units, accessories must be connected to the terminals at the back of the switch box or instrument panel. The supply terminal is usually marked "A" and the earthing terminal is "E." If an earthing terminal is not provided, the negative lead must be secured in good electrical contact with a metal part of the chassis.

With insulated return sets, the negative terminal is marked "B."

Terminals in Lucas switch boxes, junction boxes, etc., are of a

THE LIGHTING AND STARTING EQUIPMENT 99

standard grub screw type. To make efficient connection to terminals, proceed as follows—

Bare about $\frac{3}{8}$ in. of the cable, twist the wire strands together and turn back about $\frac{1}{8}$ in. so as to form a small ball. Remove the grub screw from the appropriate terminal and insert the wire so that the ball fits in the terminal port. Now replace and tighten the grub screw; this will compress the ball to make a good electrical connection.

LAMPS.

Replacement of Bulbs. When the replacement of any bulb is necessary, it is important that the same size bulb is fitted. The B.A.S. number will be found stamped on the cap of the burnt out bulb. It is strongly recommended that bulbs supplied by the makers are used, as these are arranged to be in focus and give the best results with Lucas reflectors. The methods of removing the fronts of the lamps for bulb replacement are given below.

The fronts of most types of head lamps are usually secured by means of a screw. To remove the front, slacken the screw and swing it aside from the slot. The front can then be removed. When replacing the front, locate the top first, then press on the rim at the bottom of the lamp.

Lamp fronts that are not secured by means of a screw or spring are removed by pressing the rim evenly and turning it to the left as far as possible.

With some types of tail lamps, remove the front portion of the lamp by turning it to the left and withdraw it from the base. When replacing, see that the studs locate with the slots in the lamp front, then push it home to lock it in position. With other types of tail lamps, the front can be removed by unscrewing it to the left.

Focusing the Lamps. To obtain the best results from the lamps, it is essential that they are in good alignment and that the bulbs are focused correctly.

For the best projection of light, the bulb filament must be as near as possible to the focus of the reflector. As the position of the bulb filament relative to the cap varies slightly with different bulbs, provision is made for adjusting the position of the bulb relative to the reflector.

With some types of lamps, the bulb holder is arranged so that it can be moved backwards or forwards when the clamping clip at back of the reflector is slackened. Care must be taken to tighten the clip after the adjustment. The reflector may easily be removed when focusing. With most types it is secured on three supports. Reflectors that have a cork washer in the rim are secured by a screw. Turn back the two ends of the washer at the top of the rim, the screw can then be removed and the reflector withdrawn by turning it to the left.

With other types of lamps, alternative positions are provided for the bulb in its holder. Each position should be tried for the best result.

The alignment of the lamps is very easily carried out, as they are usually fixed on a universal mounting, which is locked by a single nut.

The simplest method of adjusting and focusing the lamps is to take the car on to a straight, level road at night, and then to align them so that the beams are parallel with the road and with each other. Then focus the driving light bulbs as follows—

Cover over the one lamp and adjust the position of the bulb in the other lamp so as to obtain the most intense beam. Finally, focus the other lamp bulb in the same way.

Cleaning Lamps. The reflectors are protected by a transparent and colourless covering, which enables any accidental finger marks to be removed with chamois leather or a soft cloth without affecting the surface of the reflector. Do not use metal polishes on reflectors. Ebony black lamps can be cleaned with a good car polish. Chromium plated lamps will not tarnish and only need wiping over with a damp cloth to remove dust or dirt.

FAULTS.

Although every precaution is taken to eliminate all possible causes of trouble, failure may occasionally develop through lack of attention to the equipment or damage to the wiring. (See Figs. 54, 55 and 56.) The most probable faults are tabulated, according to the symptoms which are displayed, in the fault finding tables on pages 124 to 127.

A few hints are given on the best way to make use of these tables, as the sources of many troubles are by no means obvious. In some cases, a considerable amount of deduction from the symptoms is needed before the source of the trouble is disclosed. For instance, the engine might not respond to the starter switch; a hasty inference would be that the starter motor is at fault. However, as the motor is dependent on the battery, it may be that the battery is exhausted. This, in turn, may be due to the dynamo failing to charge, and the

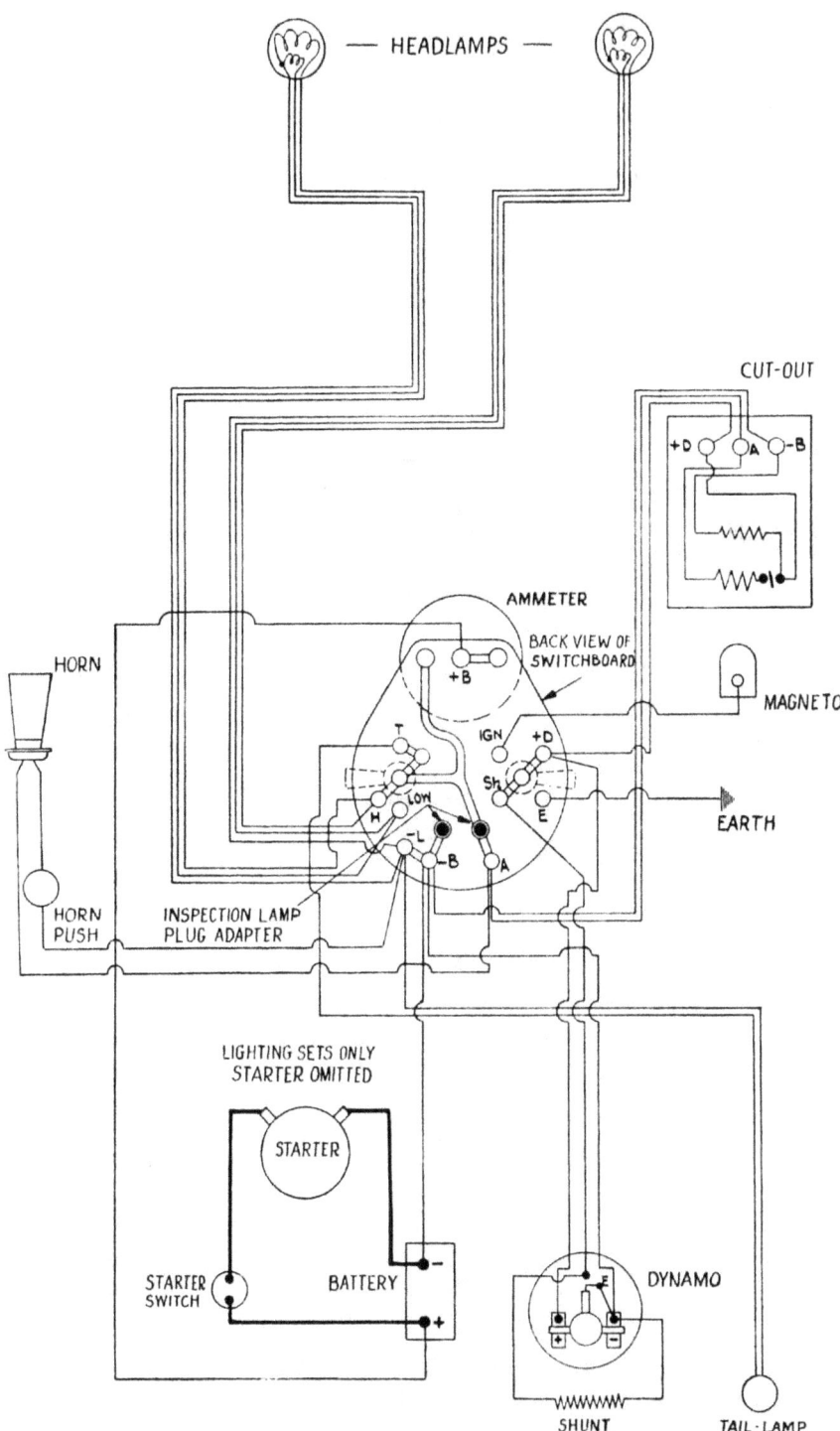

Fig. 54. Starting and Wiring Diagram (Magneto Ignition)

final cause of the trouble may be perhaps a loose terminal nut, either at the battery or elsewhere in the charging circuit.

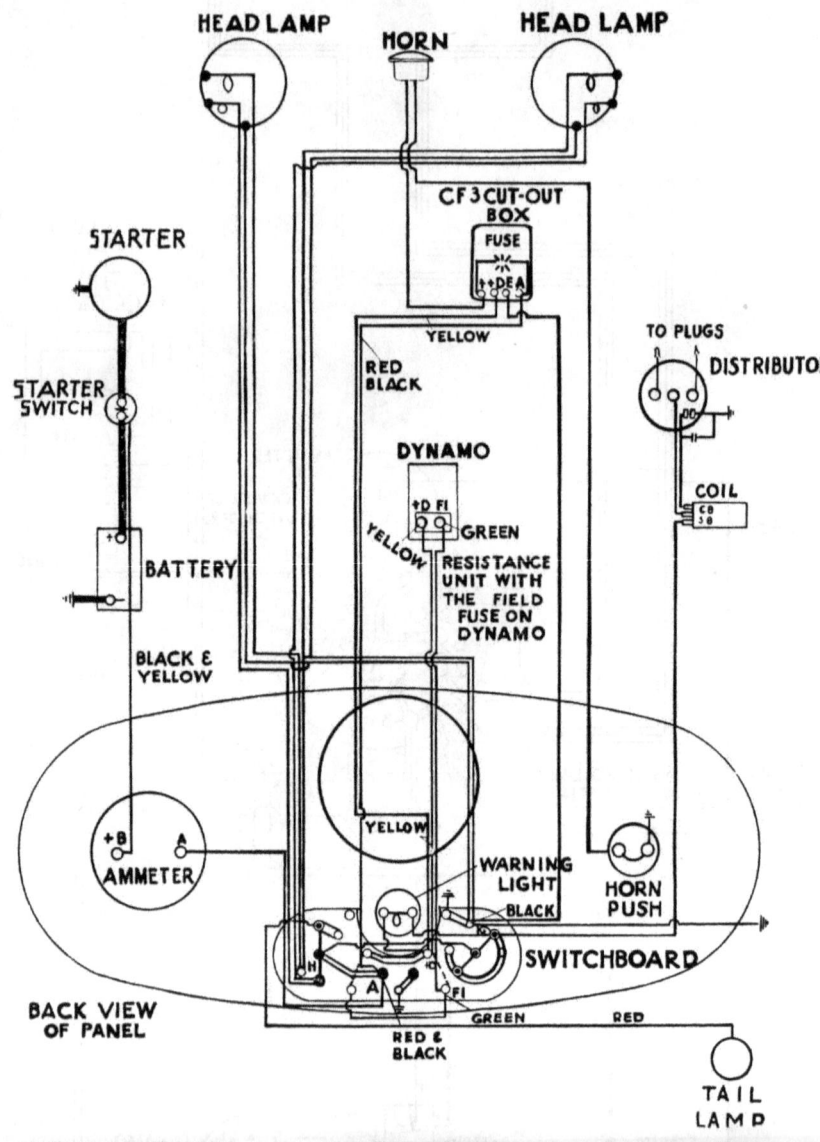

FIG. 55. THE STARTING AND LIGHTING AND COIL IGNITION WIRING DIAGRAM (1934 MODELS)

Much evidence can be gained from the ammeter. If, for instance, no charge reading is indicated when the car is running at, say, 20 miles per hour, with the charging switch in the "full charge"

THE LIGHTING AND STARTING EQUIPMENT   103

position and the lights "off," the dynamo is failing to charge. To ensure that the ammeter is not at fault, the lights should be

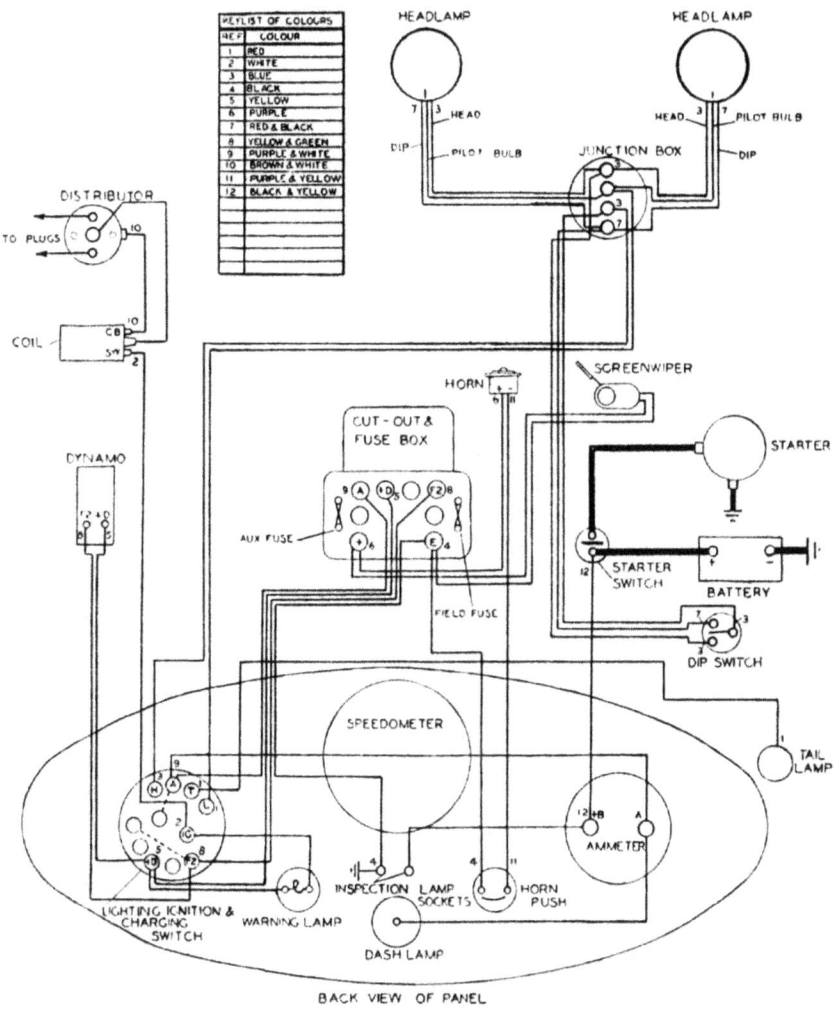

Fig. 56. The Lighting, Starting, and Coil Ignition Wiring Diagram (1935 Models)

switched on, while the car is stationary, when a reading on the discharge side of the scale should be observed. Again, if the maximum ammeter reading is much below normal when the dynamo is charging, or if the needle fluctuates when the car is running steadily, a low or intermittent dynamo output can be suspected. The dynamo may have been neglected, and the trouble could be caused by, say, worn brushes or a dirty commutator.

Should the intensity of the lights vary, or should they fail entirely, it is probably due to the battery terminals being allowed to corrode and the consequent breaking of a connection. If the cause of the trouble is not located at the battery, the switch box or the junction box should next be examined; particularly see that all the terminals are quite tight. If one particular lamp does not light, look for a broken filament or a loose connection at the lamp. When the car is stationary and the lamps light when switched on, but gradually go out, the battery is probably exhausted, due to excessive use of the starter motor and lights, or to the dynamo failing to charge.

CHAPTER VIII

TOURING

A HOLIDAY spent by means of a Morgan opens up vast possibilities and no better way of spending one's vacation comes to mind, especially when the cost of a tour can be easily kept within such reasonable limits. The open road lends a feeling of complete freedom from all the usual business and every-day worries, and the participants can make their own plans without being dependant upon trains and time-tables. Furthermore, the scope of such a holiday is considerably wider, owing to the fact that there can be a trip round fresh townships daily with ever-varying types of scenery in between.

LUGGAGE.

It is advisable to carry as little as possible on the journey, and, if necessary, a clean change should be sent on to a railway station, or hotel, to be picked up en route at the end of the first week, and the cast-off wearing apparel left to be posted on, or put on rail, either by the hotel authorities or railway officials, when the tour is concluded, and the holiday makers are home once more. A medium-sized suitcase, if this latter course is adopted, will be found amply large to accommodate the necessities for a week or two. The articles should be tightly packed to avoid damage by vibration, glass or crockery being discarded in favour of tins and enamelware wherever possible. If the suitcase is to be carried on the rear of the vehicle where it will get the full effect of any rain, it is a good tip to wrap round it an army ground-sheet or old mackintosh. The occupants of the car need, of course, take no special precautions against wet weather, as their comfort will be cared for by the hood, and possibly, side-screens if the car is so equipped. It should be borne in mind, however, that warm clothing should be the order during driving, as, no matter how hot it may be, motorists meet such a strong blast of wind whilst travelling that they are seldom uncomfortably warm. If space permits, it is well worth while carrying a spare can of petrol and a quart tin of oil. Tins to hold one gallon may be procured from any ironmonger and may be substituted for the two-gallon petrol can if luggage-carrying capacity is limited.

HOTELS.

If it is proposed to stay at hotels from night to night, one cannot do better than join one of the well-known motoring organizations who will then advise as to suitable stopping places at a price to suit one's pocket. It will then be possible to book up before starting off, thus avoiding all the trouble of finding accommodation from night to night.

MEALS.

The driver and passengers must be guided by their own tastes in this question. The most economical method is to lunch and tea at some inexpensive restaurant, and have dinner at the hotel at which one is staying the night.

CAMPING.

On the score of cheapness a camping holiday is hard to beat, and one may either take up "residence" at a definite spot, or move the "caravan" just as fancy decrees. Small collapsible tents can be purchased for a few pounds, which, when folded and packed, take up a very small amount of space. The tents shown in Figs. 57 and 58 are in every way suitable for Morgan owners, as they are compact when folded and give ample protection when in use. What few disadvantages camping has from the town-liver's point of view are easily out-weighed by the healthful and care-free properties imparted by the open-air life. With regard to cooking, this may be dispensed with except with regard to breakfast; a good hot meal on rising is strongly advocated, but lunch and tea may be of the cold variety, followed by dinner at an hotel or good restaurant. Plenty of warm bed clothing will be needed, and eiderdown quilts will be found to be worth more than their weight in gold at night.

It is a good plan to convert the quilts and blankets into sleeping bags by means of button-holes, or press fasteners.

Camping baskets containing cups, saucers, plates, etc., in addition to cooking stoves, utilizing methylated spirit or solidified fuel of a similar nature can be obtained from any sports outfitters. These outfits contain all the utensils one is likely to need and are very compact, so taking up little room.

It is highly advisable to obtain permission to pitch the tent if it is desired to camp on private property. This permission is usually readily given, although in some cases there is a small charge of a shilling or so per night. There are also camping associations in existence who will supply to members a list of recognized camping sites, but these are naturally used by other members of the association, and strict privacy is not therefore to be found. However, if one is fond of the company of others, it is highly recommended that membership of one of the camping associations be taken up. These

FIG. 57. "TINKER TENT" *(Thos. Black)*

FIG. 58. "GUINEA TENT" *(Thos. Black)*

organizations will also be found willing to give valuable assistance on all camping matters, and the beginner to this form of holiday will find their advice very useful.

ROUTE PLANNING.

Good road maps should be carried, and, if a member of one of the motoring associations, such as the R.A.C. or the A.A. either of these will suggest and map out a route or tour upon being given details as to the needs of the party. It is inadvisable to attempt to cover a large daily mileage, as the strain of long distances at comparatively high speeds is inclined to have a somewhat wearying effect upon all the occupants of the car. The better, and more restful method, is to aim at a daily run of from 100 to 150 miles, stopping to view interesting objects or scenery whenever the opportunity presents itself.

CONTINENTAL TOURING.

It is almost essential to become a member of one of the road organizations before embarking upon a holiday abroad. The process of passing the customs authorities, licensing, shipment of the vehicle and passengers and all such matters which might very conceivably become a subject of worry and annoyance to the holiday maker, can be very safely left in the hands of the representatives of the association, who will meet the tourists both at the port in this country as well as at the foreign port. They will also arrange for all the details in regard to coming home again, and it often happens that a considerable sum can be saved by making use of the facilities which these motoring associations offer to those desiring to spend a holiday a-wheel out of the United Kingdom.

CHAPTER IX

COMPETITIONS

Owing to the high degree of performance it gives, a Morgan is admirably adapted for almost any form of trial work, but it should be pointed out that the Super Sports model, owing to its low build and consequent small ground clearance, is not suitable for reliability trials of a "freak" nature in which part of the going may be of the colonial type.

No competition should be taken part in without previously going thoroughly over the whole machine, as it is essential that the engine, chassis, and all fitments be in first-class condition. Care and patience must be exercised in regard to every detail if success is to be gained, and too many drivers, it is feared, are inclined to trust to luck. It is peculiar what an amazing variety of petty troubles seem to develop in a competition in a machine which, at all other times, gives unfailing service.

The chief forms of competiton are, speed trials, usually held on a section of private road, hill-climbs which are somewhat similar events, reliability trials, sporting trials or "scrambles," and events at Brooklands track, which latter as applying to the Morgan, are usually organized by the Light Car Club. Speed trials, hill-climbs, and, of course, events at Brooklands, consist purely and simply of speed, and great skill is called for, both in preparing the machine as well as in driving it, before one can hope to bring off any award. The cost of preparing and entering the machine may amount to quite a few pounds, and unless the owner is prepared to face this, and possibly disappointment after the event, he will be wise to avoid events of this nature and try his luck at reliability trials. These are usually quite good sport and call for no heavy outlay of cash, but good driving methods and concentration on the job in hand are necessary in order to obtain a prize. There is usually an acceleration test incorporated in these events, in which the driver stops at a given point, and at a signal from one of the judges, slams the throttle open and engages the clutch as quickly as possible in order to cover a measured distance in a certain time. Practice is very necessary beforehand to accustom one's self to the violent lunge forward, and to keep the steering true and change gear at the best time.

STOP AND RESTART TESTS.

A test of this kind may also be included, wherein the driver is compelled to stop on a particularly greasy portion of an up-grade and restart at a given signal. A back tyre having a very "knobbly" tread will help the get-away very considerably, and, of course, the clutch must bite the moment the pedal is released. It is also advisable to have a lower bottom gear on the two-speed models, which is obtained by fitting a larger sprocket on the low-gear side of the back wheel. Practice also is very necessary, and knowing the hill is half the battle, although in many cases the course is kept secret until the actual start of the event.

BRAKE TESTS.

These as a rule are quite simple, but when they are combined with acceleration tests, trick driving is required. In this class of test, which is sometimes included in a reliability trial, the driver, has to accelerate from the start, stop just past a tape in the middle, run back over the tape and accelerate to the top. Overshooting the middle tape means a great loss of time, and constant practice will stand one in good stead when the actual test takes place.

" FLABBY " REAR TYRE FOR BAD HILLS.

For climbing steep or greasy hills the back tyre should have very little pressure in it, as a hard tyre causes bouncing, resulting in a spinning wheel. Therefore, before a severe hill is reached, the tyre should be deflated until it is fairly soft. This is not good for the tyre, but it may make the difference between success and failure in the competition. It is also useful to have a fair amount of weight over the back wheel, and, unless the rules preclude it, the passenger can accommodate himself on the rear part of the machine. Alternatively, one or two petrol cans filled with sand and water, may be firmly fixed over the back wheel, or sheet lead may be bolted on to the body.

NEGOTIATING WATER-SPLASHES.

Play for safety when tackling the crossing of streams, and avoid trying to make a spectacular dash across. Change to low gear as soon as the water is sighted, enter at a very low speed, and accelerate just enough to carry the machine over. Rushing tactics before entering the splash are of little avail, as the weight of water will very effectually slow down the machine the moment it strikes the water.

WATERPROOFING THE CARBURETTOR AND SPARKING PLUGS.

It is advisable to fit a long air-intake pipe to the carburettor, and this may be easily rigged up out of a length of radiator hose of suitable size. The plugs should be insulated by some form of rubber protector which can be purchased from any accessory dealer, or by wrapping the terminals round with insulation tape. The exhaust pipes will not be likely to need any alteration, as the force of the outgoing gases will keep out any water.

THE MAGNETO.

The vital points of this must be waterproofed and many old hands use Plasticine for covering over the contact breaker cover, the points where the high-tension wires lead in, and also in the vicinity of the drive.

CHAINS.

These should be cleaned and lubricated as instructed in Chapter V, and the tension carefully adjusted. A badly-worn chain, or one which has seen much service, should be replaced, and worn sprockets should be scrapped and new ones fitted.

BRAKES.

These must be adjusted up to the maximum efficiency, and care should be taken that no friction is set up by either brake rubbing, or when the time does come to use them their effect will possibly be disappointing owing to the lining having been worn down.

THE WATCH.

A reliable and accurate time-piece is essential, and the passenger may be entrusted with keeping an eye on the time, and route card. A good passenger in this capacity is a very great boon and can either add to, or detract from, one's chances of success in a great measure. The speedometer too should be his charge, and it goes without saying that this instrument should be trustworthy and give a true record of speed and mileage.

THE ROUTE CARD.

This is best carried in a route card holder which can be bought for a very moderate sum. The great feature of these is that they are proof against almost any rain, and at the same time are easily read. This is best left in the hands of a passenger, and an electric torch or good dash lamp will be of considerable assistance if the event is being run through the night, or any portion thereof.

CHAPTER X

BUYING AND SELLING

FOR financial reasons the reader may contemplate buying a second-hand machine in preference to a new one, or he may want to do so in order to have an old machine to learn the management of this make of car instead of risking damage to a brand new model. In either case, for the novice, there is as much risk in buying a second-hand motor vehicle as in buying a horse, and the inexperienced purchaser should take a friend with him who is an expert to examine the machine before making a final decision.

MAKE AND YEAR.

Competition amongst the recognized motor traders is so strong, that artificial inflation of prices is practically unknown; where a new machine is concerned, of course, the purchaser gets value according to the amount he pays, and as the prices of the new models are fixed by the manufacturers, one is not likely to be asked a figure above the catalogue price of the particular model one is seeking.

But in the case of second-hand specimens, particularly when being sold by a private owner, the seller may be asking a sum out of all proportion to the value of the machine he offers, and it is therefore advisable to obtain some idea of the current prices of whatever make of machine the reader has in view. Study of the columns of second-hand models advertised for sale weekly in the motoring and motor-cycling papers will give the prospective purchaser a very valuable guide to current prices asked for second-hand models. The year of make of the machine should be ascertained from the owner's registration book, as it is possible to "camouflage" these machines so as to bear a passing resemblance to a model of much later vintage.

EXAMINING THE MACHINE.

The chassis tubes, and all chassis lugs as far as possible, should be carefully examined for cracks, kinks, bends, or direct fractures. The condition of the chains, sprockets, wheels, tyres (and also inner tubes if there is time), wheel bearings, gear selector mechanism, bevels and bevel box should be noted.

TESTING THE ENGINE.

The engine should be turned over by means of the starting handle to ascertain that the compression is good. Then it should be rotated with the exhaust lifter raised and any knocks or signs of wear carefully listened for. If there is much wear, it will probably be most apparent in the valves and valve gear, but these parts are easily and inexpensively replaced. Have the engine started up and the throttle set to give a tick over, watching out for any signs of misfiring or uneven running, or any undue mechanical clanking, i.e. a sign of badly-worn bearings or pistons, caused either by old age or bad usage.

TRIAL RUN.

If the machine gives reasonable satisfaction from the above superficial examination, the purchaser should insist on a trial run so that he may be satisfied with the control and general running. It should be run both at speed and also slowly in top gear, and also taken up the steepest hill in the vicinity and its performances carefully noted. The efficiency of the brakes may also be tested in the course of the run, and the steering gear watched for backlash on the steering wheel, pointing to worn steering mechanism.

STOLEN PROPERTY.

The prospective buyer is advised to make quite sure that the seller is the real owner of the machine, for if he purchases, and the machine is subsequently claimed by the rightful owner, he must return the machine to the real owner and has no redress, except the doubtful one of suing the vendor—who will have probably disappeared in the meantime. Examination of the registration book will show the name and address of the owner, and comparison of signatures on any letters that may have passed and that on the registration book will help to show whether the vendor is the genuine owner.

The best proof of ownership is by the vendor producing the invoice and the receipt for the cash he paid for the vehicle. Cases have been known where a person having acquired a machine under the hire-purchase system has made attempts at selling it before the whole of the instalments have been paid. In such cases, one is justified, before taking the machine away, in asking the seller to produce receipts for all his instalments, or alternatively, his final receipt which should also carry a note signifying that he has met all his obligations in the matter of purchasing the machine.

THE DEPOSIT SYSTEM.

If the vehicle is purchased through the trade paper advertisements of second-hand machines, it is usually possible for the vendor to deposit his purchase money with the editor of the paper concerned. Then, when the purchaser is satisfied with the machine and agrees to purchase it, the paper hands over the money to the vendor.

SELLING THE MACHINE.

The foregoing information indicates to some degree the questions a purchaser is likely to ask, and before attempting to sell the machine it should be put in a reasonable selling condition. If this is done a higher price is commanded, correspondence and complaints after the sale are completely avoided, and it saves making excuses when the prospective purchaser points out any defects.

SELLING THROUGH AN AGENCY.

Several firms undertake to sell second-hand machines, the usual procedure being to value the machine and to allow the agent a commission on that price. Such agents usually sell the machine at a higher price than the owner would obtain privately, so that it is usually well worth while to adopt this method, so long as a reliable firm is dealt with.

SELLING BY ADVERTISING.

This is an excellent method of selling, because the trade papers classify the various makes of machine, so that the man wishing to purchase a Morgan has only to look down the small advertisement columns of one of the motoring journals to compare prices. The fact cannot be ignored that a prospective purchaser of a second-hand model probably looks at one of these papers, and therefore this method is to be highly recommended.

Money can be more easily wasted in advertising than in any other form of money-spending, so that the seller should carefully consider the features of his vehicle before writing out his advertisement. If price is the strong point, put it boldly at the beginning of the advertisement so that the figure stands out. As the first word of these advertisements usually appears in capital letters, the choice of the word is important.

The seller's genuine name and address is usually better than a box number in obtaining replies, as purchasers are often, though needlessly, suspicious of the latter. The season of the year should

BUYING AND SELLING

be considered; a better price is obtained in the spring than in, say, the month before the annual Motor-cycle Show at Olympia in which show Morgans are exhibited. If the tax has been paid make a point of this in the advertisement.

REGISTRATION FORMALITIES.

The rules contained in the registration book should be carefully complied with when the machine changes hands. And, finally, if the purchaser pays by cheque, get it cleared before parting with the machine, unless he is known personally as reliable.

CHAPTER XI

THE WATER-COOLED MODELS AND WINTER PRECAUTIONS

IN spite of the absence of either pump or fan, the Morgan radiator and cylinder water jackets are of such ample dimensions that boiling is never likely to occur. Keep the radiator almost full, and it is advisable to use only rain water for this purpose, as ordinary hard water contains lime, which will become deposited throughout the cooling system and possibly set up over-heating owing to the radiation being affected. Any leaks at the hose connections should be corrected by tightening the clips, or, if necessary, re-making the joint. Naturally, only clean water should be used, and it is as well to filter the water through linen in order to make sure that no foreign matter can enter the radiator, which would clog up its tubes. The radiator may be cleansed by putting a handfull of ordinary household soda in, and leaving it to dissolve when it will effectually break up all foreign matter. It is best to leave the soda in until the water has been thoroughly warmed up by the engine two or three times, after which the radiator should be drained, and the cooling system flushed out with ordinary tap water, before refilling with soft water.

Never add cold water whilst the engine is hot, particularly if the level appears to be very low. This may be ascertained by using a stick or some such instrument into the radiator via the filler spout. The radiator drain tap is fitted at the offside of the radiator and faces forward.

In winter, great care must be exercised so that the water does not freeze whilst the car is standing in the garage. If this takes place, considerable damage will be done by the ice bursting the radiator and cylinders and it will be advisable to drain the water off each night. On the other hand, a radiator lamp may be placed near the engine. These lamps are made on the principle of miner's lamps and are absolutely fireproof. Special anti-freezing mixtures may now be obtained, which, when emptied into the water will be proof against freezing. Common or garden glycerine is also a good frost preventive, the necessary quantity being four pints of glycerine to each gallon of water, this being sufficient to stand against almost any degree of temperature likely to be found in this country. Any evaporation can be made good by simply adding water. Slow combustion stoves of the safety type can also be installed in the garage, and, providing all possible sources of draughts are stopped, these are quite good. Naturally, if the car is not being taxed during the winter months, the best and safest way is to leave the cooling system empty. The petrol, oil, and battery solution will not freeze in any temperature encountered in the British Isles. To start up easily in winter, it is a good tip to fill the radiator with warm water.

CHAPTER XII

LEGAL MATTERS

MEMBERSHIP of either the Automobile Association or associate membership of the Royal Automobile Club will be found to be well worth while in case of accident or police prosecution. These organizations provide free legal defence and will give all possible help in any trouble appertaining to motoring.

ACCIDENTS.

It cannot be too strongly emphasized that in an accident of any kind, the most important thing to do is for all those concerned to keep calm, and say as little as possible. The natural tendency is to become flurried and perhaps make some rash statement which may be regretted at a later date.

The first thing to do, in the case of any person being injured, is to obtain medical assistance and a policeman. This may, in some circumstances, be rather difficult should the mishap occur in an out-of-the-way place, but it is almost always possible to find a telephone within at least a mile from any spot, in England at any rate. Having done all that is possible in this connection, take the names and addresses of all available witnesses, particularly any disinterested parties. Get the policeman to take note of the positions of the damaged vehicles, and of any marks on the road which may be of help at a later date. A rough sketch-map showing any features which might prove helpful may also be made.

Do not omit to report the matter to your insurance company within twenty-four hours from the time of the accident; also advise your motoring association should you be a member of one. Should a policeman not be available, the accident must be reported within 24 hours at any police station. Do not deal with any correspondence yourself. This should be posted to your insurance company, road association, or solicitor as the case may be. Never offer any money to an injured person or witness at any time, as this may be taken as admitting liability. A motorist is compelled to give his name and address to anyone complaining in any way regarding his driving. The penalty for refusal or supplying a fictitious name is a heavy one. Furthermore, a police constable has power to arrest without a warrant any motorist in respect of an alleged motor offence. The police

LEGAL MATTERS

official need not necessarily be in uniform, in which latter case, he can, of course, be asked to produce papers confirming his powers.

ENDORSEMENT OF LICENCE.

All convictions for motoring offences may be endorsed on the back of the driver's licence, with the exception of that of obstruction. Any licence so endorsed may, at the expiration of three years, be reissued as a "clean" licence on payment to the Licensing Authorities of a fee of 5s. providing no further convictions have been recorded in the meantime.

USE OF HORN.

What is legally termed "audible warning of approach" must always be given when necessary by sounding the horn. It is an offence to fail to give this warning under certain circumstances. A recent order has established what are known as "Silence Zones," and it is an offence to sound the horn in these zones (built-up areas) between the hours of 11.30 p.m. and 7 a.m.

OBSTRUCTION.

The vehicle must not be left for an unreasonable or unnecessary time on any road, so as to cause an obstruction. A police constable has the power to decide as to whether a machine is an obstruction or not, and he may request its removal. Failure to comply will, of course, render the owner or driver subject to prosecution. Many towns have official parking places, which are distinguished by a post bearing a large "P." The period during which a machine may be parked at this spot varies, the usual time being two hours limit. Some Municipal Authorities make a charge for this concession whilst others do not. And in most car parks it is not necessary to leave the lights on at night unless the "park" happens to form part of a wide thoroughfare. In country towns the local market place answers the description of a car park on all except market days.

A policeman must inform a motorist at the time of the offence that a summons will be issued against him.

SPEED LIMIT.

A general speed limit of 30 m.p.h. in built-up areas came into force on the 10th March, 1935. Hundreds of motorists have been stopped through exceeding this limit, and it behoves you to keep one eye on the speedometer. It should be remembered that, in certain areas, such as the Royal and municipal parks, there are definite limits to the speed of road vehicles.

PEDESTRIAN CROSSINGS.

Crossing places for foot passengers are indicated by means of white lines, "Belisha beacons," metal studs, etc. Each local authority decides which method it proposes to adopt, but it must be one of those authorized.

Drivers approaching must proceed at a speed that will enable them, if required, to stop before reaching the crossing. Where the crossing is not controlled by a police officer or light signals, pedestrians have right of way over all vehicular traffic at these crossings.

LIGHTING-UP TIME.

Under the Road Transport (Lighting) Act of 1928, hours of darkness are defined as from one hour after sunset to one hour before sunrise during "summer time." During the remaining portion of the year the definition of hours of darkness is from half an hour after sunset until half an hour before sunrise. A Morgan must carry two head lamps and a tail lamp, the latter to show a red rear light to the rear, and the tail lamp must also show a white light to illuminate the marks on the number plate. The head lamps must each be within a distance of eight inches from the extreme outside of the vehicle. A Morgan owner, however, need not bother about the regulations as to lamps, as the manufacturers of the car arrange these so as to comply with the needs of the law.

NOTES

APPENDIX

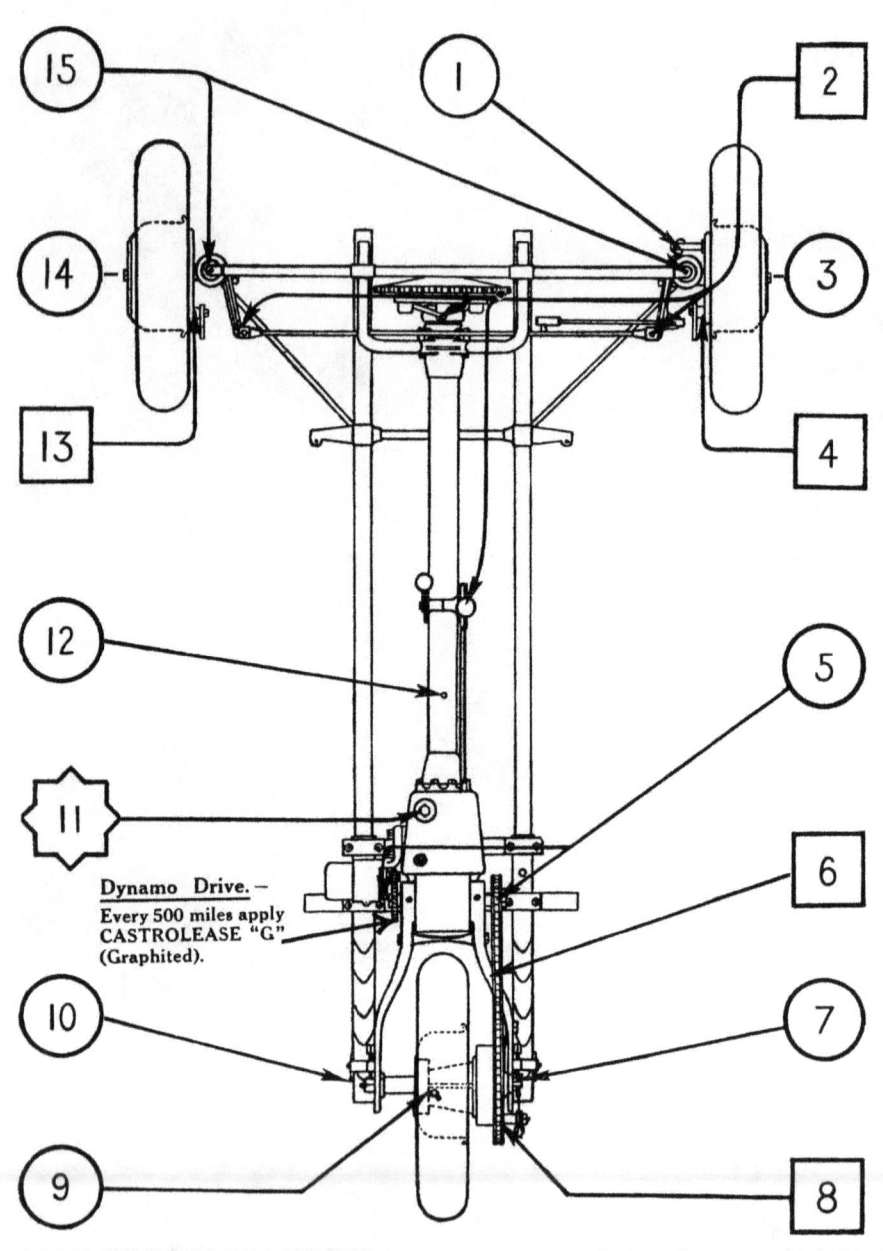

Dynamo Drive.—
Every 500 miles apply
CASTROLEASE "G"
(Graphited).

Lubrication Diagram

APPENDIX

KEY TO LUBRICATION DIAGRAM

1. SPEEDOMETER GEARBOX
   Remove cap and repack with *Castrolease* Medium every 1,000 miles.

2. UNIVERSAL BALL JOINTS, CLUTCH TOGGLE ARMS AND GEAR CHANGE LEVER
   Every 1,000 miles apply Patent *Castrol XL* with the oilcan.

3. FRONT WHEEL HUB
   Every 2,000 miles remove cap and repack with *Castrolease* Medium.

4. FRONT BRAKE CAMSHAFT
   Every 500 miles apply a few drops of Patent *Castrol XL* with the oilcan.

5. REAR FORK ARM BEARINGS
   Every 1,000 miles apply *Castrolease* Medium.

6. CHAIN
   Keep well oiled with Patent *Castrol XL* oil or *Castrolease* "*G.*" Every 1,000 miles remove and soak in *Castrolease* "*G.*"

7. SHACKLE SLIPPERS
   Every 500 miles apply *Castrolease* Medium.

8. REAR BRAKE CAMSHAFT
   Every 500 miles apply Patent *Castrol XL* with the oilcan.

9. REAR WHEEL HUB
   Every 2,000 miles apply *Castrolease* Medium.

10. SHACKLE SLIPPERS
    Every 500 miles apply *Castrolease* Medium.

11. GEARBOX
    Every 500 miles test level of oil with the dip-stick provided and as necessary refill with Wakefield Patent *Castrol* "*D*" in summer or Patent *Castrol Swanshot* in winter.

12. TRANSMISSION CENTRE BEARING
    Every 1,000 miles apply *Castrolease* medium with the grease gun.

13. FRONT BRAKE CAMSHAFT
    Every 500 miles apply a few drops of Patent *Castrol XL* with the oilcan.

14. FRONT WHEEL HUB
    Every 2,000 miles remove cap and repack with *Castrolease* Medium.

15. SLIDING AXLE GEAR
    Every 500 miles apply Wakefield *Castrolease* Medium with the grease gun.

FAULT FINDING TABLE FOR DYNAMO

- **DYNAMO NOT CHARGING**
  - DYNAMO
    - Broken or loose connections.
    - Charging switch off.
    - Switchbox fuse blown.

- **CHARGING INTERMITTENTLY OR LOW OUTPUT**
  - DYNAMO
    - Belt slipping.
    - Loose Terminal Nuts.
    - BRUSHES
      - Greasy or dirty.
      - Worn.
      - Tight in holders.
      - No spring tension.
      - Shunt brush position altered.
    - COMMUTATOR
      - Greasy or dirty.
      - Worn or rough.
      - Copper dust between segments.
  - SWITCHBOX
    - Loose fuse or connections.
  - BATTERY
    - Broken or loose connections.

- **CHARGING WITH EXCESSIVE OUTPUT**
  - SHUNT CIRCUIT
    - Brush position altered.
    - Brush not bedding.

LAMPS
├─ INSUFFICIENT ILLUMINATION
│   ├─ Lamp badly set on bracket.
│   ├─ Bulb discoloured through use.
│   ├─ Out of focus.
│   ├─ Dirty reflector or bulb.
│   └─ Battery exhausted.
├─ LIGHT WHEN SWITCHED ON, BUT GRADUALLY DIMINISHES
│   └─ Battery exhausted.
├─ BRILLIANCE VARIES WITH SPEED OF CAR
│   ├─ Battery exhausted or low level of acid.
│   └─ Battery connection loose or broken.
├─ LIGHTS FLICKER
│   ├─ Loose connection.
│   └─ Lamp adapter contacts faulty.
└─ NO LIGHTS
    ├─ Battery exhausted.
    ├─ Broken or loose connections.
    └─ Lamp filament broken.

FAULT FINDING TABLE FOR LIGHTING

FAULT FINDING TABLE FOR THE STARTING MOTOR

- **MOTOR SLUGGISH OR FAILS TO MOVE ENGINE**
  - Engine partially or entirely seized.
  - Oil too thick for winter use.

- **ENGINE TURNS FREELY AND FIRES WHEN CRANKED BY HAND**
  - **MOTOR**
    - Loose terminal nuts
    - **BRUSHES**
      - Greasy or dirty.
      - Worn.
      - Tight in holders.
      - No spring tension.
    - **COMMUTATOR**
      - Greasy or dirty.
      - Worn.
  - **OPERATING SWITCH**
    - Loose Terminal connections.
  - **BATTERY**
    - Exhausted.
    - Broken or loose connections.
    - Acid level low.

APPENDIX 127

CONDITION	METHOD OF DETECTION OF POSSIBLE CAUSES	REMEDY
	Starter will not turn engine and lamps do not give good light. Battery discharged.	Start engine by hand. Battery should be recharged by running car for a long period during day time with charging switch in full charge position. Alternatively recharge from an independent electrical supply.
	Controls not set correctly for starting.	See that ignition is switched on, petrol turned on, and everything is in order for starting.
Engine will not fire.	Remove lead from centre distributor terminal and hold it about ¼ in. away from some metal part of the chassis, while engine is turned over. If sparks jump gap regularly, the coil and distributor are functioning correctly. If the coil does not spark, the trouble may be due to any of the following causes:—	Examine the sparking plugs, and if these are clean and the gaps correct, the trouble is due to carburettor, petrol supply, etc.
	Fault in low tension wiring. Indicated by (1) No ammeter reading when engine is slowy turned and ignition switch is on, or (2) No spark occurs between the contact points when quickly separated by the fingers when the ignition switch is on.	Examine all cables in ignition circuit, and see that all connections are tight. See that battery terminals are secure.
	Dirty or pitted contact points.	Clean with fine emery cloth and afterwards with a cloth moistened with petrol.
	Contact breaker points out of adjustment. Turn engine until contacts are fully opened and test gap with gauge on spanner.	Adjust gap to gauge.
Engine Misfires.	Dirty or pitted contact points.	Clean with fine emery cloth and afterwards with a cloth moistened with petrol.
	Contact breaker points out of adjustment. Turn engine until contacts are fully opened and test gap with gauge on spanner.	Adjust gap to gauge.
	Remove each sparking plug in turn, rest it on the cylinder head, and observe whether a spark occurs at the points when the engine is turned. Irregular sparking may be due to dirty plugs, or defective high tension cables. If sparking is regular at all plugs, the trouble is probably due to engine defects.	Clean plugs and adjust the gaps to about 20 thousandths of an inch. Replace any lead if the insulation shows signs of deterioration or cracking. Examine carburettor, petrol supply, etc.

FAULT-FINDING TABLE FOR IGNITION

NOTES

INDEX

ACCIDENTS, 118
Amal carburettor, 47
Anti-freezing mixtures, 116
Audible warning of approach, 15
Automatic air valve, 60

BATTERY, 92
—— charging switch, 94
Bevels, dismantling, 75
Big ends, testing, 33
Bodywork, 5
Brakes, 81, 82
Buying and selling, 112

CARBURETTOR, 47
Chains, 77, 78
Changing down, 25
Clutch, 69, 72
Coil ignition, 41, 55
Competitions, 109
Contact breaker, 54
Controls, 17
Crankcase, flushing out, 34
Cut-out, 97
Cylinder heads, 29, 32, 63
Cylinders, removing, 32

DECARBONIZING, 28, 62
Distributor, 55
Dog sprockets, removing, 74
Drain pump trap, oil, 59
Driving, 17
—— licence, 10, 11
Dynamo, 96

EASY starting device, 60
Engine maintenance, 28
Engines, Matchless, 4

FAMILY models, 7
Flushing out the crankcase, 34
Four cylinder engine, 53
Freeing a stuck rocker cam, 40
Front hubs and spindles, 81
Fuel pump, 58

GEARBOX, 73
General specification, 6
Generator, oiling, 57
Grinding-in valves, 66

HORN, use of, 119
Hydrometer, how to use, 94

IGNITION timing, 38, 39, 57
Insurance, 13

JETS, removing, 60

LAMPS, 99
Legal matters, 118
Licence, driving, 10
——, endorsement of, 119
Lighting regulations, 15
—— and starting equipment, 90
Lubrication charts, 122
—— system, 20

MAGNETO, care of, 39
——, timing, 37
Models, range of, 1

NUMBER plates, 13

OBSTRUCTION, 119
Oil pump filter, cleaning, 62

PEDESTRIAN crossings, 120
Plugs, sparking, 43
Pump filter, cleaning, 58

RANGE of models, 1
Rear wheel removal, 79
Registration, 12
Removing overhead valves, 30
Renewing the driving licence, 11
Retiming valves, 35
Rich mixture, 52
Rocker arm, freeing stuck, 40
Running-in, 17, 26

SPARKING plugs, 43
—— ——, gap, 46
—— ——, testing, 45
Speed limits, 119
Sports family model, 8
Springing, 84
Starting motor lubrication, 58
—— the engine, 18
Steering gear, 85

Steering wobble, 88
Sump level, 61, 62

TAPPETS, 53
Testing battery, 93
Timing gear, 35
—— ignition, 38, 57
—— magneto, 37
—— valves, 35, 54
Topping-up the battery, 92
Touring, 105

Transmission, 69
Tyre pressures, 27

VALVE grinding, 31, 66
Valves, retiming, 35, 54

WARNING of approach, audible, 15
Water-cooled models, 116
Weak mixture, 52
Wheel removing, 79
Wiring diagrams, 101-103

VELOCEPRESS MANUALS - MOTORCYCLE

1930'S BRITISH MOTORCYCLE CARBS & ELEC COMPONENTS (BOOK OF)
1930'S BRITISH MOTORCYCLE ENGINES (OVERHAUL & MAINTENANCE)
1930'S BRITISH MOTORCYCLE GEARBOXES & CLUTCHES (BOOK OF)
AJS 1932-1948 SINGLES & TWINS 250cc THRU 1000cc (BOOK OF)
AJS 1945-1960 SINGLES 350cc & 500cc MODELS 16 & 18 (BOOK OF)
AJS 1955-1965 SINGLES 350cc & 500cc (BOOK OF)
ARIEL 1932-1939 PREWAR MODELS (BOOK OF)
ARIEL 1933-1951 (WORKSHOP MANUAL)
ARIEL 1939-1960 4 STROKE SINGLES (BOOK OF)
ARIEL 1958-1964 LEADER & ARROW (BOOK OF)
BMW R26 R27 (1956-1967) FACTORY WORKSHOP MANUAL
BMW R50 R50S R60 R69S (1955-1969) FACTORY WORKSHOP MANUAL
BSA BANTAM ALL MODELS FROM 1948 ONWARDS (BOOK OF)
BSA SINGLES & V-TWINS UP TO 1927 (BOOK OF)
BSA SINGLES & V-TWINS UP TO 1935 (BOOK OF)
BSA SINGLES & V-TWINS 1936-1939 (BOOK OF)
BSA SINGLES & V-TWINS 1936-1952 (BOOK OF)
BSA OHV & SV SINGLES 250-600cc 1945-1954 (BOOK OF)
BSA OHV & SV SINGLES 250-600cc 1954-1970 (BOOK OF)
BSA OHV SINGLES 350 & 500cc 1955-1967 (BOOK OF)
BSA TWINS 1948-1962 (BOOK OF)
BSA TWINS 1962-1969 (SECOND BOOK OF)
DOUGLAS 1929-1939 PREWAR ALL MODELS (BOOK OF)
DOUGLAS 1948-1957 POSTWAR ALL MODELS FACTORY SHOP MANUAL
DUCATI 160cc, 250cc, & 350cc OHC MODELS FACTORY SHOP MANUAL
HONDA 50 ALL MODELS UP TO 1970 INC MONKEY & TRAIL (BOOK OF)
HONDA 90 ALL MODELS UP TO 1966 (BOOK OF)
HONDA 125-150cc TWINS C/CS/CB/CA FACTORY WORKSHOP MANUAL
HONDA 250-305 TWINS C/CS/CB FACTORY WORKSHOP MANUAL
HONDA C100 SUPER CUB FACTORY WORKSHOP MANUAL
HONDA C110 SPORT CUB 1962-1969 FACTORY WORKSHOP MANUAL
HONDA TWINS & SINGLES 50cc THRU 305cc 1960-1966 (BOOK OF)
HONDA TWINS ALL MODELS 125cc THRU 450cc UP TO 1968 (BOOK OF)
J.A.P. ENGINES 1927-1952 & MOTORCYCLES 1934-1952 (BOOK OF)
LAMBRETTA 1947-1957 ALL 125 & 150cc MODELS (BOOK OF)
LAMBRETTA 1957-1970 LI & TV MODELS (SECOND BOOK OF)
MATCHLESS 1931-1939 ALL MODELS 250cc THRU 990cc (BOOK OF)
MATCHLESS 1945-1956 350 & 500cc SINGLES (BOOK OF)
MATCHLESS 1955-1966 350 & 500cc SINGLES (BOOK OF)
NEW IMPERIAL ALL SV & OHV FROM 1935 ONWARDS (BOOK OF)
NORTON 1932-1939 PREWAR MODELS (BOOK OF)
NORTON 1932-1947 (BOOK OF)
NORTON 1938-1956 (BOOK OF)
NORTON 1955-1963 MODELS 19, 50 & ES2 (BOOK OF)
NORTON 1955-1965 DOMINATOR TWINS (BOOK OF)
NORTON 1957-1970 TWINS FACTORY WORKSHOP MANUAL
NSU PRIMA 1956-1964 ALL MODELS (BOOK OF)
NSU QUICKLY 1953-1963 ALL MODELS (BOOK OF)
PANTHER 1932-1958 LIGHTWEIGHT MODELS 250 & 350cc (BOOK OF)
PANTHER 1938-1966 HEAVYWEIGHT MODELS 600 & 650cc (BOOK OF)
RALEIGH MOPEDS 1960-1969 (BOOK OF)
RALEIGH MOTORCYCLES 1919-1933 (BOOK OF)
ROYAL ENFIELD 1934-1946 SINGLES & V TWINS (BOOK OF)
ROYAL ENFIELD 1937-1953 SINGLES & V TWINS (BOOK OF)
ROYAL ENFIELD 1946-1962 SINGLES (BOOK OF)
ROYAL ENFIELD 1958-1966 250cc & 350cc SINGLES (SECOND BOOK OF)
ROYAL ENFIELD 736cc INTERCEPTOR FACTORY WORKSHOP MANUAL
RUDGE 1933-1939 (BOOK OF)
SUNBEAM 1928-1939 (BOOK OF)
SUNBEAM 1946-1957 S7 & S8 (BOOK OF)
SUZUKI 50cc & 80cc UP TO 1966 (BOOK OF)
SUZUKI T10 1963-1967 FACTORY WORKSHOP MANUAL
SUZUKI T20 & T200 1965-1969 FACTORY WORKSHOP MANUAL
TRIUMPH 1935-1939 PREWAR MODELS (BOOK OF)
TRIUMPH 1935-1949 (BOOK OF)
TRIUMPH 1937-1951 (WORKSHOP MANUAL)
TRIUMPH 1945-1955 FACTORY WORKSHOP MANUAL
TRIUMPH 1945-1958 TWINS (BOOK OF)
TRIUMPH 1956-1969 TWINS (BOOK OF)
VELOCETTE 1925-1970 ALL SINGLES & TWINS (BOOK OF)
VESPA 1951-1961 (BOOK OF)
VESPA 1955-1963 125 & 150cc & GS MODELS (SECOND BOOK OF)
VESPA 1955-1968 GS & SS (BOOK OF)
VESPA 1963-1972 90, 125 & 150cc (THIRD BOOK OF)
VILLIERS ENGINE UP TO 1959 INC. 3 WHEELERS (BOOK OF)
VILLIERS ENGINE UP TO 1969 (BOOK OF)
VINCENT 1935-1955 (WORKSHOP MANUAL)

VELOCEPRESS TECHNICAL BOOKS – MOTORCYCLE

CATALOG OF BRITISH MOTORCYCLES (1951 MODELS)
INDIAN PONYBIKE, BOY RACER & PAPOOSE ILL PARTS LIST & SALES LIT
MOTORCYCLE ENGINEERING (P.E. Irving)
SPEED AND HOW TO OBTAIN IT (Motor Cycle Magazine UK)
TUNING FOR SPEED (P.E. Irving)

VELOCEPRESS MANUALS - THREE WHEELER'S

BSA THREE WHEELER (BOOK OF)
VINTAGE MORGAN THREE WHEELER (BOOK OF)

VELOCEPRESS MANUALS - AUTOMOBILE

AUSTIN-HEALEY 6-CYLINDER WORKSHOP MANUAL
AUSTIN-HEALEY SPRITE & MG MIDGET 1958-1971 WSM
BMW 600 LIMOUSINE FACTORY WORKSHOP MANUAL
BMW 600 LIMOUSINE OWNERS HAND BOOK & SERVICE MANUAL
BMW 2000 & 2002 1966-1976 WORKSHOP MANUAL
BMW ISETTA FACTORY WORKSHOP MANUAL
CORVAIR 1960-1969 WORKSHOP MANUAL
CORVETTE V8 1955-1962 WORKSHOP MANUAL
JAGUAR E-TYPE 3.8 & 4.2 WORKSHOP MANUAL
METROPOLITAN FACTORY WORKSHOP MANUAL
MGA & MGB OWNERS HANDBOOK & WORKSHOP MANUAL
MG MIDGET TC, TD, TF & TF1500 WORKSHOP MANUAL
PORSCHE 356 1948-1965 WORKSHOP MANUAL
PORSCHE 912 WORKSHOP MANUAL
TRIUMPH TR2, TR3, TR4 1953-1965 WORKSHOP MANUAL
VOLKSWAGEN TRANSPORTER, TRUCKS & WAGONS 1950-1979 WSM
VOLVO 1944-1968 ALL MODELS WORKSHOP MANUAL

VELOCEPRESS TECHNICAL BOOKS - AUTOMOBILE

FERRARI 250/GT SERVICE AND MAINTENANCE
FERRARI GUIDE TO PERFORMANCE
FERRARI OWNER'S HANDBOOK
FERRARI TUNING TIPS & MAINTENANCE TECHNIQUES
HOW TO BUILD A FIBERGLASS CAR
HOW TO BUILD A RACING CAR
HOW TO RESTORE THE MODEL 'A' FORD
MASERATI OWNER'S HANDBOOK
OBERT'S FIAT GUIDE
PERFORMANCE TUNING THE SUNBEAM TIGER
SOUPING THE VOLKSWAGEN
SOLEX CARBURETORS (EMPHASIS ON UK & EU AUTOMOBILES)
SU CARBURETORS (EMPHASIS ON UK AUTOMOBILES)
WEBER CARBURETORS (EMPHASIS ON ALFA & FIAT)

VELOCEPRESS BOOKS & GUIDES - AUTOMOBILE

ABARTH BUYERS GUIDE
COMPLETE CATALOG OF JAPANESE MOTOR VEHICLES
FERRARI 308 SERIES BUYER'S AND OWNER'S GUIDE
FERRARI BERLINETTA LUSSO
FERRARI BROCHURES AND SALES LITERATURE 1946-1967
FERRARI BROCHURES AND SALES LITERATURE 1968-1989
FERRARI OPP, MAINTENANCE & SERVICE H/BOOKS 1948-1963
FERRARI SERIAL NUMBERS PART I - ODD NUMBERS TO 21399
FERRARI SERIAL NUMBERS PART II - EVEN NUMBERS TO 1050
FERRARI SPYDER CALIFORNIA
HENRY'S FABULOUS MODEL "A" FORD
MASERATI BROCHURES AND SALES LITERATURE

VELOCEPRESS BOOKS – RACING

CARRERA PANAMERICANA - MEXICAN ROAD RACE (BOOK OF)
DIALED IN - THE JAN OPPERMAN STORY
IF HEMINGWAY HAD WRITTEN A RACING NOVEL
LE MANS 24 (THE BOOK THAT THE FILM WAS BASED ON)
VEDA ORR'S NEW REVISED HOT ROD PICTORIAL

AUTOBOOKS WORKSHOP MANUALS & BROOKLANDS ROAD TEST PORTFOLIOS

FOR A COMPLETE LISTING OF THE AUTOBOOKS & BROOKLANDS TITLES THAT WE CURRENTLY HAVE AVAILABLE, PLEASE VISIT OUR WEBSITE.

Our website www.VelocePress.com includes secure online ordering via PayPal and also provides detailed descriptions of the titles listed above.

Please check our website:

www.VelocePress.com

for a complete up-to-date list of available titles

www.ingramcontent.com/pod-product-compliance
Lightning Source LLC
Chambersburg PA
CBHW070554170426
43201CB00012B/1835